The Penny Bank Book

THE PENNY BANK BOOK
by Andy and Susan Moore

The Penny Bank Book is a tour through the Moores' *Penny Door* collection, one of the largest and most important collections in the country. Nearly 1700 still banks are presented in full color — including more old cast iron banks than are pictured in any other book. This well-documented book includes an extensive appendix, which provides additional information on most of the banks. Detailed information on each bank includes a scarcity rating, measurements, names of manufacturers and dates of manufacture when known.

Conversion charts enable the reader to quickly cross-reference banks found in other still bank books with the same piece in the Moores' book. Sections on reproductions and conversions will help the reader learn to identify them. A chapter on cleaning, preserving and restoring banks will enable the collector to keep his banks in good condition. The Moores also share their extensive knowledge on purchasing banks at auction and from dealers, and on determining a fair price.

The Penny Bank Book contains a comprehensive look at the history of major manufacturers of still banks, more than eighty copies of original U.S. patent papers and more than 250 illustrated pages from early toy company and jobber catalogs, covering in excess of 1100 banks.

The Penny Bank Book makes its predecessors obsolete; no enthusiast should be without this well-organized, entertaining work.

Andy Moore is President and Chairman of the Board of the Beverly Bank, Chicago. Susan Moore was an editor of children's books at Science Research Associates, Chicago, and now pursues a career as a freelance writer. The Moores are members of the Still Bank Collector's Club of America — of which Moore is currently president, the Mechanical Bank Collectors of America and The Antique Toy Collectors of America.

The Penny Bank Book

Collecting Still Banks
Through The Penny Door

Revised & Expanded 4th Edition

Andy & Susan Moore

Additional photos
and updated price
guide by Mike Henry

4880 Lower Valley Road, Atglen, PA 19310 USA

Revised price guide: 2008
Copyright © 1997, 2000, and 2008 by Andy & Susan Moore
Library of Congress Control Number: 2007935610

Designed by "Sue"
Typeset in Zurich BdXCn BT/Souvenir Lt BT

ISBN: 978-0-7643-2842-8
Printed in China

Published by Schiffer Publishing Ltd.
4880 Lower Valley Road
Atglen, PA 19310
Phone: (610) 593-1777; Fax: (610) 593-2002
E-mail: Info@schifferbooks.com
Please visit our web site catalog at www.schifferbooks.com
We are always looking for people to write books on new and related subjects. If you have an idea for a book, please contact us at the above address.

This book may be purchased from the publisher.
Include $3.95 for shipping.
Please try your bookstore first.
You may write for a free catalog.

In Europe, Schiffer books are distributed by:
Bushwood Books
6 Marksbury Ave.
Kew Gardens
Surrey TW9 4JF
England
Phone: 44 (0)208 392-8585
Fax: 44 (0)208 392-9876
E-mail: Info@bushwoodbooks.co.uk
Website: www.bushwoodbooks.co.uk
Free postage in the UK. Europe: air mail at cost.
Try your bookstore first.

This Book is Lovingly Dedicated
To Our Children
Sarah and Drew
And the Next Generation of Collectors

"He that bloweth not his own Horn,
the same shall not be blown."

PREFACE

At a recent toy show a young enthusiast said to me, "I'd like to collect penny banks, but it is too late. Most of them are already in the hands of collectors, and those that aren't are too high priced."

I had the same concern fifteen years ago when Susan and I began to collect. After seeing a few large collections, we were convinced there was nothing left to be found.

Nothing could be farther from the truth. Bank collecting has been popular with a few collectors for a long time. Only within the last few years, however, have banks caught the attention of a wider audience. The hobby is young. Thousands of banks await the new collector in the marketplace.

In the pages of this book you will learn about many reasonably priced banks you may expect to find in The Search. You will not be alone. Of the hundreds of collectors we've known over the years, we have yet to meet one who has completed his collection. Happy Hunting!

All of the banks made by James M. Harper, Chicago, with the exception of *Board of Trade. Two Kids* is included because the authors believe it is a Harper bank.

ACKNOWLEDGMENTS

One of the great joys of having a collection is sharing it with others. Susan and I had talked about writing a book, but we did not envision it happening this soon. In July, 1983 we talked to a publisher who wanted to print a book on still banks, but whose production schedule dictated a November 1st deadline. We were overwhelmed but challenged, and decided to try.

Contributing to the body of knowledge on still banks is our continuing interest. Having received so much from others, we wanted to share what we have learned with our fellow collectors. The question was, could we gather enough additional information in a brief time period to produce a book?

We began by re-reading all issues of *The Penny Bank Post,* the newsletter of the Still Bank Collectors' Club of America, ably edited first by Elaine Werbell and then by Carl White. It is a valuable resource, containing numerous articles by the pioneers of research in still bank collecting. To add to this existing body of knowledge we needed to acquire early catalog and patent papers. Many still banks remained unidentified.

We told our collector friends what we wanted to do, and the response was overwhelming. First a package arrived from Harry Ulman, containing all of his catalogs. Bob McCumber's catalogs, reflecting his interest in J. & E. Stevens, came in the mail that same day. Then a phone call from Bernie Ellinghaus: "I'll go over to Frank Whitson's and copy everything he has." And he did. Later, Frank shared his expertise on Hubley.

Donal Markey phoned and said he would go to Dave Davison's home and see what he had. Don sent us a long letter identifying several heretofore unidentified banks. A day later, an envelope arrived from Leon Perelman, containing a spectacular Kyser and Rex catalog we'd never seen. A chat with Dale Kelley brought a quick invitation to the library of *Antique Toy World Magazine,* where he made everything he had available to us. A phone call to Bob Saylor, the meticulous Kenton historian, produced his willing help. Then Harry Ulman phoned again. He had come across a collection of catalogs and would bring it to the Mechanical Bank Convention in Hendersonville, North Carolina.

The night before I was to leave for the convention, Ernie Long called to say that Al Davidson wanted us to have his patent papers on still banks. Ernie offered to sort them out and mail them. That same day, a package containing catalogs and historical data arrived from Anthony Annese. John Haley, with whom I was to travel to the convention, arrived at our home that night. Susan and I picked his tired brain, and he promised to send more information on English banks by mail.

John and I flew to Hendersonville. Harry's material was great, and Don Markey had found another catalog. While there, mechanical bank collectors shared their expertise on still banks. Susan phoned to say that we had received a letter from Gertrude Hegarty, the first lady of toy collecting. She graciously put her library at our disposal.

Back to Chicago. Al Davidson phoned and said I must come East and peruse his library. I went with Susan's admonitions about the deadline ringing in my ears. Home again and off to lunch with Joseph Eisendrath, recently retired president of Banthrico.

The next day, Bob and Joan Brown came to visit. These good friends from Wales shared their knowledge of pottery banks. Shortly after we said goodbye to them, our close friends, Bruce and Blossom Abell, appeared at our door with their toy library in hand. Behind them was the mailman with two packages, one from Dave Davison and another from Aaron Schroeder. We began to worry about having too much material for a single book!

Our friends had been so supportive, but we had to ask them for more help. We wanted to rate the banks as to scarcity but didn't want to rely on our judgment alone. I made a few calls to collectors who are exposed to a great number of banks, and they went to work. In addition John Haley helped with the English banks and Gerhard Riegraf with the German ones. Gordon Jorgenson, a collector of dime registering banks, helped us rate them. Betty Hale gave advice on candy container and pottery banks.

Norm Bowers and Bruce and Blossom Abell's research on Harper is reflected in the book, as is Fred MacAdam's lifelong research on Arcade. Ralph Dye, Brian Cleary and Bill Robison came to our aid, as did Carl White and Bill Burkey. Don Duer shared his expertise on building banks.

We had what we needed for the book but there was too much material to handle and order by ourselves. Four wonderful women at Beverly Bank, Betty Melnyk, Sandra Tome, Sandra Grupka and Lorraine Klimas helped us with typing and the use of that wondrous tool, the word processor. Throughout, our publisher, Peter Schiffer, was patient and helpful in solving technical problems. Joel Snyder, a long-time friend, professional photographer and author, was our photographic consultant. And in the final weeks before the deadline, we called on Susan's mother, Sadie Nesbitt, and on our dear friends, Lou Ann Cover, Sue Delves, Dave Egler, Pam Hillstrom, Marge Karlic, Frannie Kyes, Eugenie Petschel, Barbara Schriver, Audrey Sullivan and Maxine Sullivan, for help with editing, proof reading, and typing.

Certainly there are others who helped, and we apologize if their names have been omitted. Many have helped over the years without realizing it. We owe a particular posthumous thank you to Louis Filler, George Knerr, Leslie Lewis, Edwin Mosler and Hubert Whiting.

We also owe a special debt of gratitude to three groups to which we belong, the Still Bank Collectors' Club of America, the Mechanical Bank Collectors of America, and the Antique Toy Collectors of America. We owe much to each of them for the friendship we have enjoyed and the knowledge we have gained. This journey through our collection is our expression of gratitude.

Some of our favorite banks.

TABLE OF CONTENTS

Who Made the Banks, continued

HOW IT ALL BEGAN

Building a Collection

Late in the summer of 1969, we were visiting a friend in Michigan who suggested we go antiquing. We complained that we loved antiquing but didn't collect anything. "How about penny banks," said our friend, "since you're a banker?" The idea appealed to us, so we set off in search of an old penny bank, determined not to spend more than ten dollars per bank.

In the third shop we went into, we found an old iron strong box dating from the late 1800's; the price tag read $10.00. The bank was locked, but we could hear the "old money" inside. "What a happy accident," I thought. "I can collect banks and old coins at the same time."

We could hardly wait to get home, where a large key collection failed to help us open the bank. A trip to the locksmith cost us $4.37. Nothing of value was inside the bank, and to this day we've not found a valuable old coin in a penny bank.

In the next few years, our collection burgeoned. Most of it was composed of oval deposit developers or pot metal replicas of bank buildings which bankers used as promotional pieces. They were in the right price range. Then I found Hubert Whiting's book, *Old Iron Still Banks*. Susan and I were overwhelmed. Within its pages, in color, were 452 — mostly iron — penny banks. It was Pandora's box!

Our first Whiting banks, *Be Wise Pig*, from Frannie Kyes, and *Mulligan*, from Susan, arrived that first Christmas of collecting. It's difficult to describe the special joy in matching your bank with a Whiting bank. Unfortunately, before Christmas Day was over we had declared Susan's *Mulligan* a reproduction. December 26, I found another *Mulligan* at a flea market, purchased it and discovered that it, too, was a reproduction. Over the years, our "Chicago Police Force" has multiplied; we have fourteen members and are still looking for variations in reproductions of this one bank.

In the spring of 1970, Susan and I were traveling in Southern Illinois. With minutes to spare before closing time, we found a shop in which the owner produced a box containing a stack of cast iron pieces. The price was right — $7.00. She was willing to guarantee that "it was all there," and we went home to construct our first building bank. As we did, we experienced something of the joy and frustration of the bank's first owner; these banks are true puzzles to assemble. When the puzzle was solved, we realized we had a Stevens bank, #1126. We still delight in that moment and in envisioning the youngster who has just robbed his penny bank and "cannot put Humpty Dumpty together again." With practice, the most clumsy among us can become adroit at assembling these banks. (Rubber bands are helpful.)

So began our love affair with building, or architectural, banks. The Stevens bank was beautifully painted, nicely cast and well-proportioned. The complex construction of some building banks makes them more intriguing than that of many mechanicals.

Toy Shows and Conventions

The same year, we discovered the Antique Toy World Show of Dale Kelley and Jack Reagan. It was all the Christmas mornings of our youth wrapped into one! We had gone to the show to learn something about a broken and repaired dog and cat bell toy we had purchased. We approached a booth manned by two friendly-looking people, Bruce and Blossom Abell.

Bruce said it was a nice toy. Would we like to make a trade? I coveted a mantle clock in his booth, but Bruce said he'd acquired it for his collection. Susan then spotted an old cap pistol, *The Chinese Must Go*, and we traded.

At the Conrad Hilton antique show the following month, I met Don Beck, a collector and bank dealer. Don had a fine collection of quality banks, but the one that caught my eye was not a Whiting bank. It was a wonderful, stubby cast iron figure with a full beard, top hat and long pipe. *Transvaal Money Box* was embossed on the hat, and I knew I had to have it. I had a little over $100 in my hobby budget, but the toy was marked $400. Too much for me to spend. Then I noted a sign stating that Don collected and traded old cap pistols. "The Chinese *indeed* must go!" I thought. Don agreed to hold the bank for me, and I phoned Susan to bring the cap gun to the show. Don then agreed to the trade but said he'd need another $100. (Don always seems to know how much I have in my pocket!)

As Susan would say, "Andy bounced all the way home." And I had found my favorite bank, which became the logo of our collecting when, one Christmas morning several years later, Susan presented me with *The Penny Door* stationery.

In 1972, we learned of the Still Bank Collectors' Club of America. A letter of inquiry brought a warm reply from Club President, Lynn Pickle, admitting us to the club and inviting us to the next convention. Susan felt some trepidation, wondering what sort of strange people would collect penny banks and gather to talk about them. Meanwhile, I had studied *The Penny Bank Post*, the Club's thrice yearly newsletter. I also received a catalog reprint and copy of "Favorite Banks," a compilation of each member's favorite banks. That day, I learned that there were hundreds of wonderful old banks not found in the Whiting book.

We were warmly received at our first convention, and Susan's fears quickly vanished. We spoke a common language — Still Banks.

It was a particularly momentous convention, as just a few months earlier, in December of 1972, two members of the Club had entered into an agreement with Burt Whiting to divide his collection among the three of them. The split was the talk of the convention. "Who went first?" "What was your first choice?" "How did you choose?" Excitement reigned! It probably was the most significant event that had ever occurred in still bank collecting. The men had agreed to divide in thirds all of Whiting's collection, some 700 banks, many of which were not in his book. They had gathered on a Saturday morning, December 2, 1972, and Burt brought out a deck of cards. They were to "cut" to determine the order of selection. They drew a four, a deuce and a three.

Whiting's first choice was the *Ark* and the others, in turn, chose the *Cannon* and *Tug Boat*. *Board of Trade*, *Doc Yak* and the *Hippo* went next, followed by *Moody & Sanky*, *Fortune Ship* and Harper's *Red Riding Hood*. And so it went through the day until 768 banks had been sold. A uniform price for each bank had been agreed upon before the sale. Now that is the stuff of which collectors' dreams are made!

One of the men sold his collection, including his Whiting banks, in 1979. After Whiting's death in 1982, his banks were sold at auction. The last of the three collectors sold his banks in 1983.

The Whiting banks have been cast to the winds, landing back in the hands of collectors. Just recently, the remarkable collection of the late Ed Mosler was returned to the collectors in his own special way. The collecting cycle has no end.

It's hard to recapture and convey the mood at a collectors' convention. The first day, everyone scurries from room to room, looking, buying and trading. A short business meeting follows dinner, after which members huddle here and there to continue negotiations. Late at night, there is time for reminiscing about the past year of collecting.

The following morning there is an auction of members' duplicate banks. A convention highlight, the auction is a wonderful opportunity for both buyer and seller. Afterwards, members dash back and forth, closing deals, doing last minute buying and selling. The afternoon is spent traveling to the homes of members who have been kind enough to invite the group to view their collections. The final event is a banquet followed by an informative program. Then members gather once again in rooms to converse long into the night. No one wants the convention to end.

If you want to immerse yourself totally in this kind of hobby, you should become a collector-dealer. At toy shows, dealers have the opportunity to shop before the doors open to the public. With an inventory of toys on your table you can often start a trade for a bank that otherwise could not be bought. We now enjoy searching for good inventory items as much as we enjoy hunting for banks. We have limited our dealing mostly to the Antique Toy World Shows, held three times a year just an hour's distance from our home. Every show is a mini-convention, where we make new friends, gain new knowledge and sometimes find additions to our collection.

More of our favorite banks.

WHAT IS A STILL BANK

No definition of a still bank will satisfy everyone. Ask two or more collectors and as many definitions will be proffered.

We differentiate in this way: mechanical banks perform, and still banks don't. A mechanical bank performs for the saver as he deposits or removes a coin. Over the years, a few banks that do not strictly meet this definition have been included in the mechanical bank category. Similarly, in this book, we have included a few banks that seem to meet the definition of a mechanical bank but which we deem to be still banks. We also have included registering banks in the still bank category as do mechanical collectors.

Some of the banks which are found both in still and mechanical collections are called Trick Drawer banks. When a coin is placed in the drawer and the drawer is then closed and reopened, the coin disappears as if by magic. (Example: *Freedman's Bureau*, #1286) Other banks some people consider mechanical are the Trick Opening banks. Their performance begins once the bank is full, triggering a spring-loaded trap which opens the bank for coin removal. (Example: *Safety Locomotive*, #1476) The balance of performing still banks are puzzle banks or banks which have wheels, a moving part, a combination opening, or an apparatus to register coins as they are deposited.

STILL BANK CONVERSIONS

"Why do you want that?" fellow collectors have asked, pointing with disdain at a bank on our shelf. "It's a conversion." The truth is that we like it and consider the piece a tribute to the ironmonger's art.

There are at least four types of converted cast iron banks. We collect the first three. The first type is the production conversion, altered at the factory where it was made. An example is Arcade's *Hot Point Stove*, #1346, produced first as a toy and then converted and advertised as a bank.

The second type of conversion also took place at the factory but was done by workers who took a part of a mechanical bank or toy that appealed to them, added a slot, painted it and took it home. An example of one of these end-of-day "whimsies" is the *Bad Accident Donkey*, #1642.

The third type of conversion took place away from the factory. A caring collector or loving father, attracted by a certain toy, converted it to a bank, carefully cutting a slot, at a time when the value of the piece was much less than the value of the time he spent.

The fourth type of conversion includes those banks which have been doctored by those who intend to deceive collectors.

Types of Conversions

Paper weights, door stops, toys and parts of toys are the most popular subjects for bank conversions. Some of the best known examples are the *Bulldog* (#403) and *Elf* (#309) doorstops, the *Oriental Boy on Pillow* #186, the *Rhesus Monkey* #778, *Bull on Base* #539, *Doc Yak* #30, *Tiny Tot* #1270, *Transvaal with Cigar* #262, *Small Ox* #1644, *Organ Grinder Man* #216 and *Boyscout* #39.

Detecting Conversions

The general rules for detecting a conversion are:
1. Beware if you are not familiar with a bank.
2. Beware of a cast iron bank that has no screw or coin trap to ease coin removal. Conversions are often riveted.
3. Beware of questionable coin slots. A good one should have draft, be logically positioned and balanced. Examine the slot for signs of original paint. Except for an occasional mismatching, where the slot has been cast on either side of the bank, we've rarely seen a poorly made slot on a production bank, early Grey Iron Casting Company banks excepted!

For us, dealing with conversions is easy. If we like a piece, if it has a slot, and if the item is priced right — we buy it.

REPRODUCTIONS AND THEIR DETECTION

Reproductions are modern copies of early pieces, sometimes cast from the original pattern. They have been made by someone other than the original manufacturer. Many reproductions are sold by companies who purchased patterns made originally by Hubley or Grey Iron Casting Company and are now selling them at the price one would expect to pay for a new cast iron bank. Reproductions like these, which are not intended to deceive, are easy to detect:

1. They have bright, modern paint or are painted dead black or bright, shiny gold.
2. Many are made of brass, aluminum or other metals not used in making the original bank.
3. The bank's halves aren't joined neatly or tightly.
4. Reproductions are not painstakingly finished. Rough parts aren't tumbled smoothly, and little attention is given to painting detail.
5. Reproductions in cast iron are heavier and thicker than the originals. The finish is rough or pebbly, a bit like cement. Modern production sand does't give the smooth finish of the early castings; the new does not have the quality of the old.

A more challenging problem is dealing with the work of the opportunist who **does** intend to deceive. He may bury a bank, causing it to oxidize and rust, soak it in salt or acid to accelerate oxidization, burn it to produce a brown or tan cast, cover it with lacquer or varnish, or remove its bright paint.

To thwart the opportunist, follow these rules:

1. Don't buy a bank that has a rough, granular finish.
2. Don't buy a rusted bank; new or old, a pitted bank is unattractive and undesirable.
3. Beware of banks with a brownish hue; they may have been fired to achieve the look of age. A bank darkened by age has uniformly deep colors.
4. Check the bank's size. Recast banks are often smaller.
5. Check the paint. Modern paint doesn't chip. If the paint appears to have been scratched off—beware.
6. Look for smooth wear spots. Few old banks survive in "mint" condition.
7. Take the bank apart. Most early banks were dipped in paint. It should appear around the slot and other openings in the casting. The casting should be smooth.
8. Don't buy, if still in doubt. If the price seems too good to be true, it probably is.

Many collectors lose objectivity when hunting for banks, causing them to make unwise purchases. Our acquisitiveness sometimes causes our mind and eyes to glaze over when in the presence of a bank we want. More than once I've bought a piece only to discover later, upon close examination, that the bank had been touched up or repainted. The rarer the piece, the greater the disaster, especially if one has paid a fair price. To protect yourself from this type of tragedy buy from collectors and dealers who stand behind their merchandise. Don't be afraid to ask if a piece is "all right." Ask dealers if they guarantee what they sell and if you may have return privileges within a reasonable amount of time.

Fortunately, most reproduction banks are the common ones. They were popular years ago, and they remain so today. The only scarce bank reproductions we know of are the *Hen* #549, *Two-Faced Devil* #31, *Baby in Cradle* #51, *Transvaal Money Box* #1, *Model T Ford* #1483, *Bear Stealing Pig* #693, *Polish Rooster* #541 and the *North Pole Bank* #1371.

The reproduction *Hen* is gilded rather than japanned, the surface is pebbly and holes have been cut in the base to make it lighter. Despite the holes, it is still heavier than the original. The *Devil* is painted bright red, not deep maroon as was the original. It is heavier, has more grinding marks, and the two pieces of the casting do not always meet well. The *Hen* and *Devil* were cast from original patterns, so they are the correct size.

Baby in Cradle is brightly painted and has the slot in the headboard instead of the blanket. The *Transvaal Money Box* has been reproduced in iron and in brass. The common reproduction is a two-piece casting; the original three-piece bank has a separate iron baseplate with holes cast in it. The reproduction *Transvaal* has a granular surface, the imprinting is not clear, and there is no hole for a pipe. There were also a few American made, three-piece reproductions of *Transvaal*. They are shorter, and the imprinting is not as clear as the original.

The reproduction *Model T Ford* is painted a dead black, the casting is heavier and thicker, and the bank has a pebbly finish. (A few deceptive reproductions are the reverse; they are too smooth!) The original Arcade auto banks have *ARCADE* boldly embossed underneath. The reproductions do not.

Bear Stealing Pig has been recast in brass. The *Polish Rooster*, recast in iron, is heavy, lacks good detail and has a pebbly finish. The reproduction *North Pole Bank* is not nickeled or electroplated; all of the originals were, including those which were painted over a nickel base. The reproduction has all of the other characteristics of a modern bank mentioned above.

CARE AND PRESERVATION OF STILL BANKS

Cleaning Banks

Most metals are vulnerable to moisture and salt, even to air. Ten collectors will provide you with ten different ways to clean and protect a bank. I did ask a few collectors I respect how they care for their cast iron banks. Here are their answers:

"I clean my banks in a mild mixture of Ivory Flakes and lukewarm or cool water, using a soft brush. I dry the bank thoroughly, and finish with a coat of Simonize Liquid Blue. If I use a hairdryer to speed the drying process, I'm careful to hold it away from the bank."

"I submerge the piece in lukewarm water and mild soap. I use a soft scrub brush to remove the dirt. I begin by putting a paper towel on the sink bottom. If the paint is water soluble, it will color the towel, and I quickly remove the bank. I dry the bank carefully and give it a light coat of oil, probably W-D 40."

"I like the look of age, so I don't do much. If a bank is particularly dirty, I spray it with Pledge and use a clean brush to loosen the dirt. If I'm still not happy, I spray again, and wait a while before using the brush. (Pledge has a water base; it may take a moment to loosen the dirt.) Dry with a turkish towel and buff with a soft cloth."

"I don't touch them. I like them the way I find them."

All methods probably work if the collector proceeds with caution. Do not attempt any of the above methods without first taking the bank apart. If you are the least bit fearful, experiment on a piece that doesn't matter, or follow the advice of Collector #4!

Now for the *DONT'S!*
1. Don't hurry.
2. Don't use hot water or abrasive cleaners.
3. Don't use a spray, brushed lacquer or varnish unless the paint is falling off or the paper label you want to preserve is deteriorating. In that case, consult a fine arts dealer and ask for the name of a museum-quality product that will preserve the bank safely.
4. Don't use water on a glass bank accessed only by a slot, as water may cloud it permanently.

Dust and examine your banks frequently. If you detect a problem, get professional help.

Removing Paint And Rust

Occasionally you will have the opportunity to purchase an original bank that has been repainted. Removing paint from a bank should be attempted only after you have gained a lot of experience working on pieces of little or no import. Many collectors refuse to touch a bank under any circumstances. Should you decide to walk where others fear to tread, do so carefully.

Some modern paints wash off. Many will come off with acetone (nail polish remover). Some collectors I know have had success with Easy-Time. Whichever liquid you use, proceed in a spot on the bank where mistakes won't be noticeable. Work a small area at a time, stopping frequently to observe the results. Use a cotton swab to get in the cracks and crevices. If necessary, remove the cotton and sharpen the stick. Do the recessed spots first; otherwise you may get too much of the product on the high spots and remove the paint you're trying to expose.

The best advice on rust removal is: Don't! You may also remove paint. I've not had much luck removing rust, but I'm not a patient person. You can carefully scrape a spot and seal it to prevent further rust. I'm told that naval jelly or electro-static cleaners work. I'm inclined to spray the bank or soak it in W-D 40 and use #0000 steel wool on the rust spots. One collector I know uses Lock-Ease, and rubs the spot with the same steel wool. After buffing with a soft cloth, he seals the bank with Klear liquid wax. I have heard that soaking a frozen part in Oilson will free it, but I have not experimented with that product.

Restoring Cast Iron Banks

Bank restoration is a controversial subject. There are collectors who are adamant in their belief that an original piece should not be doctored in any way. They are entitled to their own opinion; however, I delight in seeing a bank I love made whole again, particularly when it is a fine specimen of a rare bank, in need of minor work. A mast may be missing, a crack or chip may need to be filled, or the paint retouched.

Repairing and repainting banks is a costly process which should be undertaken only by craftsmen. The man I would recommend to undertake restoration of a rare piece is Russ Harrington of Baltimore, Maryland. Five banks in our collection have been graced by Russ. Can you find them?

A word of caution: home repairs, while satisfying to the collector, are devastating to the investment value of a piece.

RATING THE BANKS

Rating the banks is a difficult and controversial task. Emotions tend to run high when the subject is discussed among collectors. We all have a tendency to give the highest ratings to the favored specimens in our own collections, to those banks which have eluded us, or to those which have brought high prices in the marketplace.

My rating system is based on scarcity alone, and because I wanted my assessment to be as accurate as possible, and not unduly skewed by my *own* bias, I asked for the help of collector friends whose judgment I respect, and who have handled a great many banks over the years. I am greatly indebted to them for their help. I could not — and would not — have done it alone!

Rating Cast Iron Banks

A - Common banks. Any collector can readily find a specimen to add to his collection.

B - Still common, but a quality specimen is more likely to be found in the hands of a bank dealer, in a good general-line antique shop, or at an antique toy show.

C - Starting to become difficult to find, particularly nice specimens.

D - Scarce banks. Most are found in collections; only rarely will another specimen turn up.

E - Rare. Few are known to exist and they are in collections. A collection must change hands or be broken up for another to become available.

F - Nearly extinct.

M - Modern; made after 1945.

Several earlier guides for still banks used five rating bands — **A** through **E**, which I prefer over other systems. In the last few years, however, the increased interest in still bank collecting has caused some specimens, previously regarded as scarce, to appear on the market. This is particularly true of banks made in this country, which have caught the attention of the general public. Banks have left the attic and have entered the marketplace. Therefore, we expanded the rating band by one letter, to **F**, only for cast iron and brass banks. Because we know more about their availability, ratings on the cast iron banks are the most accurate.

Rating Banks Made of Other Materials

1 - Common banks. Other specimens will show up

2 - Difficult - good specimens are hard to find

3 - Scarce

M - Made after 1945

Banks made of other materials are rated within their own categories. A lead bank that has a 2 rating indicates the bank's relative scarcity within the lead group, not in the world of still banks as a whole. And a word of caution about rating banks made of other materials: they are more difficult to rate accurately. Because the level of interest in collecting these banks is just beginning to rise, we are not able to make an accurate judgment of their availability. As a rule, they are fragile, making their survival in large numbers questionable. Finally, because there has been less interest in them than in cast iron, the market has not been strong. Large numbers of them may rest in attics both here and abroad. When we first began to collect lead banks, we thought each addition to our collection was one-of-a-kind. After a few years of searching we realized that more of them did exist.

As banks made of lead, metal alloys, glass and composition are more avidly collected, their quantities will become known, and additional rating bands will be needed for them. For now, they will be rated *1* through *3*.

Rating Conversions and Variations

Bank conversions also are rated, the rating reflecting the scarcity of the piece itself. There are several casting and paint variations in the book. Those variations which the collector may have difficulty locating are rated one band higher. For example, *Baseball Player* #18 is a **C**, while its blue brother, #19, a later bank is a **D**. The easiest *Baseball Player* to find, #20, is rated **B**.

FACTORS WHICH AFFECT THE PRICE OF BANKS

Ratings as an Indicator of Value

The rating guide is only an *indicator* of value. As a rule, banks made of cast iron command the highest prices. (There are a few early tins that prove the exception, but the main competition is from the tin toy collector rather than the bank collector.) Within a particular category, such as cast iron or lead, price is greatly influenced by desirability. Many an **E** bank will sell for less than a highly desirable **D** bank. *Andy Gump* #217, *Two Kids* #594, and *Bear Stealing Pig* #693, are good examples of **D** banks which sell at **E** prices.

Subject matter is also a factor. The character banks are the most popular, followed by a few of the animal banks. There are also many highly coveted miscellaneous banks, as well as trolleys, autos and ships. Building, or architectural banks, are just coming into their own. With the exception of a few, such as the *Palace* #1116, prices had remained rather low for many years. There is increasing interest in the beautiful, highly detailed safe banks, but they are not widely collected yet.

Cross-collectibility can have have a great effect on price. For example, bank collectors must compete with collectors of political, comic, sports and world's fair memorabilia. And who will ever know for sure how many Tammany Tiger banks rest on the desks of New York City politicians?

Pottery is cross-collectible and is yet to be appreciated by any but a handful of bank collectors. A pottery pig purchased as a bank for a few dollars, might have gone for several hundred dollars at a pottery auction to someone who didn't care whether or not it had a slot!

In conclusion, ratings have been provided to help the collector determine how often he might encounter a certain bank. Knowing a bank's relative scarcity may help him determine what condition he is willing to tolerate and what price he is willing to pay.

Determining A Fair Price

Banks rated **A** and **B** tend to trade at known prices. Collectors can check their prices by attending swap meets, conventions, antique and toy shows, and by studying the price lists of established bank dealers. These banks have moved up slowly in recent years, and price changes are consistent with inflation's affect on the dollar. Condition has the greatest influence on the price of an **A** or **B** bank. **C** and **D** banks are the heart of most collections. Prices of these banks have risen consistently and best reflect the general health of our hobby. Even during the early 1980's, these prices were stable and rising, although our national economy was in a decline.

E and **F** banks are a major investment, and like precious metals, rare stamps and other commodities, reflect activity in the marketplace. Prices of these banks are greatly affected by our perception of the general economy. If the market anticipates an accelerated and rising rate of inflation, bank prices will skyrocket, even doubling and trebling in value. Once inflation has been brought under control, and people believe that it will *stay* under control, prices can fall precipitously. A scarce bank should be a good long-term investment, but the price will fluctuate depending on the state of the market. Rare, high quality collectibles are in diversified portfolios of several major bank trust departments for just this reason.

Buying a bank is not like investing in the stock market. Corporations are affected by quality of management, technological change, and so forth. Penny banks have intrinsic value much as diamonds and gold. There is a floor to their value; they cannot go out of business or into bankruptcy.

BUYING BANKS AT AUCTION

Auction prices can be unreliable and confusing to a new collector. Prices vary greatly, depending on the number of banks being auctioned, the extent to which the auction has been advertised, the number of collectors, dealers and mail bidders involved, and the condition of the banks.

Condition is all important. Looking at the auction catalog picture doesn't always tell us what we need to know about a bank. It might be one of the finest specimens known; it might have a small crack or repair;

it might be a repaint. It could even, Saints preserve us, be a reproduction or a conversion.

Be wary of placing too much stock in auction prices. A collector who has traveled a great distance and at great expense isn't going to be too concerned about the price he must pay to acquire a single bank. And if two such collectors get involved in a bidding war on that bank, the price may become astronomical.

A common bank may sell at a high price if a collector needs it to complete a series, if he collects only that type of bank, or particularly covets that specimen.

A beginning collector can often do well at an auction, particularly an auction featuring many banks. Bank dealers usually won't let a piece go too cheaply, yet they would rather handle scarce pieces or those in extra fine condition. The beginner may be able to buy good specimens of common banks at low prices.

Don't be afraid to place an auction bid by mail, but phone the auctioneer prior to the auction and discuss the condition of the banks he has. Because bank auctions occur infrequently, it is a nuisance for auction houses to handle returns; most will not accept returns unless a bank has been misrepresented in the catalog.

Ask yourself these questions before making a purchase: "Do I like it? Will it make me happy to keep it for a long time? Can I afford it? Does the price make sense?" If the answer to each question is *yes*, buy it.

BUYING BANKS BY MAIL
Communicating With Dealers

Don't shy away from buying by mail. Problems that arise are generally the result of a lack of communication between buyer and seller. I have purchased many banks by mail from dealers and collectors. I have yet to encounter a seller who wouldn't take back a bank if I weren't satisfied. Agree with the seller in advance of your order that you would like a short return period. Three days is reasonable, and a week is not unusual. If you do return an item, do it immediately; better yet, call or write the seller, advising him that the bank is in the mail so that he can resell it while his ad is still current.

If you receive a bank by mail that doesn't meet your expectations, chances are a breakdown in communications has occurred. Perhaps the seller's idea of condition wasn't the same as yours; perhaps the bank was broken, repaired or restored, and the seller failed to communicate this information or failed to notice the problem. Obviously, good communication can save you and the dealer time and trouble.

Defining Condition

Dealers who handle a large number of banks try to communicate well. They will describe the condition of their merchandise as accurately as possible to avoid the cost and nuisance of having banks returned. Problems occur among dealers and collectors who only occasionally handle banks. Certain terms should be agreed upon to help ease communication. Mechanical bank collectors use the terms *mint*, *pristine*, *choice*, *average* and *below average* to describe the amount of paint found on a bank. I use these terms and an additional one, *above average*, to describe the condition of paint found on still banks.

Mint is the most abused term in the world of collecting. A mint bank has 100% of its paint and has not been handled noticeably by the original owner or seller. Many banks advertised as *mint* or *mint-in-the-box* are not actually in that condition, and there is no such thing as *near mint*. The word mint, like the word rare, cannot be modified.

A *pristine* bank retains 98% or more of the original paint. Only a few scattered chips are visible. A *choice* bank is one that still has 90% or more of the original paint. *Average* describes the amount of paint found on most banks — 60% or more. Any bank having less than 60% paint is considered to be in *below average* condition. (*Poor*, a synonym for below average, is a term seldom used by sellers for obvious reasons!)

An additional term, *above average* is needed in describing still banks. While mechanical banks often sat on a shelf awaiting a deposit, still banks were multi-purpose toys. Animal banks, for example, saw double--duty as zoo or farm toys. Therefore, the term *above average* is used to describe those stills which retain 80% or more paint. (The use of a plus or minus following a percentage figure will allow a more accurate description of an item.)

Note that these terms refer only to paint condition. If a bank has been repainted or repaired, if it is rusty or has replaced screws or turnpins, these factors must also be communicated by the seller.

Determining the percentage of paint which remains on a bank is a difficult task at best. However, collectors must make the effort to avoid misunderstandings.

FOR BEGINNERS ONLY

When we began to collect, we often heard the adage, "Buy one scarce bank instead of ten common ones." Had I followed this advice, I might have lost interest in collecting still banks! I love the hunt, and I love bringing something home. One rare bank would have depleted the budget and taken me out of circulation for a long time.

When out of circulation, you miss the hunt and the opportunities it affords, such as finding a rare bank at a common price, or following a lead that pays off later. In order to learn, I had to make mistakes. Certainly more can be learned from handling a number of common banks than from handling a few rare ones. Each acquisition helps to develop your collecting taste, which ultimately affects the character of your collection.

Over time, I have sold hundreds of banks that had appealed to me at an earlier date. I enjoyed handling them, but eventually sold them to make room for banks I learned to enjoy more. Some of the banks in this book will probably be sold someday to make room for something else; other banks are waiting to be upgraded. When I find a duplicate of a bank I own, and the condition of the duplicate is better than mine, I'm as delighted to acquire it as I would be to acquire a bank I don't have at all. Plus it gives me another trader!

Today, we have a broad-based collection, focusing on cast iron and high quality lead banks, with a good representative sampling of other materials. Other collectors will have a different focus. The world of still bank collecting is so vast, it must be narrowed according to each collector's taste and wallet.

WHO MADE THE BANKS

ARCADE MANUFACTURING COMPANY
"Arcade Toys — They Look Real"

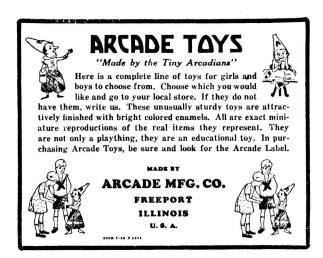

The *Arcadians*, a booklet published by Arcade in 1927 and distributed by their sales representatives, contained a poetic sales pitch. Elf-like creatures, called Arcadians, encouraged children to ask for the company's toys. An excerpt from the poem shows the vigor with which Arcade fought for its share of the market during its golden years as a toy manufacturer. The poetry isn't great, but the message apparently reached its audience:

> Our toys are not like other toys
> Which soon in pieces lie.
> They're made so strong that you can hardly
> Break them if you try!
> Make sure that you these letters see —
> A-R-C and A-D-E!

Like other early toy manufacturers in this country, Arcade began as a producer of iron goods for home and industry. And like their competitor, A.C. Williams, their production was interrupted by a devastating fire. Arcade's occurred in 1892, just seven years after the company opened its doors. The first still banks appeared in the Arcade line at the turn of the century. *The Bank of*

Columbia, patented in 1891, may have been the first bank. *The Globe on Wire Arc* is circa 1900, and a 1902-3 catalog pictures, among others, the *Dewey*, *Sampson*, and *U.S. Navy* safes. The *Teddy Bear* and *U.S. Mailbox* were two other early banks produced before 1910.

Arcade's able president, L.L. Munn, had the foresight to hire Isaac Gassman as the firm's secretary and sales manager. Gassman's ingenuity resulted in Arcade, located in Freeport, a small Illinois town, becoming a major manufacturer of cast iron toys. In 1921, Gassman struck a deal with the Yellow Cab Company of Chicago. Arcade produced a cast iron Taxi, and the cab company had the sole rights to use the toy in its advertising. The Taxi made a fortune for Arcade and the company went on to produce a popular line of beautifully made automotive toys.

During the Depression, Arcade was teetering on the brink of extinction when the Chicago World's Fair, "The Century of Progress", opened in 1933. Arcade had taken advantage of the previous Chicago Fair in 1893, producing the *Bank of Columbia* at that time. In 1933, the Fair saved Arcade. The company negotiated and won the right to produce official souvenirs. Their replica of the G.M.C. Greyhound Trailer bus that toured the fairgrounds was an immediate success. Bank collectors are enriched because Arcade also made a *Century of Progress* building bank.

Gassman may or may not have been party to other lucrative agreements Arcade made with companies such as General Electric, Roper, Hotpoint, Majestic, Kelvinator, Peters Weatherbird and Red Goose Shoes. The company also capitalized on popular comic strips of the day, making an Andy Gump toy and a bank, and the *Good Luck Horseshoe* bank, which includes Buster Brown and Tige.

World War II signalled the death knell for Arcade, as it did for so many other early toy companies. Arcade produced war materials and briefly resumed toy production immediately after the war. In 1946, L.L. Munn, Jr. sold Arcade to Rockwell Manufacturing Company of Pittsburgh and the Arcade name, so boldly embossed on many of their toys and banks, disappeared shortly thereafter.

BANTHRICO INC.

Banthrico was founded in 1931, when Jerome B. Aronson and his brother-in-law, Joseph L. Eisendrath, acquired the assets of the bankrupt Bankers Thrift

Company. Bankers Thrift had done some acquiring of its own, having absorbed the Stronghart Company in 1929. Stronghart had been in business since 1914. Bankers Thrift and Stronghart both produced banks for the banking industry.

Banthrico prospered under President Aronson and Secretary-Treasurer, Eisendrath. The *American Home Bank*, possibly the first penny bank made of plastic, was the first bank produced by the newly-formed company. Another early bank was *Snug Harbor* #1374. Thousands of new bank designs were introduced in the years that followed. After Aronson died in 1955, Joseph Eisendrath became president, followed by his son, Peter, after Joseph's retirement in 1982.

Joseph Eisendrath is particularly proud of Banthrico's replica of the new *First National Bank of Chicago, #1222*. First National placed an initial order for 5000 replicas, but had to reorder before the building was completed; construction workers at the site purchased 3000 of them as souvenirs.

Banthrico exports its banks and sells some of them through retail outlets, but the majority of its items are sold to financial enterprises.

The company's metal banks are made of a zinc-aluminum alloy, composed of 95% zinc and 5% aluminum. Some banks are made of vinyl plastisol. Eisendrath advises collectors who have a problem with oxidization of metal banks to preserve them with a coat of clear lacquer.

Banthrico banks can be dated easily. The company added the Banthrico name to its products twenty years ago. The first coin trap was a riveted key-lock with a diagonal slot. A horizontal slot identifies banks made in the early 1970's, and by 1974, a slotted base plate was in use. This device was replaced by a slotted, metal pry-off cap. Today, the cap is made of plastic. Key-lock traps are still in use on a few banks.

GEORGE BORGFELDT & COMPANY

Borgfeldt was an important dealer-distributor of dolls between 1881 and 1925. The company distributed Hubley toys and produced glass, candy-container banks.

GEORGE W. BROWN & COMPANY

This firm was founded by Brown and Chauncey Goodrich, in 1856. Located in Forestville, Connecticut, the firm ceased to exist when Stevens & Brown Manufacturing Company was formed. Brown designed fanciful building banks made of tin, which are pictured in the *George Brown Toy Sketchbook*.

CHAMBERLAIN & HILL

Chamberlain and Hill, Walsall, England, was a major manufacturer of cast iron still banks, as well as numerous other products made of iron. The company also manufactured a few mechanical banks. Chamberlain & Hill, still in business, casts its products at the Chuckery Foundry, Walsall. *See* Sydenham & McOustra, page 24.

J. CHEIN & COMPANY

Fanciful tin toys, lithographed in bright colors, were the hallmark of the Chein Company, a small, family-

owned business that produced at least sixty-five different banks. The company started up in 1903 in New York City with the production of small, tin toys. Most toy companies made safes before making other kinds of banks and Chein was no exception. The earliest known Chein banks are the *Child's Fireproof* and *Mascot Safes*, circa 1906.

Julius Chein moved his company to Harrison, New York, in 1907 and the toy line was expanded. Samuel Hoffman, Chein's brother-in-law, became president upon Chein's death in 1926 and his creativity manifested itself during the 1930's in an outpouring of whimsical and useful toys, including mechanical banks.

Chein ceased all toy production during World War II, and when the war ended the company faced a problem — the proposed route of a new highway was in line with the Chein factory. This time the company moved out of state to Burlington, New Jersey where household items such as globes were added to the line. Toys at this time included a great many items for the very young — tops, sets of dishes for little girls, playthings for the sandbox. A globe, one of Chein's most enduring banks, was introduced before 1934 and made until 1977. It can occasionally be found on a store shelf.

Hoffman retired in 1970 and was succeeded by Irving Sachs. It is not known when the manufacturer's name was changed from Chein Company to Chein Industries but Sachs did close the toy division of his busness in 1977.

Production clues can be used to date Chein banks. A number of different traps was used. The earliest trap was a square one with a flat surface, the lock sunk in a circular mound. After 1934, the trap was flattened and the traditional keyhole opening appeared. In 1938, the round keyhole gave way to an irregularly shaped one.

A big change occurred in 1941, as Chein substituted a round, twist-type trap for the square one. This trap was made of heavy, silvered metal with raised edges. After World War II, a shallow, twist-type trap made of scrap metal was used. It is found in assorted colors.

Another dating clue is the Chein logo which changed over the years. Until about 1930, the company identification — *J. Chein & Co. Made in U.S.A.* — was printed in a semi-circular design. In the 1930's, the wording was encased in a shield. A modern, spiral design replaced the shield in 1972 and was the last type used.

DENT HARDWARE COMPANY

The Dent Hardware Company was founded by Henry H. Dent of Fullerton, Pennsylvania, in 1895. The company was a major producer of cast iron toys from 1898 until 1937. Dent's still banks, never an important part of the company's line, include the *Air Mail* bank and *Stop and Save*. Dent remained in business until 1973.

ENTERPRISE MANUFACTURING COMPANY

Enterprise, located in Philadelphia, was a hardware manufacturer. The 1876 Centennial Exposition, held in that city, marked 100 years of American independence. Enterprise took full advantage of the celebration by producing a series of still banks including the large (#1242) and small (#1244) Independence Hall banks and the *Independence Tower* (#1205). The company continued to produce banks until about 1888.

GREY IRON CASTING COMPANY

The Grey Iron Casting Company, Mount Joy, Pennsylvania began in 1881 under the name, Wrightsville Hardware Company. Like many other toy companies, Wrightsville Hardware joined the National Novelty Company toy trust in 1903. That trust failed, as did its successor, The Hardware and Woodenware Manufacturing Company. In 1912, the toy company was incorporated under the name The Grey Iron Casting Company, and went into business on its own.

Over the years, Grey Iron produced all sorts of cast iron toys, including military miniatures. Early Grey Iron banks — the *Warship Maine*, *Globe on Arc* and the *Domed Mosques* — appeared in 1903. Toward the end of World War I, Grey Iron produced the *Doughboy* bank and a splendid bust of General Pershing. A George Washington bust bank of equal quality was produced sometime in the 1920's. The last production date known for a Grey Iron bank is 1925 when the *U.S. Treasury* building was made.

In a 1928 catalog, Grey Iron boasted: "All our banks have a slot large enough to accomodate a half dollar or English penny." It is on the basis of that boast that the the authors have determined that certain unidentified banks were made by Grey Iron. The *Mermaid* and *Dolphin*, the *Husky*, the *Dutch Boy* and *Dutch Girl*, the *Cat with Long Tail* and others all have unusually large and rather irregular coin slots which accept half dollars. Grey Iron's banks were also cast differently than banks made by others. The casting halves flow irregularly with the form of the banks.

In 1969, John Wright of Wrightsville, Pennsylvania, acquired Grey Iron and all of its old patterns along with some of Hubley's. A number of these banks are now being made by John Wright.

Note: Columbia Grey Iron Company, Columbia, Pennsylvania, was a separate company, producing toys twenty miles away from its similarly named competitor. Columbia Grey Iron produced the *Columbia Tower* bank, the *Street Car* bank, and the *Deposit* and *State* banks. The *Deposit* and *State* banks were also made by several other companies.

J.M. HARPER

A mystery man named James M. Harper designed and copyrighted a group of fifteen banks which are considered among the most beautifully executed still banks. A Chicagoan, Harper jobbed out the production of the banks to the Chicago Hardware Foundry Company in North Chicago, Illinois. The banks all bear copyright dates including the years 1902 through 1909. This is a summation of the known facts about Harper and his beautiful banks!

We can assume he was proud of what he designed because his name appears on all of them except the two Pig banks, which are copyrighted. To date, Harper banks have been seen in only one catalog, John M. Smyth's, a Chicago store that now sells furniture. In a 1903 Smyth advertisement under the heading, *Portrait Banks*, the following description appears:

> The bank is made of iron. Size 6 x 2½ inches and is surmounted by a portrait of either Washington, Lincoln, Grant, McKinley, Cleveland or Roosevelt, in

bronze. Handle is nickel plated. Money cannot be shaken out. Our price, 20 cents.

The Smyth advertisement only adds to the mystery as only two Harper bust banks are known to exist — Washington and Grant. For further evidence of the authors' frustration with James M. Harper and his splendid banks, see Appendix #594.

JOHN HARPER & COMPANY, LTD.

Harper was England's foremost producer of mechanical and still banks. Located in Willenhall, Staffordshire, England, as was its foundry, Albion Works, Harper produced all kinds of decorative iron goods beginning in the 1800's.

The last banks Harper made in iron were the *Crown* and *Throne*, produced in 1953 to commemorate Elizabeth II's coronation.

As so little is known about the American bank designer, James M. Harper, collectors sometimes confuse him with the English Harper. There is no evidence to support any connection between the two.

O. & M. HAUSSER

Otto and Max Hausser founded this venerable German firm in Ludwigsberg, a town near Stuttgart, in 1904. Hausser was a manufacturer and wholesaler of dolls and toys, including military miniatures.

The early military miniatures were made out of a composition material Hausser trademarked in 1926 under the name "Elastolin." Between the world wars, Hausser produced a large number of non-military figures, including a complete zoo. From 1929 to 1939 the company produced its Elastolin banks. No banks appear in Hausser's 1939-1940 catalog.

Hausser managed to stay in business during World War II, although the company's records were destroyed in bombing raids. Hausser manufactured toys made of polystyrene and plastic until June of 1983, when the company went into bankruptcy.

THE HUBLEY MANUFACTURING COMPANY

"Lancaster Brand Iron Toys"

John Hubley founded this important toy company in 1894. While other early manufacturers began to produce toys only as a sideline to their hardware business, Hubley emphasized toys from the beginning. The preface to a 1906 Hubley catalog reads:

> Our exceptional facilities for the production of iron toys and the high grade work required in this line, enable us to be in a position to make a superior grade of light gray iron castings and light machine work of every description for the trade. We would respectfully solicit a trial.

The catalog is filled with trains, hansom cabs, surreys, farm wagons, banks and every imaginable piece of horsedrawn fire equipment.

Jacob Brubacker was one of the principal designers of Hubley toys. From the late 1800's until the early 1940's, Hubley also contracted with leading sculptors of the day to design some of the company's toys. Fearful of harming their reputations as serious sculptors, the artists did not permit Hubley the use of their names!

After WWII, Hubley produced paperweight replicas of banks. They are highly coveted by collectors. The company was sold to Gabriel Industries in 1955, and that company became a division of CBS in August of 1978.

Among Hubley's earliest banks were those first made by the Wing Company of Chicago. Hubley acquired the patterns and introduced *Santa Claus* #59, *Rabbit* #570, *Foxy Grandpa* #326, *Small Elephant* #470, *Billy Bounce* #15, and *Darkey* #167 in 1906. Hubley also introduced some of its own designs at that time.

In 1914, Hubley produced two of its finest banks, the *Boy with Large Football* and *Baseball on Three Bats*. That same year, the company established a relationship with Grace Drayton, creator of wide-eyed characters such as *Fido*, *Puppo* and *Cutie*. These Banks were highly successful and *Fido* and *Puppo* were produced well into the 1940's.

IVES

Tiffany of Toy Manufacturers? The expression *does* seem excessive, but histories of Ives are filled with superlatives and for good reason. The company which underwent numerous name changes — E.R. Ives & Co.; Ives, Blakeslee & Co.; Ives, Blakeslee & Williams; Ives & Williams; The Ives Manufacturing Co.; and finally, the Ives Corporation — was founded in Plymouth, Connecticut in 1868 and moved to Bridgeport shortly thereafter.

Edward Ives, his brother-in-law Cornelius Blakeslee, Cornelius' father Joel, and Ives' son Harry C., were all connected with the business. Edward G. Williams, apparently not a family member, was the sales manager.

In business until 1930, Ives produced the best toy trains, clockwork, tin, steam and iron toys. Each is an exquisite piece, a joy to behold. Without question, Ives was the best known of all American toymakers without rival at home or abroad.

Now for the sad news: Ives produced few still banks, perhaps only one — the *Palace* — our most beautiful building bank. The *Electric Railroad* had been attributed to Ives. However, recently discovered patent papers identify it as a Shimer bank. Shimer is to be congratulated on the superior quality of its product! The *Santa with Removeable Tree* is still attributed to Ives, although there is no catalog evidence to support it.

As Ives was a jobber for other toy companies, it is often difficult to identify its banks. Ives catalogs contain mechanical and still banks that were not produced by them.

A number of remarkable still banks remain unidentified. Perhaps some of them will someday be found in a yet-undiscovered Ives catalog. Hope springs eternal.

JUDD MANUFACTURING COMPANY

The Judd Manufacturing Company, Wallingford, Connecticut, is best known for its manufacture of mechanical banks beginning in about 1882. The company was started circa 1830 by Morton Judd. By 1855, when his three sons had joined him in business, the firm's name had been changed to M. Judd & Sons. In 1887, H.L. Judd, who had gone into business on his own in Brooklyn, N.Y., bought his father's company and concentrated all metal manufacturing operations in Wallingford.

Most Judd banks are finished in brown or maroon lacquer, often washed with green. The *Snappit* banks, the two *1876 Building* Banks and the *Clock with Moveable Hands* are all good examples of Judd's craftsmanship.

The authors believe that *Lost Dog* is also a Judd bank as casting details are virtually identical to the large and small mechanical *Rabbit* banks and *Bull Dog Standing* bank.

KENTON

"The Real Thing in Everything but Size"

The Kenton (Ohio) Lock Manufacturing Company opened its doors in May of 1890. Nearly one hundred years later, Kenton is remembered more for the locks on its banks than for the door and ice box locks it made.

In 1894, Kenton added toys to its line and changed its name to the Kenton Hardware Manufacturing Company. Perhaps, it was the 1893 World's Fair in Chicago that sparked Kenton's interest in penny banks because the earliest known stills are the Columbia series, designed for the Fair.

1903 was a turbulent year for Kenton. The factory was destroyed by fire and foreign competition kept profits down. Rebuilding its factory in four months, Kenton then sold out to the National Novelty Company, a toy trust formed to help reduce the cost of manufacturing and selling toys. In 1904, National Novelty purchased Wing Manufacturing Company of Chicago and moved to the Kenton plant. Sometime after that, Wing's toys appeared in Kenton catalogs.

National Novelty proved unprofitable and in 1907 a new trust, the Hardware and Woodenware Manufacturing Company of New York, was formed. Even less successful than National Novelty, this second trust went into receivership in 1908, though it was permitted to continue operations.

The Kenton plant was closed from February, 1908 until February, 1910. Their patterns were shipped to J. & E. Stevens, Jones & Bixler and Grey Iron Casting Company. (This may partially explain why the same bank appears on the pages of different companies' catalogs.)

In 1912, the court ordered the sale of Hardware and Woodenware. L.S. Bixler, Woodenware's hard-working agent at Kenton, quickly formed a new corporation, the Kenton Hardware Company. As its president, Bixler was largely responsible for a huge outpouring of wonderful toys and banks from Kenton. He led the firm until his death in 1951. Kenton's clever radio banks, the *Roosevelt New Deal Bust*, the mailbox banks and the lovely elephant and donkey pair, were produced during the Bixler regime.

KINGSBURY MANUFACTURING COMPANY

This concern, located in Keene, New Hampshire began making toys in 1890 under the name Wilkins Toy Company. The firm was purchased in 1895 by H.T. Kingsbury, who continued to sell toys under the Wilkins name until 1919. Kingsbury produced no toys after World War II.

GEORGE C KNERR

George Knerr (1911-1979) of Williamsport, Pennsylvania, was a dedicated member of the Still Bank Collectors' Club of America. This well-loved man designed and painted thirteen iron still banks between 1968 and 1976. The *Uncle Sam Hat* was the last bank Knerr made.

Knerr, whose banks were cast at the Williamsport Foundry Company, enjoyed having collectors visit him at his home. Those who did received a special gift, Knerr's *Nickel Bank*, which he distributed only in this fashion.

KYSER & REX

Louis Kyser and Alfred C. Rex opened the doors of their company in 1879 in Frankfort, Pa. outside Philadelphia. They manufactured iron castings and hardware, match safes and other similar goods. Had these able men limited their line to these items, they would have been long forgotten. However, they also produced mechanical and still banks and bellringer toys.

Kyser, a native Philadelphian, and Rex, born in Germany, were both inventors. They were assisted by Rudolph Hunter, a mechanical engineer and attorney. These men were not the most prolific producers of still banks but they were certainly among the best. During an eight year period from 1882 until about 1890 they produced the *Apple*, the *Kneeling Camel*, a beautiful series of safe banks and the magnificent triad — *Tower*, *Globe Savings Fund* and *Coin Registering* building banks.

Perhaps this explosion of productivity was too much for the partners. In 1884 Kyser left the firm, which then became Alfred C. Rex and Company. Rex continued to patent mechanical banks but licensed them to other manufacturers. This splendid company which, like Ives, was devoted to uncompromising quality, ceased to exist in 1898.

NICOL & COMPANY

"White City Trick or Puzzle Banks"

Virtually everything we know about this Chicago-based company can be read on the pages of the 1895 company catalog that follows. The Nicol banks, which appear on page 105, are cleverly designed and well made. For an explanation of the unique opening devices on the Nicol banks, see the Appendix, page 155.

J. & E. STEVENS

The name Stevens evokes memories of mechanical banks; yet this venerable Connecticut firm, the oldest toy company in America, also manufactured a large number of still banks, toy stoves, cap pistols and pull-toys.

Located in Cromwell (in a spot known locally as Frog Hollow), Stevens was founded in 1843 by John and Elisha Stevens. Their first line was hardware, which kept them afloat until John Hall walked in the door with a design he had patented for a bank with moving parts. He called it *Excelsior* and the toy was to revolutionize the world of cast iron toys.

Stevens produced *Hall's Excelsior* around 1870 and his *Lilliput* shortly thereafter. Within two or three years, the company began to produce its own banks in prodigious numbers and varity. By 1890, Stevens had dropped its hardware line and produced only toys. One of the company's top designers, the famed Charles A. Bailey, designed the *Bismark Pig*. Mechanical and other varieties of that bank, which we assume included the *Bismark* still bank, were made from the same pattern.

Like so many other companies Stevens became a branch of the National Novelty Company in 1903. Stevens survived its stint with National Novelty better than some others and in 1912 was on its own again, doing business through Riemann, Sebrey and Co., N.Y. Mechanical bank production ceased in 1928 and during World War II the factory closed due to iron shortages. The resilient Stevens reopened under new ownership after the war, producing toys, mostly cap pistols, until the 1950's.

The earliest Stevens stills are the *Lilliput*, 1875; the *Crown Building Bank* series, 1883; the *Roof Bank*, 1887; and the *National Safes*, circa 1898.

In 1905 and 1906, the *Kodak*, *Oregon* and the *Four Tower* bank were introduced. Although this book suggests that Stevens reserved people and animals for its mechanical banks, there are two notable exceptions — *General Butler*, considered one of the finest still banks, and the *Barrel with Arms*, a creative piece made not only as a bank but as an inkwell and table lighter.

The semi-mechanical *Pay Phone*, patented in 1928, was probably the last new bank introduced by J. & E. Stevens.

CHARLES V. REYNOLDS

Charles Reynolds, a teacher of industrial arts, lives in Falls Church, Virginia. He has produced a series of mechanical and still banks in sand-cast aluminum at a foundry on his property. Reynolds' first still bank was the *Amish Man* #238, produced in 1980. In the fall of 1983, Reynolds designed a miniature foundry that produced the tiny *State Bank* #1660 for a special exhibit of architectural banks at the Cooper-Hewitt Museum in New York City.

SHIMER

Jacob and William Shimer, German immigrants, founded Shimer and Company. Also, William's sons, Milton and Irwin, were part of the firm. Located in Bethlehem, Pennsylvania, the company manufactured hardware, sad irons, scales and toys. In 1899, the company's name was changed to William Shimer and Son Co. and by 1914, Shimer was the largest independent foundry in the United States. Following a disastrous fire in 1915, Shimer closed its doors, ending the history of one of the great pioneers in the toy industry.

SMITH & EGGE

Friend William Smith and Frederick Egge organized the company bearing their names in 1874 and incorporated it in 1877. The plant was across the street from Ives, leading to speculation that Smith & Egge may have produced banks under contract from Ives. It is known that Smith & Egge made parts for Ives.

Banks made by Smith & Egge include the large and small *Boston State House*, perhaps the most beautiful pair of building banks. They also made the unusual *Moody and Sanky* bank with its inset pictures of the religious leader and his music director.

STEVENS & BROWN MANUFACTURING COMPANY

In 1868, this firm became the successor to George W. Brown & Company. (John Stevens was also one of the founders of the J. & E. Stevens Co.) Stevens & Brown of Cromwell, Connecticut was founded to merge the tin toy line of Brown with the cast iron toy line of J. & E. Stevens. The two firms founded the American Toy Company in New York City to distribute their toys.

The partnership lasted until 1872. Eight years later Stevens and Brown was dissolved by the Connecticut State Assembly for failure to file organization papers.

SYDENHAM & MC OUSTRA

Sydenham and McOustra, whose trademark was Beacon Products, was located in Walsall, Staffordshire, England on a site near Chamberlain & Hill. The company was formed in 1908 by McOustra, an ex-foreman at Chamberlain & Hll, and Sydenham, a local surgeon. A fierce rivalry existed between the two companies. They copied one another's ideas and even those of J.M. Harper Co., Ltd. A crisply written note in an old Harper catalog threatened prosecution of people who were copying the company's banks.

The smaller of two *Eiffel Tower* banks, #1974, was made by Sydenham & McOustra at Beacon Foundry and the larger one was made by them or by Chamberlain & Hill. We may never know for sure.

One or the other of these feuding companies produced the beautiful series of *Empire, Coronation* and *Dreadnought* banks pictured on page 124, and *Save and Smile,* #24.

Chamberlain & Hill bought its rival company in the 1950's and continues in business today.

TRESOR-VERLAG
&
TRESOR-PORCELLAINE ROYAL

Tresor-Verlag, Affalterbach, West Germany and Porcellaine Royal, Kronach, West Germany are two of the three companies owned by Gerhard Riegraf, the most important manufacturer of still banks in Europe.

Only banks made of porcelain are produced at Tresor-Porcellaine Royal, a company founded in Dresden in 1892. In 1979, this firm produced the lovely *Mother with Child,* #323, in a limited edition.

Riegraf, a member of the Still Bank Collectors' Club of America, has generously produced a number of special banks for the Club.

VINDEX COMPANY

Vindex was a sewing machine company located in Belvidere, Illinois. Although we know little about this firm, they made cast iron toy autos, racing cars, farm equipment and at least two still banks — the *Owl,* #597, and the aluminum and cast iron *Boston Bull Terriers,* #423 and #425.

A.C. WILLIAMS COMPANY

Empire stoves, flat irons and pruning tools were among the goods produced by the A.C. Williams Company, Chagrin Falls, Ohio when A.C., Jr. entered the family business in 1872. By 1886, he had purchased the company from his father. Just three years later, fire destroyed the factory but Williams rebuilt it the next year. Fire destroyed it again in 1892. That might have been enough bad luck for some people but Williams moved to Ravenna, Ohio and started over. Bad luck was behind him.

To improve sales, Williams provided his traveling salesmen with miniature samples of the company's hardware. A Detroit buyer, S.S. Kresge, pointed out that the samples would make nice toys. Soon A.C. Williams was the world's largest toy and still bank manufacturer. The Woolworth chain was among the company's customers.

Patent papers tell us what little we know about the early Williams banks since none appeared in company catalogs until 1904. Williams himself, may have designed what we believe to be his company's first still bank, the *Domed Bank,* in 1899. Williams is also named as the inventor on patents for the *Skyscraper* in 1900 and the *Two-Faced Indian, Two-Faced Black Boy* and *Baseball Player* in 1901. He patented the *Two-Faced Devil* in 1904, the *Elephant with Howdah* in 1905 and *Aunt Jemima* in 1906.

We don't know how many other banks were designed by Williams. We have patent papers for just a few. We do know that the company's treasurer, James H. Bigelow, designed the *Clown Bank* which he patented in 1908. Certainly, there were other designers whose names have been lost in time.

A.C. Williams was a giant in the world of still banks, producing character banks, animals, trolleys, airships, mail-boxes, cannons, clocks and buildings until the advent of World War II, when our country's iron products were in the hands of soldiers instead of children, housewives and handy-men. Although the company continued to make toys until 1977, bank production never resumed.

WING

Peter Gerhardt Wing of Chicago opened the doors of the Wing Manufacturing and Plating Company in 1894. By 1900, the company name had been shortened to Wing Manufacturing Company.

Like several other toymakers, Wing sold out to the National Novelty Company in 1904. That company moved the Wing operation to Kenton, Ohio where it became part of the Kenton Hardware manufacturing branch of National Novelty. Although Peter Wing joined the firm as head of the mechanical department, the sale of his company must have been difficult for him as he returned to Chicago within the year.

By 1906, Wing's creations, *Grandpa, Darkey, Billy Bounce, Santa Claus, Elephant, Rabbit* and *Statue of Liberty,* were being made under the Kenton and Hubley names.

Wing founded another Chicago-based company in 1907 and patented and produced at least one still bank — a toy safe. Wing died in 1962 at the age of 105.

JOHN WRIGHT

This firm purchased the Grey Iron Casting Company in 1969 and since then has reproduced toys cast from the original Grey Iron and Hubley patterns.

WRIGHTSVILLE HARDWARE COMPANY

Wrightsville Hardware Company was formed in 1881 in Mount Joy, Pennsylvania. The firm later became the Grey Iron Casting Company.

24

MANUFACTURER CATALOGS

ARCADE MANUFACTURING COMPANY

Freeport Ill. ·U·S·A·

Toy Iron Banks. 1902

No. 20

Per Gross

No. 20. State Bank, 4 x 3 x 2¼, Nickel Plated, Comb. Lock.........$44.00
Packed 6 in a paper box, 1 gross in wood case 8½ x 13 x 25¼ inches.
Net weight 100 lbs. Gross weight 113 lbs. per case.

No. 45. State Bank, Steel Back and Sides, Nickel Plated..............$32.00
Packed 6 in a paper box, 1 gross in case 13¾ x 17¼ x 26½ inches.
Net weight 39 lbs. Gross weight 49 lbs. per case.

Per Gross

No. 90. American Bank, 4 x 3 x 3, Nickel Plated, Key.................$44.00
Packed 6 in paper box, 1 gross in case 8½ x 13 x 25½ inches.
Net weight 96 lbs. Gross weight 110 lbs. per case.

37

Toy Iron Banks. 1902

No. 25.

Per Gross

No. 25. Daisy Bank, 3½ x 2½ x 2½, Nickel Plated, Key............$17.00
No. 25-X. Steel sides and back.......................................14.00
Packed 6 in paper box, 1 gross in wood case 8¾ x 11¼ x 21 inches.
Net weight 50 lbs. Gross weight 61 lbs. per case.

No. 26.

Per Gross

No. 26. U. S. Navy Bank, 3½ x 2½ x 2¼, Nickel Plated, Key......$20.00
No. 26-X. Steel sides and back..17.00
Packed 6 in paper box, 1 gross in wood case 8¼ x 12¼ x 24¼ inches.
Net weight 55 lbs. Gross weight 65 lbs. per case.

34

Toy Banks. 1902

No. 40.

Per Gross

No. 40. Sampson Bank, 6 x 4¼ x 4½, Nickel Plated, Comb. Lock ...$85.00
No. 40-x Steel Sides and Back...76.00
No. 40. Size 5¼ x 4 x 4. Packed one in paper box, 3 doz. in wood case 10½ x 14 x 28½ inches.
Net weight 108 lbs. Gross weight 120 lbs. per case.
No. 40-x differs from No. 40 only in the sides and back which are of steel.

No. 30.

Per Gross

No. 30. National Bank, Nickel Plated, Comb. Lock.................$66.00

No. 30-x. Steel Sides and Back..........$60.00

No. 30. 4¾ x 3¾ x 3½. 1 only in a paper box, ½ gross in wood case 10 x 12½ x 24½.

No. 30-x differs from No. 30 only in the back and sides which are of steel.

Net weight 87 lbs. Gross weight 95 lbs. per case.

58

Toy Banks.

Steel Back and Sides.

Per Gross

No. 110. In White Plate finish, 3 x 2½ x 2½..........................$22.00

No. 210. Nickel Plated and Polished 3 x 2½ x 2½..........35.00

Packed ½ doz. in a paper box, 1 gross in wood case 20 x 16¼ x 9 inches.

Net wgt. 54 lbs. Gross wgt. 64 lbs. per case.

The GLOBE.

Made entirely of metal, enameled with the most attractive colors.

The globe is 3 inches in diameter, 4¼ inches high.

Each packed in a paper box, ½ gross in a case 30 x 14 x 10½ inches.

Net weight 54 lbs. Gross weight 70 lbs. per case.

No. 50. Cast top and bottom steel sides, aluminum finish.

Per gross....................$9.00.

2 inches high, 1¾ in. square.

Packed 12 in a paper box, 1 gross in wood case. Measurements of case 8½ x 12½ x 18 inches.

Net weight 32 lbs. Gross weight 45 lbs. per case.

39

Toy Iron Banks. 1902

No. 5.

Per Gross

No. 5. Cottage Bank, 3 x 2 x 2, coppered...........................$8.00
1 dozen in paper box, 1 gross in case 9¼ x 13½ x 17 inches.
Net weight 72 lbs. Gross weight 82 lbs.
No. 6. Same as No. 5 only Nickel plated.

No. 15.

Per Gross

No. 15. Castle Bank, 3¼ x 2⅞ x 2, Aluminum and Bronze..........$15.00
6 in box, ½ gross in case.
Net weight 48 lbs. Gross weight 60 lbs.

Toy Iron Banks.

SECURITY BANK.

No. 100.

No. 100. Security Bank, 6½ x 5 x 4½, Nickel Plated, Combination Lock......................per gross $150.00

Packed each in a paper box, 1 dozen in wood case 6¾ x 15½ x 20¾ inches.

Net weight 60 lbs. Gross weight 70 lbs. per case.

Toy Iron Banks. 1902

ARCADE

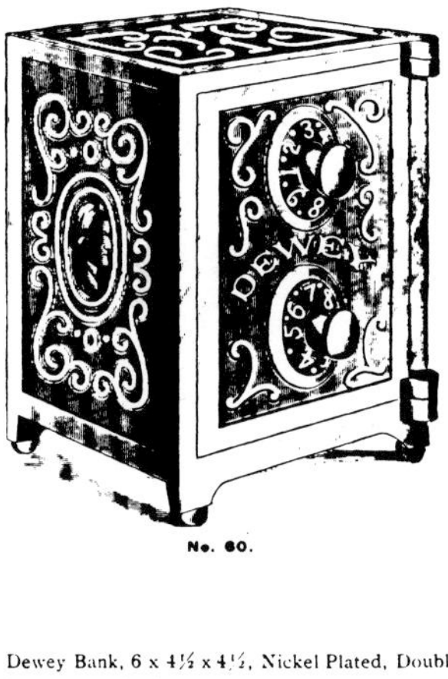

No. 60.

No. 60. Dewey Bank, 6 x 4½ x 4½, Nickel Plated, Double Combination Lock.....................per gross $96.00

Packed each in a paper box, 3 dozen in wood case 10½ x 14 x 28¼ in.

Net weight 115 lbs. Gross weight 130 lbs. per case.

35

Toy Banks. 1902

Carefully finished in nickel plate and operated by the most perfect combination lock used on a toy safe.

No. 60. 5¼ inches high. 1 doz. in case 19¼ x 14 x 6½.
Net weight 30 lbs. Gross weight 40 lbs. per case.
No. 65. 5 inches high. 1 doz. in case 18¾ x 13 x 5¼.
Net weight 28 lbs. Gross weight 38 lbs. per case.

No. 120. Safe stands 4 in. high; has same lock and finish as No. 60 and 65.

Each packed in a paper box, 3 doz. in wood case 17½ x 10 x 8¾ inches.

Net weight 40 lbs. Gross weight 60 lbs. per case.

General Sheridan Bank

c 1910

It would be difficult to show in cast iron a more vigorous picture of the famous general than this bank portrays. The illustration does not do it justice.
The horse and figure are finished in gold lacquer. The pedestal is in green and gold. It holds a large amount of coin.
All outlines are sharply defined. Sells very readily all through the year.
Extreme height 6 inches. Extreme length 6 inches.
Size of pedestal 4x2¾ inches.
Packed, each in a box, ½ gross in a case.
Case weight, net 55 pounds, gross 71 pounds.
Case measurements, 20x13x13 inches.

Bull Dog Paper Weight

This savage animal makes an excellent paper weight.
Finished only in gold lacquer. A very fine article.
Extreme length 4¾ inches. Extreme height 2¾ inches.
Packed ½ dozen in a paper box, ½ gross in a case.
Case weight, net 35 pounds, gross 44 pounds.
Case measurements, 17x10x10 inches.

220

Sun Dial Bank c 1910

A modern adaptation of the ancient method of telling time.

By placing the bank in the sun with the point "N" toward the north, the shadow of the gnomon on the dial will indicate the hour.

It is 4½ inches high. The pedestal, base and top are beautifully finished in gold bronze. The numerals and dial are outlined in crimson.

It holds a large number of coins— 25 cent pieces or smaller.

It is the most unique ten cent toy bank of the year.

Packed 1 dozen in a box, ½ gross in a case.

Case weight, net 50 pounds, gross 65 pounds.

Steam Boat Bank

An attractive inducement for a cargo of pennies. Combines an attractive toy and a large bank. A small kid and a piece of string will put this steamboat into active operation.

It is 7½ inches long and is stoutly made of cast iron, decorated in aluminum bronze with crimson striping—an interesting combination.

Packed 1 each in a heavy paper carton, ½ gross in a case.

Case weight, net 30 pounds, gross 39 pounds.

Case measurements, 27x8x7 inches.

209

Cow Bank c 1913

The cow bank is one which will sell freely at all times of the year.

The outlines are clear cut and the finish attractive.

Packed ½ dozen in a box, ½ gross in a case.

Case weight, net 38 pounds, gross 47 pounds.

Case measurements, 21x12x8 inches.

Pig Bank

This bank is a perfect image of a thoroughbred porker.

It is finished in jet black enamel, the eyes, mouth and tusks being outlined in crimson and gilt.

The extreme length is 4 inches.

Packed ½ dozen in a paper box, ½ gross in a case.

Case weight, net 37 pounds, gross 46 pounds.

Case measurements, 19x10x8 inches.

193

Cash Register Bank c 1913

The illustration shown above will give a very clear idea of the construction of this bank. It resembles a real Cash Register near enough to satisfy the demands of the young store keeper. The coins can be slipped in the slot at the side of the frame.

The bank is opened by unscrewing the bolt which holds it together. It is handsomely decorated in bright enamel and gold bronze.

Dimensions, 3¾x2½x3¾ inches.

PACKING

Packed 1 each in a carton, ½ gross in a case.

Case weight, net 27 pounds, gross 47 pounds.

Case measurements, 26½x13½x10 inches.

Drum Bank

This little bank will make a splendid item on your counter. The main frame of the bank is made of steel mesh coated with bright enamel. The metal ends are in gilt. The merry jingle of the coins in this bank will offer much amusement.

26 Size, 2⅜x2½ inches.

PACKING

Packed 1 dozen in a carton, 1 gross in a case.

Case weight, net 32 pounds, gross 56 pounds.

183

Clock Bank 1910

Every child is interested in a clock. The clock bank, therefore, has a double claim on the child's attention as it combines a clock and bank.

The front and back plates are of cast iron and the sides are formed of one piece of steel. The figures on the dial are in relief and are carefully gilded. The body of the bank is finished in black satin lacquer.

Height 3¾ inches.

Packed ½ dozen in a paper box, ½ gross in a case.

Case weight, net 29 pounds, gross 39 pounds.

Case measurements, 24x13x7 inches.

Gold Dollar Bank

We call this the Gold Dollar Bank for the reason that the face is made to represent a dollar and this is finished in a brilliant gold lacquer.

It is an exceedingly attractive bank and has great lasting qualities owing to the fact that it is constructed of cast iron and steel.

The money is inserted in the back. Height 3½ inches.

Packed ½ dozen in a paper box, ½ gross in a case.

Case weight, net 29 pounds, gross 39 pounds.

Case measurements, 24x13x7 inches.

210

Possum Bank c 1913

A lifelike reproduction. A very satisfying bank.

No. 1. Finished in aluminum bronze, with red trimmings.

No. 2. Finished in gold lacquer, with red trimmings.

Extreme length 4¼ inches. Extreme height 2½ inches.

Packed ½ dozen in a paper box, ½ gross in a case.

Case weight, net 46 pounds, gross 56 pounds.

Case measurements, 21x11x9 inches.

Rabbit Bank

The design of this bank is very carefully drawn and is decorated in a manner that gives it a very lifelike appearance. Gray and white are used in the color scheme.

Extreme length 4 inches. Extreme height 3¾ inches.

Packed ½ dozen in a box, ½ gross in a case.

Case weight, net 38 pounds, gross 48 pounds.

Case measurements, 19x10x10 inches.

192

New Crystal Bank c 1913

The very large sale of the first pattern of the Crystal Bank has encouraged us to improve the appearance by changing the design of the castings. The illustration clearly shows the result. We now avoid breakage of the glassware by packing each bank in a separate carton. We guarantee these banks to be delivered without breakage. Don't fail to place some of these in your holiday order. Size 3½x3½ inches.

PACKING

Packed one each in a carton, ¼ gross in a case.

Case weight, net 21 pounds, 29 pounds gross.

Case measurements, 15½x13½x11 inches.

Horseshoe Bank

The good luck feature of this bank is one reason its sale has been so large. Another is the attractive finish. The castings are finished in bronze and the steel mesh is dull black. It will hold a large quantity of small change. Its extreme length is 3½ inches, height 3¾ inches.

PACKING

Packed one each in a carton, ⅓ gross in a case.

Case weight, net 33 pounds, gross 56 pounds.

Case measurements, 27x13x10 inches.

182

Rhinoceros Bank c 1913

One of our latest patterns. Very attractive and a great seller.

No. 1. Finished in black lacquer with white horns, gilt and red striping.

No. 2. Finished in gilt lacquer, outlined in red and gold.

Extreme length 5 inches. Extreme height 2¾ inches.

Packed ½ dozen in a paper box, ½ gross in a case.

Case weight, net 60 pounds, gross 78 pounds.

Case measurements, 19x12x11 inches.

Elephant Bank

From the illustration you will see that this is an excellent bank.

Finished in a brilliant gold lacquer. This is one of the best animal banks that we make.

Extreme length 4¾ inches. Extreme height 3 inches.

Packed 1 dozen in a paper box, 1 gross in a case.

Case weight, net 57 pounds, gross 72 pounds.

Case measurements, 20x11x10 inches.

190

Cat Bank c 1913

The cat bank is an accurate likeness of an animal that is very attractive to every child. It is finished in gold enamel, outlined with gilt and crimson.

The extreme height is 4½ inches.

Packed ½ dozen in a paper box, ½ gross in a case.

Case weight, net 57 pounds, gross 68 pounds.

Case measurements, 23x12x8 inches.

Dog Bank

Nothing is more interesting to children than a toy in the form of a dog and this bank is a splendid looking animal of the Newfoundland type. The shaggy coat is well depicted.

It is finished in gold lacquer outlined in crimson and gold.

Extreme length 5½ inches. Extreme height 3¾ inches.

Packed ½ dozen in a box, ½ gross in a case.

Case weight, net 52 pounds, gross 66 pounds.

Case measurements, 25x13x18 inches.

194

Toy Banks c 1913

No. 10
State House Bank

An attractive little bank that is having a wide sale. A standard design and a sure seller.

Finished in gold bronze.

Size, 4x3x2¼ inches.

PACKING

½ dozen in a box, ½ gross in a case.

Case weight, net 54 pounds, gross 75 pounds.

Case measurements, 23x13½x11 inches.

Mail Box Banks.

These banks are beautifully finished with the best grade of baked enamel—not paint. One of the largest sellers in our entire line.

Size, 3½x2¾x1½ inches.

No. 1. Red enamel with gilt lettering.

No. 2. Green Enamel with gilt lettering.

PACKING

½ dozen in a paper box, ½ gross in a case.

Case weight, net 64½ pounds, gross 72 pounds.

Case measurements, 24x13x7½ inches.

203

The World Time Bank c 1913

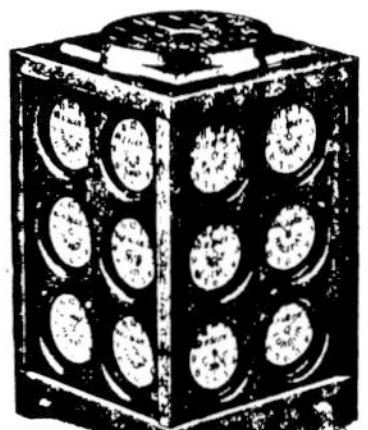

This is a most instructive bank and toy. On the top a large dial is shown with the hands pointing to 12 o'clock noon. On the sides are 24 dials showing the time in 24 different cities throughout the world when it is 12 o'clock noon at Washington.

It has a very large capacity for coin and is substantially built of cast iron. When the bank is full the contents can be easily taken out by removing a single screw.

Extreme height 4¾ inches.
Extreme width 2⅞ inches.

No. 1. Arcadian bronze finish.
No. 2. Gold lacquer.

PACKING

Packed ½ dozen in a paper box, ½ gross in a case.
Case weight, net 70 pounds, gross 87 pounds.
Case measurements, 27x13x9 inches

Bird Cage Bank

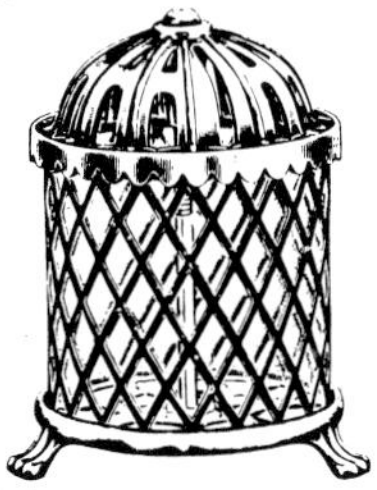

A child will have great fun in caging his change in this bank. Some of the pleasure comes from having the coins in view. Another source of joy will be in hearing the change rattle. The steel wire mesh is strong and will stand hard usage. The castings are finished in gold bronze and the steel body is dull black enamel, an attractive combination. Size, 4x3½ inches.

PACKING

Packed 1 each in a carton, ¼ gross in a case.
Case weight, net 17 pounds, gross 25 pounds.
Case measurements, 15¼x13¼x11 inches.

184

Rooster Bank c 1913

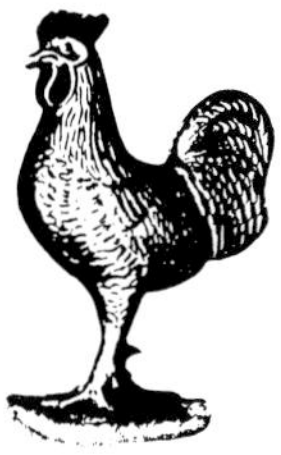

This bank is so realistic that one almost expects it to walk off or crow.
It is beautifully finished in black lacquer, while the comb is painted a bright crimson. The eyes and other features are outlined in black.
Finished in gold enamel when desired.
The extreme height is 4¾ inches. Extreme length 3¼ inches.
Packed ½ dozen in a paper box, ½ gross in a case.
Case weight, net 45 pounds, gross 55 pounds.
Case measurements, 22x12x9 inches.

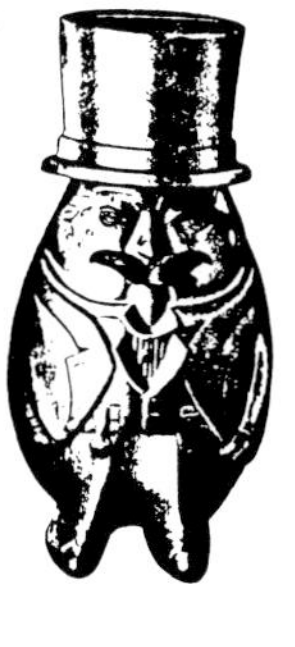

Egg Bank

This amusing bank is heavily made of cast iron finished in brilliant gold bronze with black trimmings.

It has a large capacity for change and it will prove a large seller in every locality.

Extreme height 4¼ inches.

Packed ½ dozen in a paper box, ½ gross in a case.

Case weight, net 59 pounds, gross 72 pounds.
Case measurements, 25x12x8 inches.

105

ARCADE IRON TOYS 1923

ANDY GUMP

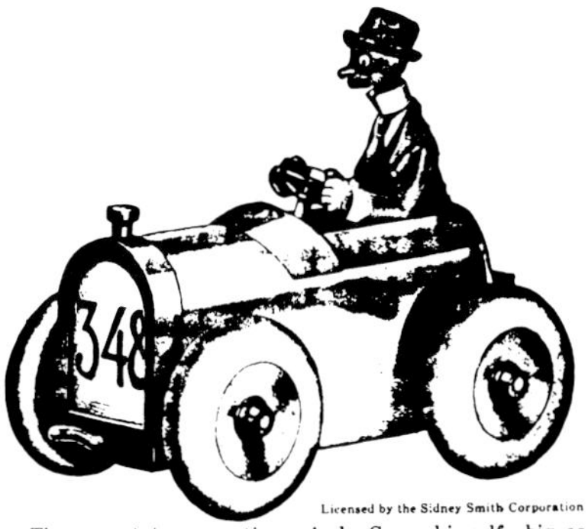

Licensed by the Sidney Smith Corporation

The newest toy sensation. Andy Gump himself—big as life. And the old veteran 348,—a perfect reproduction of Andy's celebrated auto. Well known all over the country through Sidney Smith's cartoons, Andy Gump sells himself on sight. Both grown-ups and kiddies go wild about him.

Andy and his car are solidly made from grey iron and go over the toughest roads without a break-down. This toy is beautifully colored. Andy has a red tie, white shirt, blue suit, and brown sport hat with a green hat band. Old 348 has a bright red body with green trimmings, green disc wheels with red hub caps, white tires, and aluminum license plates. Size: Length over all 7¼ inches, wheel base 4⅞ inches, height 6 inches, width 4 inches.

PACKED:

Each in a decorated paper carton, 12 in a case. Case net 35 pounds, gross 45. Case measurements 19x12¼x8¼ inches.

ARCADE MFG. CO. FREEPORT, ILL.

139

ARCADE IRON TOYS

HORSE BANKS 1923

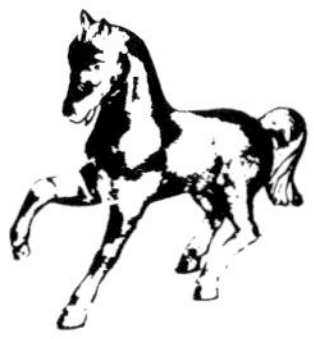

No. 1

A very attractive bank. An active design which will catch a child's attention. It is sturdily made of cast iron and will stand hard knocks. Dimensions 4¼x4¾ inches. Finished in gold bronze.

PACKED:

½ dozen in a box, ½ gross in a case. Case net 50, gross 63 pounds. Case measurements 23x12½x9 inches.

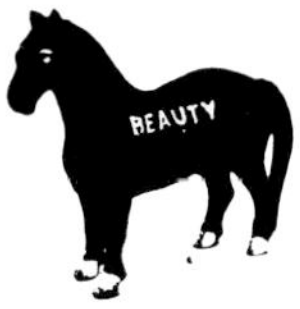

No. 2

A bank which makes a big hit with children. Black Beauty is always popular and this bank especially because of its handsome appearance. Like our other animal banks, the money may be removed by taking out a machine screw. Size 5x4¼ inches. Finished in black, satin enamel, trimmed and lettered in gold.

PACKED:

½ dozen in a paper box, ½ gross in a case. Case net 54, gross 67 pounds. Case measurements 23x12½x9 inches.

ARCADE MFG. CO. FREEPORT, ILL.

174

ARCADE IRON TOYS

HORSE BANKS 1923

No. 3

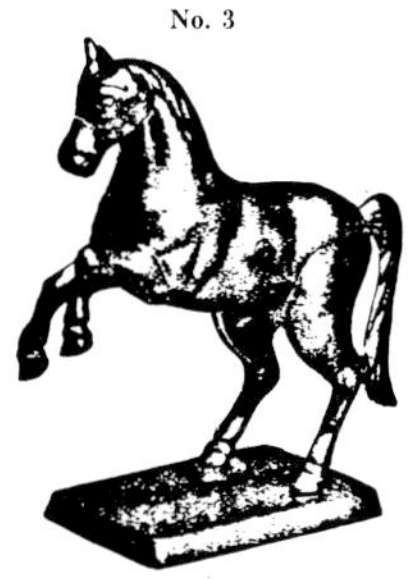

A very life-like bank of striking appearance. It is strong and heavy with a large coin capacity. Sure to fascinate children. Size 7¼x6¾ inches. Finished in gold bronze.

PACKED:

Each in a paper box, ¼ gross in a case. Case net 78, gross 95 pounds. Case measurements 27x17x11 inches.

No. 4

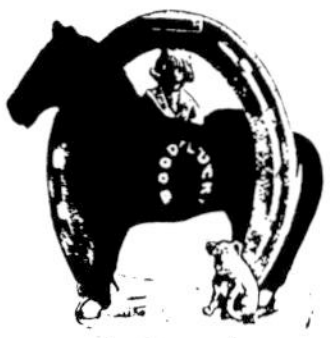

Combines a horse, a boy, a dog, a horseshoe, and a bank—five things every child delights in. Size 4⅛x5 inches. The horse is black trimmed in gold; the rest of the toy is gold bronze.

PACKED:

Each in a paper box, ¼ gross in a case. Case net 38, gross 50 pounds. Case measurements 19x14½x10 inches.

ARCADE MFG. CO. FREEPORT, ILL.

175

ARCADE IRON TOYS

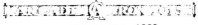

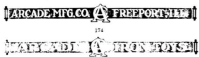

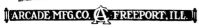

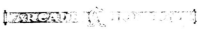

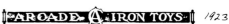

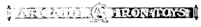

POLAR BEAR BANK 1923

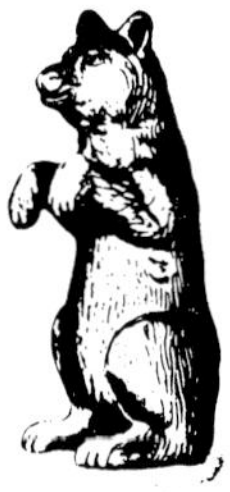

A large, capacious bank of excellent proportion and attractive design. Height 5¼ inches. Finished in gold bronze.

PACKED:

½ dozen in a paper box, ½ gross in a case. Case net 72, gross 87 pounds. Case measurements 23x13½x11 inches.

TEDDY BEAR BANK

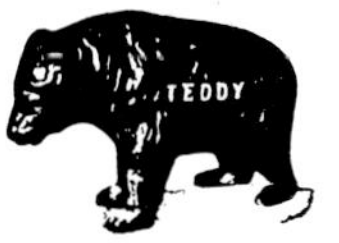

This is the most life-like model of a bear we have seen in a cast iron toy. These banks are always favorites with children. Length 4 inches, height 2½ inches. Finished in gold bronze.

PACKED:

½ dozen in a paper box, ½ gross in a case. Case net 40, gross 50 pounds. Case measurements 20x10x9 inches.

ARCADE MFG. CO. FREEPORT, ILL.

178

ARCADE IRON TOYS

ROOSTER BANK 1923

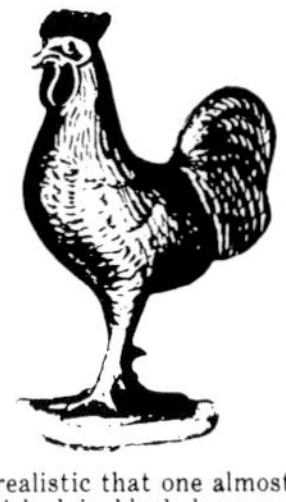

This bank is so realistic that one almost expects it to crow. It is beautifully finished in black lacquer, while the comb is painted a bright crimson. The eyes and other features are striped in with aluminum bronze and black. Extreme height 4¾ inches, extreme length 3¼ inches.

PACKED:

½ dozen in a paper box, ½ gross in a case. Case net 45, gross 57 pounds. Case measurements 23x12½x9 inches.

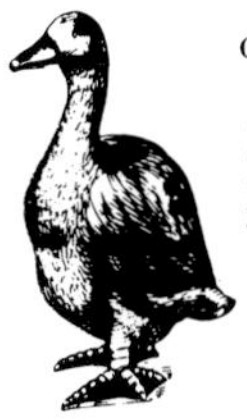

GOLD GOOSE BANK

The Gold Goose which lays the golden eggs is an old favorite with children. This Gold Goose Bank is well modeled and is very attractive. Extreme height 3⅞ in. Finished in gold bronze.

PACKED:

1 dozen in a paper box, 1 gross in a case. Case net 64, gross 76 pounds. Case measurements 23x12½x9 inches.

ARCADE MFG. CO. FREEPORT, ILL.

182

ARCADE IRON TOYS

RHINOCEROS BANK 1923

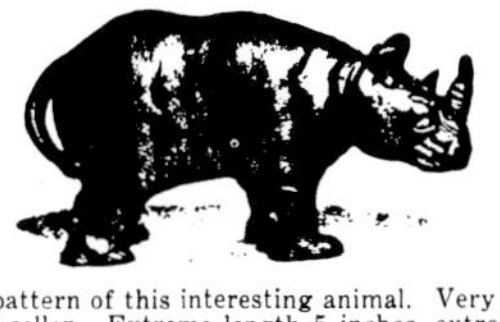

A good pattern of this interesting animal. Very attractive and a great seller. Extreme length 5 inches, extreme height 2¾ inches. Finished in gold lacquer.

PACKED:

½ dozen in a paper box, ½ gross in a case. Case net 65, gross 78 pounds. Case measurements 23x12½x9 inches.

BUFFALO BANK

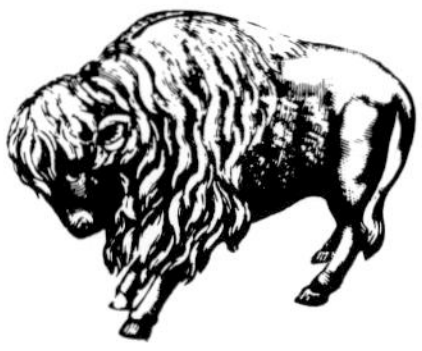

Children will like this Buffalo Bank. His shaggy coat and huge head and shoulders are well depicted. A very good animal bank. Extreme height 3 inches, extreme length 4¼ inches. Finished in gold bronze.

PACKED:

½ dozen in a paper box, ½ gross in a case. Case net 49, gross 62 pounds. Case measurements 23x12½x9 inches.

ARCADE MFG. CO. FREEPORT, ILL.

179

ARCADE IRON TOYS

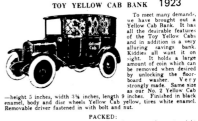

TOY YELLOW CAB BANK 1923

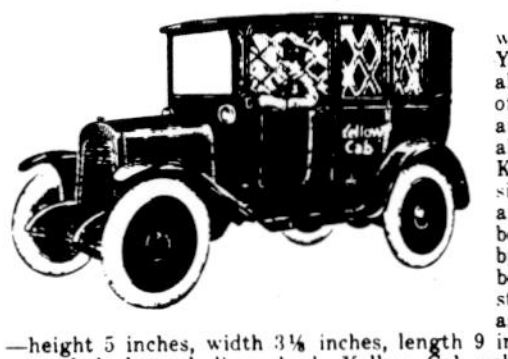

To meet many demands, we have brought out a Yellow Cab Bank. It has all the desirable features of the Toy Yellow Cabs and in addition is a very alluring savings bank. Kiddies all want it on sight. It holds a large amount of coin which can be removed when desired by unlocking the floor-board washer. Very strongly made. Same size as our No. 2 Yellow Cab—height 5 inches, width 3¼ inches, length 9 inches. Finished in black enamel, body and disc wheels Yellow Cab yellow, tires white enamel. Removable driver fastened in with bolt and nut.

PACKED:

Each in a paper carton, one dozen in a case. Case net weight 35 pounds, gross 42. Case measurements 19¾x10⅝x9 in.

TOY COUPE

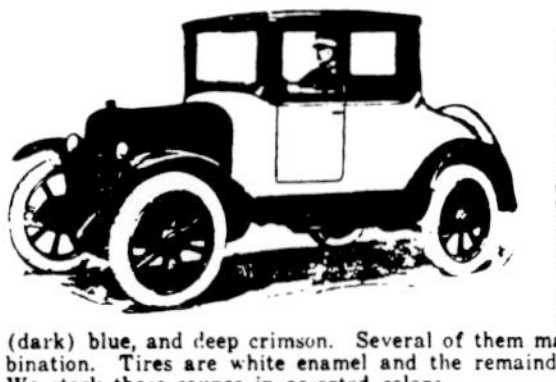

Built in the same unbreakable way as the Toy Yellow Cab. A beautiful model, it is sure to appeal strongly. Every boy will want one or more to add to his toy motor fleet. The bodies of these Coupes are strikingly finished in the following colors: Dust grey, Yellow Cab yellow, Suburban (dark) blue, and deep crimson. Several of them make a beautiful combination. Tires are white enamel and the remainder of the car black. We stock these coupes in assorted colors.

SPECIFICATIONS. Extra tire. Removable driver. Extreme length 9 inches, wheel base 6⅛ inches, height 4¼ inches, width 3½ inches.

PACKED:

Each in a paper carton, one dozen (3 of each color) in a case. Case net weight 37 pounds, gross 45. Case measurements 19⅝x11⅝x10 inches.

ARCADE MFG. CO. FREEPORT, ILL.

128

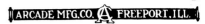

1923

ARCADE IRON TOYS

CLOCK BANK

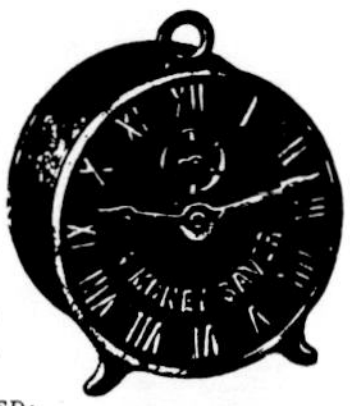

This item combines a clock and a bank and so is of unusual interest to children. The front and back are cast iron, and the sides are formed of one piece of steel. The figures on the dial are cast in relief. The bank may be opened by a machine screw in the back. Height 3½ inches.
No. 1. Finished in gold bronze.
No. 2. Finished in black enamel, figures in gold.

PACKED:

⅛ dozen in a paper box, ½ gross in a case. Case net weight 30 pounds, gross 40. Case measurements 24x13½x7 inches.

HALL CLOCK BANK

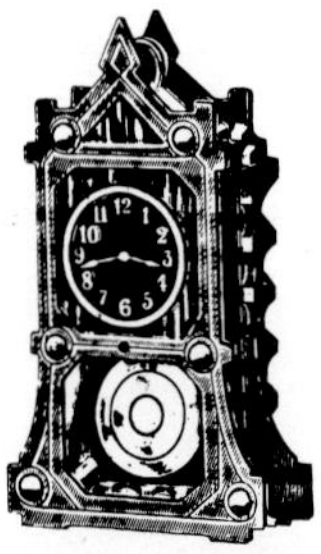

A novel bank which never fails to please youngsters. As shown in the illustration it is a perfect model of a grandfather's hall clock. The pendulum works freely over a sharply ground wedge and once started will swing for fifteen minutes without stopping. The rear of the clock contains a capacious bank. Size 5¾x3¼x1⅞ inches. Finished in black enamel with face of clock and pendulum gold.

PACKED:

Each in a paper carton, ¼ gross in a case. Case net 34, gross 45 pounds. Case measurements 20x15x7 inches.

ARCADE MFG. CO. FREEPORT, ILL.

187

1925

ARCADE IRON TOYS

TOY 05 LIMOUSINE YELLOW CAB

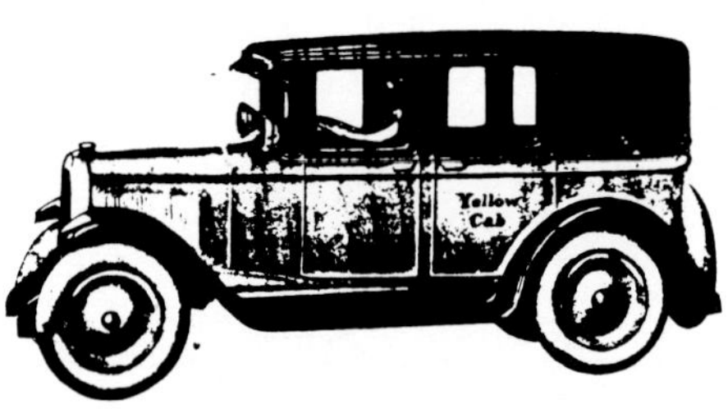

The toy 05 Limousine Yellow Cab is a splendid cast iron reproduction of this newest type of cab in use everywhere. Attractively finished as shown, with body in regulation Yellow Cab yellow, and black body stripe. Top and fenders are black enameled. Radiator and headlights finished in aluminum bronze, and the driver is nickel plated. Spare tire at rear.

Length 8½ inches, width 3½ inches, height 3⅜ inches. Furnished with nickel plated metal tires; or real rubber tires can be supplied at nominal extra cost.

Yellow Cab—Toy No. 155 with metal tires.

Yellow Cab—Toy No. 1550 with rubber tires.

PACKED

Packed one each in a paper carton, one dozen in a case. Case gross weight 38 lbs., net 47 lbs. Case measurements 21¼x12x9¾ inches.

ARCADE MFG. CO. FREEPORT, ILL.

27

1925

ARCADE IRON TOYS

LIBERTY BELL BANK

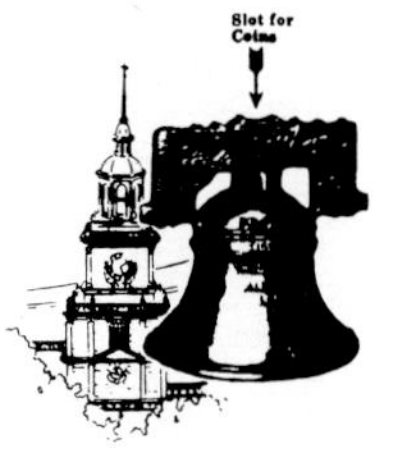

This bank miniature of the historic old Libery Bell will appeal to every red blooded American boy and girl as an added incentive to save. An emblem of the greatest episode in our history it is of great educational value to the children. Finished in attractive bronze standing 3¾ inches high and 3⅝ inches wide. A label giving a brief history of the old Liberty Bell is attached to the bottom.

PACKED

Packed one each in a carton, 3 dozen in a case. Net weight of case, 39 lbs.; gross weight 50 lbs. Case measurements, 15¼x13x10¾ inches.

ARCADE MFG. CO. FREEPORT, ILL.

63

ARCADE IRON TOYS

TOY FORD TOURING CAR 1925

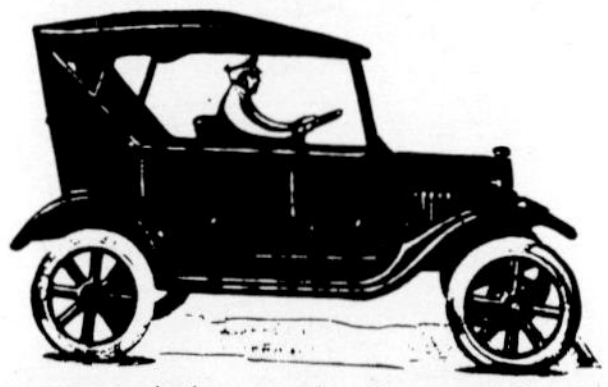

Every youngster in the country is a live prospect for one of these popular toys. They are realistic and beautiful models of the Ford Touring Car. Well made of cast iron, they will stand up under all kinds of hard service. They contain no clock work to require the attention of the garage man. The iron driver is removable. Furnished with or without rubber tires. Size: Length 6½ inches, height 4 inches, width 3 inches.

FINISH: A black enamel body. Tires white enamel. Man nickeled.

PACKED:

One each in a paper box, ¼ gross in a case. Case net 65, gross 80 pounds. Case measurements 23¾x14¼x12¾ inches.

FORD BANK

Slot in rear window for quarters, nickels, dimes and pennies. Bank compartment in back seat to hold $5.00 or more. Otherwise built same as Ford Touring shown above, of cast grey iron. Furnished with or without rubber tires.

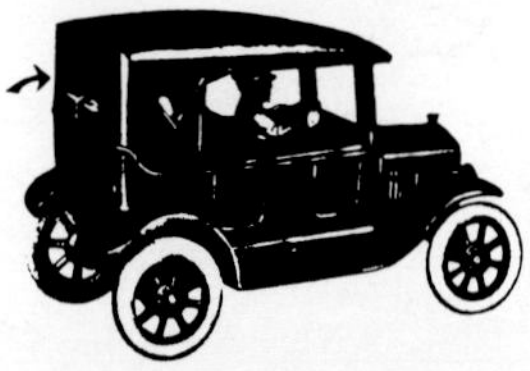

PACKED:

One each in a carton, ¼ gross in a case. Case net weight, 83 lbs.; gross, 100 lbs. Case measurements, 23¾x14¼x12¾ in.

ARCADE MFG. CO. FREEPORT, ILL.

8

ARCADE IRON TOYS

REINDEER BANK 1923

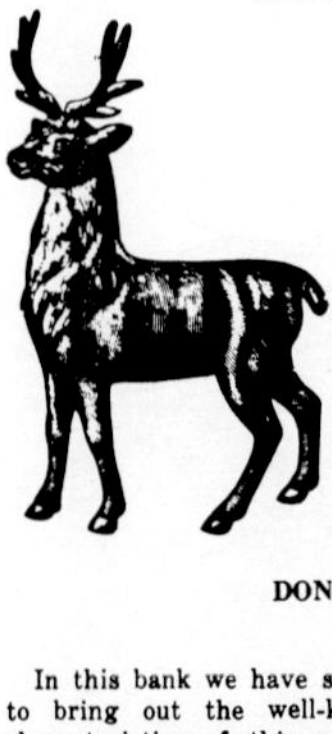

A reindeer is always coupled in a child's mind with Santa Claus and all the other delights of Christmas. Hence this life-like and graceful bank is sure to make a quick appeal to the average child. Always an item of large value. Height 6¼ inches, length 3¾ in. Beautifully finished in gold bronze.

PACKED:

⅛ dozen in a box, ⅛ gross in a case. Case net 49, gross 64 pounds. Case measurements 20x13x11 inches.

DONKEY BANK

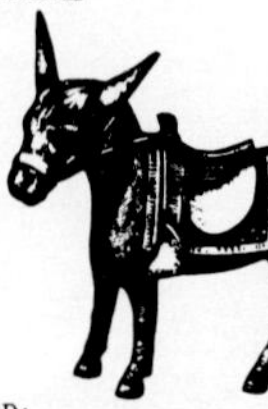

In this bank we have sought to bring out the well-known characteristics of this patient animal that are the delight of all children. It is heavily made and like its full-sized model, will stand all sorts of grief. Finished in gold bronze. Size 4½ inches high; 4½ inches long.

PACKED:

⅛ dozen in a box, ⅛ gross in a case. Case net 46, gross 61 pounds. Case measurements 23x13½x11 inches.

ARCADE MFG. CO. FREEPORT, ILL.

65

ARCADE

FACTORY PHOTO

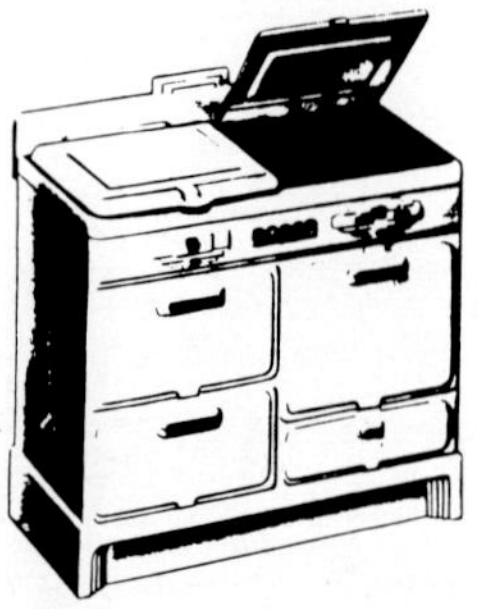

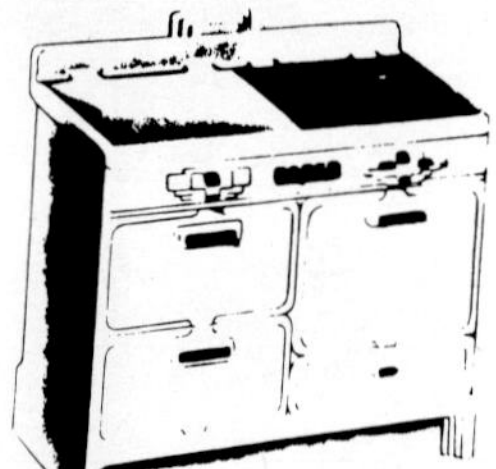

ARCADE

FACTORY PHOTO

1925

ARCADE IRON TOYS

HOTPOINT STOVE BANK

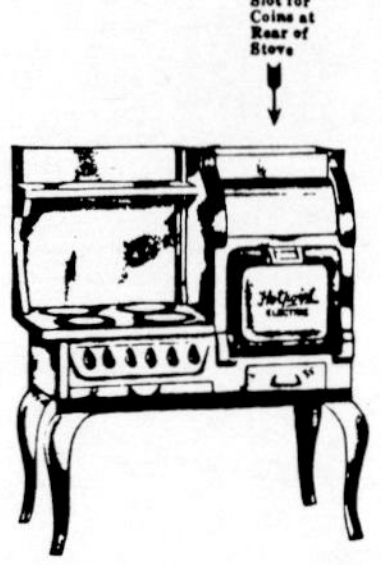

This Hotpoint Stove makes an unusual and attractive bank model and it appeals to the little girl's saving and maternal instinct. It is a miniature reproduction of the real Hotpoint Stove and serves the double purpose of bank and a part of the doll house furniture.

It is attractively finished in hard white lacquer and trimmed in gray and black, standing 8¼ inches high, 5¾ inches long and 2¾ inches wide.

PACKED

Packed one each in a carton, 3 dozen in a case. Net weight of case, 72 lbs.; gross weight 90 lbs. Case measurements, 22½x19x14¼ inches.

ARCADE MFG. CO. FREEPORT, ILL.

62

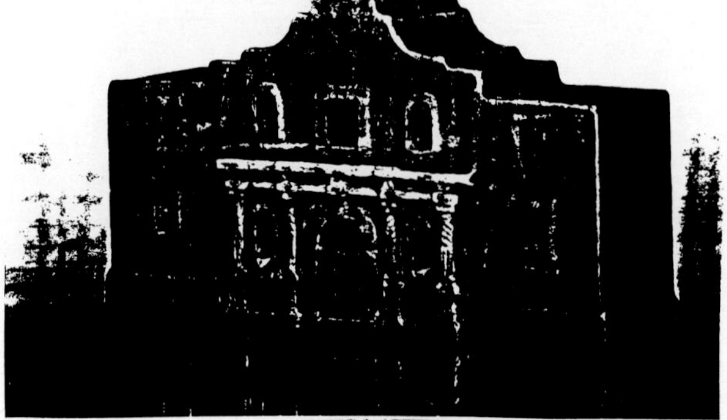

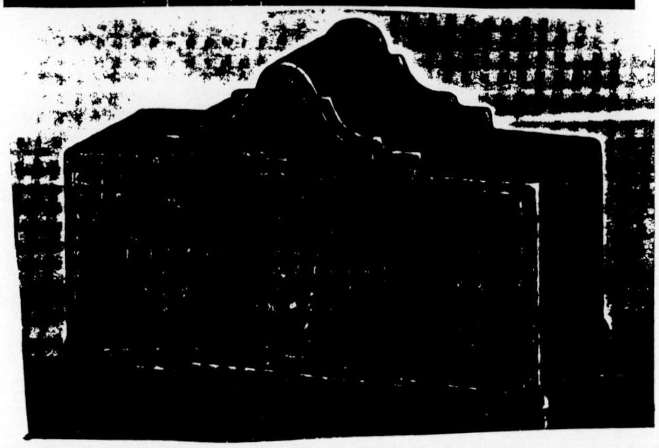

ARCADE CAST IRON TOYS

1934

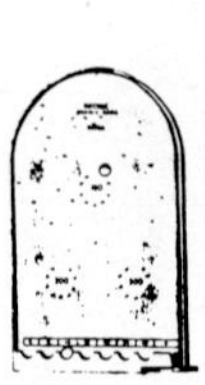

No. 889 Marble Game

Length 16½ inches, width 10¼ inches, height 2¼ inches.

An exciting game at small cost. Stops count from 5 to 300.

Board slopes toward player. Three marbles supplied. Rules on box cover. Nickeled spring gun.

Finished in apple green with black figures and decorations. Improvements in finish not shown in illustration.

Packed 1 in carton, 1 dozen in case.

Case net weight 27 pounds, case gross weight 32 pounds.

Case measurements: 11½x17x20 in.

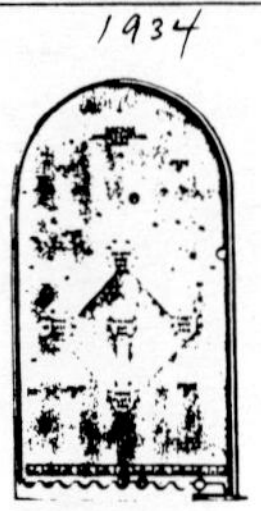

No. 890 Baseball Game

Length 23¼ inches, width 13½ inches, height 2½ inches.

The sensation in marble games,—two games in one,—the game counting by points for the younger child and the baseball game for the older children.

The baseball game has all the handicaps and thrills of the real game. Rules on the box cover. The board slopes toward the player to allow the balls to roll back, bouncing from one pin to another. Five marbles supplied.

Finished in green with tan diamond, varnished rim and notched board. Printed figures on playing surface and other attractive additions not shown in illustration.

Packed in carton, ½ dozen in case.

Case net weight 23 pounds, case gross weight 27 pounds.

Case measurements: 10x14½x24 in.

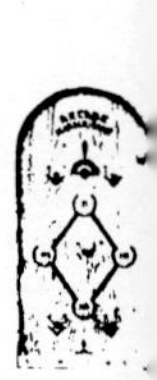

No. 888 Marble G

Length 17¼ inches, inches, height 3 inche

Finish: Varnished natu with red printed nu decorations.

Spring snap gun. Brass marbles supplied.

Packed 1 in envelope, case.

Case net weight 33 po gross weight 36 poun

Case measurements: 18

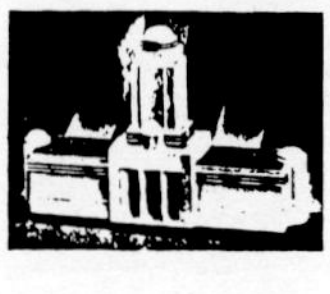

No. 869 "A Century of Progress" Ban

A miniature of a modernistic building at the World's Fair.

Finished in ivory trimmed in blue.

A coin slot on roof at either side of the Tower. Bank opened by unscrewing bo screw driver.

Width overall 7 inches, height 4¾ inches, de inches.

Packed 1 in carton, 1 dozen in case.

Case net weight 23 lbs., case gross weight

Case measurements: 7x10x14½ inches.

ARCADE CAST IRON TOYS 1934

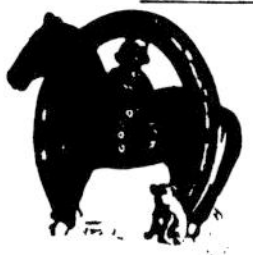

No. 801 Good Luck Bank

inches, width 1¾ inches, height 4¼ inches. Black with gold bronze horseshoe and ...
on top of horse.
in carton, 3 dozen in case.
weight 37 lbs., case gross weight 42 lbs.
urements: 11x13x16 inches.

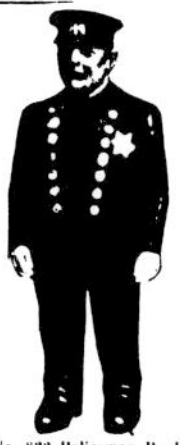

No. 822 Policeman Bank

Width 2¼ inches, depth 1⅜ inches, height 5⅝ inches.
Color: Blue with aluminum finish on gloves and star. Buttons gold. Black shoes. Face and hands flesh color.
Coin slot in back.
Packed 6 in carton, 6 dozen in case.
Case net weight 60 lbs., case gross weight 68 lbs.
Case measurements: 7x13½x23½ inches.

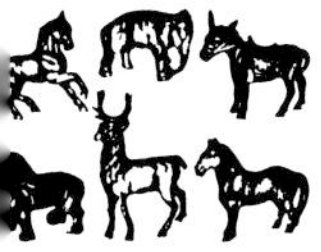

No. 863 Animal Bank Assortment

Red Horse 4¾x1¼x4¼ inches.
Blue Horse 5x1¼x1¼ inches.
Red Reindeer 5x1¼x6 inches.
Green Donkey 4½x1⅜x4⅜ inches.
Green Lion 4½x1½x3¾ inches.
Blue Elephant 4½x1½x4¼ inches.
in top of each animal.
sorted 6 in carton, 6 dozen in case.
weight 55 lbs., case gross weight 63 lbs.
surements: 9x12½x33 inches.

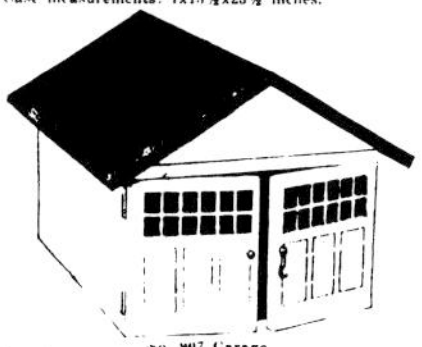

No. 907 Garage

Length 15 inches, width 10¾ inches, height 9½ inches.
Made of wood. Cream color with green trim and green roof.
Hinged double doors.
Packed 1 in shipping case.
Case weight each 5 pounds.
Case measurements: 10x11x16 inches.

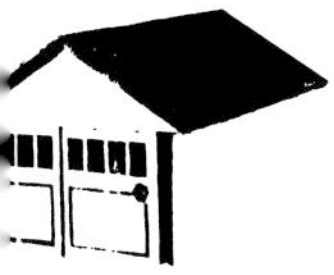

No. 908 Garage

2¾ inches, width 10 inches, height 8½ ...
wood. Cream color finish with green trim ... reen roof. Steel hinged door.
in shipping case.
ht 4 pound
surements: 9¾x10½x14 inches.

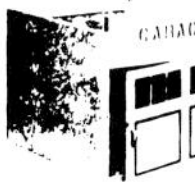

No. 906 Garage

Length 8 inches, width 7 inches, height 6½ inches.
Made of wood with hinged single steel door. Cream color with green stenciled door.
Packed 1 in carton, 1 dozen in case.
Case net weight 22 lbs., case gross weight 26 lbs.
Case measurements: 13x16x22 inches.

ARCADE CAST IRON TOYS 1934

ANIMAL BANKS

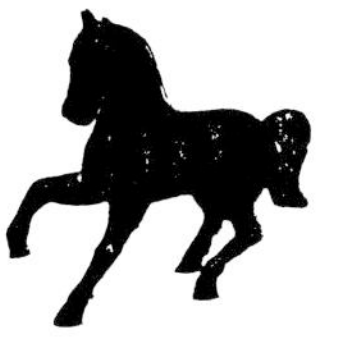

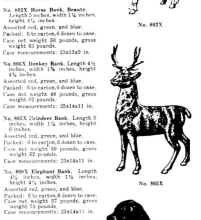

No. 801X

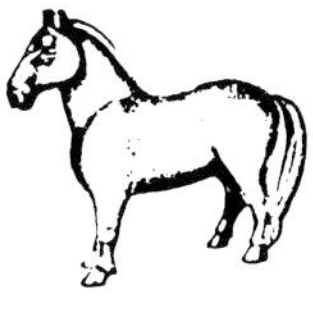

No. 802X

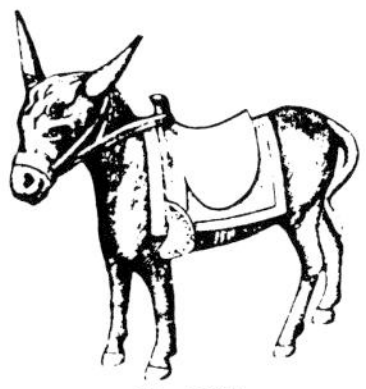

No. 806X

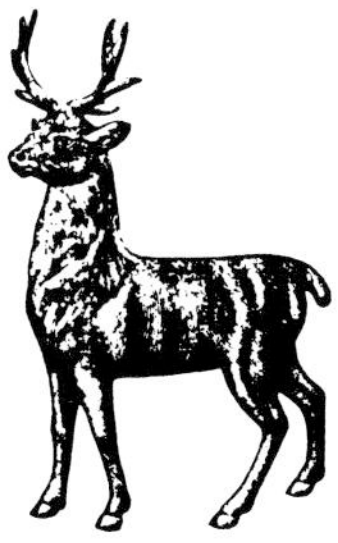

No. 805X

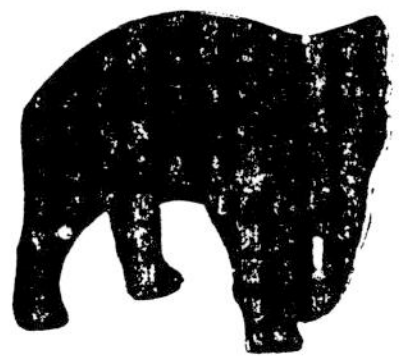

No. 808X

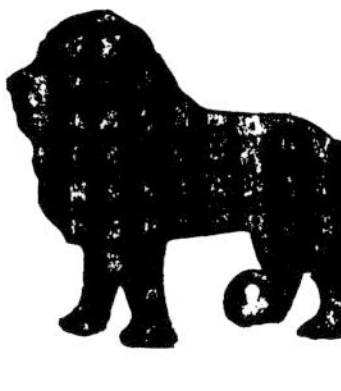

No. 807X

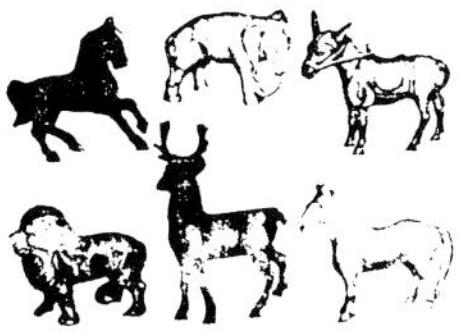

No. 863

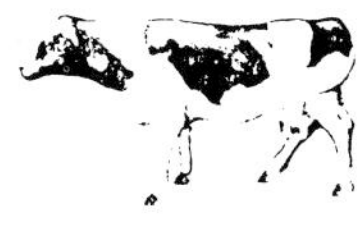

No. 816

No. 801X Horse Bank. Length 4¾ inches, width 1¼ inches, height 4¼ inches.
Assorted red, green, and blue.
Packed: 6 to carton, 6 dozen to case.
Case net weight 45 pounds, gross weight 60 pounds.
Case measurements: 23x13x9 in.

No. 802X Horse Bank, Beauty. Length 5 inches, width 1¼ inches, height 4¼ inches.
Assorted red, green, and blue.
Packed: 6 to carton, 6 dozen to case.
Case net weight 50 pounds, gross weight 63 pounds.
Case measurements: 23x13x9 in.

No. 806X Donkey Bank. Length 4½ inches, width 1⅝ inches, height 4⅜ inches.
Assorted red, green, and blue.
Packed: 6 to carton, 6 dozen to case.
Case net weight 48 pounds, gross weight 62 pounds.
Case measurements: 25x14x11 in.

No. 805X Reindeer Bank. Length 5 inches, width 1¼ inches, height 6 inches.
Assorted red, green, and blue.
Packed: 6 to carton, 6 dozen to case.
Case net weight 50 pounds, gross weight 62 pounds.
Case measurements: 23x14x11 in.

No. 808X Elephant Bank. Length 4½ inches, width 1½ inches, height 4¼ inches.
Assorted red, green, and blue.
Packed: 6 to carton, 6 dozen to case.
Case net weight 57 pounds, gross weight 73 pounds.
Case measurements: 25x14x11 in.

No. 807X Lion Bank. Length 4½ inches, width 1½ inches, height 3⅝ inches.
Assorted red, green, and blue.
Packed: 6 to carton, 6 dozen to case.
Case net weight 50 pounds, gross weight 66 pounds.
Case measurements: 25x14x11 in.

No. 863X Assortment Bank. Includes: 801 Horse, Red; 802 Horse, Blue; 805 Reindeer, Red; 806 Donkey, Green; 807 Lion, Green; 808 Elephant, Blue. (Description of individual items will be found above.)
Packed: 6 to carton, 6 dozen to case.
Case net weight 61 pounds, gross weight 66 pounds.
Case measurements: 25x14x11 in.

No. 816 Holstein Cow Bank. Length 4½ inches, width 1⅛ inches, height 2½ inches.
White, with black markings.
Packed: 6 to carton, 6 dozen to case.
Case net weight 35 pounds, gross weight 46 pounds.
Case measurements: 21x10x9 in.

ARCADE CAST IRON TOYS 1934

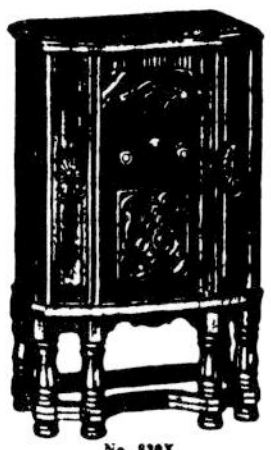

No. 830X

No. 838

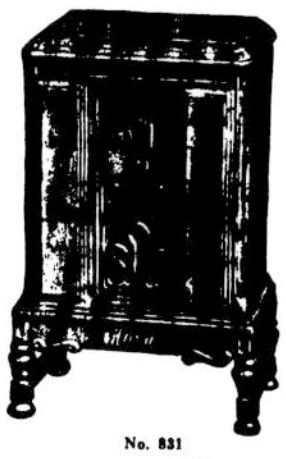

No. 831

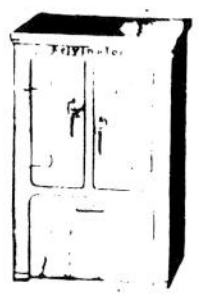

No. 832

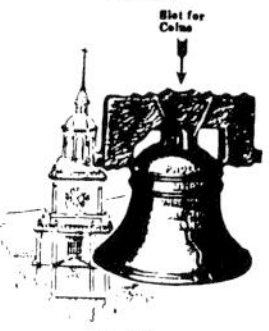

Slot for Coins

No. 859

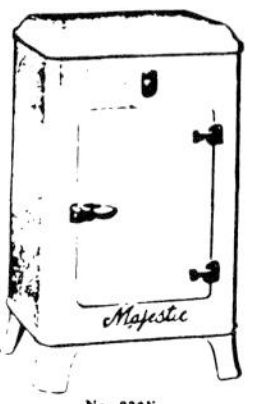

No. 833X

No. 830X G. E. Radio Bank

Height 4 inches, width 2⅛ inches, thickness 1¼ inches.
Color: Assorted red, green, blue, with gold trim.
Special key for opening. Coin slot in back.
Packed 6 in carton, 3 dozen in case.
Case net weight 27 pounds, case gross weight 30 pounds.
Case measurements: 5½x6½x12 inches.

No. 838 Mail Box Bank

Height 3¾ inches, width 1⅝ inches, thickness 1⅝ inches.
Color: Green.
Package slot opens for insertion of coins.
Packed 6 in carton, 6 dozen in case.
Case net weight 42 pounds, case gross weight 48 pounds.
Case measurements: 8x13x18 inches.

No. 832 Kelvinator Bank

Height 4½ inches, width 2½ inches, depth 1⅝ inches.
Same as illustrated but with legs.
Color: White, trimmed in grey.
Coin slot in back.
Packed 1 in carton, 3 dozen in case.
Case net weight 43 pounds, case gross weight 47 pounds.
Case measurements: 9x9x14 inches.

No. 831 Majestic Radio Bank

Height 4½ inches, width 3 inches, thickness 1⅞ inches.
Color: Mahogany finish.
Coin slot in back. A special key supplied for opening.
Packed 1 in carton, 1 dozen in case.
Case net weight 13 pounds, case gross weight 15 pounds.
Case measurements: 5½x6½x13 inches.

No. 833X Majestic Refrigerator Bank

Height 4⅛ inches, width 2⅝ inches, thickness 1⅞ inches.
Color: Assorted red, green and blue with gold trim.
Coin slot in back. A special key supplied for opening.
Packed 1 in carton, 1 dozen in case.
Case net weight 14 pounds, case gross weight 17 pounds.
Case measurements: 12½x6¾x5¼ inches.

No. 9580 Table Bell

Same design as 859 Liberty Bell Bank but smaller in size. Made of brass with a brass knocker. Has a clear ring. An exceptionally practical table bell.
Finished in lacquered antique verde.
Top bar 2¾ inches wide, height overall 2¾ inches. Bell 2½ inches diameter.
Packed 6 in carton, 3 dozen in case.
Case net weight 18 pounds, case gross weight 22 pounds.
Case measurements: 6x9x13 inches.

No. 859 Liberty Bell Bank

Width 3¾ inches, height 3¼ inches.
Color: Antique bronze finish.
Special key supplied for opening.
Packed 1 in carton, 3 dozen in case.
Case net weight 39 pounds, case gross weight 46 pounds.
Case measurements: 11x12x15 inches.

BANTHRICO

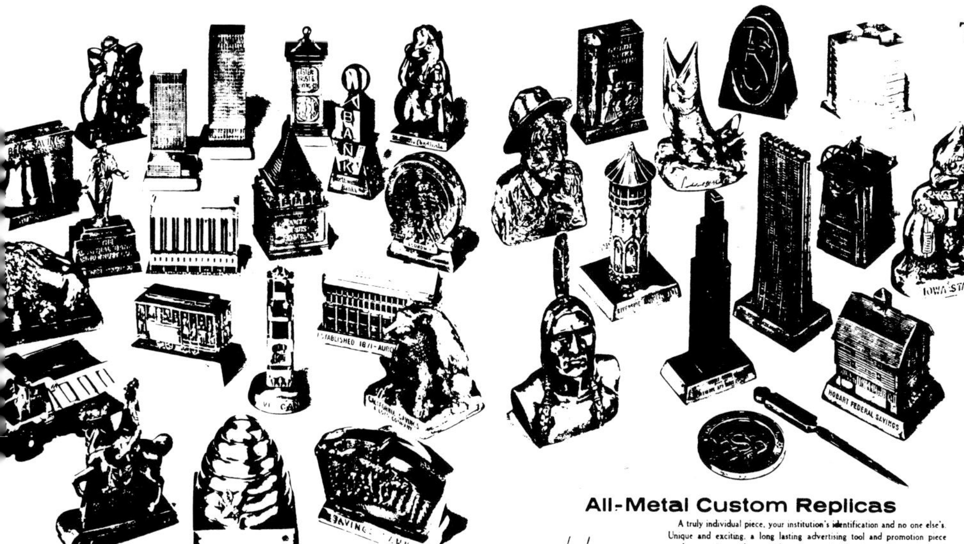

Banthrico has made replicas of many things: an Idaho Potato, Ear of Corn Trophy, a Buffalo Sculpture by a famous artist, a unique water tower, the Sears Tower of Chicago (the world's tallest building) and many more

All-Metal Custom Replicas

and they are coin banks too!

A truly individual piece, your institution's identification and no one else's. Unique and exciting, a long lasting advertising tool and promotion piece used as a savings and a general account opening motivator or as a service to your customers. Custom designed paperweights and letter openers also are available.

Made to exacting specifications, scaled down from blueprints, photos or drawings. Replicas can take the form of buildings,(old or new) sponsor a landmark, bust of a famous person, animals, school mascots, statues or well known objects of your city or state.

Each piece is hand-cast by skilled craftsmen. These replicas have strength and durability. Valued in the home or office as paperweights, bookends, or accessories, with the dual-use feature of both replica and coin bank. Over the years many have become collector pieces.

BANTHRICO, INC
4615 W. ROOSEVELT ROAD
CHICAGO, ILLINOIS 60650
312 242-0963 OR 656-7815

BANKERS THRIFT CORPORATION

BANKERS THRIFT CORPORATION CHICAGO

THE HORSE SHOE POCKET SAVINGS BANK

The Symbol of "Good Luck"

This Pocket Bank is truly a pocket piece. Holds $3.00 in dimes.

Made of steel, highly nickeled.

Opens with a Key.

Bank ad is reproduced in celluloid finish and is very attractive.

Advertisement can be produced in any color, or color combinations.

Attractive Window Display; Display Cards and Newspaper Cuts and Copy furnished.

These Banks can be Vended through a Distributing Machine.

We furnish Venders with either 10c or 25c slot deposit.

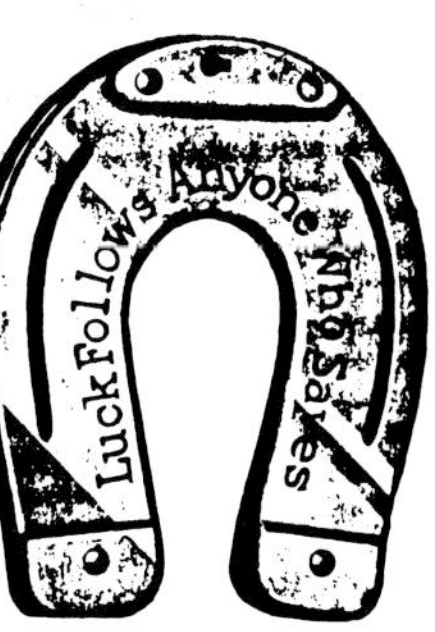

BACK VIEW
ACTUAL SIZE

PRICES

Lot 250	30c each
500	27c "
1000	25c "
2500	23c "
5000 or more	22c "

NKERS THRIFT CORPORATION CHICAGO

BANKERS "DE LUXE" POCKET BANK

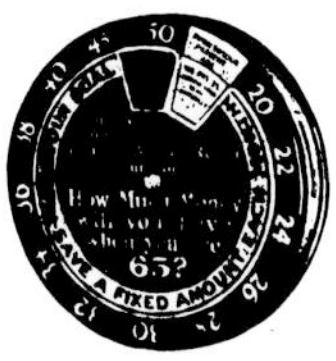

Size, 2½" Diameter

With Either "65" or "50" Dial
COPYRIGHTED AND PATENTED

Made to hold Quarters and smaller coins. Made of steel, highly nickeled. Round in shape. Size 2½" in diameter, ½" thick. Advertisement reproduced in colors on one side.

Age "50" or "65" dials on other side.

Dial is made of etched brass and rotates over celluloid scale, showing figures and amounts necessary to save to reach a definite Goal.

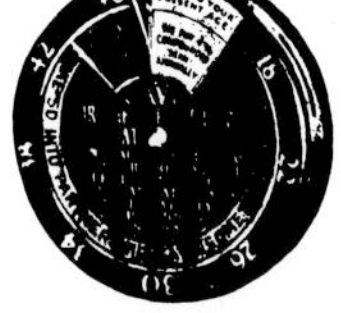

Size, 2½" Diameter

' Dial, shows how much to save
ı month in order to have a definite
. at age 65. This shown by a rotary
. Made in all interest rates.

Prices

250	27¾c each
500	25 c "
,000	23 c "
,500	22 c "
,000	21 c "

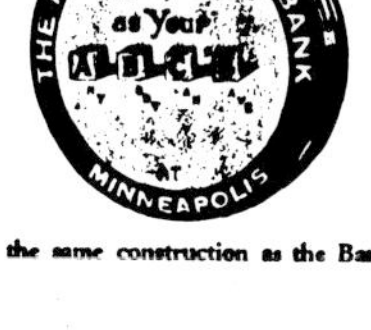

"50" Dial, shows how much to save each week in order to have a definite sum at age 50. This is shown by a rotary dial. Made in all interest rates.

Larger quantities same price as last given. Two colors allowed.

Extra charge made for cuts and special drawings.

This bank is of the same construction as the Bankers Pocket Bank.

BANKERS THRIFT CORPORATION CHICAGO

THE BANKERS JR.

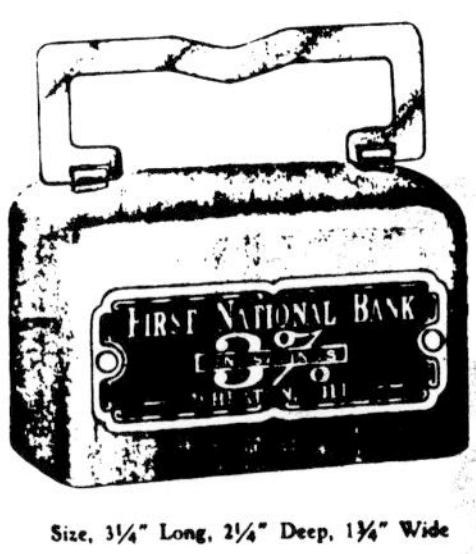

Size, 3¼" Long, 2¼" Deep, 1¾" Wide

PRICES

125	75c each
250	70c "
500	65c "
1000 or more	60c "

2c each for numbering.

A Good Home Savings Bank, strong—durable—convenient to carry. Holds all coins and paper money.

Finished nickel plated.

Holds from $12.00 to $25.00.

Bank's advertisement on etched brass plate.

Packed in individual boxes.

Etched Brass Name Plates furnished with Bank's ad on our copyrighted A B C Design. This design comes finished in red enamel. Very attractive. Display Cards and electrically controlled Display Lamps gratis with order of 125 or more Bankers Jrs.

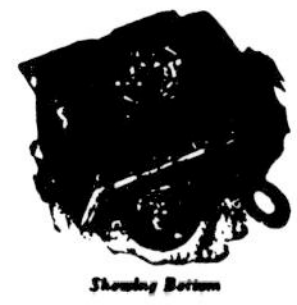

Showing Bottom

BANKERS THRIFT CORPORATION CHICAGO

BANKERS POCKET BANK

Made to Hold Quarters and Smaller Coins

(PATENTED)

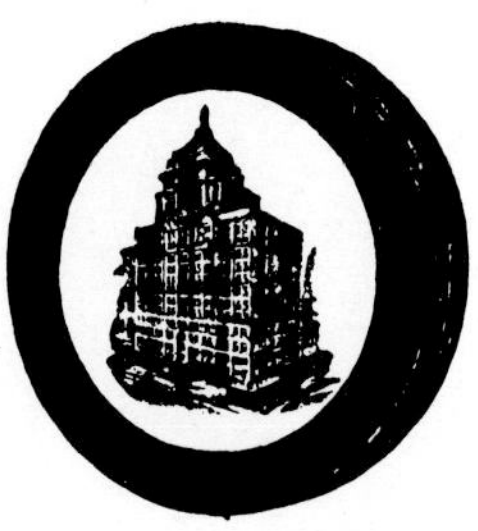

Round in shape. Size 2½" in diameter, ½" in thickness.

Made of metal, beautifully finished.

Advertising space on both sides of the bank.

Advertisement reproduced on celluloid in attractive color schemes.

Opens with a Key. Holds $6.00 in dimes or $3.00 to $5.00 in assorted coins.

PRICES

Lot 250	22c each
500	20c "
1000	17½c "
2500	16c "
5000 or more	15c "

A Charge of 1c per bank is made for numbering.

Above prices include two color printing. See "Special Information" when more than 2 colors are wanted.

Actual charge made for cuts and special drawings.

BANKERS THRIFT CORPORATION CHICAGO

THE "REAL HOME" BANK

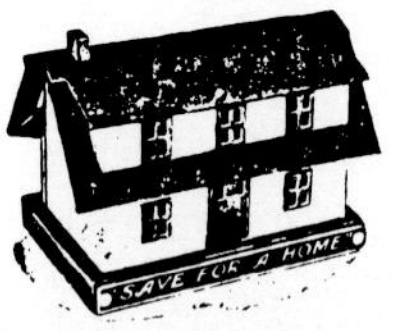

Size, 3¼" Long, 2¼" High, 2¼" Wide

Made in Assorted Colors. Most Attractive. Scientifically Constructed. Strong and Durable

125	95c Each	500	85c Each
250	90c Each	1,000	80c Each

2,500 or more....75c Each

ADV. CAMPAIGN FURNISHED

Add 2c each for numbering.

Price includes 2 etched brass name-plates, one reading—"Save For a Home", and the other with the name of the customer.

Limit copy to two lines.

THE "Real Home" Bank is a practical Home Safe, made of a very unusual design, with a genuine appeal to Savers. It is protected by U. S. Patent.

Strongly built of steel; beautifully finished in attractive baked enamel colors.

Coin trap and lock are in the bottom.

Guaranteed in every respect to be one of the strongest, and most attractive banks on the market.

Will receive all coins and paper money.

Complete advertising display furnished without charge.

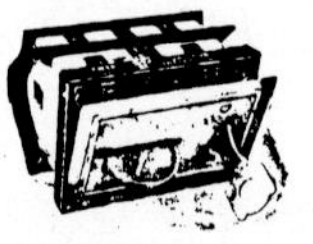

Showing bottom with coin trap and lock

DENT

1920

DENT TOYS

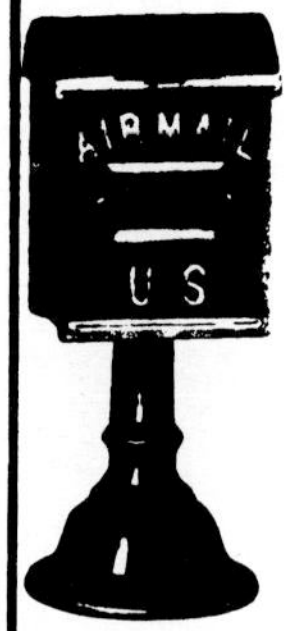

Air Mail Bank

A real up-to-date Air Mail Bank painted in bright red with blue and white trimmings.

Number	Height	Width
298	6¼"	2¾"
Packed per Box	**Doz. per Case**	**Wt. per Case**
1	3	55 lbs.

Stop and Save Bank

Finished in bright colors, assorted in a box, gilt trimmings.

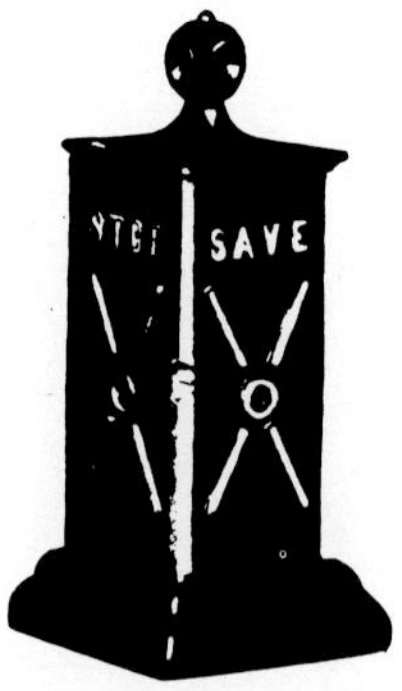

Number	Height	Width
288	5¾"	2½"
Packed per Box	**Doz. per Case**	**Wt. per Case**
6	6	58 lbs.

IRON TOYS

36

10 THE DENT HARDWARE COMPANY

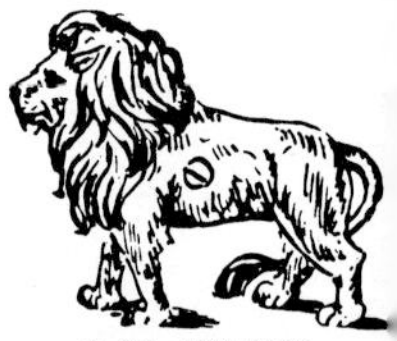

No. 201. LION BANK.

Packed 3 in box. 12 dozen

No. 201. Length, 5½ inches

Weight, 225 lbs.

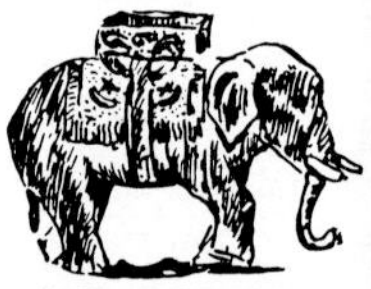

No. 200. ELEPHANT BANK.

Packed 3 in box. 12 dozen

No 200. Length, 5 inches.

Weight, 230 lbs.

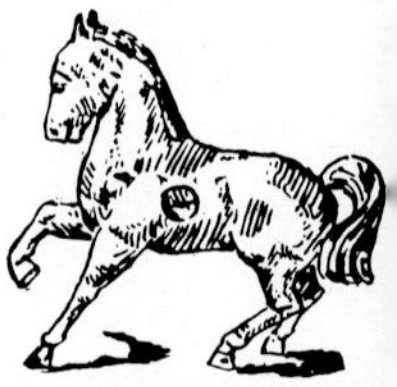

No. 203. HORSE BANK.

Packed 3 in box. 12 dozen i

No 203. Length, 4½ inches

Weight, 200 lbs.

GREY-IRON-CASTING-CO. MOUNT JOY, PA., U.S.A.

1903-1904 **TOY BANKS.**

THE GUARANTEED LINE

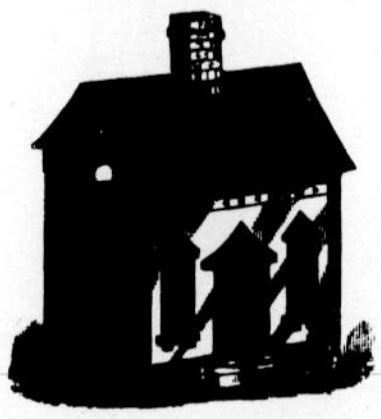

No. 5. Bank. Coppered. Height, 3¼ inches; width, 2¼ inches; depth, 2¼ inches, per gross.
One dozen in box. Five gross in case. Approximate weight, 450 pounds.

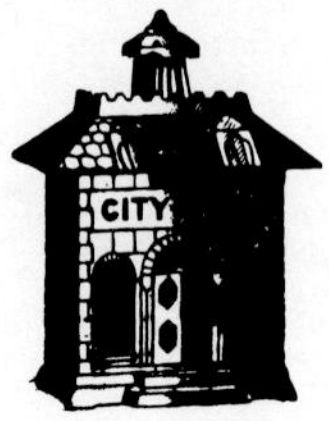

[illegible] Coppered. Height, 3¼ ins.; width, 2½ inches; depth, 2 ins. per gross.
[illegible] in box. Five gross in case. Approximate weight, 470 pounds.

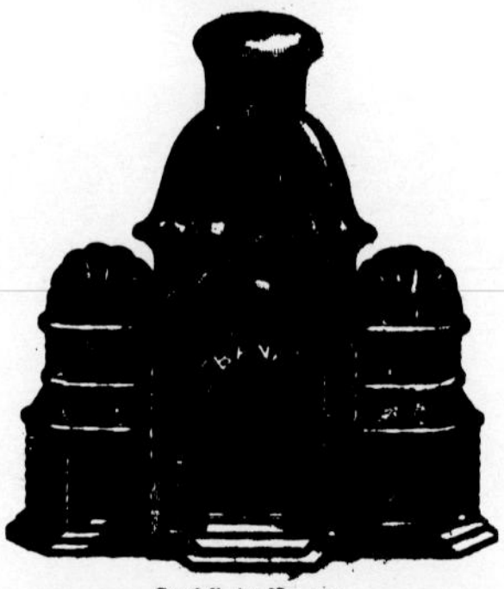

Cut full size No. 205.

No. 205. Coppered. Size, 3¼ in. high, 3⅛ in. wide, 2 in. deep.
No. 206. Bronze, Painted. Size, 3⅛ in. high, 3⅛ in. wide, 2 in. deep.
One dozen in box. 5 gross in case, per gross.

No. 210. Coppered. Size, 4¼ in. high, 4¼ in. wide, 2⅜ in. deep.
No. 211. Bronze, Painted. Size, 4¼ in. high, 4¼ in. wide, 2⅜ in. deep.
One-half dozen in box. Two and one-half gross in case, per gross.

No. 225. Bronze, Painted. Size, 5⅛ in. high, 5¼ in. wide, 3 in. deep. Combination Lock.
One in box. One-half gross in case, per gross.

Approximate Weight, Case No. 205, 500 pounds.
" " " No. 210, 450 "
" " " No. 225, 190 "

TOY BANKS.

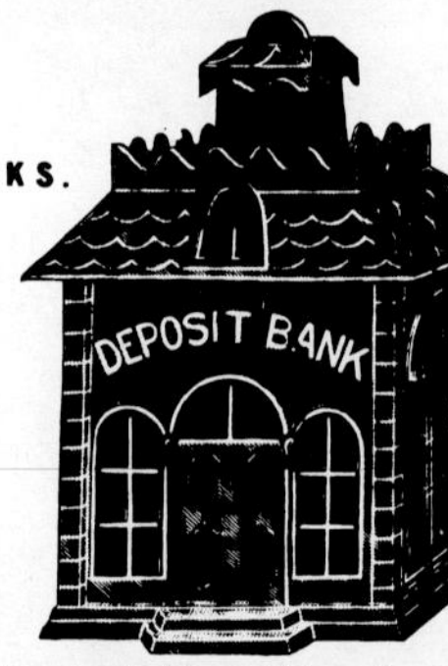

No. 9. Berlin Bronze, Painted Assorted Colors. Size, 4½ in. high, 3 in w
2½ in. deep, per gross.
One dozen in box. Two and one-half gross in case. Approximate weigh
case 320 pounds.

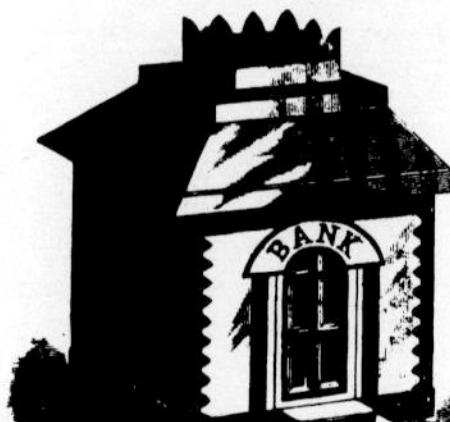

No 10. Berlin Bronze
Painted, Assorted Color
per gross.

No. 15. Gold Bronze, per g

Size, 4 in. high, 3 in. w
2½ in. deep.

One-half dozen in box.
and one-half gross in case.
proximate weight of case,
pounds.

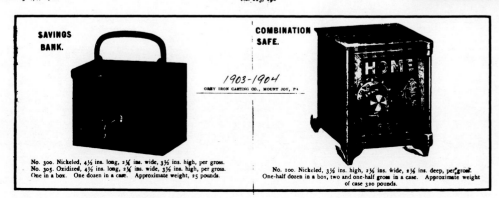

SAVINGS BANK.

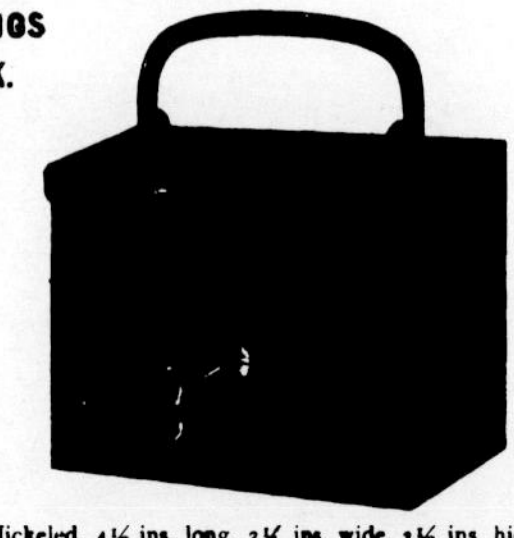

No. 300. Nickeled, 4½ ins. long, 2¾ ins. wide, 3½ ins. high, per gross.
No. 305. Oxidized, 4½ ins. long, 2¾ ins. wide, 3½ ins. high, per gross.
One in a box. One dozen in a case. Approximate weight, 25 pounds.

1903-1904

GREY IRON CASTING CO., MOUNT JOY, PA

COMBINATION SAFE.

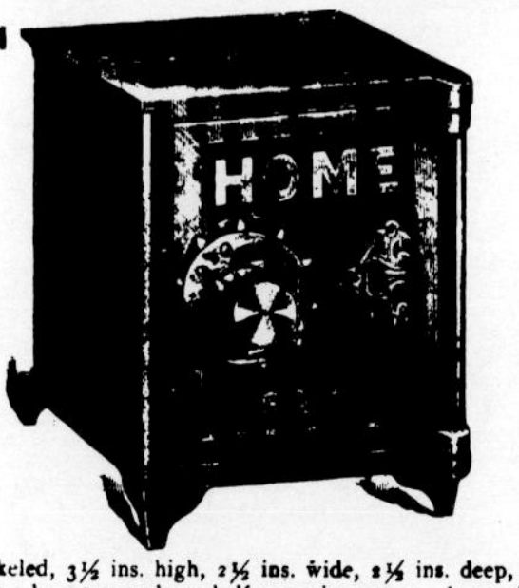

No. 100. Nickeled, 3½ ins. high, 2½ ins. wide, 2½ ins. deep, per gross.
One-half dozen in a box, two and one-half gross in a case. Approximate weight of case 320 pounds.

GLOBE BANK.

Full size cut.

No. 35. Bank. Enameled Red and Blue, height, 5½ inches, per gross. One half dozen in box. Two gross in case. Weight of case 380 pounds.

COIN DEPOSIT BANK.

250. Size 4½ ins. high, 3 ins. wide, 2½ ins. deep. Packed three in a box, half gross in a case. Weight of case 130 pounds, per gross.

500. Size 5¼ ins. high, 4¼ ins. wide, 3½ ins. deep. Packed one in a box, one-fourth gross in a case. Weight of case 275 pounds, per gross.

1000. Size 6¼ ins. high, 5¾ ins. wide, 4½ ins. deep. Packed one in a box, one-sixth gross in a case. Weight of case 170 pounds, per gross.

Entirely new design; highly polished and nickeled; a beautiful safe with good combination.

COMBINATION BANKS.

Very popular.

Beautifully Finished.

Excellent combination lock.

642. Highly Polished and Nickel Plated.
642B. Finished in Blue Enamel.
6¾ inches high. 5 inches wide. 4¾ inches deep.
1 in a box. 2 dozen in a case. 130 lbs. per case.

Fine combination lock.

Attractive Design.

All Iron.

638. Highly Polished and Nickel Plated.
638B. Finished in Blue Enamel.
5½ inches high. 4¼ inches wide. 4 inches deep.
1 in a box. 3 dozen in a case. 130 lbs. per case.

WARSHIP MAINE TOY BANK.

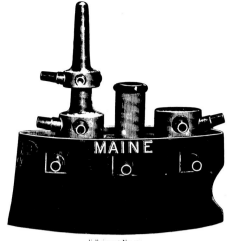

Full size cut No. 20.

No. 20. Berlin Bronze, size 4½ in. long, 2¾ in. wide, 4¾ in. high, per gross.
No. 21. Enameled and Gold, size same as No. 20, per gross.
No. 25. Enameled and Gold, size 6¾ in. long, 2¾ in. wide, 5¼ in. high, key lock, per gross.

Nos. 20 and 21, one-half dozen in box. One and three-quarter gross in case.
No. 25, one-sixth dozen in box. One-half gross in case.
Approximate weight of case, Nos. 20 and 21, 300 pounds.
Approximate weight of case, No. 25, 150 pounds.

No. 105. Highly Polished and Nickel Plated.
5½ inches high. 4¼ inches wide. 4 inches deep.
1 in a box. 3 dozen in a case. 90 lbs. per case.

Embossed steel sides and back.

Finely Finished.

Good combination lock.

Handsomely Finished.

Good combination lock.

Embossed steel sides and back.

No. 50. Polished and Nickel Plated.
5 inches high. 3¾ inches wide. 3¾ inches deep.
1 dozen in a box. 6 dozen in a case. 125 lbs. per case.

COMBINATION BANKS.

TOY BANK.

No. 119. Gold Bronze Painted, per gross.
No. 900. Berlin Bronze, per gross.

Size, 5¼ inches high, 3¼ inches wide, 3 inches deep.

One-half dozen in box. One gross in case. Approximate weight of case 350 pounds.

1928

COMBINATION BANKS.

Handsome Design.

Highly Polished and Finished.

A high grade safe with accurate combination.

No. 2000.

No. 2000. Highly Polished and Nickel Plated.
7 inches high. 5¼ inches wide. 4½ inches deep.
1 in a box. 2 dozen in a case. 165 lbs. per case.

No. 535. Highly Polished and Nickel Plated.
Design similar to No. 2000, but with steel sides and back.
6 inches high. 4¼ inches wide. 3½ inches deep.
1 in a box. 3 dozen in a case. 115 lbs. per case.

No. 535W. Nickel Plated. Same as No. 535, but not so highly polished.
1 in a box. 3 dozen in a case. 115 lbs. per case.

No. 285W. Nickel Plated. Steel sides and back.
4¾ inches high. 3 inches wide. 2½ inches deep.
1 in a box. 6 dozen in a case. 100 lbs. per case.

No. 275. Same as No. 2000, except as to size.
Highly Polished and Nickel Plated.
4½ inches high. 3 inches wide. 2½ inches deep.
1 in a box. 6 dozen in a case. 125 lbs. per case.

GREY IRON CASTING COMPANY

ESTABLISHED 1881
INCORPORATED 1913

MANUFACTURERS OF

HARDWARE
HOUSEFURNISHING SPECIALTIES
IRON TOYS

CATALOGUE No. 28

MOUNT JOY, PA., U.S.A.

1928

COMBINATION BANKS.

New Design. Well Finished.
Good Combination Lock.
Steel Sides and Back.

No. 600. Nickel Plated.
No. 600B. Finished in Blue Enamel.
Height, 4¾ inches.
Width, 3¼ inches.
Depth, 3¼ inches.
½ dozen in a box. 1 gross in a case.
190 lbs. per case.

No. 600.

Handsome New Design.
Good Combination Lock.
Embossed Steel Sides and Back.

No. 80. Nickel Plated.
Height, 4 inches.
Width, 2¾ inches.
Depth, 2¾ inches.
½ dozen in a box. 1 gross in a case.
145 lbs. per case.

No. 80.

New Design. Finely Finished.
Good Combination Lock.

No. 150. Nickel Plated.
Height, 3¼ inches.
Width, 2½ inches.
Depth, 2¾ inches.
1 dozen in a box. 2 gross in a case.
200 lbs. per case.

No. 150.

31

1928

90 **GREY-IRON-CASTING-CO. MOUNT JOY, PA., U.S.A.**
THE GUARANTEED LINE

MERRY-GO-ROUND BANK.

Distinctly New and Novel.

Handsomely Designed and Finished.

Bank Revolves on Base.

Patented.

No. 40D. Decorated in colors.
Height, 5 inches. Diameter, 4½ inches.
1 in a carton. 6 dozen in a case. 140 lbs. per case.

SAFE DEPOSIT BANKS.

Very Popular Banks.

Strongly Made and Well Finished.

No. 206. Bronze Decorated. 3¼ ins. high. 3⅛ ins. wide. 2 ins. deep.
1 dozen in a box. 2 gross in a case. 200 lbs. per case.

No. 211. Decorated in colors. 4¼ ins. high. 4¼ ins. wide. 2⅞ ins. deep.
1½ dozen in a box. 1 gross in a case. 180 lbs. per case.

(All our Banks have slot large enough to accommodate a half dollar or English penny.)

1928

GREY-IRON-CASTING-CO. MOUNT JOY, PA., U.S.A. 91
THE GUARANTEED LINE

SAFE DEPOSIT BANKS.

No. 10A.

Always Popular.
Excellent Values.

No. 10A. Decorated in colors.

Height, 4 inches.
Width, 3 inches.
Depth, 2½ inches.

½ dozen in a box.

1 gross in a case.

175 lbs. per case.

These Banks Are Always Popular.
Strongly Constructed and Well Finished.

No. 119. Decorated in colors.

Height, 5¼ inches.
Width, 3¾ inches.
Depth, 3 inches.

4 in a box. ½ gross in a case.

185 lbs. per case.

No. 119.

No. 4.

No 4. Coppered.

Height, 3¼ inches.
Width, 2⅜ inches.
Depth, 2⅛ inches.

1 dozen in a box. 2 gross in a case.

165 lbs. per case.

(All our Banks have slot large enough to accommodate a half dollar or English penny.)

1928

92 **GREY-IRON-CASTING-CO. MOUNT JOY, PA., U.S.A.**
THE GUARANTEED LINE

BUNGALOW BANK.

Patented.
No. 20.

A Perfect Model of a Beautiful
Designed Bungalow.
Absolutely New.
Must Be Seen To Be Apprecia[ted]

No. 20D. Decorated in Colo[rs]

Height, 3½ inches.
Width, 3½ inches.
Depth, 3½ inches.

1 in a carton.
6 dozen in a case.
115 lbs. per case.

UNITED STATES TREASURY BANK.

Handsomely Modeled and Complete
in Every Detail.
Nothing Like It On The Market.

No. 45D. Decorated in Colors.

Height, 3¼ inches.
Width, 3¼ inches.
Depth, 4 inches.

1 in a carton.
6 dozen in a case.
115 lbs. per case.

Patented.
No. 45.

(All our Banks have slot large enough to accommodate a half dollar or English penny.)

1928

GREY-IRON-CASTING-CO. MOUNT JOY, PA., U.S.A. 93
THE GUARANTEED LINE

LIBERTY BELL BANK.

No. 1776.

A splendid reproduction in miniature of the Old Liberty Bell that announced the Adoption of the Declaration of Independance.

Instills Thrift and Patriotism in the Child's Mind.

Handsomely Finished in Bronze Plate.
Raised Portions Polished.

1 in a carton. 6 dozen in a case.
100 lbs. per case.

ICE CREAM FREEZER BANK.

No. 440.

Attractively Finished in Colors.

Height, 4½ inches.

1 in a carton. 6 dozen in a case

110 lbs. per case

1928

94 **GREY-IRON-CASTING-CO. MOUNT JOY, PA., U.S.A.**
THE GUARANTEED LINE

ANIMAL BANK ASSORTMENT.

New Designs. Faithful Delineations. Attractively Finished.

No. 404. Pony.
5½ ins. long. 4½ ins. high.

No. 406. Sheep.
5½ ins. long. 3⅜ ins. high

No. 405. Cat.
4½ ins. high.

No. 407. Dog.
4⅝ ins. long. 4¼ ins. high

Finished in Brilliant Gold Lacquer.
No. 422. Assortment.
3 each, Nos. 404, 405, 406 and 407 in a box
1 gross pieces in a case.
170 lbs. per case.

(All our Banks have slot large enough to accommodate a half dollar or English penny.)

Columbia Grey Iron Company

20

Street Car Bank.

Bronzed.

No. 12. Bronzed, Assorted Colors, per gross, $12 00
One-half dozen in box.
One gross in case.

Columbia Bank.

Japanned and Green.

32

No. 30. Size 2⅞x2⅞ inches, 3½ inches high, per gross, $18 00

New York Office and Salesroom, 35 Warren St.

Columbia Tower Bank.

No. 50. Columbia Tower Bank, Nickeled, per gross, $30 00
" 60. " " " Bronze and Gold, per gross, ... 32 00

Height, ... 7 inches.
Diameter, ... 3¼ "

Packed one-fourth dozen in box.

Columbia Grey Iron Co., Columbia, Pa. 21

New York Office and Salesroom, 35 Warren St.

Deposit Bank.

Bronzed.

19

Size 3x2½ inches.
4½ inches high.

No. 11. Bronzed, Painted Assorted Colors, per gross, ... $14 00

One-half dozen in box.
One gross in case.

State Banks.

Bronzed.

Size 4½x3 inches.
5½ inches high.

No. 10. Bronzed, Painted Assorted Colors, per gross, . . $28 00

Size 2½x2½ inches.
2⅞ inches high.

No. 20. Bronzed, per gross, ... $12 00

One-half dozen in box.
One gross in a case.

New York Office and Salesroom, 35 Warren St.

1903 **JOHN M. SMYTH COMPANY'S Dictionary (1043) of Econom[y]**

No. 58—Chicago, U. S. A.

IRON TOYS.—Continued.

BELL TOYS.

REVOLVING CHIMES.
H2283 Our price, each, 18c
Metal wheels with rubber tire and wire spokes. Size, 8¾ inches. Sweet gong bell 2¾ inches, nickel plated, has silk cord.
Postage, extra, 10c.
H2285 Same as above except 5¼ inch wheels with double hubs and tandem spokes, 3¼ inch bell.
Our price, each........................40c
Weight, 20 ozs.

THE EAGLE BELL RINGER.
H2296 The eagle swings and rings the bell. Eagle painted in patriotic colors.
Price, each..............20c

RACE HORSE CHIMES.

H2288 Single, 7x3, with iron frame and suspended copper bell. Weight 20 ounces. Price, each........15c
H2290 Double, 9x4, with two bells and horses. The horses take a jumping motion. Weight 34 oz.
Price, each........................35c

THE ELEPHANT BELL RINGER.
H2299 The elephant stands on a four wheel pedestal, and rings the large nickeled bell. Size 8x5½. Each.....42c
Weight 24 ounces.

SAVINGS BANKS.

DIME POCKET SAVINGS BANK.
H2320 The "Little Gem" is a very popular "Money Saver." Convenient to carry in the pocket. Will open when $5.00 has been saved.
Price, each........................7c
Postage, extra, 2c.

PENNY SAVINGS BANK.
H2321 Same as Dime Savings Bank except that it holds 50 pennies.
Our price, each........................7c
Postage extra, 2c.

READY CHANGE COIN HOLDER.
Holds pennies, nickles dimes and quarters. Nickel plated. Convenient for the pocket.
H2437 Our price each........................8c
Postage extra, 2c.

POSTAL SAVINGS BANK.
One of the prettiest banks made. Heavy sheet steel. Registers the money as fast as dropped in. For pennies, nickles and dimes. Size 5¼x5x2¼. Nickel and oxidized finish.
H2359 Our price each..............75c
Weight, 25 oz.

BANKS—Continued.

PORTRAIT BANKS.
The bank is made of iron. Size, 6x2½ inches, and is surmounted by a portrait of either Washington, Lincoln, Grant, McKinley, Cleveland or Roosevelt, in bronze. Handle is nickel-plated. Money cannot be shaken out.
H2361 Our price, each....20c
Weight, 1 lb.

Baltimore Printing Presses.

These presses give the possessor valuable lessons in manual training and help educate him or her for the battle of life. While they are in some sense toys they are "money getters" if rightly used.

H2370 Will print a form 1⅝x2⅜ inches; weight of press and outfit, 3 lbs. Price of press, with roller and outfit, including one font of No. 1 short type, twenty-five blank cards, ink and furniture........................70c

H2372 This is a complete little printing office, and includes a font of type, roller, ink and 25 blank cards, furniture and leads. Every press is tested before it is packed; complete with type and drawer; will print a form 1⅝x2⅜ inches. Weight of press and outfit, 7 lbs.
Price........................95c

BANKS—Continued.

CHICAGO ANIMAL BANKS.

A new form of iron bank; size 8¼x2½ with slot [in] back. Money cannot be shaken out; holds penn[ies] nickels and dimes. Each one lifelike in finish and des[ign].

H2331 Pig.
H2332 Elephant.
H2334 Lamb.
H2335 Rabbit.
H2336 Cat.
H2338 Bear.
H2340 Hunter Dog.
Price, each........
Three for........
Postage, 12c extra each.

ST. BERNARD BANK.

H2344 An exact representation of the St. Bernard dog; size, 9x5; very strong; tongue moves when coin is dropped; money cannot be shaken out; improved this season; weight, 32 ounces.
Price, each.........20c

JUMBO ELEPHANT BANK.

H2342 Finished in bla[ck] with bronze trimmings; [will] hold $5.00; raises trunk ev[ery] time you deposit money; wei[ght] 32 ounces. Price, each .....
These animal banks [are] pretty, durable toys for children.

"THE TRUNK" DOUBLE REGISTERING SAVINGS BANK.

H2355 A money saver that shows the amount deposited at all times and that cannot be opened until $10.00 is saved. Made to receive pennies and dimes, and to register them as fast as received. Strongly made of cast iron, full nickel plated and polished. Size, 5 x 3 x 4½ inches. Exactly like the cut. Weight, 36 oz. Price, each..........

TRICK DOG BANK

H2658 Length, [...] inches. Place the c[oin] in the dog's mou[th] press the lever, d[og] jumps through ho[op] and deposits the coin [in] bank; finished in fa[st] colors. Weight 5 lbs.
Price, each ....

SECURITY BANKS.

H2350 Nickle plated with perfect working combination lock. Handsome model of a large safe. Size, 4¾x3½ x3½. Weight, 28 oz.
Price, each.........18c

H2352 Same bank, different size. Size, 5½x 4x4½. Weight, 30 oz.
Price, each 28c

Self-Inking Presses.

Cabinet not included with Presses.

H2374 Size of form, 2¼x3¼; has one font of lo[ng] type, 100 blank cards, bronze, ink and necessary fur[ni]ture; strong and simple and will not get out of ord[er]. Weight, complete, 12½ lbs.
Price, each........................$1

H2376 Will print a form 2¼x3¼ inches; weight [of] press and outfit, 15 pounds; one roller and outfit of [one] font No. 408 type, 50 blank cards, ink and furnitu[re].
Price........................$2

H2378 Self-Inking. Will print a card 2¾x4 inch[es]. This size is specially adapted for printing small jo[bs] such as cards, envelopes, etc., and is in every way [a] complete self-inking press. One roller and outfit, [in]cluding one font of No. 217 type, 50 blank cards, ink a[nd] furniture in a box. Weight of press and outfit, 21 lbs.
Price, each........................$4

H2380 Self-Inking. Will print a form 2¾x4. Ex[tra] finish, with two rollers, with outfit of two fonts of N[o.] 80 and 84 type, 50 blank cards, ink and furnitu[re]. Weight, 25 lbs.
Price, each........................$5

H2381 Self-Inker. Will print a form 4½x6¾. T[wo] rollers; has four fonts of type, composing stick, plan[er,] cards, ink and other furniture. Weight, 50 lbs. A goo[d] strong job press.
Price, each........................$16

CABINETS FOR PRINTING OUTFITS.

H2382 A three-drawer cabinet that every one ow[n]ing a press should have. Holds the type and furnitu[re] and keeps them in good condition. Also makes the wo[rk] easier and the press can be fastened to the top of t[he] cabinet. Sold with or without the presses. See cut abov[e]. Price, each........................

Haussers Elastolin-Fabrikate

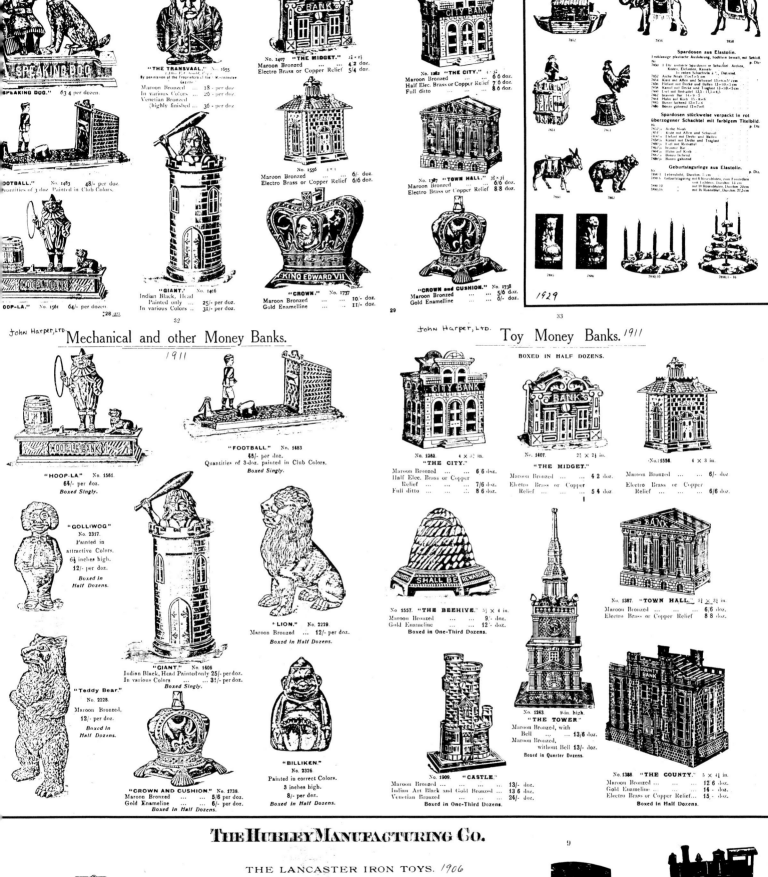

Finished in Attractive Colors, and Packed One in a Box.

"SPEAKING DOG."   63 4 per dozen.

"THE TRANSVAAL."   No. 1655
(Late J. & T. Gould, B'g'm)
By permission of the Proprietors of the *Westminster Gazette*
Maroon Bronzed ... 18 - per doz.
In various Colors ... 26 - per doz.
Venetian Bronzed
(highly finished ... 36 - per doz.

No. 1407   "THE MIDGET."   2¼ × 2¼
Maroon Bronzed ... ... 4.2 doz.
Electro Brass or Copper Relief 5/4 doz.

No. 1282   "THE CITY."   4 × 3¼
Maroon Bronzed ... ... 6 6 doz.
Half Elec. Brass or Copper Relief 7 6 doz.
Full ditto ... ... 8 6 doz.

No. 1556   4 × 3
Maroon Bronzed ... ... 6/- doz.
Electro Brass or Copper Relief 6/6 doz.

No. 1387   "TOWN HALL."   3¼ × 3¼
Maroon Bronzed ... ... 6/6 doz.
Electro Brass or Copper Relief 8.8 doz.

"FOOTBALL."   No. 1483   48/- per doz.
Quantities of 3 doz. Painted in Club Colors.

"OOP-LA."   No. 1561   64/- per dozen

"GIANT."   No. 1406
Indian Black, Head
Painted only ... 25/- per doz.
In various Colors ... 31/- per doz.

"CROWN."   No. 1737
Maroon Bronzed ... ... 10/- doz.
Gold Enamelline ... ... 11/- doz.

"CROWN and CUSHION."   No. 1738
Maroon Bronzed ... ... 5/6 doz.
Gold Enamelline ... ... 6/- doz.

28   32   29   33

Boxed in Half Dozens.

1929

John Harper, LTD.   Mechanical and other Money Banks.   1911

"HOOP-LA."   No. 1561
64/- per doz.
Boxed Singly.

"FOOTBALL"   No. 1483
48/- per doz.
Quantities of 3-doz. painted in Club Colors.
Boxed Singly.

"GOLLIWOG"   No. 2317
Painted in attractive Colors.
6½ inches high.
12/- per doz.
Boxed in Half Dozens.

"GIANT."   No. 1406
Indian Black, Head Painted only 25/- per doz.
In various Colors ... ... 31/- per doz.
Boxed Singly.

"LION."   No. 2229.
Maroon Bronzed ... 12/- per doz.
Boxed In Half Dozens.

"Teddy Bear."   No. 2228.
Maroon Bronzed,
12/- per doz.
Boxed In Half Dozens.

"CROWN AND CUSHION"   No. 1738.
Maroon Bronzed ... ... 5/6 per doz.
Gold Enamelline ... ... 6/- per doz.
Boxed In Half Dozens.

"BILLIKEN."
No. 2326
Painted in correct Colors.
3 inches high.
8/- per doz.
Boxed In Half Dozens.

John Harper, LTD.   Toy Money Banks. 1911

BOXED IN HALF DOZENS.

No. 1282.   4 × 3¼ in.
"THE CITY."
Maroon Bronzed ... ... 6 6 doz.
Half Elec. Brass or Copper Relief ... ... 7/6 doz.
Full ditto ... ... 8 6 doz.

No. 1407.   2¼ × 2¼ in.
"THE MIDGET."
Maroon Bronzed ... ... 4 2 doz.
Electro Brass or Copper Relief ... ... 5 4 doz.

No. 1556.   4 × 3 in.
Maroon Bronzed ... ... 6/- doz.
Electro Brass or Copper Relief ... ... 6/6 doz.

No. 1557.   "THE BEEHIVE."   3½ × 4 in.
Maroon Bronzed ... ... 9/- doz.
Gold Enamelline ... ... 12/- doz.
Boxed in One-Third Dozens.

No. 1243.   9-in. high.
"THE TOWER"
Maroon Bronzed, with Bell ... ... 13/6 doz.
Maroon Bronzed, without Bell 13/- doz.
Boxed in Quarter Dozens.

No. 1387.   "TOWN HALL."   3¼ × 3¼ in.
Maroon Bronzed ... ... 6/6 doz.
Electro Brass or Copper Relief 8 8 doz.

No. 1909.   "CASTLE."
Maroon Bronzed ... ... 13/- doz.
Indian Art Black and Gold Bronzed ... 13 6 doz.
Venetian Bronzed ... ... 24/- doz.
Boxed in One-Third Dozens.

No. 1388.   "THE COUNTY."   5 × 4½ in.
Maroon Bronzed ... ... 12 6 doz.
Gold Enamelline ... ... 14 - doz.
Electro Brass or Copper Relief... 15 - doz.
Boxed in Half Dozens.

THE HUBLEY MANUFACTURING CO.

THE LANCASTER IRON TOYS. 1906

9

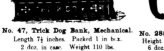

No. 276, Bank.
Height 4 inches. Packed 3 in box.
6 doz. in case. Weight 150 lbs.

No. 277, Bank.
Height 6 inches. Packed 2 in box.
3 doz. in case. Weight 150 lbs.

No. 47, Trick Dog Bank, Mechanical.
Length 7½ inches. Packed 1 in box.
2 doz. in case. Weight 110 lbs.

No. 285, Large Elephant Bank.
Height 5 inches. Packed 2 in box.
6 doz. in case. Weight 230 lbs.

No. 48, Monkey Bank, Mechanical.
Length 8 inches. Packed 1 in box.
2 doz. in case. Weight 100 lbs.

No. 286, Cash Register Bank.
Length 4 inches. Height 5 inches.
Packed 1 in box. 3 doz. in case.
Weight 150 lbs.

No. 43, Locomotive, Mechanical.
Length 8 inches. Packed 1 in box.
3 doz. in case. Weight 70 lbs.

No. 79, Locomotive, Mechanical.
Length 9¼ inches. Packed 1 in box.
3 doz. in case. Weight 100 lbs.

1906

No. 279, Santa Claus Bank.
Height 6 inches. Packed 1 doz. in box.
12 doz. in case. Weight 140 lbs.

No. 280, Rabbit Bank.
Height 4½ inches. Packed 6 in box.
12 doz. in case. Weight 120 lbs.

No. 281, Foxy Grandpa Bank.
Height 5½ inches. Packed 6 in box.
12 doz. in case. Weight 110 lbs.

No. 12. Cab.
Length 15½ inches. Packed 1 in box.
3 doz. in case. Weight 195 lbs.

No. 125, Spider Phaeton.
Length 13½ inches. Packed 1 in box.
3 dozen in case. Weight 180 lbs.

No. 146, Express Wagon, Two Horses.
Length 15 inches. Packed 1 in box.
3 doz. in case. Weight 140 lbs.

No. 73, Phaeton.
Length 17 inches. Packed 1 in box.
3 doz. in case. Weight 170 lbs.

No. 204, Surrey, Two Horses.
Length 15 inches. Packed 1 in box.
3 doz. in case. Weight 175 lbs.

No. 95, Farm Wagon, no Driver.
Length 15 inches. Packed 1 in box.
3 doz. in case. Weight 150 lbs.

No. 282, Small Elephant Bank.
Height 3¾ inches. Packed 6 in box.
12 doz. in case. Weight 180 lbs.

No. 283, Billy Bounce Bank.
Height 5 inches. Packed 6 in box.
12 doz. in case. Weight 110 lbs.

No. 573, Darkey Bank (Pat).
Height 5½ inches. Packed 6 in box.
12 doz. in case. Weight 110 lbs.

No. 26, Trap, Two Horses.
Length 13½ inches. Packed 1 in box.
3 doz. in case. Weight 140 lbs.

No. 22, Large Elephant and Chariot.
Length 12½ inches. Packed 1 in box.
3 doz. in case. Weight 180 lbs.

No. 177, Surrey, Two Horses.
Length 13½ inches. Packed 1 in box.
3 doz. in case. Weight 150 lbs.

Assortment A.   Packed Six in Box.   12 Dozen in Case.

No. 98, Bell Toy, Two Horses Galloping.
Length 9½ inches. Packed 1 in box.
3 doz. in case. Weight 100 lbs.

No. 147, Surrey, Two Horses.
Length 13½ inches. Packed 1 in box.
3 doz. in case. Weight 110 lbs.

No. 175, Buckboard.
Length 14 inches. Packed 1 in box.
3 doz. in case. Weight 150 lbs.

No. 605. Ox Cart.
Length, 5¾ inches, 12 in box, 24 doz. in case, weight 170 lbs.
No. 605S. Without Driver.

No. 601. Pony Cart.
Length, 5 inches, 12 in box, 24 doz. in case, weight 140 lbs.

No. 600. Pony Cart.
Length, 4 inches, 12 in box, 24 doz. in case, weight 115 lbs.

BANKS.

No. 55, Surrey, with Driver.
Length 13½ inches. Packed 3 in box.
6 doz. in case. Weight 155 lbs.

No. 37, Buckboard.
Length 13½ inches. Packed 3 in box.
6 doz. in case. Weight 120 lbs.

No. 97, Bell Toy, 1 Horse Galloping.
Length 6½ inches. Packed 2 in box.
6 doz. in case. Weight 115 lbs.

No. 813. Base Ball Bank.
Design Patented.
Aluminum Ball and Red Bats.
Height, 5¼ inches, 6 in box, 12 doz. in case,
weight, 160 lbs.
No. 813G. White Ball and Gold Bats.

No. 33, Pony Cart, Length 11½ inches.
Packed 3 in box. 6 doz. in case. Weight 185 lbs.

No. 107, Coupe.
Length 9½ inches. Packed 6 in box.
6 doz. in case. Weight 155 lbs.

No. 19, Small Elephant & Chariot.
Length 8½ inches. Packed 6 in box.
6 doz. in case. Weight 130 lbs.

No. 814. Foot Ball Bank.
Design Patented.
Aluminum Ball, Red Man.
Height, 5¼ inches, 6 in box, 12 doz. in case,
weight, 150 lbs.
No. 814M. Polished Nickel Ball, Red Man.

No. 807. Grandpa Bank.
Height, 5¾ inches, 12 in box, 24 doz. in case, weight 220 lbs.
No. 810. Darkey Bank.
Height, 5¾ inches, 12 in box, 24 in case, weight 220 lbs.
No. 809. Billy Bounce Bank.
Height, 5 inches, 12 in box, 24 doz. in case, weight 220 lbs.

No. 821. Hall Clock Bank.
Height, 6¼ inches, 12 in box, 24 doz. in case, weight, 140 lbs.
No. 825. Camel Bank.
Height, 4¼ inches, 12 in box, 24 doz. in case, weight 160 lbs.
No. 844. Boy Scout Bank.
Height, 6 inches, 12 in box, 24 doz. in case, weight 210 lbs.

No. 802. Office Bank.
Height, 5¾ inches, 12 in box, 24 doz. in case, weight 210 lbs.
No. 803. Sailor Bank.
Height, 5¾ inches, 12 in box, 24 doz. in case, weight 280 lbs.
No. 804. Soldier Bank.
Height, 6¼ inches, 12 in box, 24 doz. in case, weight 240 lbs.

No. 819. Ball Player Bank.
Height, 6 inches, 12 in box, 24 doz. in case, weight 200 lbs.
No. 808. Elephant Bank.
Height, 3¾ inches, 12 in box, 24 doz. in case, weight 280 lbs.
No. 806. Rabbit Bank.
Height, 4¼ inches, 12 in box, 24 in case. weight 240 lbs.

No. 812. Horse Bank.
Height, 5 inches, 12 in box, 24 doz. in case, weight 260 lbs.
No. 843. Clown Bank.
Height, 6¼ inches, 12 in box, 24 doz. in case, weight, 210 lbs.
No. 824. Rooster Bank.
Height, 4¼ inches, 12 in box, 24 doz. in case, weight 180 lbs.

No. 801. Indian Bank.
Height, 6¼ inches, 12 in box, 24 doz. in case, weight 280 lbs.
No. 826. Dog Bank.
Height, 4½ inches, 12 in box, 24 doz. in case, weight 270 lbs.
No. 811. Bear Bank.
Height, 5¾ inches, 12 in box, 24 doz. in case, weight 290 lbs.

No. 817.
Bull Dog Bank.
Height, 4 inches, 6 in box, 12 doz. in case, weight 190 lbs.

No. 822.
Cutie Bank.
Height, 4 inches, 12 in box, 24 doz. in case, weight 250 lbs.

No. 818.
Lion Bank.
Length, 5½ inches, 6 in box, 12 doz. in case, weight 170 lbs.

No. 845.
Santa Bank.
Height, 6 inches, 12 in box, 12 doz. in case, weight 160 lbs.

No. 815.
Triangle Bank.
Height, 6 inches, 6 in box, 12 doz. in case, weight 180 lbs.

No. 820.
Mascot Bank.
Height, 6¼ inches, 6 in box, 12 doz. in case, weight 150 lbs.

No. 836. Policeman Bank.
Height, 5¾ inches, 12 in box, 12 doz. in case, weight 190 lbs.
No. 841. Elephant Bank.
Height, 4 inches, 12 in box, 12 doz. in case, weight 190 lbs.
No. 837. Mammy Bank.
Height, 6 inches, 12 in box, 12 doz. in case, weight 190 lbs.

No. 823.
Fido Bank, Black.
No. 823A.
White, Black Spots.
No. 823B.
White, Brown Spots.
Dolly Dimple's "Fido." Design Pat'd.
Manf'd under exclusive license from Grace G. Drayton.

No. 775. Polar Bear Cage, Two Horses, Two Bears.
Length, 16 inches, 1 in box, 1 doz. in case, weight 120 lbs.

No. 70. Baby Elephant.
Height, 2 inches, length, 3½ inches, 12 in box, 12 doz. in case, weight 90 lbs.

No. 704. Chariot.
Length, 9½ inches, 1 in box, 3 doz. in case, weight 110 lbs.

No. 827. Elephant Bank.
Height, 5 inches, length 7 inches, 1 in box, 3 doz. in case, weight 90 lbs.

No. 841. Elephant Bank.
Height, 4 inches, 12 in box, 12 doz. in case, weight 190 lbs.

No. 808. Elephant Bank.
Height, 3¾ inches, 12 in box, 24 doz. in case, weight 280 lbs.

No. 829. Trick Monkey Bank.
Length, 9 inches, height 7½ inches, 1 in box, 2 doz. in case, weight 100 lbs.

No. 828. Trick Dog Bank.
Length, 9 inches, height 7½ inches, 1 in box, 2 doz. in case, weight 110 lbs.

No. 823. Fido Bank, Black.
No. 823A. White, Black Spots.
No. 823B. White, Brown Spots.
Height, 5⅛ inches, 1 in box, 3 doz. in case, weight 100 lbs.

No. 846A. Puppo Bank, White, Black Spots.
No. 846B. White, Brown Spots.
Height, 5 inches, 1 in box, 3 doz. in case, weight 125 lbs.
Fido and Puppo manufactured under exclusive license from Grace G. Drayton.

No. 827. Elephant Bank.
Height, 5 inches, length 7 inches, 1 in box, 3 doz. in case, weight 90 lbs.

No. 841. Elephant Bank.
Height, 4 inches, 12 in box, 12 doz. in case, weight 190 lbs.

No. 822. Cutie Bank.
Height, 4 inches, 6 in box, 24 doz. in case, weight 250 lbs.

No. 801. Indian Bank.
Height, 6¼ inches, 12 in box, 24 doz. in case, weight 280 lbs.

No. 817. Bull Dog Bank.
Height, 4 inches, 12 in box, 12 doz. in case, weight 190 lbs.

PRE 1920

No. 845.
Santa Bank.
Height, 6 inches, 12 in box, 12 doz. in case, weight 160 lbs.

No. 826.
Dog Bank.
Height, 4½ inches, 12 in box, 24 doz. in case, weight 270 lbs.

No. 806.
Rabbit Bank.
Height, 4¾ inches, 12 in box, 24 doz. in case, weight 240 lbs.

No. 818.
Lion Bank.
Length, 5½ inches, 6 in box, 12 doz. in case, weight 170 lbs.

No. 811.
Bear Bank.
Height, 6¼ inches, 12 in box, 24 doz. in case, weight 290 lbs.

No. 808.
Elephant Bank.
Height, 3¾ inches, 12 in box, 24 doz. in case, weight 280 lbs.

No. 802. Officer Bank.
Height, 5¾ inches, 12 in box, 24 doz. in case, weight 210 lbs.

No. 803. Sailor Bank.
Height, 5¾ inches, 12 in box, 24 doz. in case, weight 280 lbs.

No. 804. Soldier Bank.
Height, 6¼ inches, 12 in box, 24 doz. in case, weight 240 lbs.

No. 825. Camel Bank.
Height, 4¾ inches, 12 in box, 24 doz. in case, weight 160 lbs.

No. 824. Rooster Bank.
Height, 4¾ inches, 12 in box, 24 doz. in case, weight 180 lbs.

No. 812. Horse Bank.
Height, 5 inches, 12 in box, 24 doz. in case, weight 260 lbs.

No. 807. Grandpa Bank.
Height, 5½ inches, 12 in box, 24 doz. in case, weight 220 lbs.

No. 810. Darkey Bank.
Height, 5½ inches, 12 in box, 24 doz. in case, weight 220 lbs.

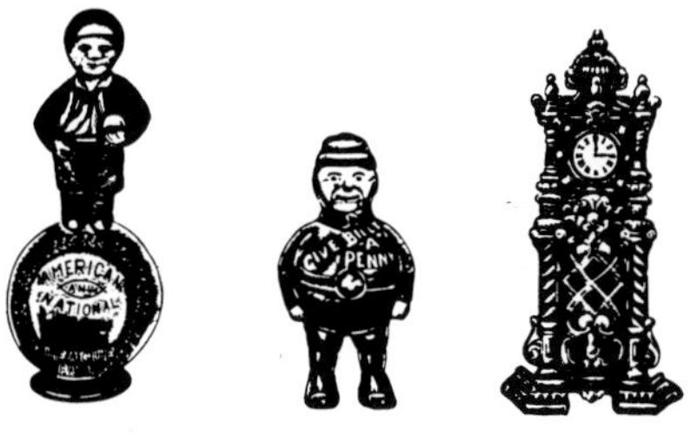

No. 820.
Mascot Bank.
Height, 6¼ inches, 6 in box, 12 doz. in case, weight 150 lbs.

No. 809.
Billy Bounce Bank.
Height, 5 inches, 12 in box, 24 doz. in case, weight 220 lbs.

No. 821.
Hall Clock Bank.
Height, 6¼ inches, 12 in box, 24 doz. in case, weight 140 lbs.

BANKS

1930

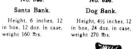

No. 817. Porky Bank
Height 6 inches
Weight 1½ lbs. each

No. 820. Kitty
Height 5¼ inches
Weight 18½ lbs. per dozen

No. 823. Fido
Height 5 inches
Weight 22 lbs. per dozen

No. 818. Mammy Bank
Height 5⅜ inches
Weight 1 lb. each

No. 819. Elephant
Height 4½ inches
Weight 13 lbs. per dozen

No. 821. Bear
Height 6¾ inches
Weight 30 lbs. per dozen

No. 827. Duck
Height 5½ inches
Weight 16½ lbs. per dozen

No. 822. Piggie
Height 7 inches
Weight 27 lbs. per dozen

No. 824. Scotty
Height 5 inches
Weight 19 lbs. per dozen

No. 825. Wire Haired Terrier
Height 4¾ inches
Weight 17½ lbs. per dozen

No. 826. Boston Bull
Height 4¾ inches
Weight 18½ lbs. per dozen

[Saving is a pleasure in Hubley's line of toy banks. Painted in bright natural colors, and packed in suitable gift boxes.]

No. 844 G. E. Bank
Height: 3½ inches
Packed 12 in box, 12 doz. to carton; weight 80 lbs
Painted White

No. 828 Trick Dog Bank
Length: 8½ inches.
Packed 1 in box, 1 doz. to carton; weight per carton, 50 lbs.
Highly Decorated in Various Colors.

No. 829 Trick Monkey Bank
Length: 8¾ inches.
Packed 1 in box, 1 doz. to carton; weight per carton, 44 lbs.
Highly Decorated in Various Colors.

No. 830 Trick Elephant Bank
Length: 8½ inches.
Packed 1 in box, 1 doz. to carton; weight per carton, 50 lbs.
Painted White, Trimmed in Color.
Coin is placed in trunk and thrown into body by lifting the tail.

No. 865 Elephant Bank.
Height 5¾ inches, 6 in box, 12 doz. in case, weight 150 lbs.

No. 861 Elephant Bank.
Height 4 inches, 6 in box, 12 doz. in case, weight 150 lbs.

No. 817 Bull Dog Bank.
Height 4 inches, 6 in box, 12 doz. in case, weight 120 lbs.

No. 846 Radio Bank.
Height 3½ inches, 12 in box, 12 doz. in case, weight 80 lbs.

No. 845 G. E. Bank.
Height 3½ inches, 1 in box, 1 doz. in case, weight 150 lbs.

No. 862 U. S. Bank.
Height 3½ inches, 12 in box, 24 doz. in case, weight 160 lbs.

No. 630—The King Midas Bank at the right is 5" high and its base is 3½" square. Made in two finishes, painted and ivory. The grotesque figure clutches a money bag at the top of which is the coin slot. Packed 1 in box.

A tag attached to it reads as follows:
"I am the greatest thing on earth.
'King Midas,' and behold!
He who keeps me always near,
Shall never want for gold."

KING MIDAS

No. 827 Duck Bank
Height: 5½ inches.
Packed 1 in box, 2 doz. to carton; weight per carton, 37 lbs.
Painted Natural Colors with Red Base and Gold Letters.

No. 820 Kitty Bank
Height: 5¼ inches.
Packed 1 in a designed box, 2 doz. to carton; weight per carton, 39 lbs.
Painted White with Pink or Blue Ribbons.

No. 822 Pig Bank
Height: 7 inches.
Packed 1 in box, 3 doz. to carton; weight per carton, 83 lbs.
Packed in box as illustrated.
Painted Ivory.
(Copyrighted by Josie McCutcheon Raleigh)

No. 819 Elephant Bank
Height: 4½ inches.
Packed 1 in a colorful box, 3 doz. to carton; weight per carton, 44 lbs.
Attractively Painted.

No. 821 Bear Bank
Height: 6¾ inches.
Packed 1 in box, 1 doz. to carton; weight per carton, 31 lbs.
Painted Natural Colors.

No. 823 Fido Bank
Height: 5 inches.
Packed 1 in box, 3 doz. to carton; weight per carton, 71 lbs.
Painted White with Black Ears.

Page 10

No. 824 Scotty Bank
Height: 5 inches. Packed 1 in box, 1 doz. to carton; weight per carton, 22 lbs.
Painted black with red collar.

No. 825 Wire Haired Bank
Height: 4½ inches. Packed 1 in box, 1 doz. to carton; weight per carton, 20 lbs.
Painted brown and white with red collar.

No. 826 Boston Bull Bank
Height: 4½ inches. Packed 1 in box, 1 doz. to carton; weight per carton, 21 lbs.
Painted black and white with red collar.

No. 828 Trick Dog Bank
Length: 8¾ inches.
Packed 1 in box, 1 doz. to carton; weight per carton, 48 lbs.
Highly Decorated in Various Colors.

No. 829 Trick Monkey Bank
Length: 8¾ inches.
Packed 1 in box, 1 doz. to carton; weight per carton, 44 lbs.
Highly Decorated in Various Colors.

No. 830 Trick Elephant Bank
Length: 8¾ inches.
Packed 1 in box, 1 doz. to carton; weight per carton, 50 lbs.
Painted White, Trimmed in Color.
Coin is placed in trunk and thrown into body by lifting the tail.

Page 11

NEW YORK OFFICE

693 BROADWAY

NEW YORK CITY

N. Y.

MANAGERS SALES COMPANY

THE KENTON HARDWARE COMPANY

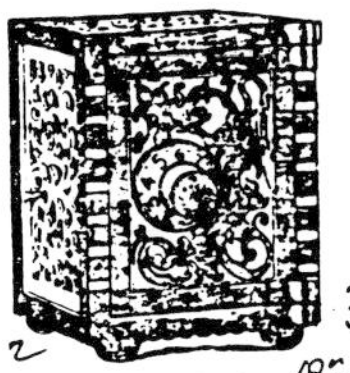

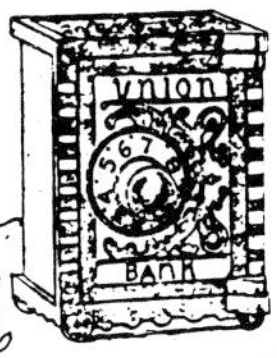

Steel Sides. Nickel Plated.

16. Steel Sides. Electro Oxydized. Height, 4¼ inches; width 3¼ inches in a box; one gross in a case. Weight of case, 225 lbs.

868. Polished and Nickel Plated. Combination lock. Height 3¾ inches; width, 2½ inches. Six in a box; two gross in a case. Weight of case, 100 lbs.

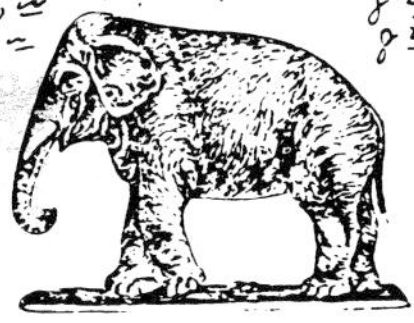

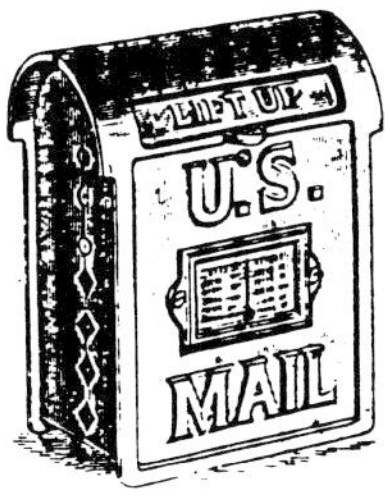

MAIL BOX BANK.

No. B69. Aluminum. Height, 3½ inches. Width, 2⅝ inches. Six in a box; two gross in a case. Weight of case, 100 lbs.

No. B70. Aluminum. Height, 4¾ inches. Width 3½ inches. One in a box; one gross in a case. Weight of case, 125 lbs.

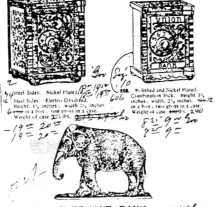

ELEPHANT BANK.

Painted. Length, 4½ inches. Height, 3 inches. One dozen in a box; one gross in a case. Weight of case, 126 lbs.

Painted. Length 4½ inches; height, 3½ inches. Six in a box; one-half gross in a case. Weight of case, 100 lbs.

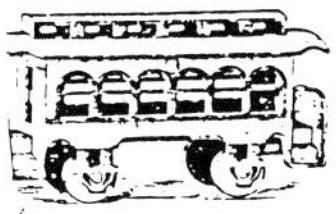

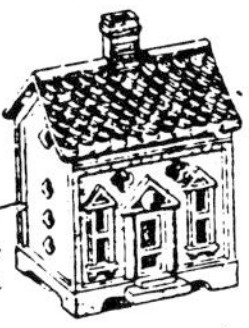

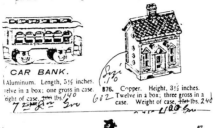

CAR BANK.

Aluminum. Length, 5½ inches. Twelve in a box; one gross in case. Weight of case, 100 lbs.

B76. Copper. Height, 3½ inches. Twelve in a box; three gross in a case. Weight of case, 150 lbs.

Kenton Line Ranges

21

No. 3½

Nickel Plated

Length, 5¼ inches. Height, 5¾ inches. Width, 5 inches. 4 pieces in a box. 6 dozen in a case. Weight of case, 170 lbs.

No. 3

Nickel Plated

No. 3A

Electro Oxydized

Length, 5¼ inches. Height, 3¼ inches. Width, 5 inches. 4 in a box. 6 dozen in a case. Weight of case, 155 lbs.

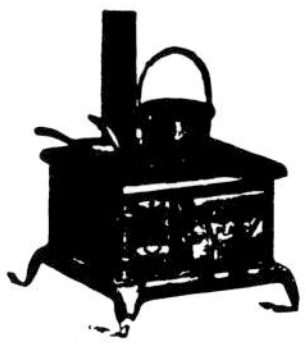

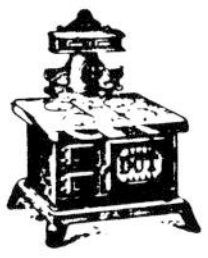

No. 900 No Utensils

No. 901 With Utensils

Nickel Plated

Length, 3¾ inches. Height, 4¼ inches. Width, 2¼ inches. 1 dozen in a box. 2 gross in a case. Weight of case, 230 lbs.

No. 1

Nicke Plated

Length, 3¼ inches. Height, 4¼ inches. Width, 2¼ inches. 12 in a box, 2 gross in a case. Weight of case, 194 lbs.

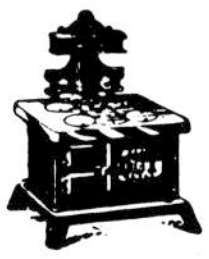

63

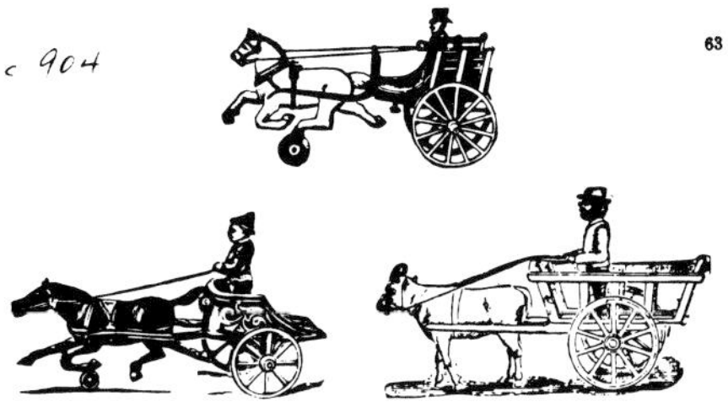

Assortment

No. 102 —Average length, 7¼ inches. 4 pieces, each toy in a box. 12 dozen in a case. Weight per case, 175 lbs.

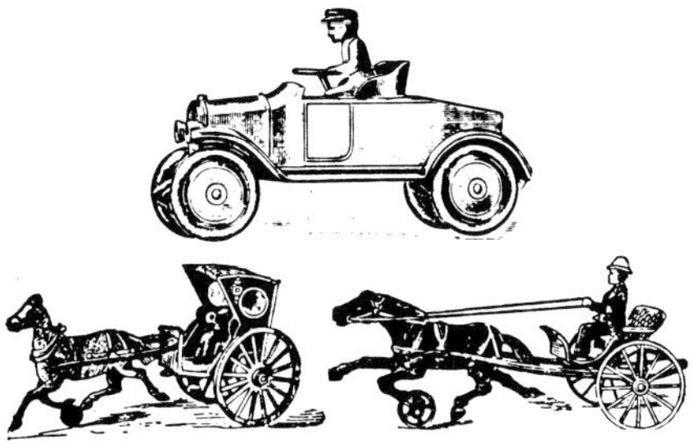

Assortment

No. 106 —Average length, 7 inches. 4 pieces, each toy in a box. 12 dozen in a case. Weight per case, 166 lbs.

67

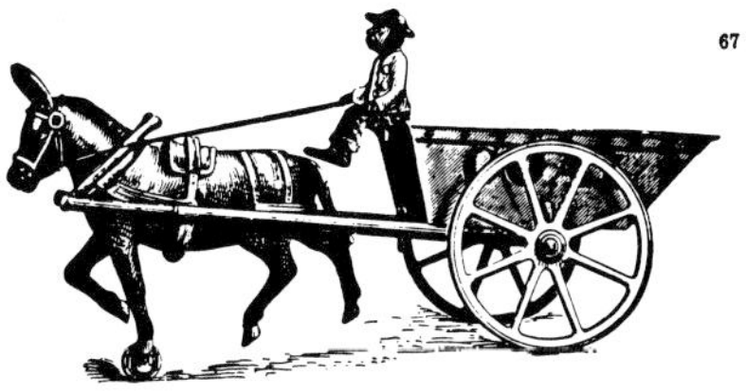

Mule and Coal Cart

No. 598 Painted. Length 14 inches. Negro Driver. Made to dump. 1 in a box. 2 dozen in a case. 162 lbs. per case.

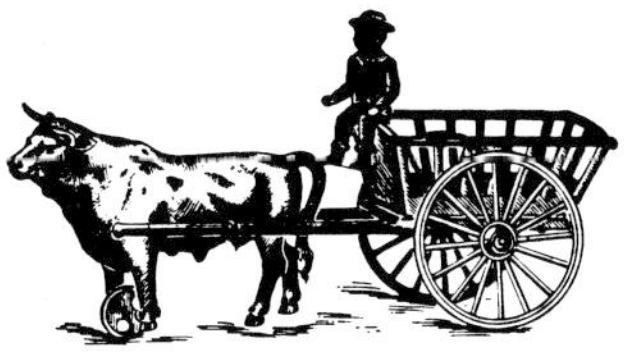

Plantation Ox Cart

No. 599 Painted. Length 13 inches. 1 in a box. 3 dozen in a case. 150 lbs. per case.

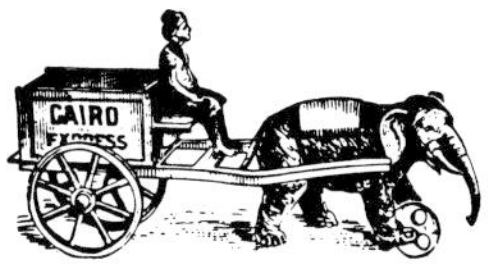

Cairo Express

No. 882

Painted. Length, 10 in.

1 in a box. 6 dozen in a case.

215 lbs. per case.

83

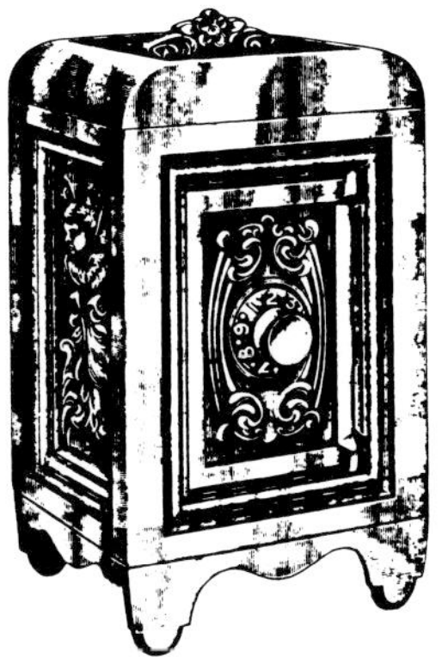

Patented
Aug. 22, 1911

Iron Clad Banks

Furnished with Combination Locks

No. 260	Nickel Plated.	Height 4¾ inches.
No. 262	Electro Oxydized. Width 3 inches. Depth 2¼ inches. 6 in a box. 12 dozen in a case. Weight of case, 200 lbs.	
No. 264	Nickel Plated.	Height 5¾ inches.
No. 266	Electro Oxydized. Width 3¾ inches. Depth 3 inches. 1 in a box. 3 dozen in a case. Weight of case, 110 lbs.	
No. 268	Nickel Plated.	Height 7¼ inches.
No. 270	Electro Oxydized. Width 4¼ inches. Depth 3¾ inches. 1 in a box. 2 dozen in a case. Weight of case, 125 lbs.	

84

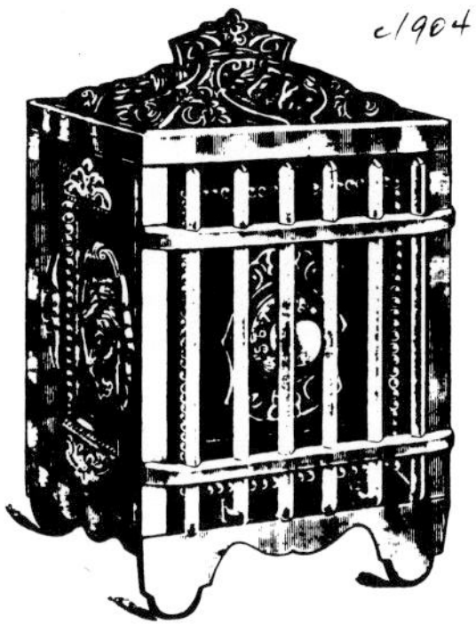

Patented
Nov. 28, 1911

Safety Vault Bank

Furnished with Combination Lock.

No. 620	Nickel Plated. Height 5¾ inches.
No. 621	Electro Oxydized. Width 3¾ inches. Depth 3¾ inches. 1 in a box. 3 dozen in a case. Weight per case, 100 lbs.
No. 640	Nickel Plated. Height 6¾ inches. Width 4¼ inches.
No. 641	Electro Oxydized. Depth 4 inches. 1 in a box. 3 dozen in a case. Weight of case, 135 lbs.
No. 644	Nickel Plated. Height 7¾ inches. Width 4¾ inches.
No. 645	Electro Oxydized. Depth 5 inches. 1 in a box. 2 dozen in a case. Weight of case, 125 lbs.

Combination Safes

85

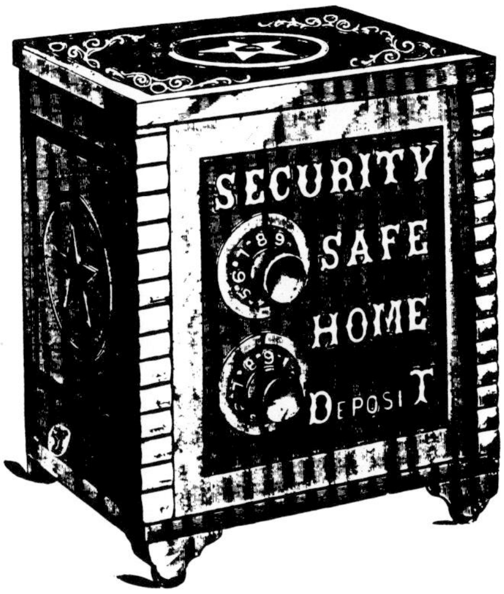

Security Safe Home Deposit

Furnished with Combination Lock

No. 145 Nickel Plated.

No. 145A Electro Oxydized. Steel Sides and Back. Height 6¾ inches. Width 5¼ inches. Depth, 4¾ inches. 1 in a box. 2 dozen in a case. 100 lbs. per case.

86

Bank of Commerce

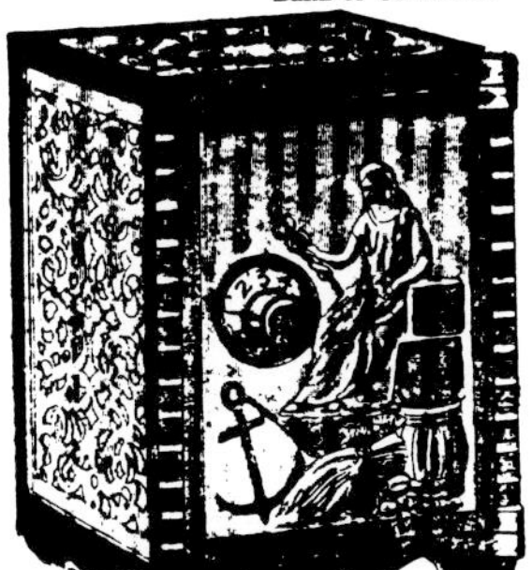

No. 642

Nickel Plated

No. 643

Electro Oxydized

All Iron Bank Furnished with Combination Lock.

Height 6¾ inches Width 5 inches 1 in a box. 2 dozen in a case. 125 lbs. per case.

Bank of Industry

No. 638

Nickel Plated

No. 639

Electro Oxydized

Furnished with Combination Lock.

All Iron Bank. Height 5¼ inches. Width 4¼ inches. 1 in a box. 3 doz. in a case. 130 lbs. per case.

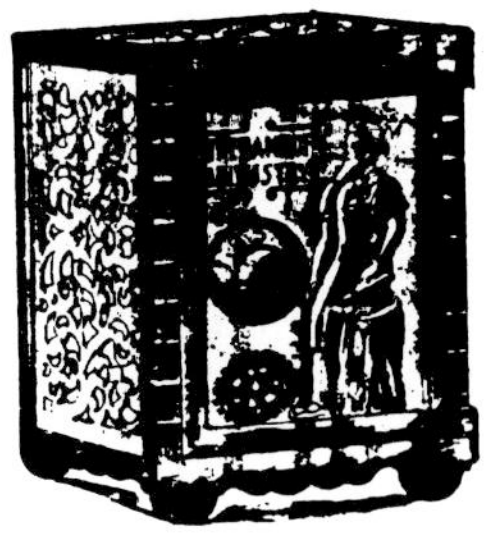

Flat Iron Building Bank

Fitted With Patented Lock.

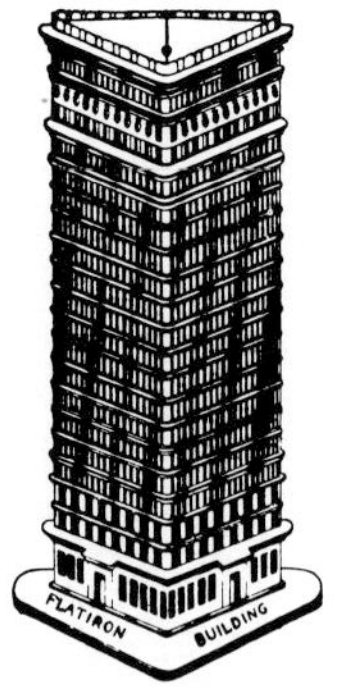

No. 605

Aluminum Finish. Height 3½ inches. 12 in a box. 24 dozen in a case. 175 lbs. per case.

No. 606

Aluminum Finish. Height 5½ inches. 12 in a box. 12 dozen in a case. 150 lbs. per case.

No. 616

Aluminum Finish. Height 6 inches. 3 in a box. 6 dozen in a case. 135 lbs. per case.

Mail Box Bank

No. 608

Aluminum Finish. Height 3⅞ inches. Width 2⅜ inches. 12 in a box. 2 gross in a case. 200 lbs. per case.

No. 609

Aluminum Finish. Height 4½ inches. Width 3⅛ inches. 12 in a box. 1 gross in a case. 150 lbs. per case.

No. 610

Fitted with Patent Lock. Aluminum Finish. Height 5½ inches. Width 3⅞ inches. 4 in a box. 1 gross in a case. 225 lbs. per case.

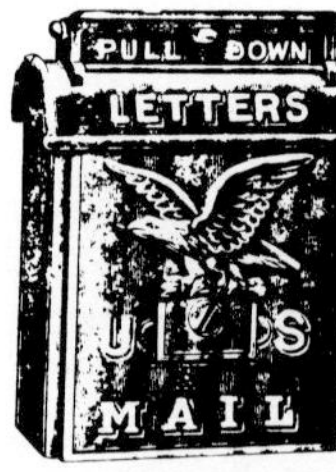

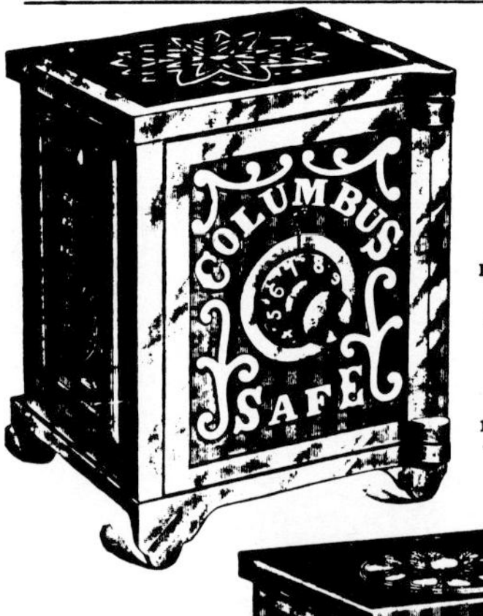

Columbus Safe

No. 105

Nickel Plated

No. 105A

Electro Oxydized

Furnished with Combination Lock.

Steel Sides and Back.

Height 5½ inches.

Width, 4½ inches.

Depth 4 inches.

1 in a box. 3 dozen in a case. 88 lbs. per case.

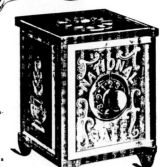

National Safe

No. 50

Nickel Plated

No. 50A

Electro Oxydized

Furnished with Combination Lock.

Steel Sides and Back.

Height 5 inches.

Width 3⅞ inches.

Depth 3⅞ inches.

6 in a box. 6 dozen in a case. 125 lbs. per case.

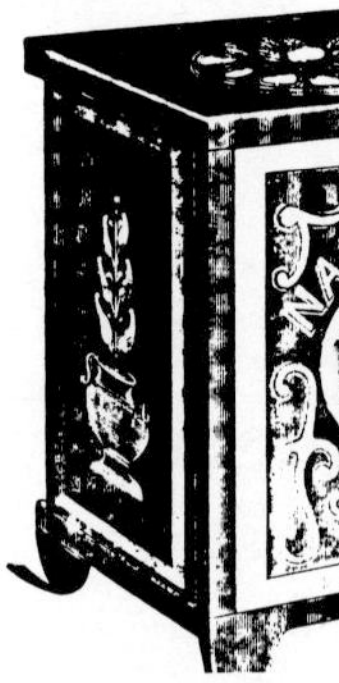

Combination Safes

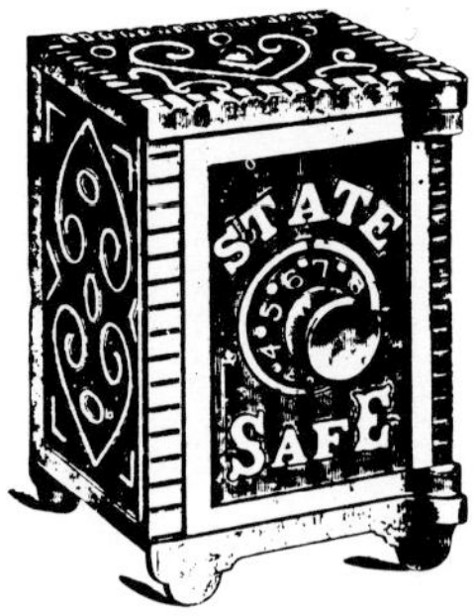

The State Safe

No. 65

Nickel Plated

No. 65A

Electro Oxydized

Furnished with Combination Lock.

All Iron Bank. Height 4½ in. Width 3 in. Depth 3 in.

6 in a box. 12 dozen in a case. 224 lbs. per case.

The Army Safe

No. 45

Nickel Plated

Steel Sides and Back.

Furnished with Combination Lock.

Height 4½ inches. Width 3 in.

Depth 3 in. 6 in a box.

12 dozen in a case.

165 lbs. per case.

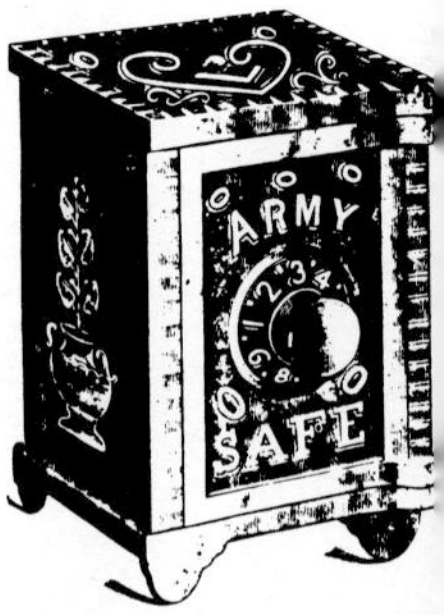

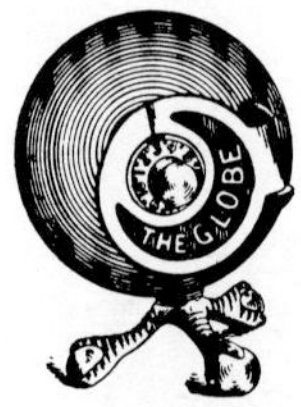

The Globe Safe

No. 55A

Electro Oxydized.

All Iron Bank is highly polished and plated. Makes a very handsome ornament for a home. Closed by combination lock with money guard. One of the most beautiful and attractive Banks made.

Height 5½ inches. Globe 4 inches in diameter being a perfect sphere

1 in a box. 3 dozen in a case.

75 lbs. per case.

The National Safe

No. 30

Nickel Plated

No. 30A

Electro Oxydized

Furnished with Combination Lock.

All Iron Bank. Height 5 inches.

Width 3⅞ inches. Depth 3⅞ inches.

1 in a box. 3 dozen in a case.

100 lbs. per case.

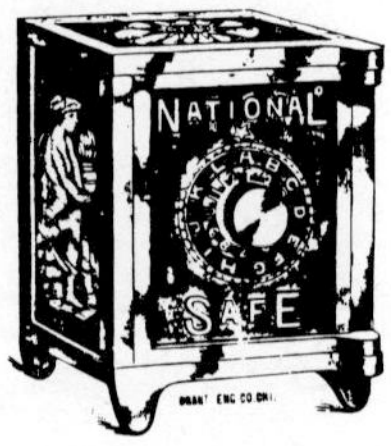

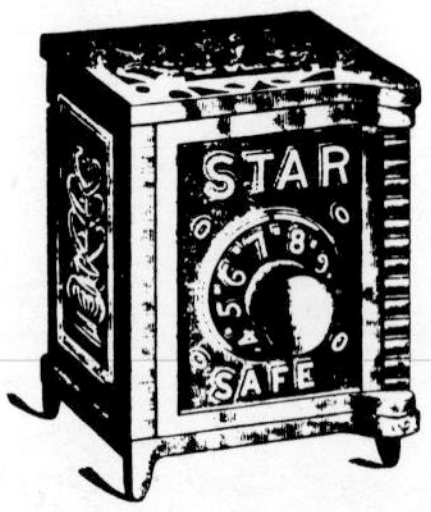

Star Combination Safe

No. 120

Polished and Nickel Plated.

Steel Sides and Back.

Height 3½ in. Width 2½ in.

Depth 2½ inches. 12 in a box.

2 gross in a case. 220 lbs. per case.

Combination Banks

No. 612 Steel Sides. Nickel Plated

No. 613 All Iron. Nickel Plated.

No. 614 Steel Sides. Electro Oxydized.

No. 615 All Iron. Electro Oxydized.

Furnished with Combination Lock.

Height 4½ inches. Width 3⅞ inches.

6 in a box. 1 gross in a case.

220 lbs. per case with steel sides

275 lbs. per case, all iron.

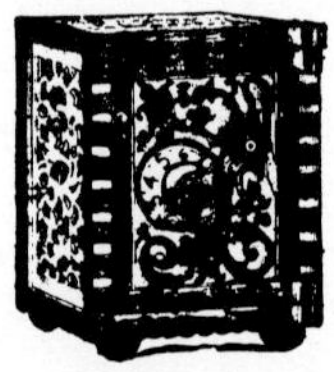

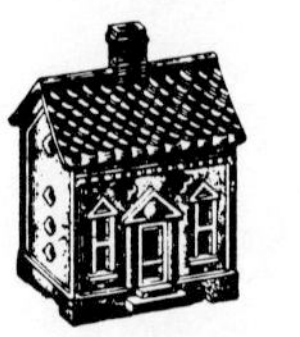

House Bank

No. 602

Coppered. Height 3½ inches.

12 in a box. 4 gross in a case.

335 lbs. per case.

The Rival Safe

No. 25

Nicely Polished and Nickel Plated.

Good lock and key. Made of steel and iron.

Height 3½ inches. Width 2½ inches.

Depth 2½ inches. 12 in a box.

2 gross in a case. 200 lbs. per case.

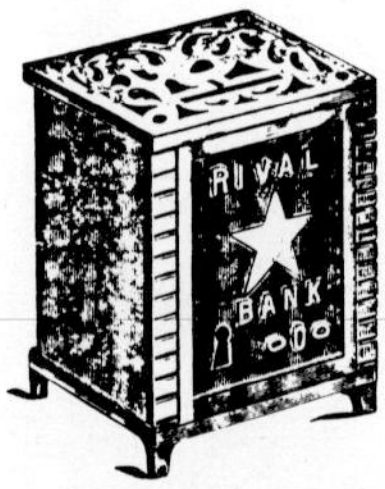

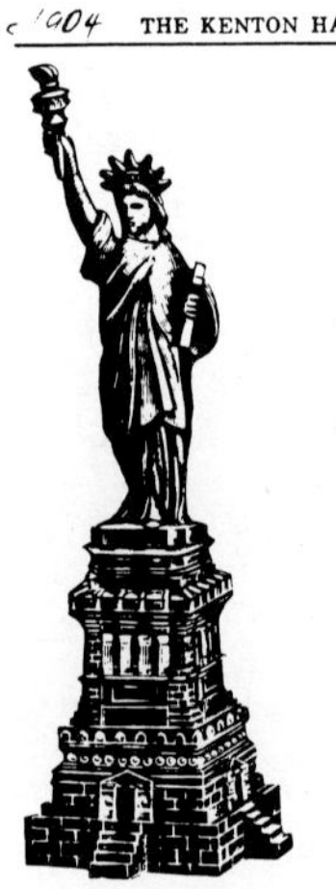

Liberty Bank

No. 630 Height 6½ inches. Width 2½ inches. 12 in a box. 24 dozen in a case. 210 lbs. per case.

No. 632 Height 9⅞ inches. Width 3½ inch. 4 in a box. 12 dozen in a case. 280 lbs. per case.

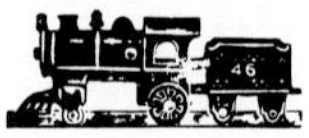

Locomotives

No. 384

Aluminum Finish. 5½ inches long. 12 in a box 24 dozen in a case. 130 lbs. per case.

No. 385

Aluminum Finish. 6 inches long. 12 in a box 24 dozen in a case. 180 lbs. per case.

No. 386

Painted. 6½ inches long. 12 in a box. 12 dozen in a case. 130 lbs. per case.

No. 387

Painted. 7 inches long. 6 in a box. 12 dozen in a case. 180 lbs. per case.

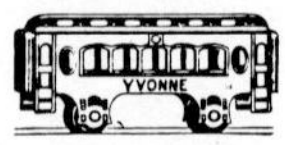

Coaches

No. 284

Aluminum Finish. Length 4½ inches. 12 in a box. 24 dozen in a case. Weight per case, 150 lbs.

No. 285

Aluminum Finish. Length 5 inches. 12 in a box. 24 dozen in a case. Weight per case, 180 lbs.

No. 286

Painted. Length 5⅜ inches. 12 in a box. 12 dozen in a case. Weight per case, 130 lbs

No. 287

Painted. Length, 6½ inches. 12 in a box. 12 dozen in a case. Weight per case, 150 lbs

Columbia Banks

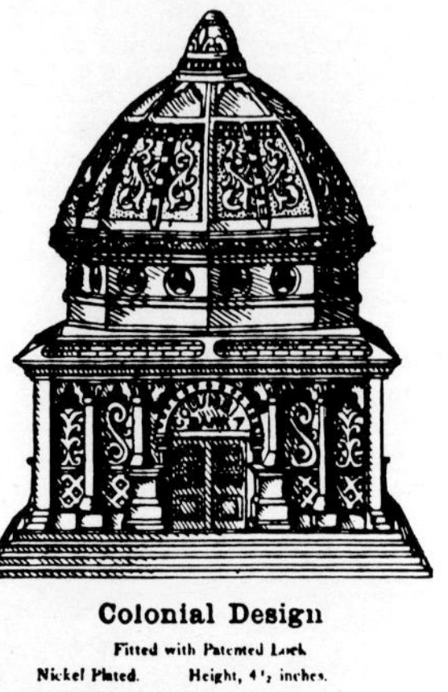

Colonial Design

Fitted with Patented Lock

No. 450. Nickel Plated. Height, 4½ inches.
No. 451. Electro Oxydized. Width, 3½ inches.
6 in a box 12 dozen in a case. 200 lbs. per case.

No. 452. Nickel Plated. Height, 5¼ inches.
No. 453. Electro Oxydized. Width, 4½ inches.
1 in a box. 3 dozen in a case. 100 lbs. per case.

No. 454. Nickel Plated. Height, 7 inches.
No. 455. Electro Oxydized. Width, 5½ inches.
1 in a box. 3 dozen in a case. 150 lbs. per case.

No. 456. Nickel Plated. Height, 9 inches.
No. 457. Electro Oxydized. Width, 7 inches.
1 in a box. 2 dozen in a case. 200 lbs. per case.

The Tower Bank

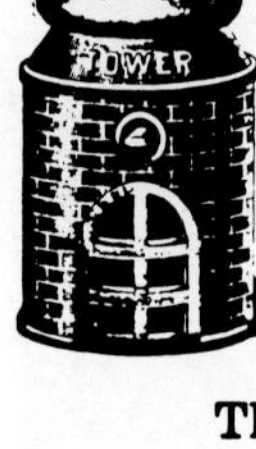

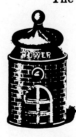

The Tower Bank

No. 10A.

Antique Oxydized Copper Plated.

Height, 4¼ inches Diameter, 2½ inches.

12 in a box. 2 gross in a case.

215 lbs. per case.

The Jewel Bank

The Jewel Bank

No. 15A.

Antique Oxydized Copper Plated.

Height, 4¼ inches. Width, 3¼ inches.

Depth, 2½ inches

12 in a box. 2 gross in a case.

275 lbs. per case.

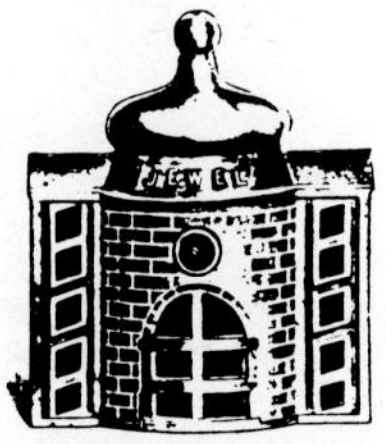

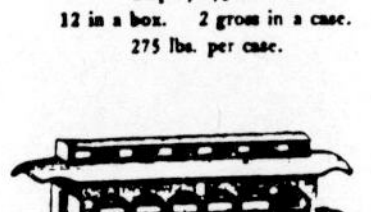

Car Bank

No. 604.

Aluminum.

Length, 5½ inches. 12 in a box.

2 gross in a case. 270 lbs. per case.

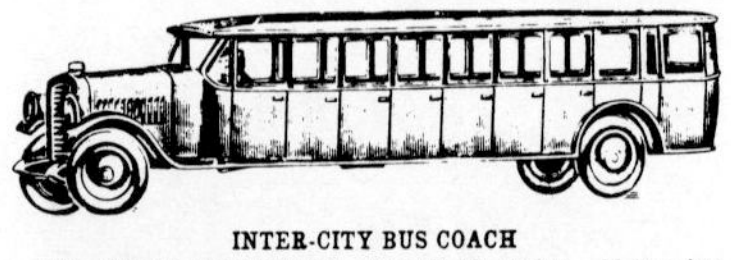

INTER-CITY BUS COACH

No. 480—Painted and decorated. Length 5⅞ inches. 12 in a box. 12 dozen in a box. Weight of case 150 lbs.

No. 482—Painted and decorated. Length 8 inches. 3 in a box. 6 dozen in a case. Weight of case 130 lbs.

No. 486—Painted and decorated. Length 11 inches. 1 in a box. 3 dozen in a case. Weight of case 135 lbs.

No. 487—Painted and decorated. Length 13¼ inches. 1 in a box. 3 dozen in a case. Weight of case 165 lbs.

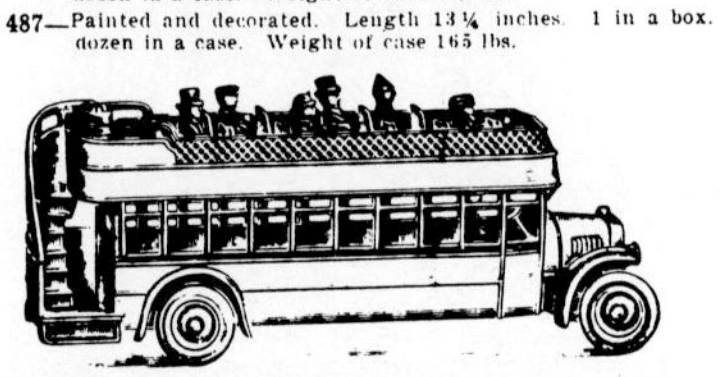

CITY BUS

No. 517—Painted and decorated. Length 6½ inches. 3 in a box. 6 dozen in a box. Weight of case 140 lbs.

No. 521—Painted and decorated. Length 7½ inches. 1 in a box. 3 dozen in a case. Weight of case 110 lbs.

No. 522—Painted and decorated. Length 10 inches. 1 in a box. 3 dozen in a case. Weight of case 155 lbs.

No. 523—Painted and decorated. Length 12 inches. 1 in a box. 2 dozen in a case. Weight of case 130 lbs.

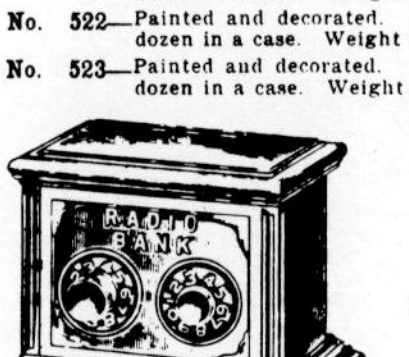

RADIO BANK

Combination Lock

No. 56

Nickel Plated. Steel sides and back. Height 3¼ inches. Width 3¼ inches. Length 4½ inches. 6 in a box. 6 dozen in a case. Weight of case 125 lbs.

RADIO BANK
New Combination Lock. All Three Dials Operate

No. 57—Painted and decorated. Length 4¾ inches. Width 3 inches. Height 3 inches. 6 in a case. 6 dozen in a case. Weight of case 125 lbs.

No. 58—Painted and decorated. Length 6⅝ inches. Width 3¼ inches. Height 3½ inches. 1 in a box. 3 dozen in a case. Weight of case 140 lbs.

NEW HEATROLA BANK
No. 59

Painted and decorated. Length 2⅝ inches. Width 2⅝ inches. Height 4⅝ inches. 6 in a box. 12 dozen in a case. Weight of case 185 lbs.

1933 « ROOSEVELT BANK »

An up-to-the-minute bank that serves a double purpose as an ornament and money saver. An astonishing realistic likeness of the President, carrying the words "New Deal" and the full name of the Chief Executive. An inspiring toy and a beautiful mantel-piece for any room. Catalog No. 33 has copper finish, while Catalog No. 33A has copper oxidized surface. While this bank presents an expensive appearance, its cost is very reasonable and allows plenty of profit.

Length	Width	Heigth	Pcs. per Box	Dz. per Case	Wt. per Case
2½"	2⅝"	5"	1	6	88

« TELEPHONE TRUCK »

KENTON'S most interesting toy for 1933. The City Telephone Truck comes supplied with four wooden poles, together with a similar number of cross arms and pole bases. By attaching string to the eyelets provided on the four cross arms, a realistic "telephone line" can be erected. A "big" item, well suited for window displays. Ask for Catalog No. 3300. Has a color combination of red, orange, and brilliant green. A winner!

Length	Pcs. per Box	Dz. per Case	Wt. per Case
9½"	1		88

THE Kentontoys listed in the pages of this supplement to Catalog 32 are, without doubt, some of the finest "buys" ever offered. New designs, timely appeals, clever ideas are all combined in the 1933 Kentontoy line. Flashy colors attract attention to these toys when displayed on your counter or in the window. The usual superior quality is found in these new Kentontoys, although prices have been made especially attractive. The demand is increasing for Kentontoys and an early showing of these interesting replicas of the real thing will bring you added profits, even before the arrival of the holiday season. May we have your order? It will have our usual prompt attention.

THE KENTON HARDWARE CO., KENTON, O.

Variety Iron Works,
TRENTON AVENUE
AND MARGARETTA STREET,
FRANKFORD, PHILADELPHIA, PA.

Mail Box Bank

No. 612—Attractive green. Height, 4¼ inches. Width, 3¼ inches. 6 in a box. 6 dozen in a case. Weight of case, 90 lbs.

No. 614—Attractive green. Height, 5 inches. Width, 3½ inches. 4 in a box. 6 dozen in a case. Weight of case, 110 lbs.

National Safe

No. 50—Nickel Plated—Furnished with Combination Lock. Steel Sides Back. Height, 5 inches. Width, 3¼ inches. Depth, 3¼ inches. 6 in a box. 6 dozen in a case. Weight of case, 135 lbs.

Iron Clad Bank

No. 260—Furnished with Combination Lock, Nickel Plated. Height 4¼ inches. Width, 3 inches. Depth, 2½ inches. 6 in a box. 12 dozen in a case. Weight of case, 225 lbs.

1933

Templeton Radio Bank

A unique method of saving money is offered the child by the Radio Bank pictured above. This is a close imitation of real radio set and is finding ready appeal among children. Finished in assorted colors.

No. 60—Length, 3¾ inches. Width, 2¾ inches. Height, 4½ inches. 6 in a box. 12 dozen in a case. Weight of case, 195 lbs.

The New Radio Bank cashes in on the popularity of the Crosley Table Model, and the advertising this famous radio is enjoying everywhere. Teaches thrift. Parents are glad to buy this toy. Radio dealers will want it for an advertising novelty. Folks will use it as an ornament in the home. Attractively colored in contrasting hues. Popular everywhere.

No. 40—Width, 4 inches. Height, 4½ inches. 6 in a box. 6 dozen in a case. Weight of case, 80 lbs.

No. 42—Width, 4½ ins. Height 5½ inches. 1 in a box. 6 doz. in a case. Weight of case, 135 lbs.

RADIO BANK
New Combination Lock — All Three Dials Operate

No.___ Finished in assorted colors and decorated. Length, 4½ ins. Width, 3 inches. Height, 3 inches. 6 in a box. 6 doz. in a case. Weight of case, 115 lbs.

KYSER & REX

1882 DOG TRAY BANK

1882 UNCLE TOM BANK

1882 TOWN HALL BANK

1882 ORIENTAL BANK

CASTLE BANK

LOG CABIN BANK

VILLA BANK

PAVILION BANK

1892 BEE-HIVE BANK

STATE BANK

APPLE BANK

1882 STAR SAFE

I X L SAFE

1882

1889 YOUNG AMERICA BANK

1889 THE ROLLER SAFE

1889 SPORT SAFE

SECURITY SAFE DEPOSIT.

39

c 1889 **SECURITY SAFE DEPOSIT.** Kyser + Rex

(Patented February 11, 188?, and March 1, 188?.)

WITH NICKEL-PLATED COMBINATION LOCK AND PATENT MONEY GUARD.

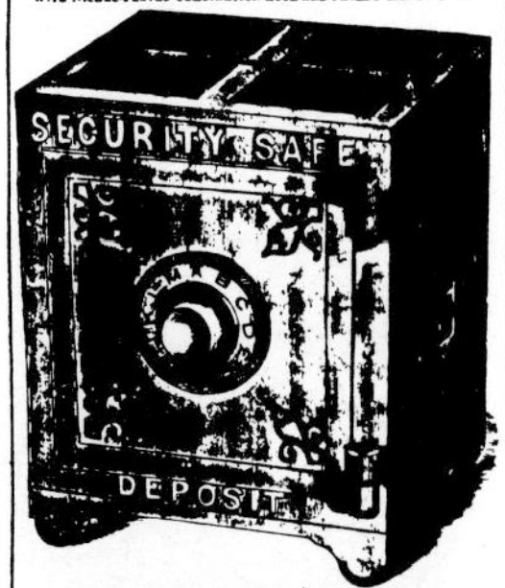

No. 300. Size, 5⅜ inches high, 4⅝ wide, 4 deep.

The external appearance of this safe has been much improved since above cut was made. It has a new and accurate combination lock. It has two dials, each containing thirteen letters, thus comprising the whole alphabet. Each safe will have attached a tag giving the letters of its combination, and directions for use plainly expressed. It will also have attached to the opening a new money guard, which will make the abstraction of money an impossibility. The safe will be finished in black and gold. Packed one in a box, and three dozen in a case. Each case will contain a number of different combinations.

Size of case, 25⅜ inches, 16⅜ x 15. Weight of case, 165 lbs.

Price, per dozen, ... $10 00

Discount, ...

No. 300N. The same, nickel-plated.

Price, per dozen, ... $15 00

Discount, ...

8

c 1889 **SECURITY SAFE DEPOSIT.** Kyser + Rex

(Patented February 19, and March 1, 188?.)

WITH NICKEL-PLATED COMBINATION LOCK AND PATENT MONEY GUARD.

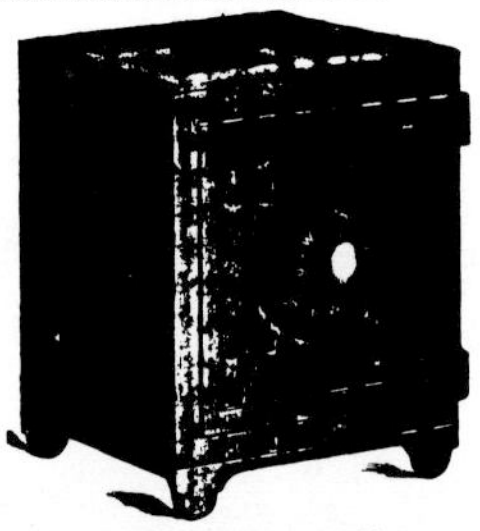

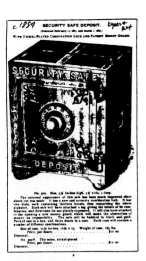

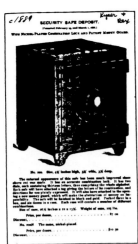

No. 200. Size, 4⅝ inches high, 3⅝ wide, 3⅝ deep.

The external appearance of this safe has been much improved since above cut was made. It has an accurate combination lock. It has two dials, each containing thirteen letters, thus comprising the whole alphabet. Each safe will have attached a tag giving the letters of its combination, and directions for use plainly expressed. It will also have attached to the opening a new money guard, which will make the abstraction of money an impossibility. The safe will be finished in black and gold. Packed three in a box, and six dozen in a case. Each case will contain a number of different combinations.

Size of case, 26½ inches x 22 x 13½. Weight of case, 225 lbs.

Price, per dozen, ... $7 00

Discount, ...

No. 200N. The same, nickel-plated.

Price, per dozen, ... $10 50

Discount, ...

9

c 1889 **GLOBE SAVINGS FUND BANK.** Kyser + Rex

(Patent Applied For.)

WITH IMPROVED COMBINATION LOCK.

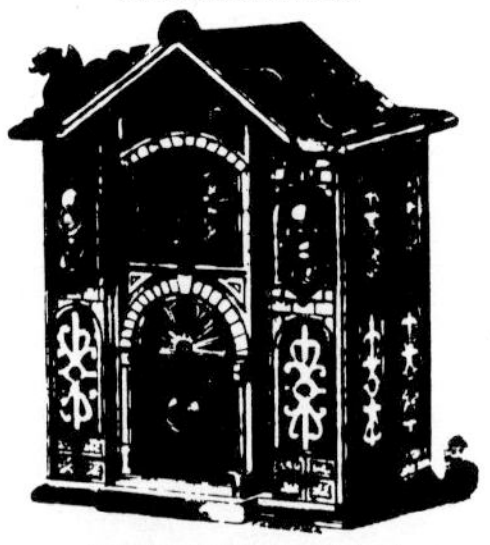

No. 450. Size, 7¼ inches high, 5⅜ wide, 4¼ deep.

In the above bank we have combined the attractiveness of a building, with the advantages of a safe with a combination lock. The lock has been improved and simplified, so that each one can be guaranteed as perfect.

Each bank will have attached a tag containing full particulars as to combination and method of changing the same.

Beautifully finished in assorted bronze colors, and packed one in a wooden box, and three dozen in a case.

Size of case, 32 inches x 15 x 12. Weight of case, 210 lbs.

Price, per dozen, ... $10 50

Discount, ...

15

c 1889 **TOWER SAVINGS FUND BANK.** Kyser + Rex

(Patent Applied For.)

WITH IMPROVED COMBINATION LOCK.

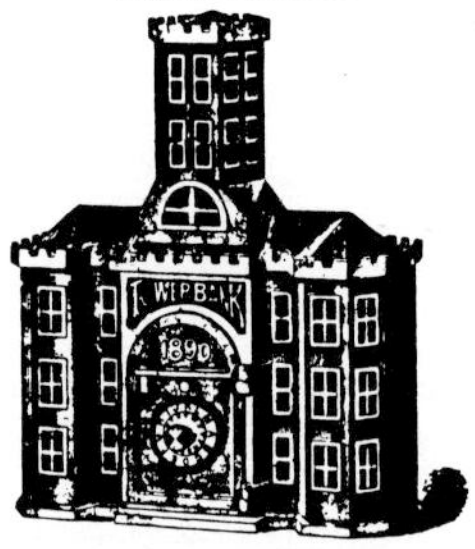

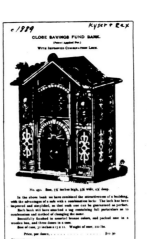

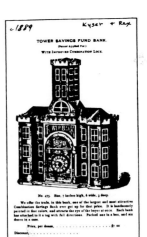

No. 475. Size, 7 inches high, 6 wide, 3 deep.

We offer the trade, in this bank, one of the largest and most attractive Combination Savings Bank ever got up for that price. It is handsomely painted in fine colors, and attracts the eye of the buyer at once. Each bank has attached to it a tag with full directions. Packed one in a box, and six dozen in a case.

Price, per dozen, ... $7 00

Discount, ...

16

c 1889 **REGISTERING 5c. AND 10c. SAVINGS BANK.** Kyser + Re

(PATENT APPLIED FOR.)

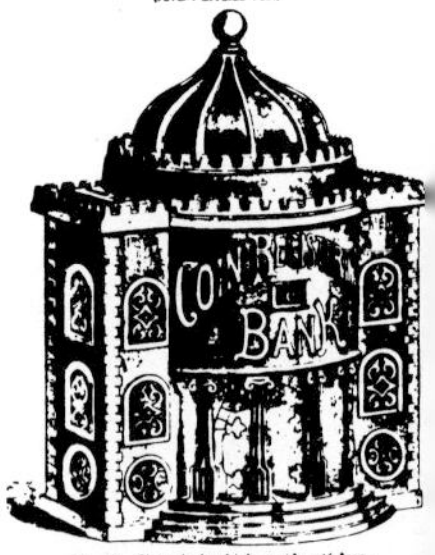

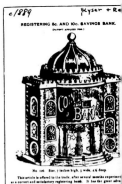

No. 126. Size, 7 inches high, 5 wide, 4½ deep.

This article is offered to the trade, after several months experimen as a correct and satisfactory registering bank. It has the great adva over other banks in the market of registering both 5 and 10-cent co the same dial. When the last 5 or 10 cents to make the total amo $5 00 is deposited, the door will fall out and the money can be withd If the directions pasted on the bottom are complied with, the bank c fail to give satisfaction. Finished in two styles, packed one in a w box, and three dozen in a case.

Price, per dozen, in fancy colors, ... $17 00

" " " nickeled, ... 22 00

Discount, ...

3

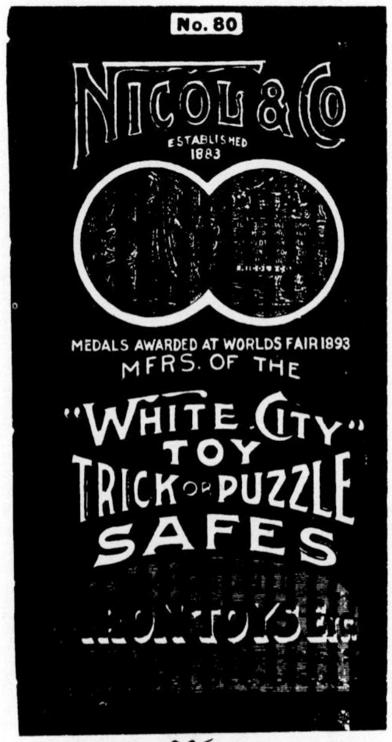

1895

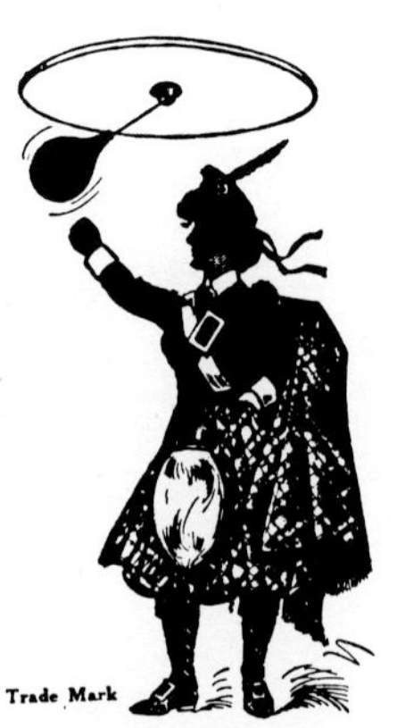

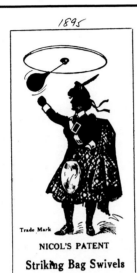

Trade Mark

NICOL'S PATENT

Striking Bag Swivels

1895

"WHITE CITY" TRICK OR PUZZLE SAFE

[Patented October 23, 1894]

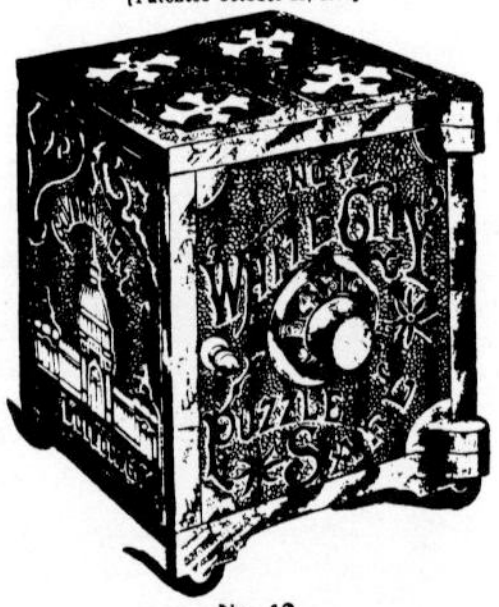

No. 12

NOT a Combination Bank

WITHOUT a doubt the most artistic and best finished banks ever put upon the market. They are of gray iron, highly nickel plated throughout, and so constructed that money cannot be shaken out. You cannot solve the problem of how these banks are opened without first being shown. Directions and solution of puzzle are packed with each safe. We guarantee each safe to be perfect, and it is utterly impossible for one of them to get out of repair. They are highly engraved with pictures of the "World's Fair" buildings, also the great Ferris Wheel.

Packed one dozen in box, one-half gross in case.

5 in. high, 4¾ in. wide and 3¾ in. deep.

No. 12. Price per dozen . . . . $

Assorted finishes, nickel plated or oxidized.

Weight per gross, 335 lbs.

5

1895

"WHITE CITY" TRICK OR PUZZLE SAFE

[Patented October 23, 1894.]

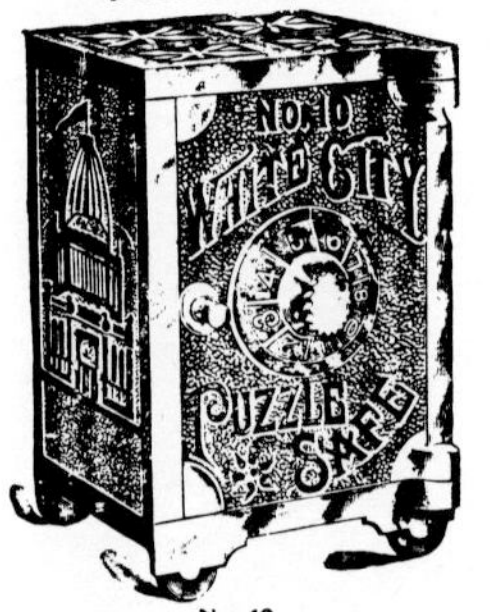

No. 10

NOT a Combination Bank

WITHOUT a doubt the most artistic and best finished banks ever put upon the market. They are of gray iron, highly nickel plated throughout, and so constructed that the money cannot be shaken out. You cannot solve the problem of how these banks are opened without first being shown. Directions and solution of puzzle are packed with each safe. We guarantee each safe to be perfect, and it is utterly impossible for one of them to get out of repair. They are highly engraved with pictures of the "World's Fair" buildings, also the great Ferris Wheel.

Packed one dozen in box, one-half gross in case.

4 in. high, 2¾ in. wide and 2¾ in. deep.

No. 10. Price per dozen . . . . $

Assorted finishes, nickel plated or oxidized.

Weight per gross, 215 lbs.

4

1895

NEW BASKET PUZZLE BANK

No. 3

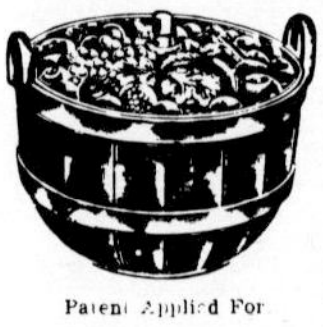

Patent Applied For

ABOVE CUT shows our new basket puzzle bank. The design is an artistic miniature reproduction of a bushel basket filled with fruits, emblematic of the generous manner of good things possible those who save early in life.

The exquisitely dainty appearance substantial construction of this bank peals to every child and parent.

The ingenious mechanical puzzle locking device is one of our numerous exclusive patented features which for practicability and substantiality has put line in a place by itself.

Packed one-half dozen in box, one-half gross in case. Size, 3 in. high, diameter 3⅝ in.

No. 361. Price, per dozen, nickel plated or oxidized . . . . $

Weight, per gross, 200 lbs.

8

1895

"WHITE CITY"

TRICK OR PUZZLE BANK

[Patented October 23, 1894]

"A BARREL OF MONEY"

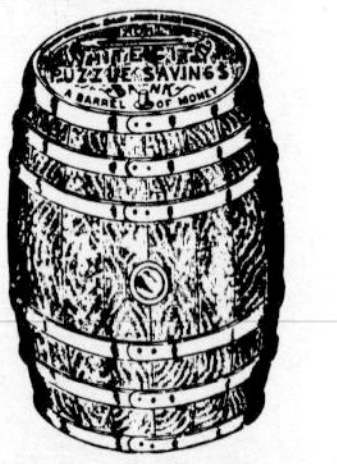

No. 1

We are the first and only firm in the United States to make and introduce the "White City" Puzzle Savings Banks. These are new and novel designs and have proven to be good sellers. They are made of gray iron, highly nickel plated, and so constructed that the money cannot be shaken out. It is impossible to solve the problem of how these banks are opened without first being shown. Directions and solution of the puzzle are packed with each bank. It is impossible for these banks to get out of order or repair as is the case with all combination or key banks on the market at the present time.

Packed one dozen in box, one-half gross in case.

4 in. high, 3¾ in. diameter.

No. 1. Price per dozen . . . . $

Assorted finishes, nickel plated or oxidized.

Weight per gross, 210 lbs.

9

1895

Just Out!

WHITE CITY PUZZLE BANK

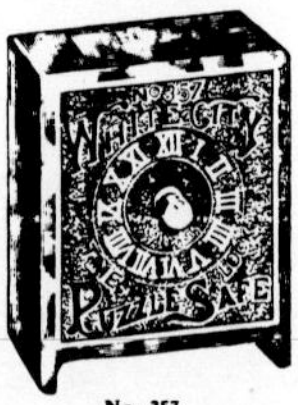

No. 357

Every person delighted and satisfied, especially the kiddies. They are made from one solid piece of grey iron and are oxidized in old copper with lacquer finish. The cutest and most novel bank ever produced and are guaranteed never to get out of repair. Order today for immediate or future delivery.

Size 2½ inches by 1½ inches. Weight, per gross, 112 lbs.

No. 357. Per Gross . . . . $

2

1895

"WHITE CITY"

TIME-LOCK PUZZLE SAFE

[Patented October 23, 1894.]

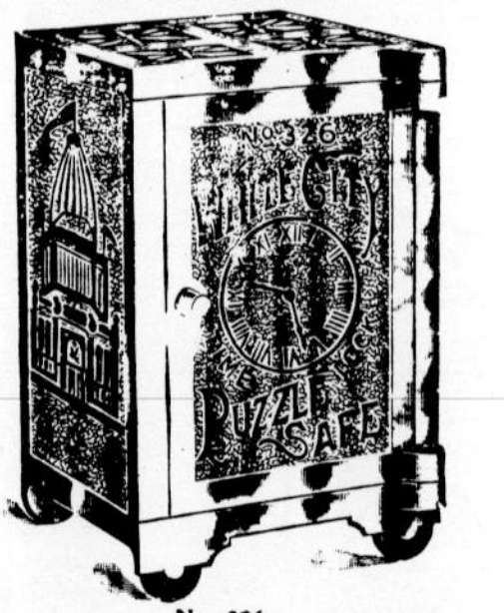

No. 326

A true representation of the burglar-proof time lock safe now in use in all bank vaults. The same size and general style as our No. 10, but without tumbler, and is not so highly finished. We claim this to be the best cheap bank ever offered for sale. Guaranteed never to get out of repair.

No. 326. Assorted Nickel Plate and Oxidized finish. Price per doz . . . . $

Weight per gross, 210 lbs.

3

1895

STATE SAVINGS BANK

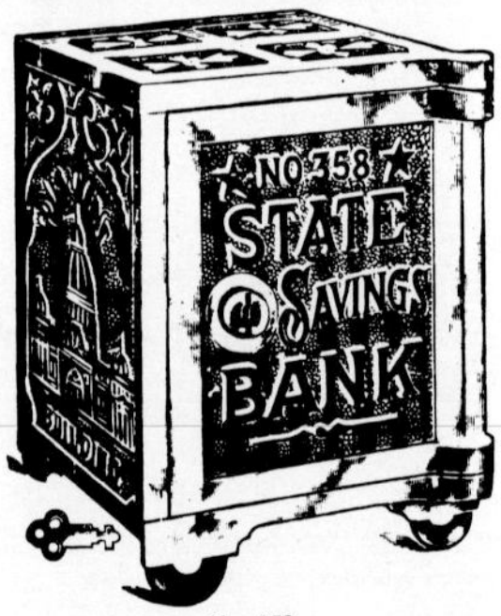

No. 358

Same size, style and finish as our No. 12 Bank. With flat key lock

Packed ½ dozen in box, ½ gross in case.

5 in. high, 3¾ in. wide and 3¾ in. deep.

No. 358. Price per dozen . . . . $

Assorted finishes, nickel plated or oxidized.

Weight per gross, including case, 335 lbs.

6

1895

"WHITE CITY"

TRICK OR PUZZLE BANK

[Patented October 23, 1894]

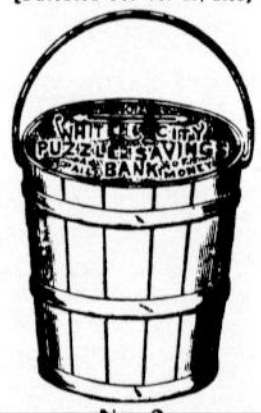

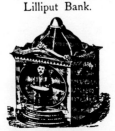

No 2

"A PAIL OF MONEY"

We are the first and the only firm in the United States to make and introduce the "White City" Puzzle Savings Banks. These are new and novel designs and have proven to be good sellers. They are of grey iron, highly nickel plated, and are so constructed that the money cannot be shaken out. It is impossible to solve the problem of how these banks are opened without first being shown. Directions and solution of the puzzle are packed with each bank. It is impossible for these banks to get out of order or repair, as is the case with all combination and key banks on the market at the present time.

Packed one dozen in box, one gross in case.

2¾ in. high, 2½ in. diameter.

No. 2. Price per dozen . . . . $

Assorted finishes, nickel plated or oxidized.

Weight per gross, 100 lbs.

7

1895

"WHITE CITY" TRICK OR PUZZLE BANK

[Patented October 23, 1894.]

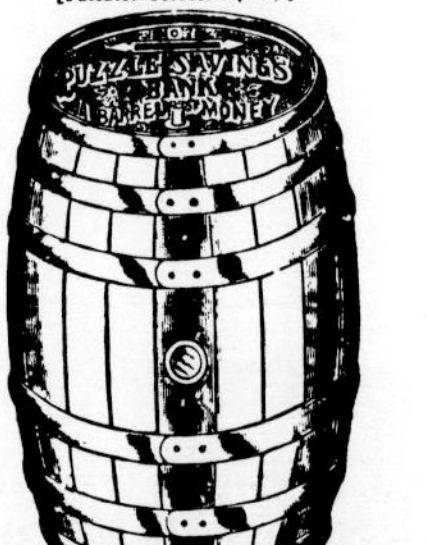

Extra Large. A Barrel of Money

We are the first and only firm in the United States to make and introduce the "White City" Puzzle Savings Banks. These are new and novel designs and have proven to be good sellers. They are of gray iron, highly nickel plated, and so constructed that the money cannot be shaken out. It is impossible to solve the problem of how these banks are opened without first being shown. Directions and solution of the puzzle are packed with each safe. It is impossible for these banks to get out of order or repair, as is the case with all combination and key banks on the market at the present time.

Packed one dozen in box, one-half gross in case

5¼ in. high and 3¾ in. diameter.

No. 3. Price per dozen . . . . $

Assorted nuishes, nickel plated or oxidized.

Weight per gross, 300 lbs

10

1895

Something Entirely New

For The Holiday Trade

A PUZZLE TOY SAVINGS BANK

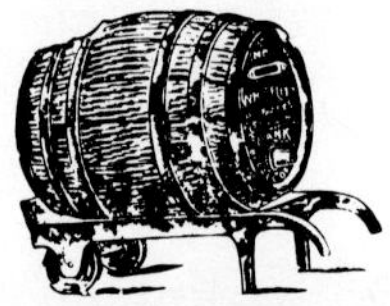

A Barrel of Money

On a miniature nickel plated truck with revolving wheels

The first of its kind ever offered to the public. It makes a very neat ornament for the mantel and a delightful toy for the little ones. The barrel can be detached from the truck at will. The truck is a facsimile of the large commercial one commonly used for handling boxes and barrels. They are handsomely nickel plated throughout. Instructions how to open sent with each bank.

Packed one dozen in box, half gross in case.

No. 324. Price per dozen . . . . $

Guaranteed never to get out of order.

Assorted finishes, nickel plated or oxidized.

Weight per gross, 250 lbs.

11

18 THE J. & E. STEVENS CO.'S 1883

Lilliput Bank.

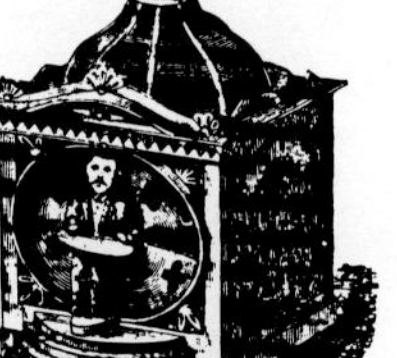

No. 150.

Height, 4½ in., Width, 3½ in., Depth, 3 in.

Pretty, tasteful, and simple in construction. Cannot get out of order.

The coin laid upon the plate is carried around by the Cashier and placed in the Bank. The figure then returns to its place, ready for another deposit.

22 THE J. & E. STEVENS CO.'S 1883

Frog Bank.

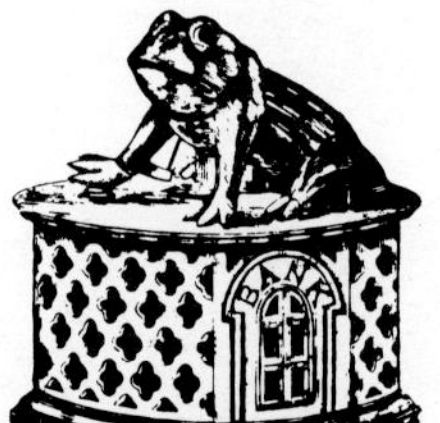

No. 110.

Height, 4¼ in., Diameter, 4½ in.

By pressing one foot, the frog's mouth is caused open to receive a coin, which is swallowed on releas the foot from pressure; the eyes thereupon give a w of satisfaction.

The J. & E. Stevens Co.,

Cashier Bank.

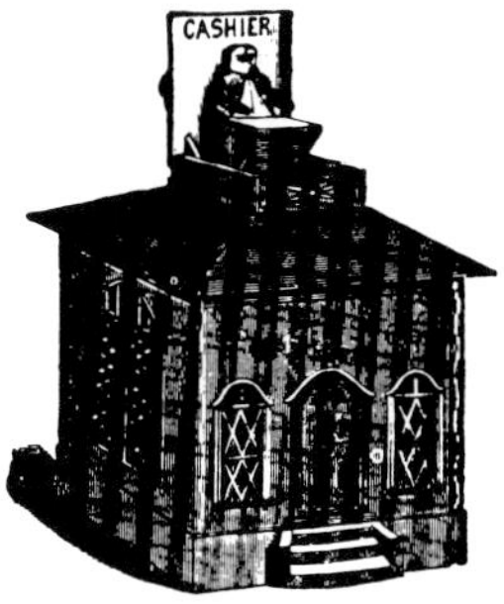

No. 108.

Height, 6 in., Width, 4 in., Depth, 4 in.

On pulling a knob, a door opens at the top of this Bank, and a figure of a Cashier appears to receive the deposit. When this is made, the door falls back to its place.

Savings Banks.

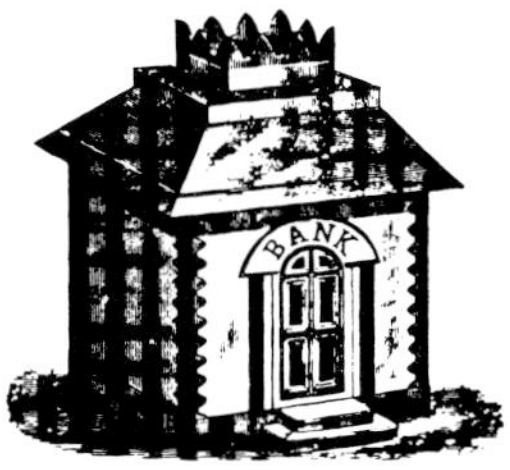

PATENTED.

No. 113. Height, 3 in., Width, 2½ in., Depth, 2⅜ in.
No. 114. " 3¾ " " 3¼ " " 2¾ "
No. 115. " 5 " " 4½ " " 3¾ "

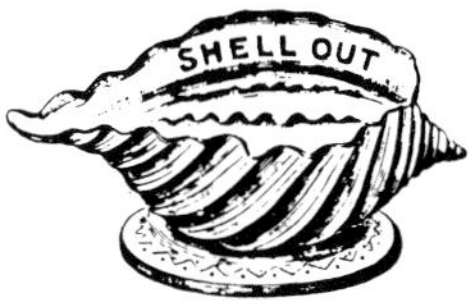

No. 116. Length, 5 in., Width, 2¾ in., Height, 2½ in.

Savings Banks.

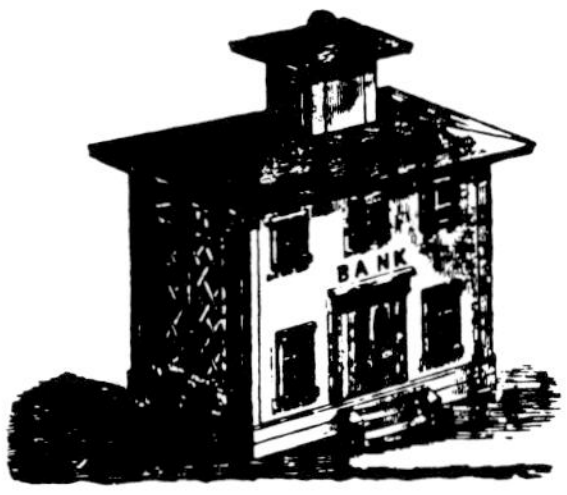

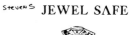

No. 103. Height, 3⅜ in., Width, 2½ in., Depth, 2⅜ in.
No. 104. " 4¼ " " 3¼ " " 2¾ "
No. 105. " 5¼ " " 4⅜ " " 3¾ "

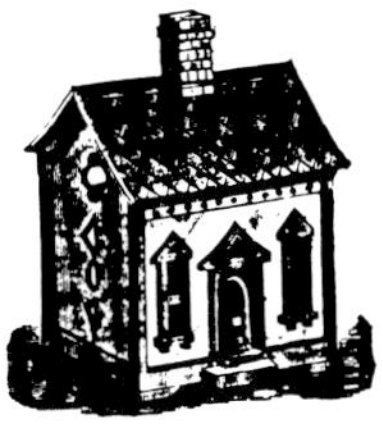

No. 112. Height, 3¼ in., Width, 2¼ in., Depth, 2¼ in.

Home Bank.

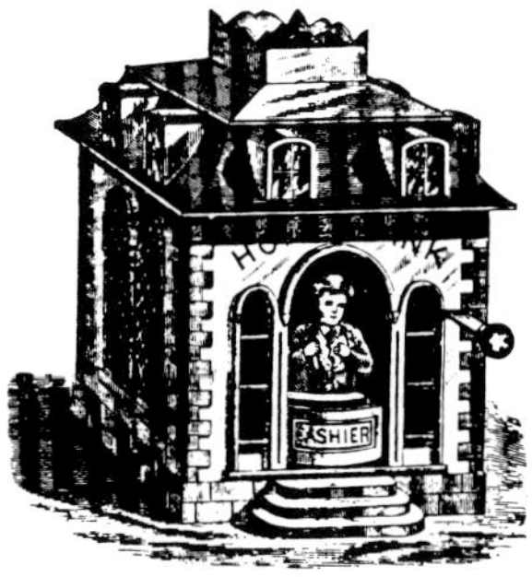

No. 1.

CASHIER.-OPEN.

Height, 5½ in., Width, 4½ in., Depth, 4½ in.

Pull the knob until it catches; place the penny on its edge in front of the Cashier; push the knob to the right, and the deposit is made in the vault at the rear of the Bank.

No. 2. Same size and design as No. 1, with the exception of the windows in the roof.

No. 3. Same size and design as No. 1, but without Cashier.

No. 4. Same size and design as No. 2, but without Cashier.

Savings Banks.

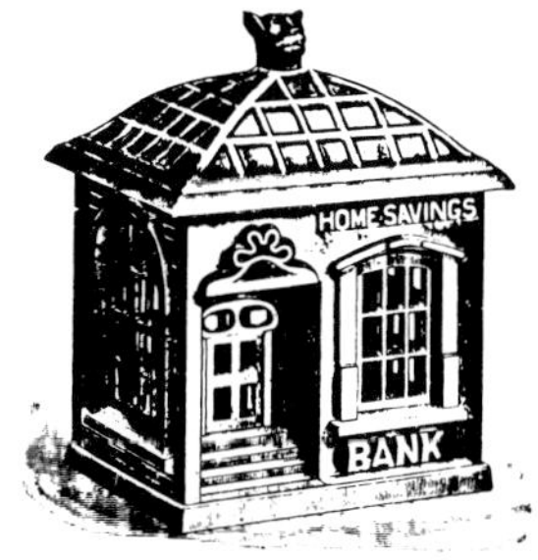

No. 113. In Colors. Height, 3½ in. Width, 2½ in. Depth, 2⅛ in.
No. 119. Dark Bronze Finish. Height, 6 in. Width, 4½ in. Depth, 3½ in.

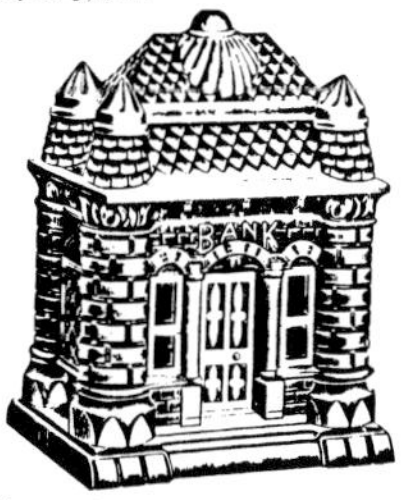

No. 120. In Fancy Colors. Height, 5¾ in. Width, 4⅜ in. Depth, 3⅜ in.

JEWEL SAFE

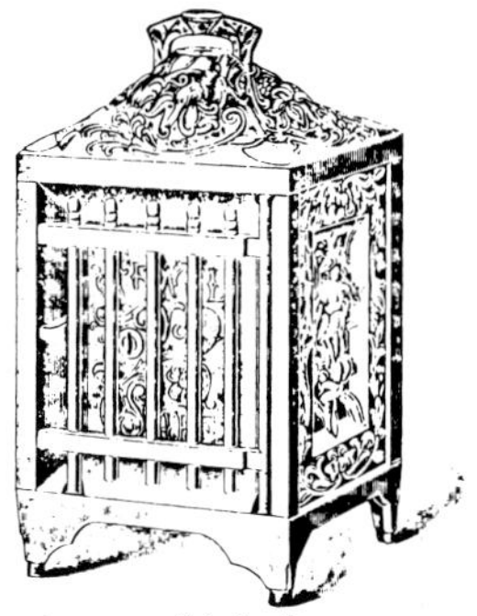

Yale Lock.

No. 43. Height, 7½ in. Width, 4½ in. Depth, 4⅛ in.
Finely Polished and Nickel Plated.
Price per Dozen, - - - - - [redacted]

Stevens

JEWEL SAFE

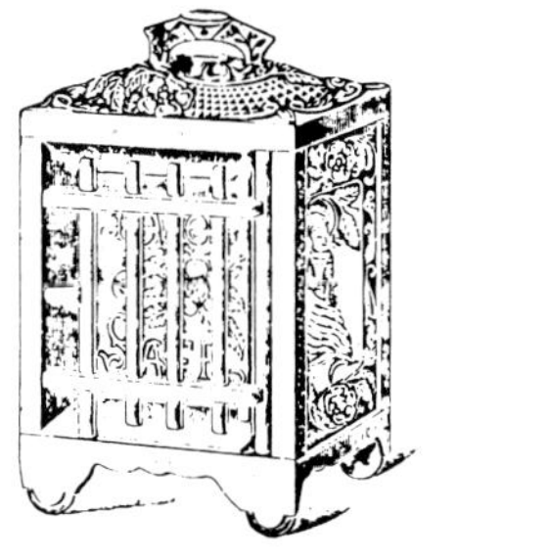

Yale Lock.

No. 47. Height, 5½ in. Width, 3⅞ in. Depth, 3¼ in.
Finely Polished and Nickel Plated.
Price per Dozen, - - - - - [redacted]

National Safes.

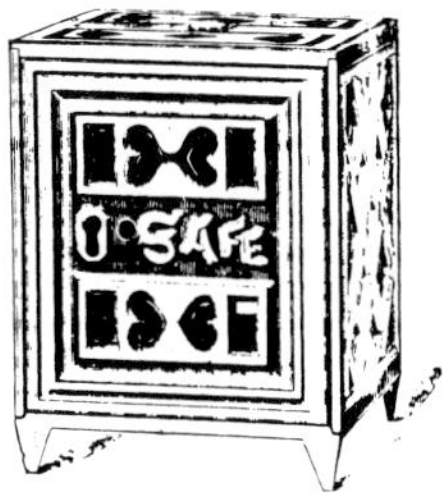

No. 4. In Colors. Height, 2⅝ in. Width, 2⅛ in. Depth, 2 in.
No. 8. In Colors. Height, 3¼ in. Width, 2½ in. Depth, 2¼ in.

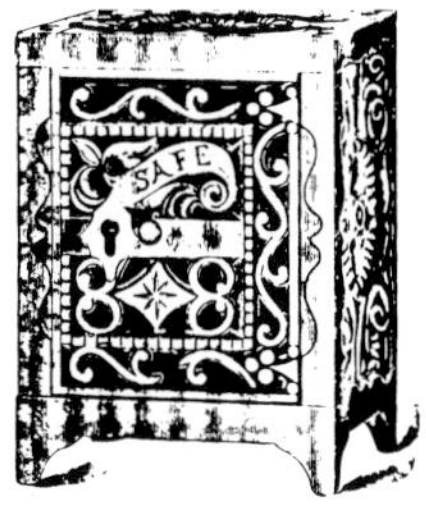

Height, 3⅜ in. Width, 2½ in. Depth, 2¼ in.
No. 9. Dark Bronze Finish.
No. 9½. Polished and Nickel Plated.

SAFE

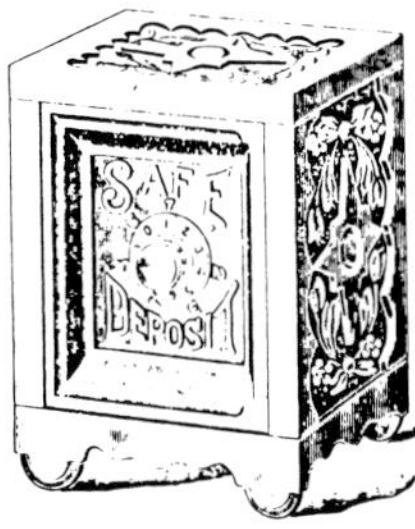

No. 50. Height, 4½ inches. Width, 3¼ inches. Depth, 2¾ inches.

Polished and Nickel Plated (spring lock).

Price per Gross, - - - - [redacted]

National Safes.

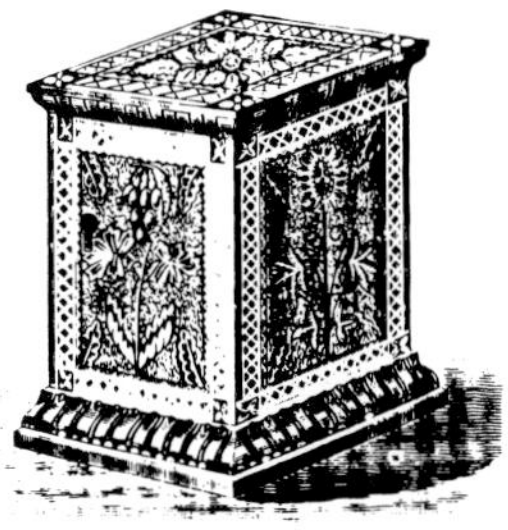

No. 23. In Colors. Height, 4¾ in. Width, 4¼ in. Depth, 4¼ in.

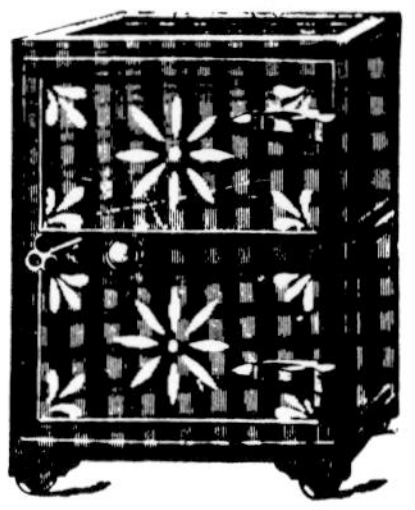

No. 10. In Colors. Height, 3¾ in. Width, 2¾ in. Depth, 2¾ in.
No. 13. In Colors. Height, 4⅛ in. Width, 2⅞ in. Depth, 2⅞ in.

Stevens

Savings Bank.

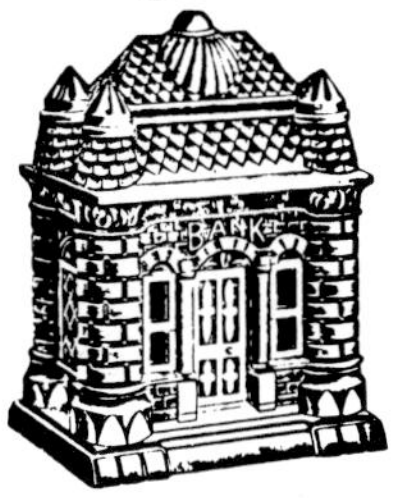

No. 120. In Fancy Colors. Retail price, 25c.
Height, 5¾ in. Width, 4⅜ in. Depth, 3⅜ in.
Packed ½ gro. in Case. Weight, 185 lbs.

U. S. Navy Bank.

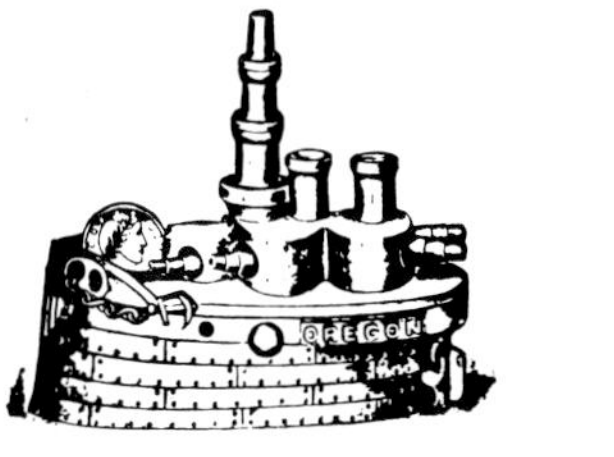

			Cases.	Weight.
No. 115.	Length, 5 in.	Height, 4 in.	18 doz.	235 lbs.
No. 121.	Length, 6¼ in.	Height, 5¾ in.	6 doz.	130 lbs.

Handsomely Painted. Retail price, 10c. and 25c.

1929

THE J. & E. STEVENS CO. CAST IRON PISTOLS AND TOYS CROMWELL, CONN., U.S.A.

"Savapound" Bank.

No. 47   Retail price, 50c.

Will only open after 16 ounces (one pound) of coins
have been deposited.

Height, 4⅛ in.   Width, 3½ in.   Depth, 3¼ in.

Packed 6 doz. in Case.   Weight, 154 lbs.

Nicely Polished and Nickel Plated.

Kodak Bank.

No. 48.   Height, 4½ in.   Width, 5 in.   Depth, 2⅞ in.

Retail Price, 50c.

Packed 4 dozen in Case.   Weight, 130 pounds.

Finely polished and nickel plated.

No. 40 Safe — Key Combination Lock
Height, 6"   Width, 4¾"   Depth, 4⅛"
Packed 1 in a box, 6 boxes to a carton
Weight per carton, 58 pounds

No. 41 Safe — Same as No. 40
with Combination Lock only

No. 47 Safe — Yale Lock
Height, 5½"   Width, 3⅞"   Depth, 3½"
Packed 1 in a box, 12 boxes to a carton
Weight per carton, 32 pounds

No. 125 Bank — Lock and Key
Height, 4¼"   Width, 3½"   Depth, 3"
Packed 3 in a box, 8 boxes to a carton
Weight per carton, 40 pounds

No. 126 Bank — Lock and Key
Height, 5¼"   Width, 4⅝"   Depth, 4"
Packed 1 in a box, 12 boxes to a carton
Weight per carton, 32 pounds

No. 45 Safe — Key Combination Lock
Height, 5⅛"   Width, 3⅞"   Depth, 3¼"
Packed 1 in a box, 24 boxes to a carton
Weight per carton, 60 pounds

The banks and safes shown above are regularly furnished in Nickel Plate finely
polished, but will be supplied painted in assorted colors when so ordered.

1929

THE J. & E. STEVENS CO. CAST IRON PISTOLS AND TOYS CROMWELL, CONN., U.S.A.

No. 117 Bank — Dark Bronze Finish
Height, 5½"   Width, 3¾"   Depth, 2¾"
Packed 24 to a carton
Weight per carton, 36 pounds

No. 118 Bank — Bronze Finish
Height, 6"   Width, 4½"   Depth, 3½"
Packed 12 to a carton
Weight per carton, 27 pounds

No. 101 Bank — Copper Bronze Finish
Height, 3¼"   Width, 2¼"   Depth, 2¼"
Packed 72 to a carton
Weight per carton, 35 pounds

No. 49 Safe — Spring Lock and Key
Height, 4¼"   Width, 3¼"   Depth, 2¾"
Packed 3 in a box, 8 boxes to a carton
Weight per carton, 40 pounds

No. 50 Safe — Spring Lock and Key
Height, 4½"   Width, 3¼"   Depth, 2¾"
Packed 3 in a box, 8 boxes to a carton
Weight per carton, 40 pounds

No. 275 — Cabin Bank
Finished in Fancy Colors
Length, 4¼"   Height, 3⅝"   Width, 3"
Packed 3 in a box, 8 boxes to a carton
Weight per carton, 38 pounds
Place the coin upon the roof above the Negro's head, move
the handle of the white-wash brush, and the Negro will be
made to stand on his head and kick the coin into the bank.

No. 310 — Jolly Nigger Bank
Finished in Bright Colors
Height, 7"   Width, 5½"   Depth, 4½"
Packed 1 in a box, 6 boxes to a carton
Weight per carton, 32 pounds
Place a coin in the hand and press the lever. As it
is deposited in the mouth, the tongue moves and
the eyes roll upwards.

No. 9½ Safe — Lock and Key
Height, 3⅜"   Width, 2½"   Depth, 2¾"
Packed 6 dozen in a carton
Weight per carton, 58 pounds

No. 48 Bank — Lock and Key
Height 4¼"   Width, 5"   Depth, 2⅞"
Packed 1 in a box, 24 boxes to a carton
Weight per carton, 60 pounds

The banks and safes shown above are regularly furnished in Nickel Plate finely
polished, but will be supplied painted in assorted colors when so ordered.

No. 128 — Pay Phone Bank
Nickel Finish
Length, 7¼"   Width, 5"   Depth, 3"
Packed 1 in a box, 12 boxes to a carton
Weight per carton, 25 pounds
Removable receiver. Three coin slots, 5 cents, 10 cents
and 25 cents. Bell rings when handle is turned or
money is deposited.

No. 128½ — Same as No. 128
in Mahogany Finish

No. 220 — Owl Bank
Height - - - - 7½"
Width - - - - 4"
Depth - - - - 3"
Packed 1 in a box, 12 boxes to a carton
Weight per carton, 32 pounds
This bank has glass eyes and is nicely ornamented in
Natural colors. Place coin on top of the branch and
press the thumb piece at the back, when the head of
the owl turns and the coin is deposited, after which
the head moves back to its former position.

No. 127 — Toy Radio Bank
Nickel Finish
Length - - - - 5½"
Height - - - - 2¾"
Depth - - - - 3"
Packed 1 in a box, 12 boxes to a carton
Weight per carton, 20 pounds
Two dials which when revolved produces two imita-
tions of static.

No. 127½ — Same as No. 127
in Mahogany Finish

No. 24 — Artillery Bank
Finished in Bright Colors
Height, 6"   Width, 4"   Length, 8"
Packed 1 in a box, 6 boxes to a carton
Weight per carton, 34 pounds
The coin is placed in the cannon (or mortar). When
the hammer is pushed back and the thumb piece
pressed upon, the coin is fired into the fort or tower.
The cannon is so arranged that paper caps may be
used if desired. The arm of the artillery man moves
up and down.

ORDERS FOR LESS THAN CARTONS on the above items 10% ADDITIONAL

SHIMER TOY CO. BETHLEHEM, PENNSYLVANIA

c1899

c1899

THE STEVENS & BROWN MF'G CO'S. 1870

No. 195. COTTAGE BANK.   per gro. $ 24.00
No. 196.   „   „   „   „   12.00

No. 200. COTTAGE BANK (with lock)   per doz. $ 9.00

1870   PRICE LIST. Stevens + Brown 19

No. 79. Large House Bank.   per gro. $ 9.00
 „ 80. Small   „   „   „   „   7.00
 „ 83. Extra   „   „   „   „ 24.00

Gothic Banks.   Clock Banks.
No. 81. large. per gro. $ 7.50   No. 193. large. per gro. 7.50
No. 82. small. „   „   6.00   No. 194. small „ „   5.00

43

SWISS COTTAGE BANK. (New)
No. 215.   per doz. $ 4.00

TOY SAVINGS BANK.

No. 103, ... per doz. $1 75.
" 104, ...   "   3 50.
" 105, ...   "   4 50.

New Pattern for Postage Currency; the Bank can be taken apart by turning a screw.

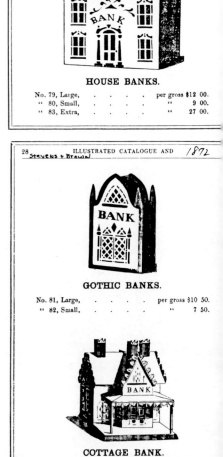

TOY TUBS.

No. 71, 7 inches diameter, . . per gross $42 00.
" 72, 6 " " . . " " 30 00.
" 73, 4½ " " . . " " 21 00.
" 74, 4¼ " " . . " " 18 00.
" 75, 3½ " " . . " " 13 50.
" 76, 3¼ " " . . " " 10 50.
" 77, 3 " " . . " " 9 00.
" 78, Nest of 5 Tubs, . per doz. 6 00.

HOUSE BANKS.

No. 79, Large, . . . per gross $12 00.
" 80, Small, . . . " 9 00.
" 83, Extra, . . . " 27 00.

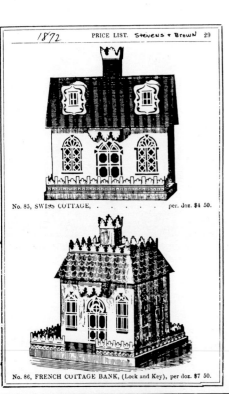

No. 85, SWISS COTTAGE, ... per doz. $4 50.

No. 86, FRENCH COTTAGE BANK, (Lock and Key), per doz. $7 50.

FRENCH COTTAGE BANK.
No. 87, ... per. doz $4 50.

TOY WAITERS.
No. 89, 3½ x 5 inches, . . per gross $4 50.
" 90, 4 x 7 " . . " 9 00.
" 91, 9 x 6½ " . . " 16 50.

GOTHIC BANKS.

No. 81, Large, . . . per gross $10 50.
" 82, Small, . . . " 7 50.

COTTAGE BANK.
(With Lock and Key.)
No. 84 . . . . . per doz. 10 00.

VINDEX

Toy No. 76
Owl Bank

Colors – Golden – Gray
One doz. in case
$6.00 doz. in case lots
$6.50 doz. in less case lots

Toy No. 61
Boston Bull Pup Bank

Colors – Red – Green – Blue
Toy No. 6
One in a box, one dozen in a case

Colors   True to Life
One doz. in a case
Price
$6.00 doz. in case lots
$6.50 doz. in less case lots

HOUSE BANK.

THE A. C. WILLIAMS CO., RAVENNA, OHIO, U. S. A.   30

Patented.

PRICE.

No. 448. Aluminum Bronze Base. Gold Bronze Roof. Aluminum Bronze Dome. 4¾ inches high, 4 inches wide, 2½ inches deep. Per gross $20 00

½ dozen in paper box; ½ gross in a case.

Shipping weight 115 lbs. per case.

THE A. C. WILLIAMS CO., RAVENNA, OHIO, U. S. A.   25

The "Sky-Scraper" Bank.

[TRADE MARK.]

Gold Bronze Roof and Towers.   Green Bronze Door Trimmings.
Aluminum Bronze Base.

Patented.   With Lock and Key.

6¾ inches high, 4⅝ inches deep, 3½ inches wide.

No. 1248. Per gross $45 00
The handsomest and most attractive 25c Bank on the market. There are over 500 open windows in this Bank.
¼ dozen in a paper box; 6 dozen in a case.
Shipping weight 265 lbs. per case.

THE A. C. WILLIAMS CO., RAVENNA, OHIO, U. S. A.   29

HOUSE BANK.

Height, 5½ inches; width, 4 inches; depth, 3 inches.
Weight, 2 lbs. 1 oz. each.
Finished in Silver, with Gold and Copper Trimmings.

PRICE.

No. 648. Per gross $30 00
½ dozen in a paper box. ½ gross in a case.
Shipping weight 170 lbs. per case.

The "Sky-Scraper" Bank.

[TRADE MARK]

THE A. C. WILLIAMS CO., RAVENNA, OHIO, U. S. A.   28

Gold Bronze Roof and Towers.

Aluminum Bronze Base.

Green Bronze Door Trimmings.

Patented.

3⅜ inches high, 1⅝ inches wide, 1½ inches deep.

No. 1848. Per gross $14 00

1 dozen in paper box; 1 gross in case.
Shipping weight 90 lbs. per case.

26   THE A. C. WILLIAMS CO., RAVENNA, OHIO, U. S. A.

The "Sky-Scraper" Bank.

[TRADE MARK.]

Green Bronze Roof and Towers.
Aluminum Bronze Base.
Green Bronze Door Trimmings.

Patented.

5⅛ inches high, 2⅜ inches wide, 2⅜ inches deep.

No. 848. Per gross $22 00
The largest and handsomest Bank ever put on the market for a 10-cent article. There are 360 open windows in this Bank.
Packed ½ dozen in paper box; one-half gross in a case.
Shipping weight 115 lbs. per case.

THE A. C. WILLIAMS CO., RAVENNA, OHIO, U. S. A.   33

TOY BANK.

Patented.

PRICES.

No. 948. 2¾ inches wide, 2 inches deep, 3 inches high. Aluminum Bronze Base, Gold Bronze Roof and Dome. Per gross $13 00
No. 1948. Same Bank as No. 948, except it is finished in Copper. Per gross 12 00

1 dozen in paper box. 1 gross in a case.
Shipping weight 80 lbs. per case.

House Bank.

THE A. C. WILLIAMS CO., RAVENNA, OHIO, U. S. A.   31

Patented.

No. 2548. 4¾ inches high, 3¼ inches wide, 2⅝ inches deep. Aluminum Bronze Base and Dome, Gold Bronze Roof, Green Bronze Door Trimmings. Per gross $19 00

Packed one-half dozen in paper box, one gross in a case.

THE A. C. WILLIAMS CO., RAVENNA, OHIO, U. S. A.   27

The "Sky-Scraper" Bank.

[TRADE MARK]

Gold Bronze Roof and Towers.
Aluminum Bronze Base.
Green Bronze Door Trimmings.

Patented.

4½ inches high, 3⅛ inches wide, 3⅛ inches deep.

No. 2848. Per gross $20 00

Packed one-half dozen in a paper box; one gross in a case.

34   THE A. C. WILLIAMS CO., RAVENNA, OHIO, U. S. A.

TOY BANK.

PRICES.

No. 748. 2½ inches wide, 1⅝ inches deep, 3 inches high. Per gross $12 00
Finished in Berlin Bronze with Gold Trimmings.
No. 1748. Same Bank as No. 748, except finished in Copper. Per gross 11 00

1 dozen in paper box. 1 gross in a case.
Shipping weight 80 lbs. per case.

1906

THE A. C. WILLIAMS CO., RAVENNA, OHIO, U. S. A.   17

1906

THE A. C. WILLIAMS CO., RAVENNA, OHIO, U. S. A.   19

16   THE A. C. WILLIAMS CO., RAVENNA, OHIO, U. S. A.

1906

Devil Head Toy Bank.

Patented.

PRICES.

No. 2648.   4½ inches high, 3¼ inches wide, 4⅛ inches deep.
Finished in dark red, black, white and yellow.
Per gross...$45 00
No. 2748.   3⅝ inches high, 2½ inches wide, 3¾ inches deep.
Finished same as No. 2648. Per gross.............. 23 50
No. 2648, packed one Bank in a paper box; six dozen in a case.
No. 2748, packed six Banks in a paper box; twelve dozen in a case.
An elegant, attractive and new design for a Toy Bank, beautifully finished, and a fine mantel ornament.

Elephant Toy Bank.

Patent Pending.

No. 3548.   Seven inches long, 4⅞ inches high; finished in
Drab; Gold and Silver Trimmings; per gross........$50 00
No. 3648.   Five and one-eighth inches long, 3⅝ inches high;
finished same as No. 3548, per gross.................... 25 00

The Trunk of the Elephant moves when coin is inserted, and Trunk automatically closes the slot as soon as coin is deposited. Coin can be removed only by taking the Bank apart.
No. 3548 packed one Bank in paper box; 6 dozen in a case.
No. 3648 packed six Banks in paper box; 12 dozen in a case.

Negro Toy Bank.

Patented.

No. 1448.   4⅛ inches high, 3⅛ inches wide, 3⅞ inches deep;
elegantly finished in Black, Yellow, White and
Red. Per gross..$45 00
No. 2448.   3¼ inches high, 2¾ inches wide, 2⅞ inches deep;
finished same as No. 1448. Per gross.................. 23 50

No. 1448, 1 bank only in a paper box   6 dozen in a case.
No. 2448, 6 banks in a paper box. 1 gross in a case.
This Negro Head Bank is really a fine work of art and was taken from life.
It is of an unique design and elegantly finished. It makes a fine ornament for the mantle and attracts the attention of everybody.

Policeman Toy Bank.

Patent Pending

No. 4248.   Elegantly finished in Dark Blue Enamel, Flesh
Colored face and Hands. Trimmed in Black and
Gold. 5¾ inches high, 3 inches wide, 2 inches
deep.

PRICE.

Per gross...$23 50

Packed 6 Banks in a Paper Box.
12 dozen in a case.

Aunt Jemima Toy Bank.

Patent Pending.

No. 4148.   Elegantly finished in Dark Blue Enamel, Dull
Black Face and Arms, Red Polka-dot Bandana,
Aluminum Apron, Gold Cake Turner. Six inches
high, 3 inches wide, 2 inches deep.

PRICE.

Per gross...$23 50

Packed 6 Banks in a paper box.
12 dozen in a case.

Indian Toy Bank.

Patented.

PRICE.

No. 1648.   Elegantly finished in Copper, Gold and Brown.
4¾ inches high, 3⅞ inches wide, 2⅝ inches deep.
Per gross...$40 00
This Indian Head Bank is of a very beautiful design and has a perfect typical Indian face. It is beautifully finished and is a fine work of art that will attract attention everywhere.
1 Bank only in a paper box. 6 dozen in a case.

1906

THE A. C. WILLIAMS CO., RAVENNA, OHIO, U. S. A.   35

22   THE A. C. WILLIAMS CO., RAVENNA, OHIO, U. S. A.

1906

THE A. C. WILLIAMS CO., RAVENNA, OHIO, U. S. A.   21

1906

THE DAISY

TOY COFFEE MILL.

PRICE.

No. 867.   Box 2½ inches wide, 2½ inches deep. 2 inches high.
extreme height over all, 3⅞ inches, per gross........ $20 00

½ dozen in paper box. 1 gross in case.

Shipping weight 90 lbs. per case.

Cat Toy Bank.

Patent Pending.

PRICE.

No. 3248.   Five and three-fourths inches long, 2½ inches
high; finished in Black with Gold Bronzed
Ball; per gross.. $23 50

½ dozen in paper box; 1 gross in a case.

Dog Toy Bank.

Patent Pending.

PRICE.

No. 2948.   Eight inches long, 5½ inches high, finished in
Brown Enamel, imitating a Water Spaniel,
trimmed in gold and silver, per gross $50 00
No. 3048.   Five and one-half inches long, 3⅞ inches high,
finished same as 2948; per gross...................... 23 50

No. 2948 packed 1 Bank in a paper box,
6 dozen in a case.
No. 3048 packed 6 Banks in a paper box,
12 dozen in a case.

1906 *1906* *1906*

24   THE A. C. WILLIAMS CO., RAVENNA, OHIO, U. S. A.   THE A. C. WILLIAMS CO., RAVENNA, OHIO, U. S. A. 23   20 THE A. C. WILLIAMS CO., RAVENNA, OHIO, U. S. A.

Frog Bank.

PRICE.

No. 1548. Elegantly finished in Green, Gold and Black. 3⅜ inches high, 2¾ inches wide, 2⅝ inches deep.

Per gross..$23 50

½ dozen in paper box. 1 gross in case.

Turkey Toy Bank.

Patent Pending.

No. 3748. Three and seven-eighths inches long, 4½ inches high, 3⅜ inches wide; finished in Bronze Enamel, trimmed in Red, Black and Gold; per gross.........$45 00

No. 3848. Three and one-fourth inches long; 3½ inches high, 2⅝ inches wide; finished same No. 3748, per gross.. 23 50

No. 3748 packed 1 Bank in paper box; 6 dozen in a case.
No. 3848 packed 6 Banks in paper box; 12 dozen in a case.

This is a new departure in Toy Banks, representing a Gobbler strutting about with wings trailing on the ground. Opening for coin between the long and short tail feathers. This is a very attractive mantel ornament as well as a beautiful Toy.

Lion Toy Bank.

Patent Pending.

No. 3348. Six and five-eighths inches long, 5¼ inches high; finished in Gold Bronze; trimmed in Red and Black, per gross.................................$45 00

No. 3448. Five and one-fourth inches long, 4 inches high; finished same as No. 3348; per gross..... 23 50

No. 3348 packed one Bank in paper box; 6 dozen in case.
No. 3448 packed six Banks in paper box; 12 dozen in case.

BILLIKEN ON THRONE TOY BANK.

No. 5748. Finished in gold bronze, trimmed in red; 6⅝ inches high, 3¼ inches wide, 4 inches deep.

PRICE.

Per gross... $50 00

Packed 1 Bank in a paper box.
6 dozen in a case.
Shipping weight 200 lbs. per case.

Billiken Toy Bank.

No. 5848. Finished in gold bronze, trimmed in red. 4¼ inches high. 2½ inches wide, 2½ inches deep.

PRICE.

Per gross $23 50

Packed 6 banks in a paper box.
1 gross in a case.
Shipping weight, 140 lbs. per case.

Ball Player Toy Bank.

Patented August 31, 1909.

No. 5448. Finished in gold bronze, trimmed in blue, flesh, aluminum and black. 5¾ inches high, 2¼ inches wide, 1½ inches deep.

PRICE.

Per gross... $23 50

Packed 6 banks in a paper box.
1 gross in a case.
Shipping weight 135 lbs. per case.

Buster Brown and Tige Toy Bank.

No. 5648. Finished in gold bronze, trimmed in blue, flesh, red, copper and black, 5¼ inches high, 3½ inches wide 2 inches deep.

PRICE.

Per gross $23 50

Packed 6 banks in a paper box.
1 gross in a case.
Shipping weight 135 lbs. per case.

Clown Toy Bank.

Patented Oct. 27, 1908.

PRICES.

No. 5148. Finished in gold bronze, trimmed in red. 6¼ inches high, 2¼ inches wide, 2 inches deep. Price per gross.............................$23 50

No. 5148½. Finished in aluminum bronze, trimmed in red. Price per gross 23 50

Packed 6 banks in a paper box.
1 gross in a case.
Shipping weight 140 lbs. per case.

Clock Toy Bank.

No. 5548. Finished in dull black, trimmed in gold. 3½ inches high, 3 inches wide, 1¾ inches deep.

PRICE.

Per gross.. $23 50

47

Packed 6 banks in a paper box.
1 gross in a case.
Shipping weight 115 lbs. per case.

1910 ## Large Rabbit Bank.

No. 4548. Finished in gold bronze, trimmed in red and black, 6½ inches high, 6 inches long.

PRICE.

Per gross..$45 00

Packed 1 Bank in a paper box.
6 dozen in a case.
Shipping weight 160 lbs. per case.

1910 ## Rabbit Toy Bank.

No. 4648. Finished in gold bronze, trimmed in red and black, 5 inches high, 2½ inches wide.

PRICE.

Per gross..$23 50

Packed 6 Banks in a paper box.
1 gross in a case.
Shipping weight 135 lbs. per case.

1910 ## Three Wise Monkeys Toy Bank.

No. 5948. Finished in gold bronze, trimmed in red, black and copper. 3½ inches high, 3½ inches wide, 1⅝ inches deep.

PRICE.

Per gross..$23 50

Packed 6 banks in a paper box.
1 gross in a case.
Shipping weight 125 lbs. per case.

HORSE BANK

PRICES.

No. 4448. Finished in gold bronze, trimmed in red and black, 4¼ inches high, 5 inches long. Price per gross........................$23 50
No. 4448½. Finished in dull black, trimmed in silver and red. Price per gross........................23 50

Packed 6 banks in a paper box.
1 gross in a case.
Shipping weight 145 lbs. per case.

Large Horse Bank.

PRICES

No. 4348. Finished in gold bronze, trimmed in red and black, 7½ inches high, 7 inches long, per gross...................$50 00
No. 4348½. Finished in dull black, trimmed in silver and red. Price per gross.........50 00

Packed 1 bank in a paper box.
6 dozen in a case.
Shipping weight 195 lbs. per case.

Rooster Toy Bank.

No. 4748. Finished in gold bronze; trimmed in red and black, 5 inches high, 3½ inches wide.

PRICE.

Per gross..$23 50

Packed 6 banks in a paper box.
1 gross in a case.
Shipping weight 140 lbs. per case.

Duck Bank.

No. 4848. Finished in gold bronze, trimmed in black, 5 inches high, 3½ inches wide.

PRICE.

Per gross..$23 50

Packed 6 Banks in a paper box
1 gross in a case.
Shipping weight 145 lbs. per case.

Bear Toy Bank.

No. 5048. Finished in gold bronze, 5½ inches high, 2 inches wide, 2½ inches deep.

PRICE.

Per gross..$23 50

Packed 6 banks in a paper box.
1 gross in a case.
Shipping weight 165 lbs. per case.

Pig Toy Bank.

No. 5348. Finished in gold bronze, trimmed in red and black, 3 inches high, 2¼ inches wide, 4½ inches long.

PRICE.

Per gross..$23 50

Packed 6 banks in a paper box.
1 gross in a case.
Shipping weight 135 lbs. per case.

Campbell Kids
Toy Bank

Manufactured under a license from Campbell's Soups, Camden, N. J.

No. 7048. Finished in gold bronze, 3⅜ inches high, 4¼ inches wide, weight 14 oz.

PRICE

Per gross $23 50

Packed 6 banks in a paper box.
1 gross in a case.
Shipping weight 155 lbs. per gross.

Darkey Bank

No. 4048. Dull black face, gold bronze hat, gold suspenders, red shirt, aluminum collar and black trousers; 5¾ inches high; 2¾ inches wide, 2 inches deep; weight 14 oz.

PRICE

Per gross $23 50

Packed 6 banks in a paper box.
1 gross in a case.
Shipping weight 160 lbs. per case.

Mutt and Jeff
Toy Bank

Manufactured under a license from H. C. Fisher, N. Y.

No. 6948. Finished in gold bronze, 5¼ inches high, 3⅜ inches wide, weight 14 oz.

PRICE

Per gross $23 50

Packed 6 banks in a paper box.
1 gross in a case.
Shipping weight 155 lbs. per gross.

Washington Monument Bank

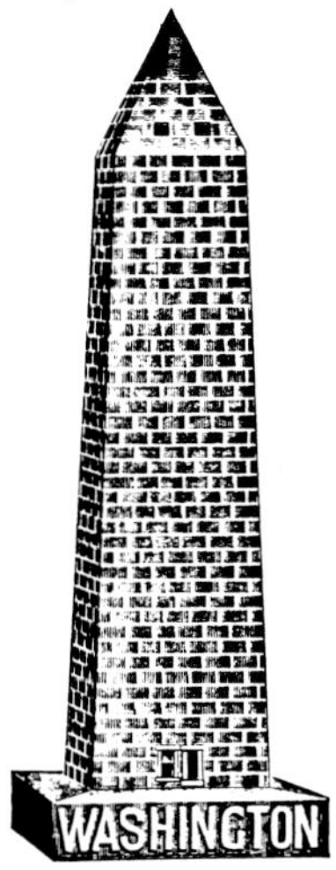

No. 7248. Finished in gold bronze, 6⅛ inches high, 2⅛ inches square at the base, weight 13 oz. Per gross $23 50

No. 7348. Finished in gold bronze, 7½ inches high, 2½ inches square at the base, weight 19 oz. Per gross $35 00

No. 7248. Packed 6 banks in a paper box.
1 gross in a case. Shipping weight 145 lbs. per gross.

No. 7348. Packed 6 banks in a paper box.
1 gross in a case. Shipping weight 200 lbs. per gross.

Statue of Liberty Toy Bank

No. 6748. Finished in gold bronze, trimmed in red, 6⅜ inches high, 2¼ inches square at base, weight 13 oz.

PRICE

Per gross $23 50

Packed six banks in a paper box.
One gross in a case.
Shipping weight 135 lbs. per gross.

Donkey Toy Bank

No. 6648. Body finished in drab, saddle brown, trimmed in red and gold, bridle black, 4⅛ inches high, 4¾ inches long, weight 12 oz.

No. 6648½ Body finished in gold, saddle and bridle in red.

PRICE

Per gross $25 00

Packed 6 banks in a paper box.
1 gross in a case.
Shipping weight 145 lbs. per gross.

Elephant Toy Bank

No. 6348. Finished in gold bronze, trimmed in red, 4⅞ inches high, 6¼ inches long, weight 1¾ lbs., per gross $50 00

No. 6448. Finished in gold bronze, trimmed in red, 3 inches high, 4 inches long, weight 12½ oz., per gross 23 50

No. 6348. Packed one bank in a paper box, six dozen in a case.

No. 6448. Packed six banks in a paper box, one gross in a case.

Shipping weight No. 6348, 175 lbs. per case.
Shipping weight No. 6448, 150 lbs. per gross.

Dog Toy Bank

No. 6848. Finished in gold bronze, trimmed in red, 4¼ inches high, 4 inches long, weight 14 oz.

PRICE

Per gross $23 50

Packed six banks in a paper box.
One gross in a case.
Shipping weight 150 lbs. per gross.

Owl Toy Bank

No. 6248. Finished in gold bronze, trimmed in black and white, 5 inches high, 2½ inches wide, 1⅝ inches deep, weight 12½ oz.

PRICE

Per gross $23 50

Packed six banks in a paper box.
One gross in a case.
Shipping weight 140 lbs. per case.

1912 THE A. C. WILLIAMS CO., RAVENNA, O., U. S. A. 107

Bird Toy Bank

No. 6048. Finished in gold bronze, trimmed in silver, green, copper and black, 5 inches high, 4¾ inches long, weight 12½ oz.

PRICE

Per gross.. $23 50

Packed six banks in a paper box.
1 gross in a case.
Shipping weight 140 lbs. per gross.

110 THE A. C. WILLIAMS CO., RAVENNA, O., U. S. A. 1912

Boat Toy Bank

No. 6548. Finished in gold bronze, trimmed in red, 7¾ inches long, 1⅝ inches wide, 2⅝ inches high, weight 1 lb.

PRICE

Per gross.. $23 50

Packed 6 banks in a paper box.
One gross in a case.
Shipping weight 165 lbs. per gross.

1912 THE A. C. WILLIAMS CO., RAVENNA, O., U. S. A. 97

Mail Box Bank

No. 4948. Finished in aluminum bronze, with red letters, 3⅝ inches high, 2¾ inches wide, 1¾ inches deep, weight 13 oz., per gross.................. $23 50

No. 4948½. Finished in aluminum bronze with red letters, 4⅝ inches high, 2¾ inches wide, 1¾ inches deep, weight 1 lb.; per gross.................. 25.00

Packed 6 banks in a paper box.
1 gross in a case.
Shipping weight No. 4948, 150 lbs. per case.
Shipping weight No. 4948½, 175 lbs. per case.

x
116 THE A. C. WILLIAMS CO., RAVENNA, O., U. S. A. 1912

Mail Box Bank

No. 7148. Finished in aluminum bronze with red letters. 4¼ inches high, 3¼ inches wide, 1⅜ inches deep, weight 15 oz.

PRICE

Per gross.. $23 50

Packed 6 banks in a paper box.
1 gross in a case.
Shipping weight 165 lbs. per gross.

1919

THE A. C. WILLIAMS CO., RAVENNA, OHIO, U. S. A. 87A

ROOSEVELT BANK

No. 1248—Gold 5½ inches high, 3½ inches wide, weight 12 oz.

Packed ½ dozen in a paper box; 6 dozen in case.
Shipping weight 120 lbs. per gross.

110D

ELK TOY BANK

No. 7748. Finished in gold, 6½ inches high, weight 11 ounces.
Packed 6 banks in a paper box.

134A THE A. C. WILLIAMS CO., RAVENNA, OHIO, U. S. A.

ARMOURED CAR BANK

No. 5367—Body red, wheels gold. 6¾ inches long, 4 inches high. Weight 24 oz.

Packed ½ dozen in a paper box; 3 dozen in a case.
Shipping weight 228 lbs. per gross.

No. 1867. Body finished in Spartan Red enamel, wheel in gold bronze, 5¾ inches long, 2¼ inches wide, 2¾

1920 THE A. C. WILLIAMS CO., RAVENNA, OHIO, U. S. A. 101

AUTOMOBILE

No. 1667—Body green, striped with gold. 9½ inches long, 3¼ inches wide, 3¼ inches high. Weight 2 lb.
Packed one each in a paper box; 2 dozen in a case.
Shipping weight 340 lb per gross.

No. 1767—Decorated same as No. 1667. 12 inches long, 4⅛ inches wide, 3⅞ inches high. Weight 3¾ lb.
Packed one each in a paper box; 1 dozen in a case.
Shipping weight 564 lb per gross.

AUTOMOBILE BANK

No. 3167—Body red enamel. Wheels gold. 6¾ inches long, 3½ inches high, 2½ inches wide. Weight 19 oz.
Packed ½ dozen in a paper box; 4 dozen in a case.
Shipping weight 180 lb per gross.

92 THE A. C. WILLIAMS CO., RAVENNA, OHIO, U. S. A. 1920

CAMEL BANK

No. 7448 —Body drab, saddle trimmed with red and gold. 5 inches high, 4 inches long. Weight 9 oz.

No. 7448½—Body gold, saddle trimmed with brown and red.

No. 7548 —Body drab, saddle trimmed with red and gold. 7½ inches high, 6½ inches long. Weight 1 lb 9 oz.

No. 7548½—Body gold, saddle trimmed with brown and red.

No. 7448 and 7448½ packed 1 dozen in a paper box; 6 dozen in a case.

No. 7548 and 7548½ packed 1 bank in a paper box; 3 dozen in a case.

Shipping weight Nos. 7448 and 7448½, 88 lb per gross.
Shipping weight Nos. 7548 and 7548½, 244 lb per gross.

1920 THE A. C. WILLIAMS CO., RAVENNA, OHIO, U. S. A. 115

HORSE ON WHEELS

No. 4067—Body gold. Wheels red. 4¾ inches long, 5¼ inches high. Weight 14 oz.
Packed ½ dozen in a paper box; 4 dozen in a case.
Shipping weight 140 lb per gross.

LION ON WHEELS

No. 4167—Body gold, wheels red. 4½ inches long, 4⅞ inches high. Weight 16 oz.
Packed ½ dozen in a paper box; 4 dozen in a case.
Shipping weight 155 lb per gross.

94 THE A. C. WILLIAMS CO., RAVENNA, OHIO, U. S. A. 1920

COW BANK

No. 7848—Plain gold. 3½ inches high, weight 13 oz.
Packed 1 dozen in a paper box; 6 dozen in a case.
Shipping weight 116 lb per gross.

BUFFALO BANK

No. 7948—Plain gold. 3½ inches high, weight 11 oz.
Packed 1 dozen in a paper box; 6 dozen in a case.
Shipping weight 102 lb per gross.

STREET CAR BANK

No. 3867—Plain gold. 6¼ inches long, 3½ inches high. Weight 20 oz.

Packed ½ dozen in a paper box; 3 dozen in a case.

Shipping weight 215 lb per gross.

ELEPHANT ON WHEELS

No. 3967—Body gold. Saddle trimmed with red. 4½ inches long, 4¼ inches high. Weight 16 oz.

Packed ½ dozen in a paper box; 4 dozen in a case.

Shipping weight 160 lb per gross.

CIRCUS ASSORTMENT ANIMAL BANKS

Patent Pending

No. 1348—Elephant, Lion and Horse on Tubs. Finished in plain gold. Packed 6 only assorted in paper box. 6 dozen in shipping case. Average height 5¼ In. Average weight each 12 oz.

CIRCUS ASSORTMENT ANIMAL BANKS

No. 1648—Elephant, Lion and Horse on Tubs. Finished in assorted colors and highly decorated.

Packed 6 only assorted in paper box. 6 dozen in shipping case.

Average height each 5¼ inches. Average weight each 12 ounces.

CLOCK BANK

Patent Pending

No. 48—Finished Red Enamel with Gold Bronze Face. Height 6 in. Weight each 10 oz.

Packed 12 in a paper box. 6 dozen in a shipping case. Shipping weight 100 lb per gross.

TOY BANK

Patented

No. 148—Aluminum. Gold dome. 3½ inches wide, 4¼ inches high. Weight 14 oz.

No. 248—Aluminum. Gold dome. 2¾ inches wide, 3¼ inches high. Weight 9 oz.

No. 348—Aluminum. Gold dome. 2¾ inches wide, 3¾ inches high. Weight 11 oz.

No. 148 packed ½ dozen in a paper box; 4 dozen in a case.
No. 248 packed 2 dozen in a paper box; 6 dozen in a case.
No. 348 packed 1 dozen in a paper box; 6 dozen in a case.
Shipping weight No. 148, 135 lb per gross.
Shipping weight No. 248, 84 lb per gross.
Shipping weight No. 348, 98 lb per gross.

DONKEY BANK

No. 7648 —Body drab, saddle brown, trimmed in red and gold, bridle black. 6½ inches high, 6¼ inches long, weight 1¾ lb.

No. 7648½—Body gold, saddle brown and red.

Packed 1 bank in a paper box; 2 dozen in a case.

Shipping weight 270 lb per gross.

ELK BANK

No. 7748—Plain gold. 6¼ inches high, weight 13 oz.

Packed 1 dozen in a paper box; 6 dozen in a case.

Shipping weight 124 lb per gross.

CIRCUS ASSORTMENT ANIMAL BANKS

Patent Pending

No. 2148—Elephant, Lion, Dog and Cat on Tubs. Finished in plain gold. Packed 12 only assorted in paper box. 6 dozen in shipping case. Average height 3⅞ in. Average weight each 9 oz.

HOUSE BANK

Patented

No. 2548—Aluminum. Gold roof. 4¾ inches high, 3 5/16 inches wide. Weight 15 oz.

Packed 1 dozen in a paper box; 4 dozen in a case.

Shipping weight 159 lb per gross.

THE "SKY SCRAPER" BANK

Trade Mark

No. 1848—Aluminum. Gold roof. 3⅝ inches high, 1⅞ inches wide, 1 15/16 inches deep, weight 9 oz.

Packed 1 dozen in a paper box; 6 dozen in a case.

Shipping weight 84 lb per gross.

MAIL BOX BANK

No. 2048—Mail Box Bank. Assorted colors, red and green with gold letters, 5¼ in. high, 3 in. wide.

Packed 1 dozen assorted in a box. 6 doz. in a case.

Shipping weight 85 lb per gross.

ELK BANK

No. 8048—Plain gold. 9½ inches high, weight 1 lb 11 oz.

Packed 1 bank in a paper box; 2 dozen in a case.

Shipping weight 300 lb per gross.

HORSE BANK

No. 8148 —Plain gold. 5½ inches high. Weight 13 oz.

No. 8148½—Black enamel. Aluminum hoofs.

Packed 1 dozen in a paper box; 6 dozen in a case.

Shipping weight 128 lb per gross.

HOUSE BANK

No. 448—Aluminum. Gold roof. 4¾ inches high, 4 inches wide, weight 1 lb 5 oz.

Packed 6 banks in a paper box; 3 dozen in a case.

Shipping weight 212 lb per gross.

TANK BANK

Patent Pending

No. 548—Plain Gold. 4½ inches long, 2½ inches high. Weight 11 oz.

No. 1148—Plain Gold. 6 inches long, 3¼ inches high. Weight 1½ lb.

No. 548 packed ½ dozen in a paper box; 6 dozen in a case.
No. 1148 packed ½ dozen in a paper box; 3 doz. in a case.
Shipping weight 548, 120 lb per gross.
Shipping weight 1148, 240 lb per gross.

TOY BANK

Patented

No. 948—Aluminum. Gold roof. 2¼ inches wide, 3 inches high. Weight 8 oz.

No. 1948—Plain Gold. 2¼ inches wide, 3¾ inches high. Weight 10 oz.

No. 948 packed 2 dozen in a paper box; 6 doz. in a case.
No. 1948 packed 1 dozen in a paper box; 6 doz. in a case.
Shipping weight No. 948, 68 lb per gross.
Shipping weight No. 1948, 90 lb per gross.

STEEL SAFE

No. 1048—Stamped steel. Black enamel finish with nickel trimmings. Combination lock. 4 inches high, 3 inches wide, 2⅞ inches deep. Weight 8 oz.

Packed 1 dozen in a paper box; 6 dozen in a case.

Shipping weight 80 lb per gross.

TOY BANKS 1927

No. 648 —Double Garage. Plain gold.

No. 648-D —Double Garage. Assorted, with red, green and blue roofs.

No. 2648 —Single Garage. Plain gold.

No. 2648-D—Double Garage. Assorted, with red, green and blue roofs.

No. 648—648-D, weight 13 oz. 6 dozen in case. Shipping weight 125 lb per gross.

No. 2648—2648-D, weight 10 oz. 6 dozen in case. Shipping weight 100 lb per gross.

FOOTBALL PLAYER BANK

No. 8348—Football Player Bank. Plain Gold. 6 inches high. Weight 11 oz.

Packed 1 dozen in paper box; 6 dozen in case.

Shipping weight 100 lb per gross.

COLONIAL HOUSE BANK 1927

No. 1248—Colonial House Bank. Plain gold.

No. 1248-D—Colonial House Bank. Assorted with red, green and blue roofs. Weight 12 oz.

Packed 6 dozen in case. Shipping weight 115 lb per gross.

COLONIAL HOUSE BANK

No. 2748 —Colonial House Bank. Plain gold or aluminum.

No. 2748-D—Colonial House Bank. Assorted, with red, green and blue roofs. Weight 1 lb, 6 oz. each.

Packed ¼ dozen in paper box. 3 dozen in case.

Shipping weight 225 lb per gross.

BANK ASSORTMENT

No. 22-A—Assorted Red, Blue and Green Enamel.

Average weight about 6 oz.

Packed 1 dozen in a paper box; 6 dozen in a case.

Shipping weight about 30 lb. per case.

GRAF ZEPPELIN

No. 968—Aluminum Finish. Rubber Tires. 5 inches long, 1⅜ inches high. Weight 5 oz.
Packed 1 dozen in a paper box; 6 dozen in a case.
Shipping weight about 25 lb per case.

No. 1868—Aluminum Finish. Rubber Tires. 5½ inches long, 1¾ inches high. Weight 7 oz.
Packed 1 dozen in a paper box; 6 dozen in a case.
Shipping weight about 35 lb per case.

AREOPLANE

No. 1168—Assorted Red, Blue, Green and Tan Bodies. Nickel Propeller. Rubber Tires. 4 inches long, 1½ inches high. Weight 4½ oz.
Packed 1 dozen in a paper box; 6 dozen in a case.
Shipping weight about 25 lb per case.

No. 9667—Assorted Red, Blue, Green and Tan Bodies. Motor & Propeller Nickel Plated. Rubber Tires. 4¾ inches long, 2¼ inches high. Weight 7½ oz.
Packed 1 dozen in a paper box; 6 dozen in a case.
Shipping weight about 35 lb per case.

SPEED BOAT

No. 2168—Assorted Red, Blue, Green and Tan Bodies. 4¾ inches long, 1¾ inches high. Weight 6½ oz.
Packed 1 dozen in a paper box; 6 dozen in a case.
Shipping weight about 30 lb per case.

No. 2268—Assorted Red, Blue, Green and Tan Bodies. Rubber Tires. 5½ inches long, 1⅞ inches high. Weight 8½ oz.
Packed 1 dozen in a paper box; 6 dozen in a case.
Shipping weight about 40 lb per case.

SULKY AND HORSE

No. 2467—Sulky, Horse and Man Aluminum. Rubber Tires. 5 inches long, 3⅛ inches high. Weight 8 oz.
Packed 1 dozen in a paper box; 6 dozen in a case.
Shipping weight about 35 lb per case.

TOY BANK

No. 1048 —Plain Gold. 2¼ inches wide, 3⅛ inches high. Weight 8 oz.

No. 1048-D—Assorted, with Red, Blue and Green Roofs.
Packed 1 dozen in a paper box; 6 dozen in a case.
Shipping weight 38 lb. per case.

COLONIAL HOUSE BANK

No. 1248 —Plain Gold. 2¾ inches wide, 3⅛ inches high. Weight 11½ oz.

No. 1248-D—Assorted, with Red, Blue and Green Roofs.
Packed 1 dozen in a paper box; 6 dozen in a case.
Shipping weight 60 lb. per case.

GRAF ZEPPELIN BANK

No. 8748—Aluminum Finish. 6¾ inches long, 1¾ inches high. Weight 10 oz.
Packed 1 dozen in a paper box; 6 dozen in a case.
Shipping weight 55 lb. per case.

WING MANUFACTURING CO

No. 807. Grandpa Bank.
Height 5¼ inches, 6 in box, 12 doz. in case, weight 110 lbs.

No. 810. Darkey Bank.
Height 5¼ inches, 6 in box, 12 doz. in case, weight 110 lbs.

No. 809. Billy Bounce Bank.
Height 5 inches, 6 in box, 12 doz. in case, weight 110 lbs.

No. 805. Santa Claus Bank.
Height 6 inches, 12 in box, 24 doz. in case, weight 280 lbs.

No. 808. Elephant Bank.
Height 3¾ inches, 6 in box, 12 doz. in case, weight 180 lbs.

No. 806. Rabbit Bank.
Height 4¾ inches, 6 in box, 12 doz. in case, weight 120 lbs.

Liberty Bank

No. 600 Height 6¾ inches. Width 2½ inches. 12 in a box. 24 dozen in a case. 210 lbs. per case.

No. 601 Height 9¼ inches. Width 3¼ inches. 4 in a box. 12 dozen in a case. 200 lbs. per case.

Locomotives

No. 384
Aluminum Finish. 5½ inches long. 12 in a box. 24 dozen in a case. 180 lbs. per case.

No. 385
Aluminum Finish. 6 inches long. 12 in a box. 24 dozen in a case. 180 lbs. per case.

No. 386
Painted. 6½ inches long. 12 in a box. 12 dozen in a case. 130 lbs. per case.

No. 387
Painted. 7 inches long. 6 in a box. 12 dozen in a case. 180 lbs. per case.

Coaches

No. 284
Aluminum Finish. Length 4½ inches. 12 in a box. 24 dozen in a case. Weight per case, 150 lbs.

No. 285
Aluminum Finish. Length 5 inches. 12 in a box. 24 dozen in a case. Weight per case, 180 lbs.

No. 286
Painted. Length 5½ inches. 12 in a box. 12 dozen in a case. Weight per case, 130 lbs.

No. 287
Painted. Length, 6½ inches. 12 in a box. 12 dozen in a case. Weight per case, 150 lbs.

SAFES

No. 60A. This beautiful safe. Is of a highly artistic pattern. Highly polished and antique oxidized copper finish. Has a double combination burglar proof lock that cannot be picked unless you have the combination. Makes a very handsome ornament for a home.

Size—Height, 6 in.
Width, 4⅜ in.
Depth, 4⅜ in.

Packed one in a box.

SAFES

No. 40. **Columbus Safe.** Is highly finished and beautifully ornamented; handsomely nickel plated; closed with a good combination lock, with the best moneyguard. Packed one in a box.
Size, Height, 5⅜ in.; Width, 4⅜ in.; Depth, 4⅜ in.

No. 40A. Same as No. 40, but finished in antique oxidised copper.

SAFES

No. 30. **The National Safe.** Combines the same artistic features as the Columbus has a new combination lock, handsomely finished in nickel.

Packed three in a box.

Size—Height, 5 in.
Width, 3⅜ in.
Depth, 3⅜ in.

No. 30A. Is antique oxidised copper finish.

SAFES

No. 120A **Sterling Safe** ... beauty. Full polished ... idized copper. Good ... lock. Embossed steel ...

Size—Height, 3⅜ ...
Width, 2⅜ in...
Depth, 2⅜ in...

Packed 1 dozen in a box.

THE COTTAGE

No. 125. **Bank.** This bank is of the country villa style. Very large and showy. Neatly polished in antique oxidised copper.

Packed one dozen in a box.

No. ... Is the same as No. 125, only nickel plated.

ELEPHANT BANK

No. 105. The Elephant ... favorite for a low-pric... polished and nickel pl...

Size, 3⅜ x 2⅜ in...

Packed one dozen ...

No. 110A. Antique oxidise...

SAFES

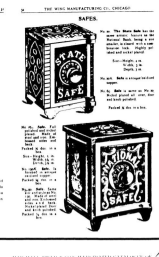

No. 50A. **Uncle Sam Security** is a safe you cannot pick. There is a large demand for a safe that boys and girls cannot open unless by permission to do so, and this safe embodies that feature the same as our No 100. It is handsomely finished in antique oxidized copper, has a blind combination with a good lock and key, and a special patent lock.

Packed one in a box.
Size—Height, 5 in.
Width, 3½ in.
Depth, 3½ in.

No. 50. **The State Safe** has the same artistic feature as the National Bank, being a size smaller, is closed with a combination lock. Highly polished and nickel plated.

Size—Height, 4 in.
Width, 3 in.
Depth, 3 in.

No. 50A Safe is antique oxidized copper.

No. 65 Safe is same as No 50. Nickel plated all over, door and knob polished.

Packed ½ doz. in a box.

No. 130C Safe. Full polished and nickel plated. Made of steel and iron. Embossed sides and back.

Packed ½ doz. in a box.
Size—Height, 4 in.
Width, 3¾ in.
Depth, 3½ in.

No. 130 Safe. Is finished in antique oxidized copper.

Packed ½ doz. in a box.

No. 90 Safe. Same finished in antique oxidized copper. No. 130. Made of steel and iron. Embossed Nickel plated. Door and knob polished.

Packed ½ doz. in a box.

THE NICKEL AND DIME SELF-REGISTERING SAVINGS BANK.

1890-1891

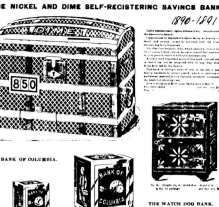

BANK OF COLUMBIA.

THE WATCH DOG BANK.

THE NATIONAL.

READ THE PREFACE BEFORE ORDERING.

TOY BANKS.

DANCING BEAR.

COLUMBUS BANK.

VILLA BANK.

PRESTO TRICK BANK.

READ THE PREFACE BEFORE ORDERING.

TOY BANKS.

READ THE PREFACE BEFORE ORDERING.

---

c. 1890's

Toy Banks.

No. 3296.

No. 3306, 3311.

No. 3078.

SNAP BANK.

WITHOUT SNAP

No. 3074, 3076.

No. 3290, 3297.

No. 3330 to 3337.

c. 1890's

Toy Banks.

Nos. 3192 to 3197.

Nos. 3182, 3187.

No. 3174, 3181.

c. 1890's

Toy Banks.

No. 3285.

No. 3320.

SANTA CLAUS.

No. 3292.

No. 3336.

c. 1890's

Toy Banks.

Nos. 3166, 3171.

No. 3292.

No. 3900.

Nos. 3540, 3543, 3546, 3550.

No. 3296, 3297.

IRON TOYS.

SAVINGS CHEST.

READ THE PREFACE BEFORE ORDERING.

TOY BANKS. 1893-1894

READ THE PREFACE BEFORE ORDERING.

BANKS.

HOME SAVINGS BANK.

CABIN BANK.

TIME LOCK BANKS.

THE EAGLE BANK.

PLANTATION DARKY BANK.

The Toy Locomotive Savings Bank.—NEW.

Very Durable. Made entirely of Iron, and Nickel-Plated.

25. This is a perfect combination of a Play Toy and Savings Bank for small children.

Price, 3.50 Per Dozen.

IRON TOYS, Etc.

Iron Freight Train.

26. Consists of a Locomotive, Tender, and two Freight cars, with Brakemen, made of solid iron, and painted neatly in red and black. PRICE, 8.00 PER DOZEN.

Iron Locomotive, Tender and One Car.—NEW.

Malleable Iron.   Price 4.50 Per Dozen.

27.

Prices Subject to Change Without Notice.

1887—SELCHOW & RIGHTER, 41 JOHN ST., N. Y.—1888.   7

Security Safe Bank.—No. 2.—NEW.

BRASS COMBINATION LOCK AND NEW MONEY GUARD ATTACHMENT.

Size, 4¾ inches high, 3¾ wide, 3½ deep.

18. This safe has a new and accurate combination lock. Price, 4.00 Per Dozen.

Security Safe Deposit.—No. 4.—NEW.

WITH NICKEL-PLATED COMBINATION LOCK AND PATENT MONEY GUARD.

Size, 6 inches high, 4¾ wide, 6½ deep.

18. This safe has an accurate combination lock.

Price, 6.00 Per Dozen.

Purse Bank.—NEW.

Size, 3½ inches long, 1½ wide, 2½ high.

20. This is a cheap and attractive little bank, finished in japan.

Price Per Dozen, 75c.

Prices Subject to Change Without Notice.

Little "Middy" Bank.

Size, 5 inches high 3 wide, 1½ deep.

19. This is a cheap and simple little bank, and calculated to please children. Finished in black japan, and packed one in a box.

Price Per Doz. 75c.

"TIME IS MONEY."

FINISHED.

Body in Gilt.
Top and Base Black Enameled.
Feet Gilded.

CLOCK SAVINGS BANK.

18. An exact imitation of a French Gilt Clock.
Size, Height, 5 in.; Width at Base, 4½ in.; Depth at Base, 3 in.

Price, 1.75 Per Dozen.

The Kicking Cow Bank—NEW.

Size, 6 inches high, 10 inches long, 3½ inches wide.

14. Place the coin in the small aperture on the cow's back, and press the lever, when the cow will kick over the man milking.

Price, 3.50 Per Dozen.

1887—CATALOGUE AND PRICE LIST OF GAMES AND NOVELTIES.—1888

"Safe Deposit" Toy Bank.

21. Instructive and secure. The Coins cannot in any way be shaken out, as there is a "Burglar Proof" Automatic Stop covering the slot. Has Silver Plated Combination Lock.

Price 7.00 Per Dozen.   CUT ½ SIZE.

Security Safe Deposit—No. 5.—NEW

NICKEL-PLATED COMBINATION LOCK.

22. Size, 8½ inches high, 6 wide, 8 deep. This safe has an accurate combination lock.

Price, 15.00 Per Dozen.

23. Car Bank.—NEW.

Imitation Horse Car.
Length, 4½ inches. Height, 3 inches. Finished in gilt and bronze. On wheels for child to pull along floor.

Price, 75c. Per Dozen.

The Palace Bank.—NEW.

24. This is one of the leading new Banks.

Price, 8.50 Per Dozen.

Prices Subject to Change Without Notice.

House Bank.

15. The above is a cut of a new Bank, which retails at 35 cents. A splendid Bank for the price.

Price, 3.00 Per Dozen.

Mansion Bank, NEW.

16. Size 3½ inches long, 4 wide, 5½ high. An entirely new design in house banks.

Price, 3.00 Per Dozen.

Security Safe Deposit.—No. 1, NEW.

WITH NICKEL-PLATED COMBINATION LOCK AND PATENT MONEY GUARD.

Size, 4¾ inches high, 3½ wide, 3½ deep.

17. This safe has a new style combination lock.

Price, 2.00 Per Dozen.

TOY SAVINGS BANKS.

1894.—CATALOGUE AND PRICE LIST OF GAMES AND NOVELTIES.—1895.

EAGLE BANK.

337. Length, 8 inches; height, 6 inches; width, 4 inches.

Place a coin in the eagle's beak, press the lever and the eaglets rise from the nest, actually crying for food. As the eagle bends forward to feed them the coin falls into the nest, and disappears in the receptacle below. Packed one in a wood box.

PRICE, 8.50 PER DOZEN.

TYROLESE BANK.

338. Length 10¼ in.; Height 6½ in. Width 9 in. Place the coin in proper position on the barrel of the rifle, when, by pressing the right foot, it is thrown into the opening, which is the bull's-eye of the target. As the coin enters, it strikes a gong bell, and the rifle is so arranged that a paper cap may be fired at the same time. Packed 1 in a package.

PRICE, 8.50 PER DOZEN.

National Safe Deposit Bank.

329. With Coppered Combination Lock, and patented Burglar Proof attachment. Finished in black and copper bronze. Size, 6 in. high: 4½ in. wide. Packed ¼ doz. in package.

Price per Dozen, 4.00.

Pail Penny Registering Bank.

330. Size, 3 inches high by 2¾ in diameter. This is the cheapest registering bank in the market and is as perfect as can be reasonably expected for the price. Put a penny in the slot and push the button to the right when the amount will be correctly registered. When 100 have been deposited the lid can be taken off. When replaced it is ready for business again and the first coin deposited locks it. Packed ½ in a box.

Price, 2.00 per dozen.

1894.—SELCHOW & RIGHTER, 390 BROADWAY, N. Y.—1895.

Security Safe Deposit. No. 1.

331. With Bronzed Combination Lock and Patent Money Guard.
Size, 4¾ inches high, 3½ wide, 3½ deep.

PRICE, 2.00 PER DOZEN.

Security Bank, No. 2.

Brass Combination Lock and New Money Guard Attachment.

Size, 4¾ inches high, 3½ wide, 3½ deep.
333. This safe has a new and accurate combination lock.

PRICE, 4.00 PER DOZEN.

Security Safe Deposit No. 4.

With Nickel plated combination Lock and Patent Money Guard.
Size, 6 inches high, 4¾ wide, 4¾ deep.
332. This safe has an accurate combination lock.

PRICE, 8.00 PER DOZEN.

Security Safe, No. 5.

USEFUL AND ATTRACTIVE, SECURE.
334. Inspire Business Ideas and habits in the young. Finished in black with gilt and decalcomania. Silver plated combination lock.

PRICE, 16.50 PER DOZEN.

Iron House Bank.

335. No. 225.
Height, 4¾ in.; 3 in. One of the 10c. Iron Banks.

Price, 75c. per dozen.

House Bank.

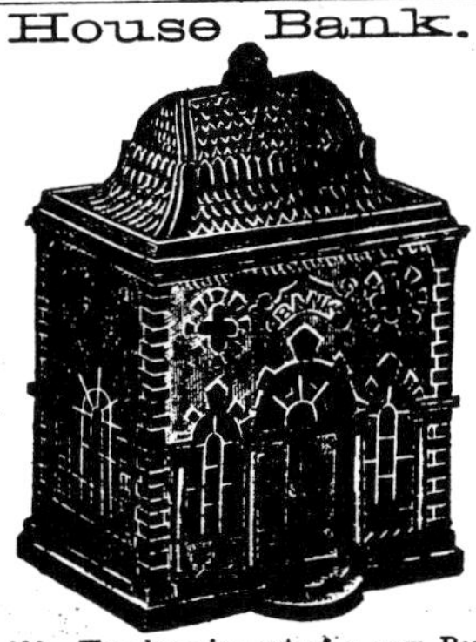

336. The above is a cut of a new Bank which retails at 25 cents. A splendid Bank for the price. Packed 6 in a package.
Price, 2 00 per Dozen.

Iron House Bank.

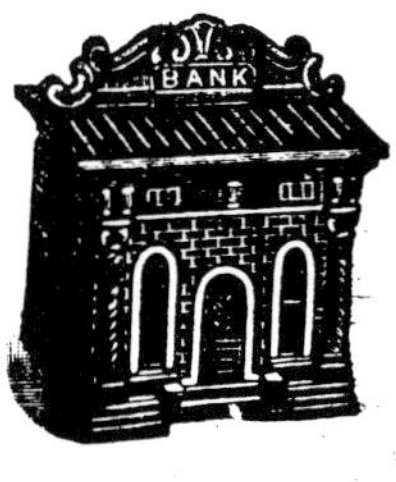

5c. Size.

Per Dozen, 38c.

337. Packed one dozen in a package.

WATERMELON BANK. NEW

Mechanical, with Lock and Key.

No. 133. Size, 6¾ inches long, 5 high, 1¼ deep.

338. This bank represents a very attractive idea to children. The money is put in a slot and remains in view until the lever is pressed, when it disappears, the dog runs out to attack the boy, whose hand is hastily withdrawn from the melon. Attractively finished in fancy colors and packed four in a box.

Price, per dozen, 4 00

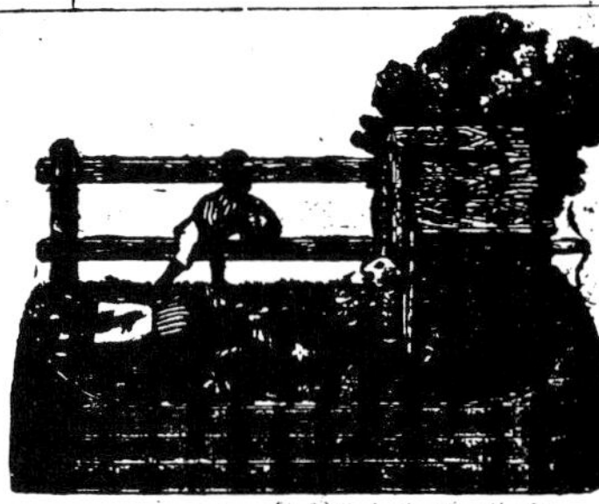

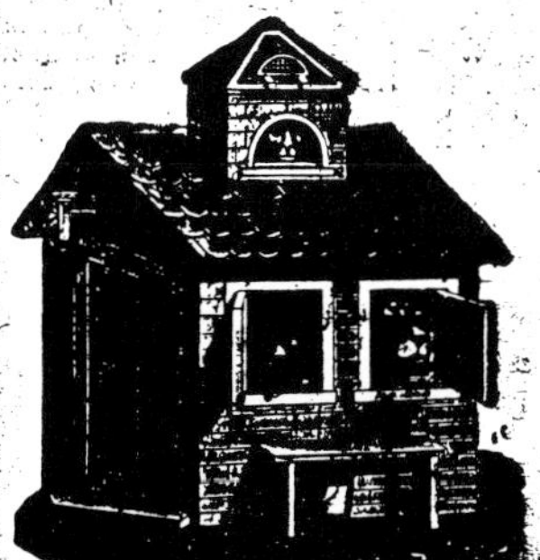

"ZOO" BANK. NEW.

MECHANICAL, WITH LOCK AND KEY.

No. 134. Size, 4¼ inches long, 4¼ high, 1¼ deep.

339. This is the cheapest mechanical iron bank in the market. The money is put in the slot and remains in sight until the monkey's face is pressed, when it falls, the shutters fly open and the lion and tiger put their faces through the windows. The shutters can be snapped shut and the bank is again ready for business. Merely as a mechanical toy, the sudden appearance of the animals is an attraction to children. Attractively painted in bright colors and packed one-half dozen in a box.

Price, per dozen, 2 00.

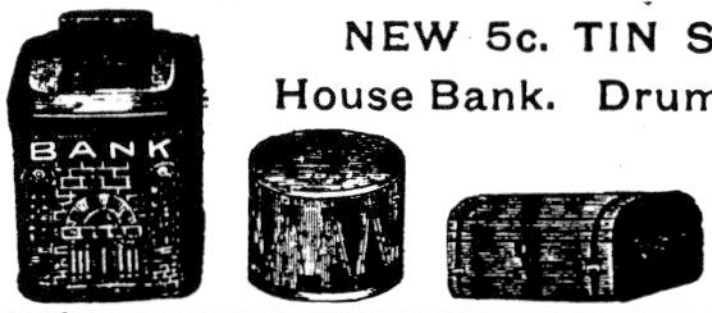

NEW 5c. TIN SAVINGS BANKS.

House Bank. Drum Bank. Trunk Bank.

340. Assorted, 4 of each, 3 kinds in each dozen. We do not break dozen boxes.
Per Dozen, 38 cents.

DANCING BEAR.---NEW.

With Clock-Work Mechanism and Chimes.

No. 132. Size 6⅞ inches long; 4¾ wide; 5¼ high.

341. In this bank is introduced some ingenious mechanism which produces very attractive results. It represents the front of a country house with an Italian organ-grinder and a bear on the lawn. After winding up the mechanism, place a coin in the slot and push the knob in front of him. He will then deposit the coin and play the organ while the bear performs his part. This bank will doubtless give great satisfaction. Handsomely painted. Packed one in a wooden box.

Price, per dozen, 8 50.

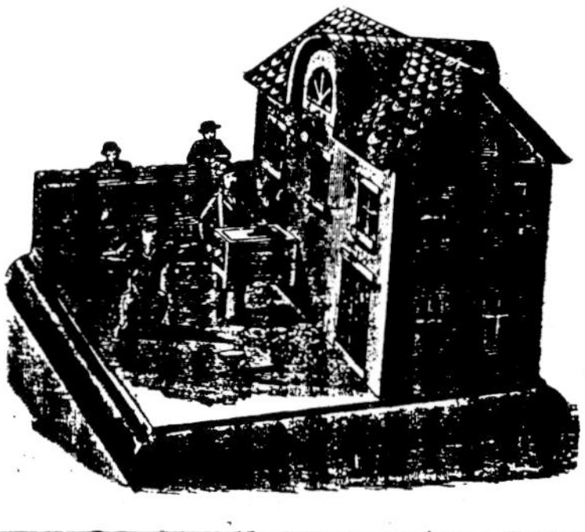

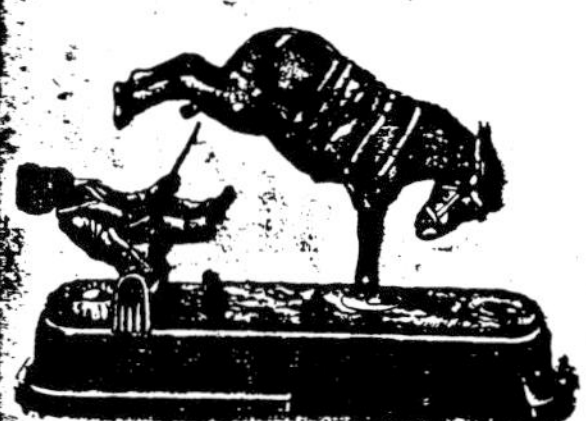

Kicking Mule Bank.

NEW PATTERN.

Length, 10 inches. Height, 6½ inches.

342. When the mule and boy are brought into position, a slight touch on the knob at the base causes the mule to turn around and kick the boy over, throwing the coin from the bench into the receptacle below.

Price, 8.50 per dozen.

"ARTILLERY" BANK.

NEW.

Size, 6 inches high, 8 inches long.

343. Made wholly of iron, highly finished. The coin is placed in the cannon (or mortar). The hammer is then pushed back; when the thumb-piece is pressed upon, the coin is fired into the fort or tower. The arm of the artilleryman moves up and down. Paper caps may also be used if desired.

Each bank packed in a small wood

Price, per dozen, 8.50.

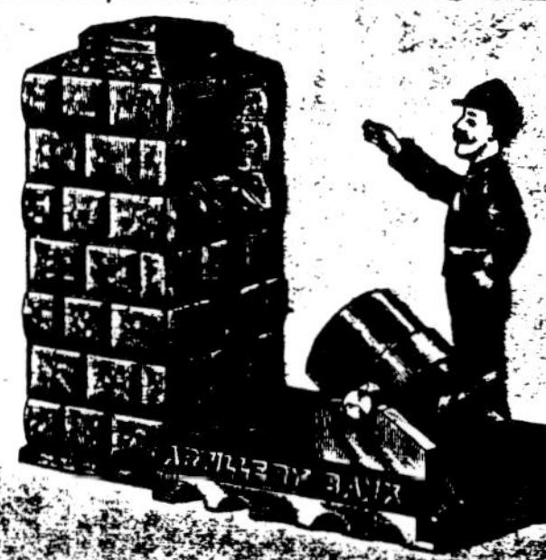

Prices Subject to Change Without Notice.

SECURITY SAFE DEPOSIT.

With Bronzed Combination Lock and Money Guard. No. 101. Size, 4½ in. high, 3¼ wide, 2¼ deep.

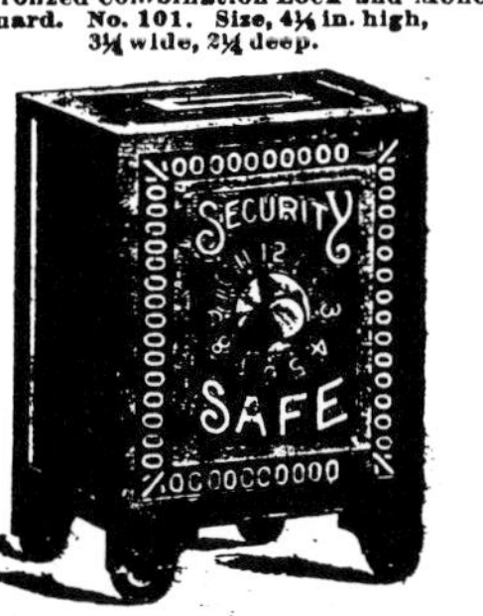

344. An altogether new safe in style and mode of construction. It has a simple but very effective combination lock with two changes. Finished in black japan relieved with bronze, with door in bright colors. Packed one-half dozen in a box.

PRICE 2 00 PER DOZEN.

"Safe Deposit" Toy Bank.

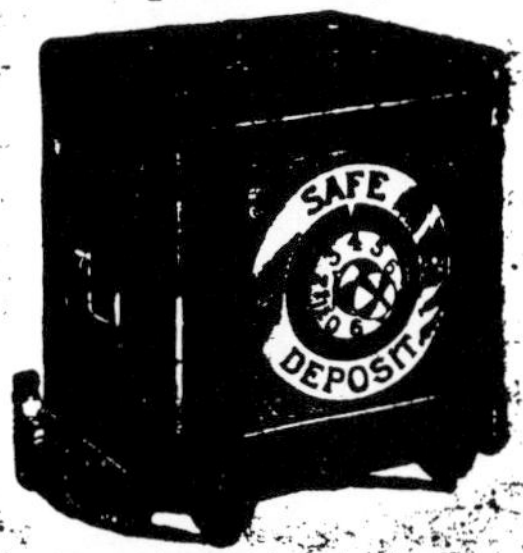

345. Instructive and secure. The coins cannot in any way be shaken out, as there is a "Burglar Proof" Automatic Stop covering the slot. Has silver plated combination lock and is otherwise handsomely finished in black, gilt and silver and ornamented in fancy colors. It is sure to please the little ones and keep their savings, and it cannot be opened except by the person knowing the combination. Packed 1 in a package.

PRICE, 6 00 PER DOZEN.

ORGAN BANK. Medium Size.

346. 6½ inches high, 4 wide and 3 deep. A fine half dollar bank. Packed one in a package.

PRICE, 4 00 PER DOZEN.

Iron Banks with Lock and Key.

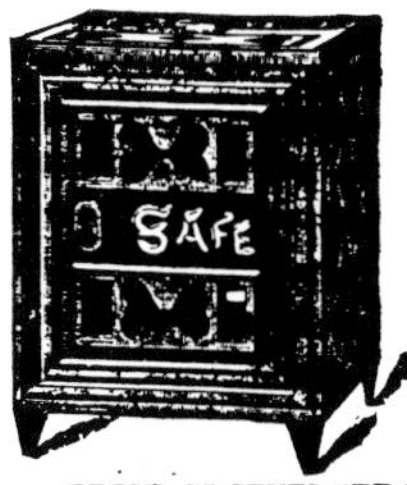

347. No. 8.

Height 3¼ in.;

width, 2½ in.;

depth, 2¼ in.

Packed ½ dozen in a package.

PRICE, 75 CENTS PER DOZEN.

Best 10c. Lock & Key Bank on the Market.

348. No. 10 Safe. Height, 3½ in; width, 2½ in. Painted in colors. Packed ¼ doz. in a package.

PRICE, 1 25 PER DOZEN.

349. No. 15 Safe. Height, 4 in.; width, 3 in. Painted in colors. Packed ¼ dozen in a package.

PRICE, 2 00 PER DOZEN.

ORGAN BANK.

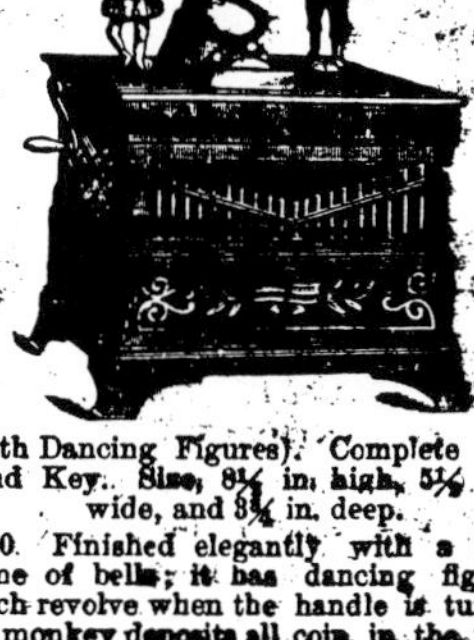

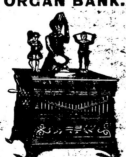

(With Dancing Figures). Complete Lock and Key. Size, 8½ in. high, 5½ in. wide, and 3¾ in. deep.

350. Finished elegantly with a large chime of bells; it has dancing figures, which revolve when the handle is turned. The monkey deposits all coin in the vault and politely raises his hat. Packed each in a wooden box.

PRICE, 8 50 PER DOZEN.

ORGAN BANK. Small.

A new size to retail at 25c.

351. One of the best quarter banks made. Same as the 50c. and 1 00 size, only smaller. Packed 6 in a package.

PRICE, 2 00 PER DOZEN.

URN SAVINGS BANK,

Brass and White Metal,

Genuine Silver Plated.

Handsome! Cheap! Useful!

PRICE, 2 00 PER DOZEN.

352.

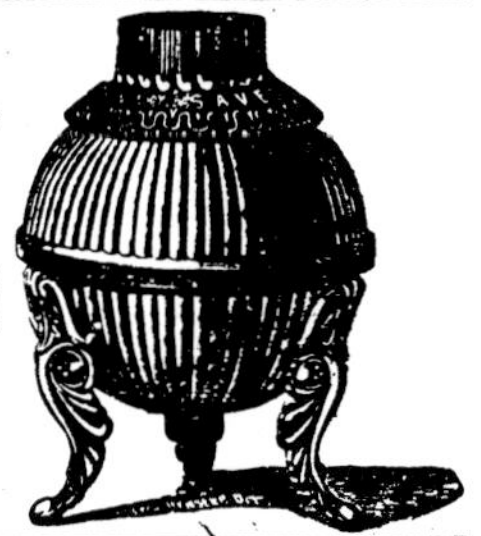

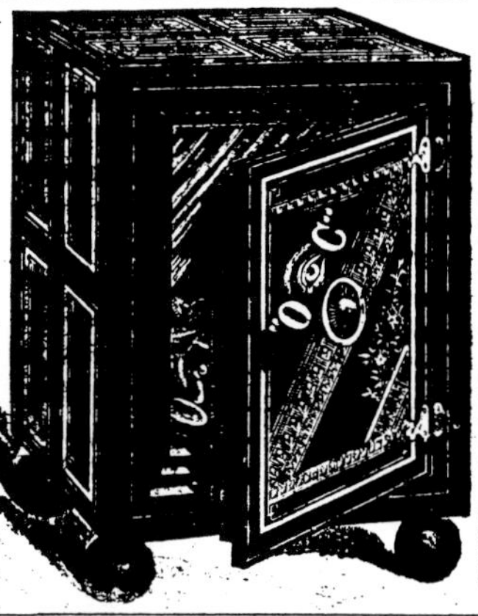

The "OIC" Safe Bank.

353. A new extra large safe, made of wood, very neatly and strongly put together and covered with a fine lithograph. Inside the door is placed a light of glass so that when the safe door is open the coins can be seen through the glass, but they cannot be handled. This is a very attractive feature. The safe can be opened from the back by removing a screw which is carefully concealed but which can be found easily by reading the directions accompanying each safe. The largest, best made, best looking, and attractive toy safe ever made at anything like so low a price. The coin is in sight but out of reach as the light of glass separates the money from the depositor or looker on.

Size 5½x5½x7 inches. The largest toy safe ever offered at so low a price. The woodwork is first-class. The lithographing very fine in black and red, brass hinge and knob.

PRICE, 1 50 PER DOZEN.

TRUNK REGISTERING SAVINGS BANK.

354. This bank indicates, at all times, exact amount contained. Coins cannot be deposited without being accurately registered, and money cannot be removed until the required amount has been deposited for which combination is set.

The first coin locks the door, which cannot be locked in any other manner, and cannot be opened until full amount has been deposited, when it will open automatically.

Another very important point of this bank over all others, is that it cannot be tampered with in any way without being detected by the figures.

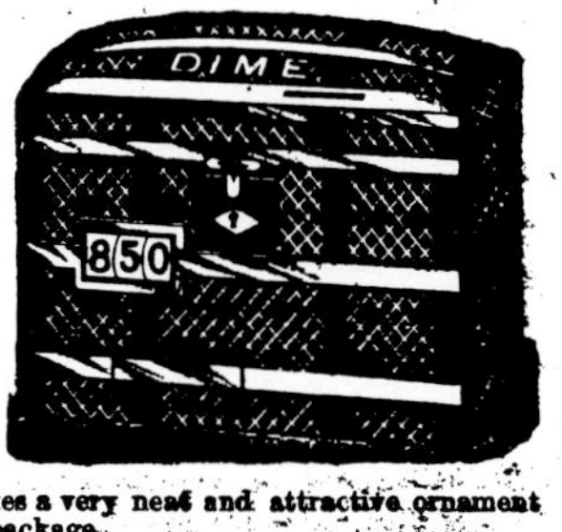

This bank is strongly made of cast iron in the above design, and handsomely nickel plated, which in addition to its usefulness, makes a very neat and attractive ornament for the mantel or dressing case. Packed 1 in a package.

To take only 10c. pieces. Each bank is made to register and open when 100 10c. coins have been deposited—$10.00 worth. Price, 8 00 per dozen.

Samples sent by express on receipt of 75c., by Selchow & Righter, New York, purchaser pay express charges. *THIS BANK IS WARRANTED NOT TO GET OUT OF ORDER.*

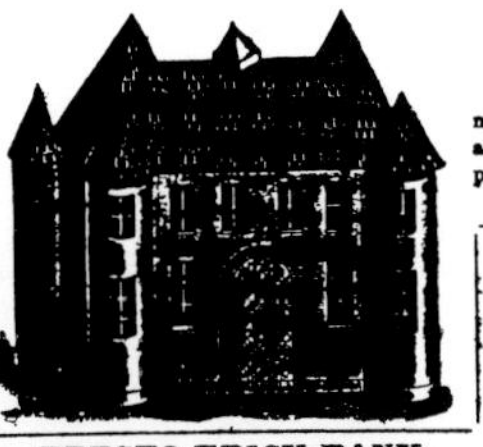

Villa Bank.

Size, 5 inches high, 5 wide, 2¾ deep.

355. This bank is in the style of a modern country villa and is very large and showy for the price. Handsomely painted. Packed ½ dozen in a box.

Price per dozen, 2 00.

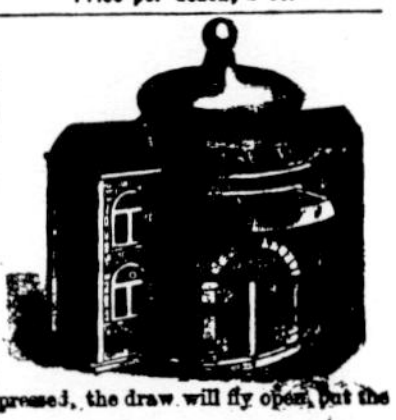

PRESTO TRICK BANK:

With Lock and Key Opening.

Size, 4½ inches high, 4 wide, 2½ deep.

356. This bank contains the novel feature of a trick drawer. Press down the button over the front door, and the drawer will fly open. Put the coin in and close it. When the button is again pressed, the draw will fly open, but the coin will have mysteriously disappeared.

The money can be removed from the bottom of the bank by means of a lock and key. Handsomely decorated, and packed one-half dozen in box.

Price per dozen, 2 00.

NO. D. **NO. F.**

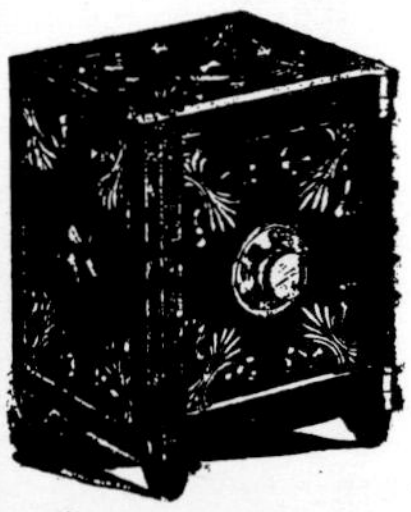

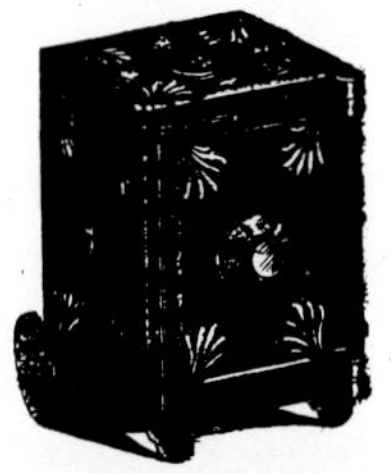

357. Nickel Plated, size, 5½ x 4 x 3¾. Price, 4.00 per dozen.

358. Nickel Plated, size, 4½ x 3½ x 2¾. Price, 2.00 per dozen.

These two Banks are Nickel Plated and are the very best value of any 25 or 50 cent Banks in the market.

Prices Subject to Change Without Notice.

THE "READY CHANGE" HOLDER.

359. The latest and most useful Coin Holder ever offered to the public. Sells at sight. Just the coin you want. Just when you want it.

The "Ready Change" Holder can be carried in the vest pocket, holding 1, 5, 10 and 25c. coins to the amount of $3.00, thus keeping your change compact and always at hand. It is simple and durable, having no complicated mechanism to get out of order, and is handsomely nickel plated.

By the use of the "Ready Change" Holder you avoid inconvenience, delay and possible error in making change. No more small coin lost. No more torn pocketbooks. Packed 1 dozen in a package.

Price, 75c. per dozen.

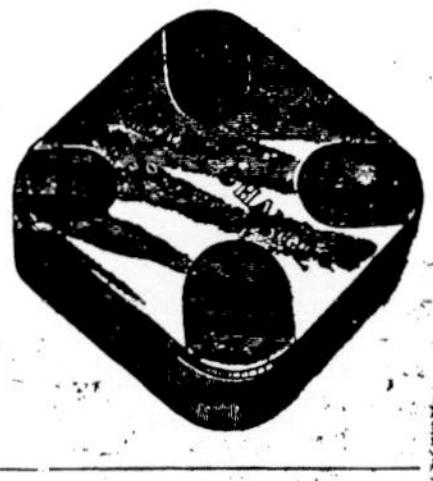

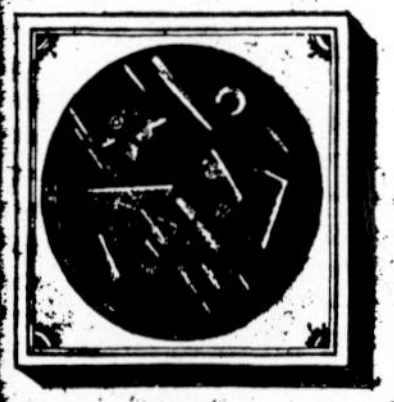

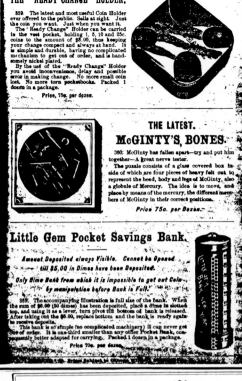

THE LATEST.

McGINTY'S BONES.

360. McGinty has fallen apart—try and put him together—A great nerve tester.

The puzzle consists of a glass covered box inside of which are four pieces of heavy felt cut to represent the head, body and legs of McGinty, also a globule of Mercury. The idea is to move, and place by means of the mercury, the different members of McGinty in their correct positions.

Price 75c. per Dozen.

Little Gem Pocket Savings Bank.

Amount Deposited always Visible. Cannot be Opened till $5.00 in Dimes have been Deposited.

Only Dime Bank from which it is impossible to get out Coin by manipulation before Bank is Full.

361. The accompanying illustration is full size of the bank. When the sum of $5.00 (50 dimes) has been deposited, place a dime in slotted top, and using it as a lever, turn pivot till bottom of bank is released. After taking out the $5.00, replace bottom and the bank is ready again to receive deposits.

This bank is so simple (no complicated machinery) it can never get out of order. It is one-third smaller than any other Pocket Bank, consequently better adapted for carrying. Packed 1 dozen in a package.

Price 70c. per dozen.

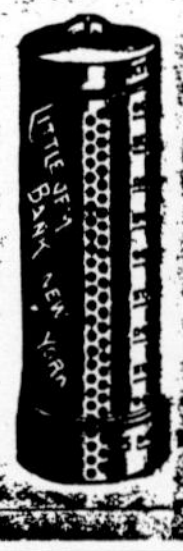

Prices Subject to Change Without Notice.

Tin Toys—*Continued.*

DUST PANS.

No.		Dozen.
11	Nicely painted, 5½ in. long, 3¾ in. wide, 1 dz. in pack,	30
12	" " 8 " 6½ " 1 " "	56
13	" " 10 " 7¼ " 1 " "	75

TIN BANKS.

No.		Dozen.
14	Rustic, small size, 2½ in. high, 1 doz. in pack, -	62
15	" large " 3½ " 1 " " -	80

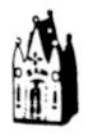

No.		Dozen.
16	Gothic, small size, 3 in. high, 1 doz. in pack, -	38
17	" large " 4 " 1 " " -	62

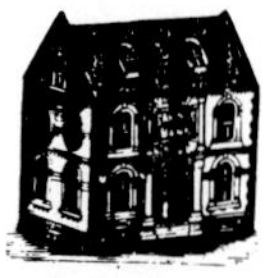

No.		Dozen.
18	House, small, fancy, 2¾ in. high, 1 doz. in pack, -	31
19	" medium, " 2¾ " 1 " " -	50
20	" " Japanned 3½ " 1 " " -	45
21	" large " 4¼ " 1 " " -	65
22	Patent " " 5 " 1 " " -	62½
23	Square, " " 4 " 1 " " -	70
23a	Drum, " " 2¾ " 1 " " -	60
23b	Clock, with movable hands, 4½ in. high, 1 doz. in pack,	80
23c	Barrel, Bronzed, 4½ " 1 " "	80

Iron Toys--*Continued.*

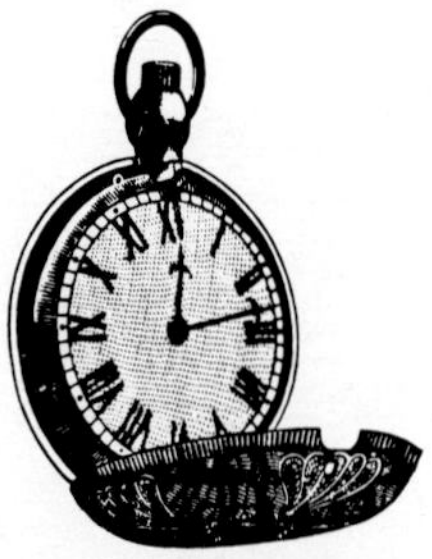

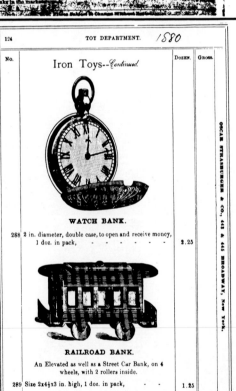

WATCH BANK.

No.		Dozen.	Gross.
288	2 in. diameter, double case, to open and receive money, 1 doz. in pack, - - - - - -	2.25	

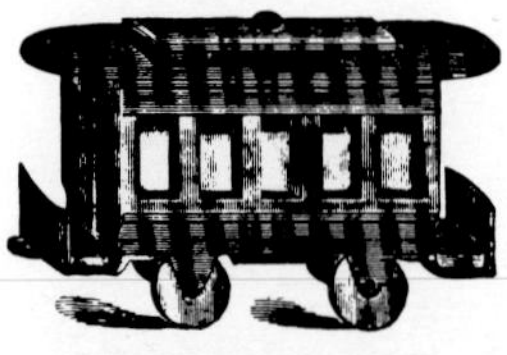

RAILROAD BANK.

An Elevated as well as a Street Car Bank, on 4 wheels, with 2 rollers inside.

No.		Dozen.	Gross.
289	Size 2x4½x3 in. high, 1 doz. in pack, - -	1.25	

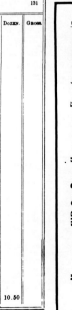

Tin Toys—*Continued*

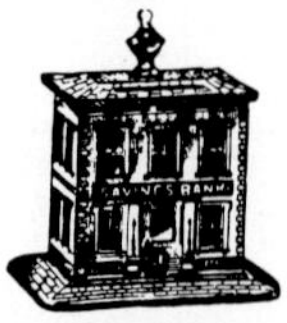

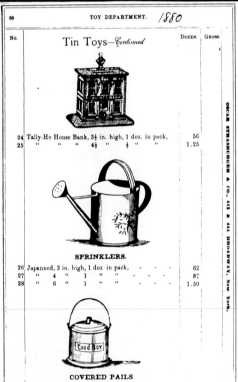

No.		Dozen.	Gross.
24	Tally-Ho House Bank, 3½ in. high, 1 doz. in pack,	56	
25	" " " 4½ " ½ "	1.25	

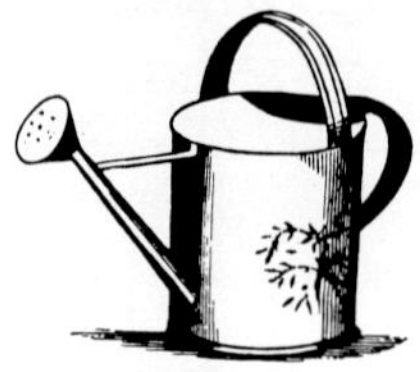

SPRINKLERS.

No.		Dozen.	Gross.
26	Japanned, 3 in. high, 1 doz in pack, - - -	62	
27	" 4 " 1 " " - - -	87	
28	" 6 " 1 " " - - -	1.50	

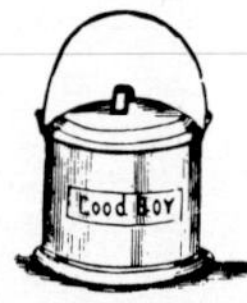

COVERED PAILS.

Iron Toys—*Continued.*

GEM BANK.

A dog, which receives the money, and deposits it in the bank.

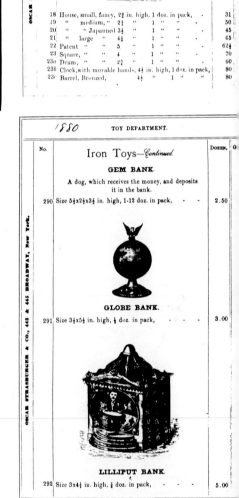

No.		Dozen.
290	Size 5½x2½x3¼ in. high, 1-12 doz. in pack, - -	2.50

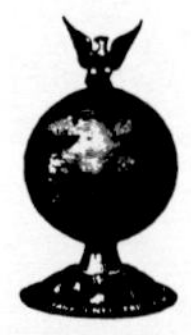

GLOBE BANK.

No.		Dozen.
291	Size 3½x5½ in. high, ½ doz. in pack, - - -	3.00

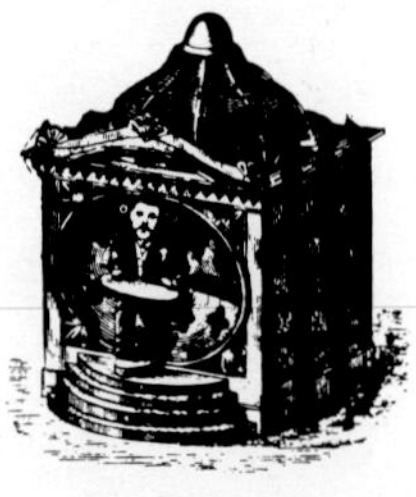

LILLIPUT BANK.

No.		Dozen.
292	Size 3x4½ in. high, ½ doz. in pack, - - -	5.00

Iron Toys—*Continued.*

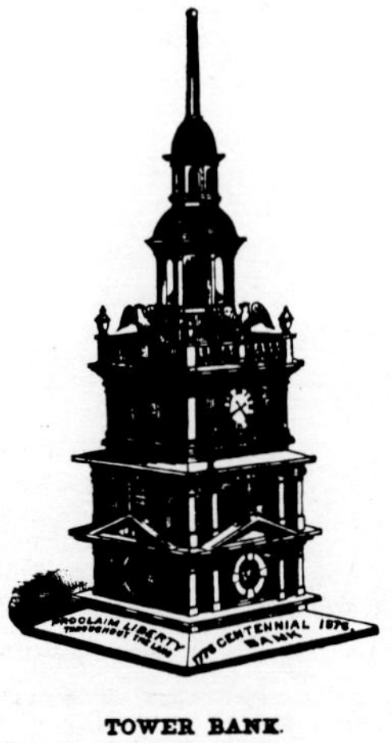

TOWER BANK.

No.		Dozen.	Gross.
300	Size 6¼x9 in. high, 1-12 doz. in pack, -	10.50	

1913

Banks, Etc., and Christmas Tree Decorations.

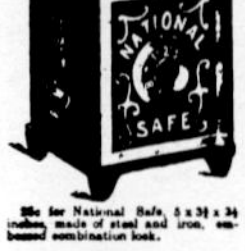

25c for National Safe, 5 x 3½ x 3½ inches, made of steel and iron, embossed combination lock.

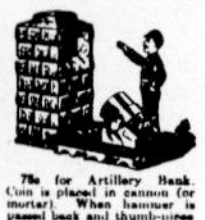

75c for Artillery Bank. Coin is placed in cannon (or mortar). When hammer is passed back and thumb-piece pressed upon, coin is fired into fort or tower. So arranged that a paper cap may be used.

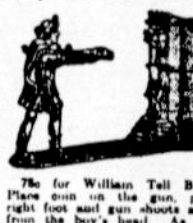

75c for William Tell Bank. Place coin on the gun, press right foot and gun shoots apple from the boy's head. As coin enters castle it strikes a gong bell. So arranged that a paper cap may be fired at same time.

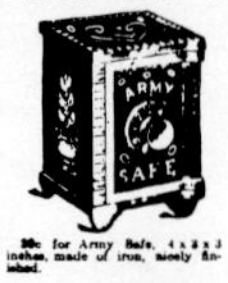

20c for Army Safe, 4 x 3 x 3 inches, made of iron, nicely finished.

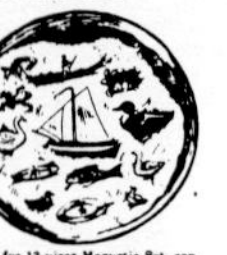

98c for 13-piece Magnetic Set, consisting of ducks, fish and boats. Others from 25c to $6.00.

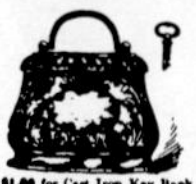

$1.00 for Cast Iron Key Bank, new shape, money can not be taken out without unlocking.

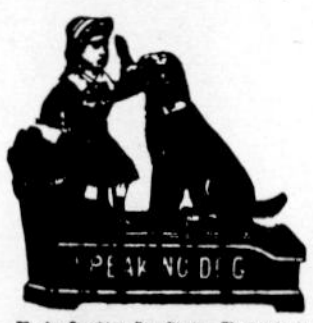

75c for Speaking Dog Bank. Place coin in plate held by girl. Thumb-piece is pressed upon, when girl's arm moves quickly and deposits coin through a trap-door in bench. At same time dog opens and closes his mouth as if "speaking," also wags his tail.

40c for Owl Bank, glass eyes, nicely ornamented in natural colors. Place coin on top of branch and press thump-piece at back, when head of owl turns and coin is deposited below, after which head moves back to its former position.

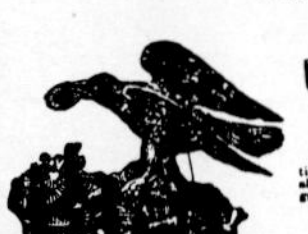

75c for the Eagle Bank. Place a coin in the eagle's beak, press the lever and the eaglets rise from the nest, actually crying for food. As the eagle bends forward to feed them, the coin falls into the nest.

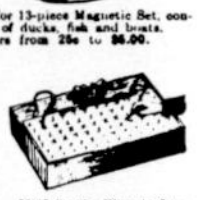

$2.45 for the Electric Questioner, guaranteed to answer all questions correctly, greatest novelty of the age.

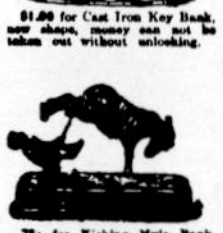

75c for Kicking Mule Bank. A slight touch on the knob at base causes mule to turn around and kick boy over, throwing coin from bench into receptacle below.

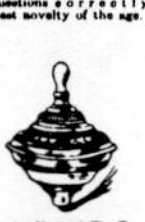

5c for Musical Tin Top, 5 inches high.
10c for Musical Tin Top, 7 inches high.
25c for Musical Tin Top, 8 ins. high, changes tunes. Others at 40c and 60c.

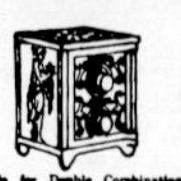

40c for Double Combination Bank, antique oxidized finish; size, 6 x 4½ x 4½ inches.

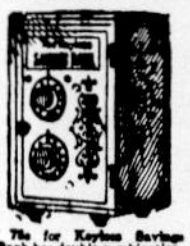

75c for Keyless Savings Bank, has double combination, very intricate, combination can be changed, made of iron, oxidized finish.

10c for Daisy Iron Bank, with lock and key, nicely nickeled.

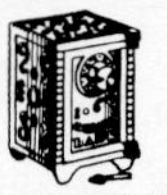

25c for American Bank, nicely nickeled and ornamented, with lock and key.

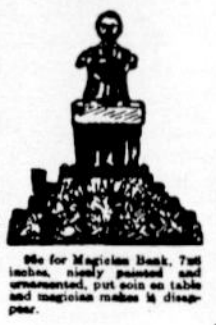

95c for Magician Bank, 7½ inches, nicely painted and ornamented, put coin on table and magician makes it disappear.

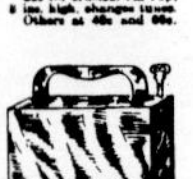

25c for New Metal Key Bank, modeled after design of those used by the banking houses of the United States.

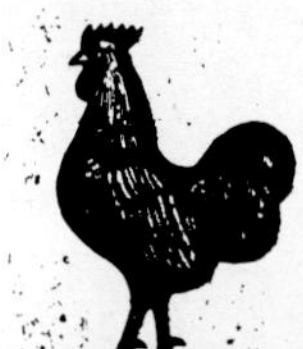

ROOSTER IRON TOY BANK, finished in gold bronze, 12 inches high. Price..10c

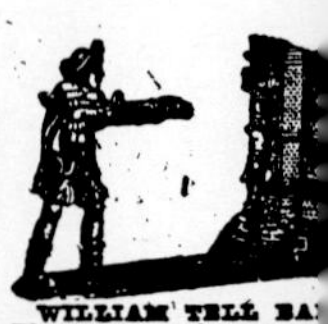

WILLIAM TELL BA… Place coin on the gun, p… right foot and gun sh… apple from boy's head. … coin enters castle it str… a gong. So arranged … a paper cap may be fire… the same time. Price..$…

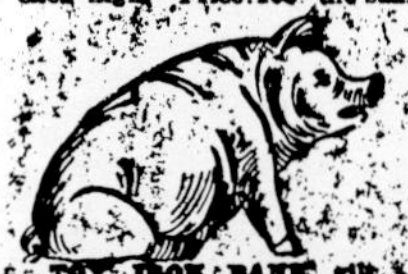

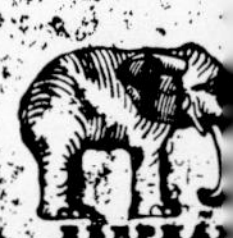

TOY IRON BANK, gilt, colored pig. Price....10c.

ELEPHA… BANK, painted g…

Black St. Bernard Dog. Price … Price …10c. Black Cat … Mary's Lamb, white and red ribbon arou… … Price …

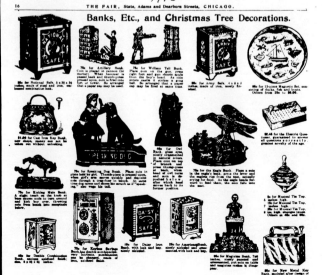

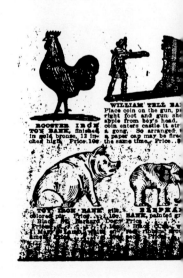

THE FAIR STORE

CHRISTMAS TREE ORNAMENTS OF ALL KINDS.

We carry the most complete line of all styles and kinds of imported Tree Ornaments. Prices Positively the Lowest.

CHILDREN'S SAVINGS BANKS.

Made from the best material, Strong, Reliable and rather difficult to extract the Money.

No. 5.

CASH REGISTER BANK.

THE LATEST OF OUR ALWAYS POPULAR TOY BANKS.

By pressing the Button at the top of the Safe, any amount from One Cent to Ten Dollars may be Registered.

This Bank has a Brass Front; the Dial is in bright colors, and the appearance of the Bank is very attractive.

Each Bank in a Wood Box with sliding cover.

Price each, $1.00.

No. 285. Height, 6¼ in. Width, 5½ in. Depth, 5½ in.
Price, ... $1.00

ILLUSTRATED CATALOGUE. 47

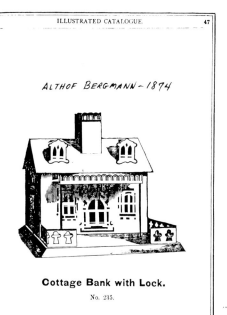

ALTHOF BERGMANN – 1874

Cottage Bank with Lock.
No. 235.

---

48 ILLUSTRATED CATALOGUE.

House Bank, Fancy.
No. 231.

Cottage Bank with Lock.
No. 236.

50 ILLUSTRATED CATALOGUE.

House Bank, Plain.
No. 229, Small.
" 230, Medium.
" 232, Large.
" 233, Large cottage shape.

Gothic Bank.
No. 228, Small.
" 227, Large.

ILLUSTRATED CATALOGUE. 49

Cottage Bank with Lock.
No. 237.

Safe-Pattern Bank with Padlock and Key.
No. 234.

II

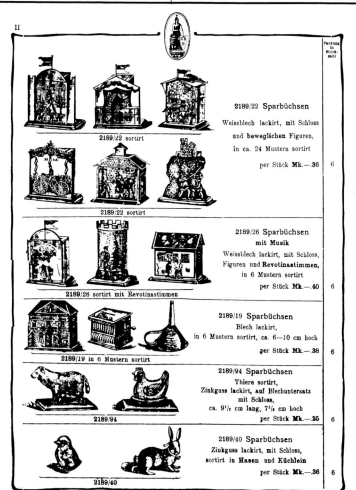

	Packung in Stückzahl
2189/22 Sparbüchsen Weissblech lackirt, mit Schloss und beweglichen Figuren, in ca. 24 Mustern sortirt per Stück Mk. —.36	6
2189/22 sortirt	
2189/26 Sparbüchsen mit Musik Weissblech lackirt, mit Schloss, Figuren und Revotinastimmen, in 6 Mustern sortirt per Stück Mk. —.40	6
2189/26 sortirt mit Revotinastimmen	
2189/19 Sparbüchsen Blech lackirt, in 6 Mustern sortirt, ca. 6—10 cm hoch per Stück Mk. —.38	6
2189/19 in 6 Mustern sortirt	
2189/94 Sparbüchsen Thiere sortirt, Zinkguss lackirt, auf Blechuntersatz mit Schloss, ca. 9½ cm lang, 7½ cm hoch per Stück Mk. —.25	6
2189/94	
2189/40 Sparbüchsen Zinkguss lackirt, mit Schloss, sortirt in Hasen und Küchlein per Stück Mk. —.36	6
2189/40	

Unter der in der letzten Rubrik angegebenen Packungsweise wird kein Artikel abgegeben.

I

	Packung in Stückzahl
Sparbüchsen Weissblech, decorirt (nicht zum Oeffnen) 2189/33 5½ cm hoch, 5½ cm Dchm. p. St. Mk. —.06½	12
Weissblech decorirt, mit Schloss 2189/14 6 cm hoch, 5 cm Dchm. p. St. Mk. —.08½	12
Sparbüchsen Weissblech, lackirt, mit Vorleger (Trommelform) 2189/7 4 cm hoch, 4 cm Dchm. p. St. Mk. —.07	12
/8 4½ " 4½ " " " " —.12	12
/9 5 " 5 " " " " —.15	12
Weissblech, lackirt, mit Schloss 2189/30 6 cm hoch, 6 cm Dchm. p. St. Mk. —.23	6
/27 7½ " 7½ " " " " —.30	6
2189/35 Sparbüchsen (Trommelform) Weissblech, ff. lackirt, mit gutem Schloss, 7 cm Dchm. 6½ cm hoch, . . p. St. Mk. —.38	6
Sparbüchsen Weissblech mit gutem Schloss 2189/105 blank, gerade Form, 9 cm hoch, p.St.Mk.—.35	6
/46 f.lackirt, " 9 " " " —.38	6
/106 blank, konische " 9 " " " —.32	6
/107 f.lackirt, " 9 " " " —.45	6
Sparbüchsen Blech bedruckt, mit Schloss 2189/41 Schweizerhaus, 6 cm lang, 5 cm hoch, p. St. Mk. —.08½	12
/31 Haus mit Hänsel und Gretel, 6 cm lang, 5½ cm hoch, p. St. Mk. —.08½	12
Sparbüchsen Blech bedruckt, mit Schloss 2189/47 Kirche, 6 cm lang, 8½ cm hoch, p.St.Mk. —.08½	12
Weissblech, fein lackirt, mit Schloss 2189/39 7 cm lang, 5½ cm hoch, p. St. Mk. —.25	6

Unter der in der letzten Rubrik angegebenen Packungsweise wird kein Artikel abgegeben. 1901. D 31 V

57

72/38 Starenhaus
fein lackiert, mit gutem Schloss
8½ cm hoch, per Stück Mk. —.40 | Pckg 6

72/35 Koffer
lackiert, mit Schloss
8 cm lang, 5 cm breit, per Stück Mk. —.65 | 5

72/90 Sparbüchsen, Weissblech
fein lackiert, mit gutem Schloss, in ca. 15 Mustern sortiert, 7—15 cm hoch, per Stück Mk. —.70 | 3

72/56 Geldsack
Zinnguss bronciert, 9 cm hoch, per Stück Mk. —.70 | 3

72/87 Reisekoffer
Zinnguss lackiert, 9½ cm lang, per Stück Mk. —.42 | 6

72/58 Max und Moritz
Zinnguss lackiert, 5 cm hoch, per Stück Mk. —.25 | 6

Sparbüchsen, vernickelt, mit gutem Schloss
73/84 Bierkrug, 9½ cm hoch, per Stück Mk. —.38 | 6
73/85 Kirche, 13 cm hoch, per Stück Mk. —.42 | 6

72/34 Portemonnaie
Blech, fein lackiert, mit gutem Schloss und vernickeltem Bügel, 8½ cm lang, 7 cm hoch, per Stück Mk. —.45 | 6

72/42 Badekarren
Blech, fein lackiert, mit gutem Schloss, 12 cm lang, 10½ cm breit, per Stück Mk. —.75 | 3

72/91 Haus
altdeutsch, mit gutem Schloss, 16½ cm hoch, per Stück Mk. —.80 | 3

72/46 Gasofen
Blech, fein lackiert, mit poliertem Kupferreflektor und gutem Schloss, 11 cm hoch, 7 cm breit, per Stück Mk. 1.25 | 2

72/28 Weissblech, lackiert, mit Schloss, 9½ cm lang, 7½ cm hoch, per Stück Mk. —.38 | 6
72/29 Weissblech, lackiert, mit Schloss, 10½ cm lang, 16 cm hoch, per Stück Mk. —.48 | 6
72/31 Weissblech, lackiert, mit Schloss, 11 cm lang, 9½ cm hoch, per Stück Mk. —.65 | 3
72/37 Weissblech f. lackiert, mit Schloss, 11 cm lang, 14 cm hoch, per Stück Mk. —.72 | 3

Sparbüchsen
Weissblech, mit gutem Schloss
71/24 blank, gerade, 9 cm hoch, p. Stück Mk. —.38 | 6
72/24 lackiert, 9 » » » » —.42 | 6
73/25 vernickelt, 9 » » » » —.65 | 6
71/26 blank, konisch, 9 » » » » —.38 | 6
72/26 lackiert, 9 » » » » —.50 | 4

72/45 Telephon mit Glocke
lackiert mit Schloss, 14 cm hoch, per Stück Mk. —.90 | 2

71/55 „Spar"-Kochherd
mit gutem Schloss, 10 cm hoch, 7½ cm lang, 6½ cm breit, per Stück Mk. —.55 | 4

72/41 Weissblech, lackiert, mit Schloss, 12 cm lang, 9 cm hoch, per Stück Mk. —.70 | 3
72/36 Weissblech, lackiert, mit Schloss, 9 cm breit, 16 cm hoch, per Stück Mk. —.70 | 3
72/43 Bratwurstglöcklein zu Nürnberg, Weissblech, f. lackiert, mit Schloss, 11 cm lang, 9 cm hoch, per Stück Mk. —.72 | 3
72/44 Weissblech, lackiert, mit Schloss, 8 cm Durchmesser, 14 cm hoch, per Stück Mk. —.72 | 3

Neben dem Preis ist die Packungsweise nach Stückzahl bezeichnet, unter welcher kein Artikel abgegeben wird.

Neben dem Preis ist die Packungsweise nach Stückzahl bezeichnet, unter welcher kein Artikel abgegeben wird.
1908 D 35*

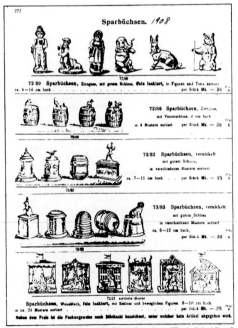

Sparbüchsen. 1908

72/89 Sparbüchsen, Zinnguss, mit gutem Schloss, fein lackiert, in Figuren und Tiere sortiert, ca. 5—10 cm hoch, per Stück Mk. —.38

72/86 Sparbüchsen, Zinnguss, mit Vexierschloss, 6 cm hoch, in 4 Mustern sortiert, per Stück Mk. —.38

73/82 Sparbüchsen, vernickelt, mit gutem Schloss, in verschiedenen Mustern sortiert, ca. 7—11 cm hoch, per Stück Mk. —.25

73/83 Sparbüchsen, vernickelt, mit gutem Schloss, in verschiedenen Mustern sortiert, ca. 8—12 cm hoch, per Stück Mk. —.38

72/21 sortierte Muster
Sparbüchsen, Weissblech, fein lackiert, mit Schloss und beweglichen Figuren, 8—10 cm hoch, in ca. 24 Mustern sortiert, per Stück Mk. —.38

Neben dem Preis ist die Packungsweise nach Stückzahl bezeichnet, unter welcher kein Artikel abgegeben wird.

14 | 1908 catalog page found in the German Patent Office by Gerhard Riegraf

Home Budget Bank

A convenient method of budgeting the income. Size, 17x6½x13½ inches. Six removable compartments which may be labeled with any desired titles. Red, blue and green baked enamel colors. Complete with key and card with 48 printed titles.
1-3983....Per doz. 16.00

Andy Panda Bank

Andy's sly smile and mischievous eyes make him an amusing novelty for a child's room. Made of wood pulp composition with a slot for coins in the back of head. Comes in black and white, blue and white, and yellow and white. Height, 5 inches.
1-3984—1 doz. in box.
N.B.—Per doz. 1.68

Copy of a Wholesale-Catalog printed 1939 (Germany)

Nr. 453a Dtz. —.75
Nr. 667 Dtz. 1.30
Nr. 667a Dtz. 1.75
Nr. 452 Dtz. —.55
Nr. 454 Dtz. 2.20
Nr. 453 Dtz. —.50
Nr. 669 Dtz. 3.95
Nr. 819 Dtz. 3.—
Nr. 668 Dtz. 2.—

Copy of a Wholesale-Catalog printed in 1939 (Germany)

| Nr. 456 | Dtz. —.60 | Nr. 457 | Dtz. 1.35 | Nr. 458 | Dtz. 1.80 | Nr. 456a | Dtz. —.88 |

| Nr. 458b | Dtz. 3.25 | Nr. 458a | Dtz. 2.40 | Nr. 458/1 | Dtz. 4.10 |

| Nr. 455 | Dtz. 3.75 | Nr. 455a | Dtz. 4.10 |

1939

BANKS

WALT DISNEY'S CHARACTER BANKS

Made of a special composition material finished in authentic colors. These highly publicized and ever-popular characters in the form of toy banks will increase your sales and profits. The complete line will take coins up to 50c size. Each bank individually boxed, complete with lock and key.

No. 259 — DONALD DUCK BANK. Extreme height 5½ inches. Per doz. $4.00

No. 260 — DOPEY BANK. Extreme height 7½ inches. Per doz. $4.00

No. 261 — MICKEY MOUSE BANK. Extreme height 6 inches. Per doz. $4.00

No. 262 — JIMMINY CRICKET BANK. Extreme height 6 inches. Per doz. $4.00

No. 263 — WORLD BANK. Diameter 4 inches, height 5 inches. Made of heavy steel appropriately lithographed. Fitted sheet steel base. Complete with key. Per doz. $1.50

No. 280 — BUDDY "L" THRIFTY ANIMAL BANK. Length 3¾ inches, height 3½ inches. Made of heavy sheet steel lithographed in four bright colors. A real incentive to child and interesting to adults to watch the oak tree fill with dimes. Packed ½ dozen in a carton. Per doz. $4.00

No. 283 — CASH BOX BANK. Length 4 inches, height 2½ inches, depth 3 inches. Made of sheet steel in black crackle finish. Steel dials trimmed in gold bronze. Fitted with nickel plated carrying handle. Each bank tagged with combination numbers. Packed one dozen in a box. Per doz. $4.00

No. 287 — HOME BUDGET BANK. Size 5x6 inches. Made of heavy sheet steel finished in glossy baked enamels. Fitted with metal corners. Six compartments, each of which may be filled separately. Packed one in a carton complete with key. Per doz. $16.00

No. 285 — TELEPHONE BANK. Size 10x2x5½x2½ inches. This old type pay station telephone is in itself a toy and also a practical savings bank. Made of heavy sheet steel finished in black or red with nickel trim. Bell rings when coins are deposited, also when receiver is removed. Opened at top by screw attachment. Packed one in a box. Per doz. $16.00

PRICES SUBJECT TO CHANGE WITHOUT NOTICE

1925

Banks

Register Banks

Prices subject to change without notice

Banks, Cash Registers and Register Banks

PRICES SUBJECT TO CHANGE WITHOUT NOTICE

Banks

PRICES SUBJECT TO CHANGE WITHOUT NOTICE

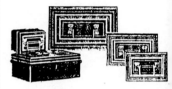

"The Little Millionaire"

Combination Savings Bank

Your First Step on the Road to Independence

No Keys to Lose. Holds Ten Dollars in Silver.

"The Little Millionaire" is a very high grade Savings Bank. There are no keys to lose. There is a special Combination to each Bank, and it is impossible to open the bank unless you know what this Combination is. The bank cannot be picked; there are numerous combinations, no one else can open yours unless they know the particular Combination to your bank. Thus every person in the family may have a Bank with a different Combination and it will be impossible to open the other although made of SOLID Brass, handsomely nickel plated, stands out three inches high, and not quite two inches in diameter. It will hold any amount of coin, with a capacity of about Ten Dollars in silver. Of course it will accommodate the coins of other countries.

No. 2874. "THE LITTLE MILLIONAIRE" Combination Savings Bank. Three for $2.00, or $7.00 per dozen, postpaid to any address **75c**

......10-Cent Trick Money Bank—A neatly made wood box, size 4½x2½, with drawer hollowed out to take coin. When drawer is pushed in the bottom drops down and "deposits" the coin. A smart rap on top or bottom respectively will lock or unlock drawer, to the bewilderment of those not "in it." **78**

......Iron Savings Bank—A great one for a dime. Strongly made of cast iron in attractive shape. Size 2½x4, 6½ inches high, neatly painted and gold trimmed. Every way the best bank for the money we ever sold. 1 doz. in box **84**

......Our "Home" Savings Bank—All iron, finished in Berlin bronze, trimmed and striped in gilt, very handsome and showy. Open windows on sides. Size 3½x2½x4, 6 inches deep. Can be opened without breaking. The largest 25-cent bank ever offered. ½ doz. in box **2 15**

......Loop Frog Bank—A clever conceit well worked out. The coin is placed in a receptacle on the top of hollow tree. When thumb piece is pressed one boy leaps over the other's back and makes the coin disappear by striking the lever in front of tree. All iron, brightly finished. Size 5 inches high, 7½ inches long. Each in wood box **7 80**

......Our Bee Hive Dime Registering Bank—The first dime "deposited" locks it and it cannot be opened till one hundred dimes (or $10.00) are put in, when it opens automatically. Made of iron, nickel plated and fancifully decorated. Each dime is registered and an indicator in front shows amount at any time. Best savings bank imaginable, as it forces economy. Each in box with full directions. **8 85**

......Lighthouse Combination Savings Bank—Sells for a dollar. Representing a lighthouse standing on a craggy rock. 10¾ inches high, 6½ inch base. The house admits of any coin to the size of a quarter, while the tower takes nickels only, registering same to the amount of five dollars, when money can be removed. Until the full amount has been deposited in the tower not a cent can be drawn. Made of iron, finished in nickel, red and bronze. Each in box **8 90**

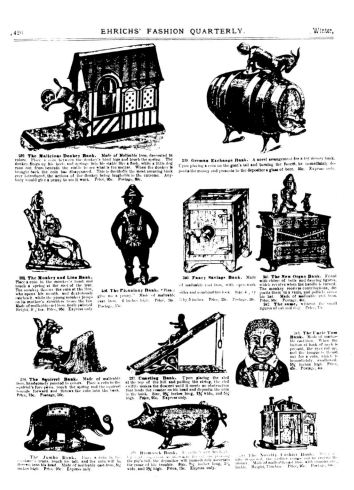

HOW TO USE THE CATALOG

Photographing the Banks

The catalog is the core of the book. The color photographs are organized by subject; that is, character banks, animals, clocks, safes, and so forth, are usually found together. A few exceptions are late acquisitions found near the end of the book. Sometimes we were arbitrary: *Pug Frog* is with the character banks, but *Thrifty Pig* is with the other pigs. Several space heater, or stove banks are in the building bank section because, until recently, most collectors believed them to be aviaries or six-sided buildings. Globes and bells are together because we liked the way they looked together. Although English banks appear throughout the book, many of them are concentrated on two pages.

Our original plan to photograph six rows of banks at a time, reproducing the six-shelf matrix on a single page, would have resulted in the bank images being too small. We compromised by photographing the top three rows, removing those banks and replacing them with the bottom three rows of banks. At times we lowered the sixth shelf to accomodate taller banks. We felt it was important that the camera never be moved, so that the reader would have an accurate feeling for relative bank sizes. How often I've said upon seeing a bank for the first time, "This is smaller than I thought it was!" By comparing a familiar bank to an unfamiliar one on the same page, one can estimate within a quarter of an inch or better the height of the unknown bank.

Variations

Paint and casting variations are included in the book to alert the collector. Most banks came in more than one finish or paint combination. At times, collectors turn down a nice specimen just because it isn't in "The Book," or differs from the manufacturer's catalog description. Sometimes the manufacturers changed the bank's finish over a period of years, offering it in a number of different color combinations. Often, the rarest paint variations are those most recently produced; fewer may have been made, or they were the first to go to the World War II scrap drives. One of the more interesting paint variations is the Arcade *Polar Bear* #716. Apparently to boost sales, Arcade painted its gold bear white during Peary's race to the North Pole.

Casting variations are equally puzzling to collectors. When the original casting proved too difficult to produce, the casting was sometimes simplified, and the difference between the two can be dramatic. A good example is Hubley's *Hall Clock*, numbers 1534 and 1535. It is interesting to note that Hubley continued to

advertise the original clock long after the design had been modified.

The addition of a printed message on a bank is a more common casting variation. (See *Mulligan* #179.) Sometimes, more than one manufacturer produced a bank, resulting in a different size, paint or detailing. (See Arcade's *Rooser* #547 and A.C. Williams' *Rooster* #548.) It is tempting to speculate that one company might have given a bank finer detailing than another, but that kind of speculation can be dangerous. Also, it may be that an early casting of a bank has finer detail than a later casting from a tired pattern.

Building, or architectural bank, variations are the most confusing. As many as four different companies produced the same bank, and they did so in different sizes. We've done our best to sort them out.

Reading the Captions

We gave each bank the manufacturer's name whenever practical to do so. If the producer merely dubbed the item "Toy Bank" or "Building," we supplied a name we thought would be more descriptive and useful. Any material within quotation marks appears on the bank itself.

Symbols and Abbreviations

★	This symbol appears before the name of a bank when we know it has been reproduced. Read *Reproductions*, page 14, before purchasing a specimen of that bank.
CI	*cast iron*
AL	*aluminum*
WM	*white metal*. The term *white metal* includes those banks made of a mixture of metals; names such as spelter, slush, pot metal and metal alloy are often used to describe the various mixtures. the term *lead* is used to describe those banks whose alloys have a heavy lead content. Banks made of this dense and smooth material may have beautiful paint and casting detail.
comp.	Any mixture of materials yielding a medium from which banks are made, other than metal, ceramic, plastic, glass or wood.
TT	*twist trap*
ST	*screw trap*
KLT	*key locked trap*
PT	*pry-out trap*
TL	*trick lock*. Appears to need a key to open, but doesn't.

Measurements

Although we tried to use common sense in measuring the banks accurately, it is a difficult task. Some banks have a single measurement, while others have two or three. Ours don't always agree with those in early toy company catalogs, whose measurements can be deceptive; some appear to be estimates, while others may be the measurement of the wooden sculpture or pattern bank. Due to metal shrinkage, the production bank would be smaller than the advertised bank.

We hoped that accurate measurements would assist anyone doing research on companies that produced seemingly identical banks, but as we went along we realized that, at best, measurements can be used as a guide only.

Manufacturers

The name of the manufacturer appears when we know who made a bank, and a question mark indicates we have made an educated guess. Refer to the Appendix or the section, *Who Made the Banks*, for evidence to support the use of the question mark. Sources we used to identify the banks included books, *The Penny Bank Post*, patent papers, manufacturers' catalogs, trade publications and jobbers' catalogs from the period. For a list of sources, including toy catalogs at our disposal, see the *Bibliography*.

Dating the Banks

Dating some of the banks was easy, because they appeared in a manufacturer's dated catalog, or we found patent papers which gave us a date close to the bank's actual production date. Other banks were harder to date; we found some in crumbling jobber and department store catalogs from the turn of the century. For the many banks we could not positively date, we tried to come as close as possible, using a "c" for *circa*. Other dates are followed by a question mark. It represents our best guess, and relates to factors such as the creation of a comic strip character, the date a building was erected, or the glory years of a movie star.

Scarcity Rating

The scarcity rating appears last, in bold print. (See *Rating the Banks*, page 16. Cast iron banks are rated on a scale of **A** to **F**, with **F** meaning *rare*. Banks made of other materials are rated **1** to **3**, with **3** being the most difficult to find. Banks made after 1945 are marked **M** for *modern* and are not rated.

Using the Appendix

If space on the catalog page permitted, we included some ancillary information. Otherwise, additional factual or historical information on the banks appears in the Appendix, following the catalog. The numbers preceding each entry correspond to the banks' numbers.

Cross References

A cross reference guide to well known books on still banks can be found on page 173. A **V** next to an entry in this section indicates that a bank in our book is a variation of one found in another. The following works are cross-referenced:

1. Duer, Don and Sommer, Bettie, *The Architecture of Cast Iron Penny Banks*, American Limited Editions, 1983.
2. Long, Ernest and Ida, and Pitman, Jane. *Dictionary of Still Banks*, Mokelumne Hill, Cal.: Long's Americana, 1980.
3. Whiting, Hubert B. *Old Iron Still Banks*, Manchester, Vt.: Forward's Color Productions, Inc., 1968.
4. *Collectable Penny Banks*. Photo project of the Still Bank Collectors' Club of America.

A number of banks which were not photographed for our book can be seen in the section on patent papers, page 165, and on the pages of the manufacturers' catalogs. Pictures of banks appearing in these sections have not been cross-referenced in the book.

A 1. ***"Transvaal Money Box"** Cl; 6 3/16 x 4 1/4; John Harper Ltd. England c1885; **E**. $2500-3000

2. **Frederick of Prussia** lead, KLT; 3 13/ x 4; Germany 1912; **3**. $600-900.

3. **Mascot** Hubley US 1905-1915; **D**. $400-600.

9. **Officer** (brass pattern); 5 13/16; Hubley US. $300-400.

10. **Boy with Large Football** Cl; 5 1/8 x 3 1/4; Hubley US 1914; **E**. $1800-2500.

11. **Football Player** Cl; 5 7/8; A.C. Williams US 1910-1931; **C**. $300-500.

12. **Frowning Face** (hanging) Cl; 5 5/8; US; **E**. $800-1400.

13. **"King Midas"** Cl; 4 1/2 x 3 3/8; Hubley US 1930; **E**. $1800-3000.

14. **Billy Bounce** Cl; 4 11/16; Wing US 1900; **C**. $600-1200.

15. **Billy Bounce** Cl; 4 11/16; Hubley US c1906; **C**. $400-700.

16. **Dutch Girl** Cl; 6 1/2; Grey Iron Casting Co.? US; **D**. $400-800.

17. **Dutch Boy** Cl; 6 3/4; Grey Iron Casting Co.? US; **D**. $400-800.

C 18. **Baseball Player** Cl; 5 3/4; A.C. Williams US 1909-1934; **C**. $300-600.

19. **Baseball Player** Cl; 5 3/4; A.C. Williams US 1920s; **D**. $400-700.

20. **Baseball Player** Cl; 5 3/4; A.C. Williams US 1909; **B**.

$200-400.

21. **Baseball Player** (wood carving); A.C. Williams US. $1200-1800.

22. **Baseball Player on Base** lead, KLT; 5 7/8; Campbell Soup Co. premium US 1969; **M**. $50-100.

23. **"Mother Hubbard"** Safe Cl; 4 3/8 x 2 3/8; J.M. Harper US 1907; **E**. $4000-7000.

24. ***Save & Smile Money Box** Cl; 4 1/4 x 4; Sydenham & McOustra or Chamberlain & Hill, England; **C**. $400-600.

25. **Little Red Riding Hood Safe** Cl; 5 1/16 x 2 1/2; J.M. Harper US 1907; **E**. $4000-8000.

26. **Mariner at Wheel** silvered lead, KLT; 4 x 3 1/2; Germanyc 1905; **2**. $100-200.

27. **Sailor (small)** Cl; 5 1/4; Hubley? US; **B**. $250-400.

28. **Sailor (med.)** Cl; 5 1/2; Hubley? US; **C**. $200-400.

29. **Sailor (large)** Cl; 5 5/8; Hubley US 1905-1915; **C**. $250-450.

A 82. **Santa in Chimney** WM; 5"; US; **3.** $200-300.
83. **Two-Faced Black Boy (Negro Toy Bank)** Cl; 4 1/8 x 3 1/8; A.C. Williams US 1901-1919; **B.** $200-300.
84. **Two-Faced Black Boy (Negro Toy Bank)** Cl; 3 1/8 x 2 3/4 A.C. Williams US 1901-1919; **B.** $100-200.
85. *****Golliwog** Cl; 6 3/16; John Harper Ltd. England 1910-1925. **D.** $450-750
86. *****Golliwog** AL; 6"; John Harper Ltd. England; **2.** $100-150.
87. *****Golliwog** (early copy) brass; 5 1/2; England; **C.** $100-150.
88. **Wizard** (hat missing) tin; 5 3/8; England; **3.** $300-400.
89. **"Tired Tim"** tin; 4 3/4; Germany c1912; **2.** $150-300.
90. **"Weary Willie"** tin; 4 3/4; Germany c1912; **2.** $150-300.
91. **Santa (cloth bag)** plastic; 5 3/4; US; **M.** $20-30.
B 92. **Snowman with Broom** AL; 4 5/8; Reynolds Toys US 1981; **M.** $45-70.
93. **Santa Waving** WM; 5 1/2; US; **1.** $40-60.
94. **Santa Candy Container** tin; 2 7/8 x 4 1/4; US; **2.** $100-200.

95. **Santa** WM; 5 1/2; US; **1.** $50-100.
96. **"Copeland" Snowman (Copeland Refrigerators)** AL; 6 1/2 x4 ; US; **3.** $500-1000.
97. **Oriental Santa** silvered lead; 4"; Japan; **2.** $80-150.
98. **Santa with Book** WM, PT, 5 7/8; US; **1.** $50-100.
99. **Santa with Book** WM, PT, 5 7/8; US; **1.** $40-80.
C 100. **Hanging Santa** AL; 6 1/8; Reynolds Toys US 1980; **M.** $45-70.
101. **Standing Santa** AL; 6 1/8; Reynolds Toys US 1982; **M.** $50-100.
102. **Sleeping Santa** WM; 6 1/2; Banthrico US c1950s; **M.** $40-75.
103. **Sleeping Santa** WM; 5 7/8; Banthrico US c1950s; **M.** $30-65.
104. **Santa at Chimney** lead, KLT; 3 3/4 x 4 1/2; Miller Bank Service Co. US 1925; **2.** $350-600.
105. **Santa on Rooftop** WM, KLT; 6 1/4; **1.** $50-100.
106. **Sleeping Santa** chalk; 7"; Banthrico US 1948; **M.** $40-70.

A   107.   ***Transvaal Money Box** Cl; 6 3/16 x 4 1/4; John Harper Ltd England c1885; **D.** $1000-1200.

108.   **Eggman** (caricature of Wm. Howard Taft) Cl; 4 1/8; Arcade US 1910-1913; **E.** $2000-3000.

109.   **Taft-Sherman** Cl; 4"; J.M. Harper US 1908; **D.** $2000-3000.

110.   **Boss Tweed (Tammany Tiger)** Cl; 3 7/8; US c1873; **E.** $3000-4000.

111.   **Uncle Sam on Beehive** Lead and WM, ST; 7 x 4 1/8; US; **3.** $1500-2500.

112.   **Uncle Sam Candy Container** glass; 3 5/8 x 4; US; **3.** $400-700.

113.   **Uncle Sam Bust** pottery; 4 1/2; US c1860; **2.** $40-60.

114.   **George Washington Safe** Cl; 5 7/8; J.M. Harper; US 1903; **D.** $2000-3000.

115.   **Abraham Lincoln Safe** Cl; 5 5/8; J.M. Harper US 1903; **D.** $2000-3000.

B   116.   **Grant Bust** Cl; 5 1/2 x 4 7/8; US 1976; **M.** $40-80.

117.   **Robert E. Lee Bust** WM, KLT; 5 3/8; Banthrico US; **M.** $40-60.

118.   **Washington Bust** silvered lead, KLT; 5 1/4; A.C. Rehberger US c1920s; **1.** $40-60.

119.   **Washington Bust** WM, KLT; 5"; US; **1.** $40-60.

120.   **"Teddy"** Cl; 5 x 3 1/2; A.C. Williams US 1919; **C.** $200-400.

121.   **Washington Bust** WM, KLT; 5 7/8; Preferred Bank Service Co. US c1920s; **1.** $30-50.

122.   **Ben Franklin Bust** lead, KLT; 5 3/16; Preferred Bank Service Co. US c1920s; **1.** $20-40.

123.   **Ben Franklin Bust** WM, KLT; 5 13/16; Preferred Bank Service Co. US c1930s; **1.** $20-40.

C   124.   **"Lindy Bank"** AL, KLT; 6 1/2 x 3 7/8; Grannis & Tolton US; **2.** $75-150.

125.   **Lindberg with Goggles** lead, KLT; 5 7/8; A.C. Rehberger US 1929; **2.** $200-300.

126.   **Washington Bust on Pedestal** WM, KLT; 7 9/16 x 3 1/2 x 2 7/8; US c1920s; **3.** $200-300.

127.   **"Save for Victory"** (Gen. MacArthur) cardboard; 7 x 11; US c1943; **2.** $75-150.

128.   **Lincoln Bust on Pedestal** WM, KLT; 7 1/4; US c1920s; **2.** $150-250.

129.   **Lincoln Bust** lead, KLT; 4 13/16; A.C. Rehberger US c1920s; **1.** $40-60.

130.   **Lincoln Bust** lead, KLT; 5"; A.C. Rehberger US c1920s; **1.** $40-60.

A   131.   **Gen. MacArthur Bust** WM, KLT; 5 7/8; Banthrico US c1940s; **M.** $30-50.

132.   **Gen. MacArthur Bust** WM, KLT; 5 5/8; Banthrico US c1940s; **M.** $30-50.

133.   **Gen. Eisenhower Bust** WM, KLT; 5 1/2; Banthrico US c1940s; **M.** $30-50.

134.   **Eisenhower Bust** WM, KLT; 5 1/8; Banthrico US c1950s; **M.** $20-40.

135.   **"John F. Kennedy" Bust** WM, KLT; 5 1/4; Banthrico US c1960; **M.** $20-40.

136.   **Washington (hollow base)** Cl; 6 3/8; US c1970; **M.** $30-50.

137.   **Washington on Wood Base** Cl; fig., 6 3/8; with base, 7 1/2; US c1973; **M.** $40-60.

138.   **Washington (solid base)** Cl; 6 1/4; US; **C.** $100-200.

139.   **Lincoln Seated** WM, KLT; 6 3/16; Banthrico US c1950s; **M.** $30-50.

B   140.   **Nixon Bust** Cl; 5 5/16; Charlotte Blevins US 1972; **M.** $50-80.

141.   **Edison Bust** WM, KLT; 5 1/8; Banthrico US; **M.** $20-40.

142.   **LaSalle Bust**, WM, KLT; 5 1/8; Banthrico US; **M.** $30-50.

143.   **Beefeater** brass; 4 1/2; England; **M.** $30-60.

144.   **Bust of Man** Cl; 5"; May be modern US; **D.** $150-250.

145.   **F.D. Roosevelt** WM, KLT; 4 7/8; US 1930s; **1.** $40-60.

146.   **"F.D. Roosevelt"** WM, KLT; 5 1/16; US; **1.** $50-80.

147.   **"F.D. Roosevelt"** WM, KLT; 4 5/8; Miller Bank Service Co. US; **1.** $40-60.

148.   **Roosevelt ("New Deal")** Cl; 5"; Kenton US 1933-1936; **C.** $250-500.

C   149.   **Uncle Sam** comp., TT; 6 3/4; US c1940s; **2.** $100-200.

150.   *****Gen. "Pershing"** (bronze electroplate) Cl; 7 3/4 x 3 1/2; Grey Iron Casting Co. US patented **1918**; **B.** $60-120.

151.   ***"Pershing"** (copper finish) Cl; 7 3/4 x 3 1/2; Grey Iron Casting Co. US patented 1918; **B.** $70-120.

152.   **"Von Hindenburg"** lead; 9 1/4 x 5 x 4 7/16; Germany 1915; **3.** $350-550.

153.   **Washington, Tall Bust** Cl; 8 x 3 7/8; Grey Iron Casting Co. US late 1920s; **E.** $1500-2500.

154.   **The Trust Bank** Cl; 7 1/4; J. & E. Stevens Co. US late 1800s; **E.** $2500-5000.

155.   **Gen. MacArthur** comp., TT; 7 1/2; US c1940s; **2.** $75-150.

A 156. **Foreman** Cl; 4 1/2 x 4 1/2; Grey Iron Casting Co. US c1951; **M.** $400-800.
157. **"Mutt & Jeff"** Cl; 4 1/4 x 3 1/2; A.C. Williams US 1912-1 931; **B.** $150-250.
158. **"Saving Sam"** AL; 5 1/4; US; **D.** $400-800.
159. **"Peters Weatherbird"** Cl; 4 1/4 Arcade US; **E.** $2000-3000.
160. **Peters Weatherbird Shoes** cardboard & tin; 2 x 2 1/4; F.L. Rand Co., US; **2.** $60-80.
161. **Harold Lloyd** tin; 5 3/8; Germany c1925; **3.** $1200-1800.
162. **Policeman Safe** Cl; 5 1/4; J.M. Harper US 1907; **F.** $4000-7000.
163. *"**Campbell Kids**" Cl; 3 5/16 x 4 1/8; A.C. Williams US 1910-1920s; **B.** $250-350.
164. ***Mary & Little Lamb** Cl; 4 3/8; US 1901; **D.** $800-1500.
165. **Carpenter Safe** Cl; 4 3/8; J.M. Harper US 1907; **E.** $4000-7000.
B 166. **"Give Me a Penny"** (with screw) Cl; 5 1/2; Hubley US 1902 -1926; **C.** $300-500.
167. **"Give Me a Penny"** (turnpin) Cl; 5 5/8; Wing US c1894; **C.** $300-500.
168. ***Aunt Jemima (Mammy with Spoon)** Cl; 5 7/8; A.C. Williams US 1905-1930s; **B.** $200-400.
169. **Aunt Jemima (Mammy with Spoon)** slot between legs Cl; 5 7/8; US; **C.** $250-450.
170. **Young Negro** Cl; 4 1/2; England; **C.** $250-400.
171. **"Picaninny Money Bank"** Cl; 5 1/8 x 4 7/16; England; **D.** $400-700.

172. **Young Negro** AL; 4 1/2 x 3 1/2; England; **2.** $150-250.
173. **Darkey (Sharecropper)** toes visible on 1 foot Cl; 5 1/2; A.C. Williams US 1901; **B.** $150-300.
174. **Darkey (Sharecropper)** toes visible both feet Cl; 5 1/4; US early 1900s; **C.** $400-600.
175. **Mammy with Basket** WM, KLT; 5 1/4; US; **B.** $200-400.
C 176. ***Mammy with Hands on Hips** Cl; 5 1/4; Hubley US 1914- 1946; **A.** $200-300.
177. ***Mulligan (Policeman)** Cl; 5 3/4; A.C. Williams 1905- 1932; Hubley US 1914; **B.** $200-400.
178. **Mulligan (slot between legs)** Cl; 5 3/4; US; **C.** $300-500.
179. **Mulligan "Hamberger Boys Dept."** Cl; 5 3/4; US; **D.** $500-1000.
180. **Dutch Boy on Barrel** Cl; 5 5/8; Hubley US 1930s; **A.** $150-250.
181. **Dutch Girl Holding Flowers** Cl; 5 1/4; Hubley US 1930s; **A.** $150-250.
182. **Policeman** Cl; 5 1/2; Arcade US 1920s-34; **C.** $350-600.
183. **Dutch Girl Holding Flowers** Cl; KLT; 5 1/4; Hubley US; **B.** $150-250.
184. **Dutch Girl Holding Flowers** (iron trap in base) WM; 5 1/2; US; **1.** $100-200.
185. **Gendarme** AL; 8"; France 1930s; **3.** $200-300.

A 186. **Oriental Boy on Pillow** (conversion) Cl; 5 1/2 x 6 1/4 x 5 1/4; Hubley US c1920s; **B.** $300-400.

187. **Juliet Low Bust** WM, KLT; 5 3/4; US; **2.** $150-300.

188. **Boy Scout "A Scout is Thrifty"** comp., TT; 6 1/4; US; **1.** $50-75.

189. **The Scout Bank Book**; 6 1/2 x 8 1/8; Platt & Monk Co. US 1930; **2.** $50-75.

190. **Cub Scout** comp., TT; 6 1/4; US; **1.** $50-75.

191. **"Shirley" Temple** WM; 6 1/4; M. Yzaguirre, designer 1966 US; **M.** $25-35.

192. **Benten, Goddess of Amiability** (conversion) Cl; 5 9/16; Hubley US; **B.** $150-250.

B 193. **Amish Boy** Cl; 5"; John Wright US 1970; **M.** $20-30.

194. **Amish Girl** Cl; 5"; John Wright US 1970; **M.** $20-30.

195. **Amish Boy on Bale of Straw** Wm, KLT; 4 3/4 x 3 3/8; US; **1.** $75-125.

196. **Mickey Bank** Cl; 5 x 3 3/4; John Wright, Inc. US 1971-73; **M.** $150-250 pr.

197. **"Mickey Mouse Bank"** vinyl and metal; 4 1/4 x 3 1/8; "Zell Prods. Co." US c1930s; **2.** $100-150.

198. **Amish Boy in White Shirt** Cl; 5"; John Wright US 1971; **M.** $20-30.

199. **Amish Girl** AL, PT; 5 1/4; John Wright US 1971; **M.** $20-30.

200. **Amish Boy** AL, PT; 5 1/4; John Wright US 1971; **M.** $20-30.

C 201. ***Mickey Mouse, Hands on Hips** AL; 8 x 5 13/16; France early 1930s; **3.** $400-700.

202. **Mickey Mouse** (moveable head) comp.,; 6 x 3 1/4 x 3 1/8; Crown US c1940; **B.** $150-300.

203. **Mickey Playing Mandolin** WM, KLT; 4 11/16 x 2 3/4 diam., Arthur Shaw & Co. England 1934; **3.** $400-600.

204. **Mickey Mouse Chest** vinyl a nd metal, KLT; 2 13/16; "Zell Products Corp." US c1933; **1.** $100-200.

205. **Charlie McCarthy** WM; 6 1/4; US c1930s; **2.** $150-250.

206. **Charlie McCarthy** (moveable wood jaw) WM; 5 1/2; Vanio US 1938; **1.** $200-300.

207. **Charlie McCarthy** (moveable wood jaw) comp., 5 1/4; Crown US 1930s; **2.** $150-250.

208. **Charlie McCarthy with Monacle** WM; 7 1/2; US 1930s; **2.** $200-300.

209. **Charlie McCarthy** comp., 9 3/8; Crown US 1930s; **2.** $100-200.

A 210. **Clown with Crooked Hat** Cl; 6 3/4 x 2 1/4; US; **E.** $1000-2000.

211. ***Clown** Cl; 6 3/16; A.C. Williams US 1908; **A.** $100-200.

212. **Clown** (brass); 6 1/16 x 2 3/8; US. $75-150.

213. **Clown on Rock** bronze, KLT; 7 3/4; Germany c1850; **E.** $500-800.

214. **Chantecler** Cl; 4 5/8; US c1911; **F.** $5000-10,000.

215. **Two-Faced Indian (Indian Toy Bank)** turn pin Cl; 4 5/16 x 3 3/4; A.C. Williams US 1901-1906; **E.** $2000-4000.

216. **Organ Grinder** (conversion) Cl; 6 3/16 x 2 1/8; Hubley US; **B.** $150-250.

217. ***Andy Gump** Cl; 4 3/8 x 2 7/8; Arcade US 1928; **D.** $1000-2000.

218. **"Andy Gump Thrift Bank"** tin; 4 3/8 x 3; Gen. Thrift Products US 1920s; **3.** $200-300.

219. **"Andy Gump Savings Bank"** lead; 5 3/4 x 5 3/4; Gen. Thrift Products US 1920s; **3.** $300-500.

B 220. **Shawmut Indian** WM, KLT; 6 11/16; Banthrico US c1960-present; **M.** $40-60.

221. **Indian Bust with Full Headdress** lead, KLT; 3 1/2; Germany; **1.** $100-150.

222. **Indian Bust with Headdress** lead, KLT; 3 5/8; Europe; **1.** $150-250.

223. **Indian with Teepee** lead, KLT; 3 3/4; Europe; **2.** $400-800.

224. **"The Indian Family"** Cl; 3 5/8 x 5 1/8; J.M. Harper US 1905; **D.** $1500-2500.

225. **"Old Sleepy Eye"** lead, KLT; 3 1/8 x 3; Europe; **3.** $400-600.

226. **Pocahontas Bust** lead; KLT; 3 1/8; Europe; **2.** $150-250.

227. **Indian Bust with Headdress** lead, KLT; 3 1/8"; Europe; **1.** $75-150.

228. ***Indian with Tomahawk** Cl; 5 7/8; Hubley US 1915-1930s; **C.** $300-600.

C 229. **Indian Chief Bust** Cl; 4 7/8; US c1978; **M.** $20-30.

230. **Teepee**, WM, KLT; 4 3/8; Vanio US 1939; **B.** $60-100.

231. **Indian Bust, Profile** lead, KLT; 4 1/4; Japan; **1.** $50-100.

232. **Clown with Black Face** lead, KLT; 3 7/8; Germany; **3.** $600-1000.

233. **Clown with Pointed Nose** lead, TL; 3 7/8; Germany; **3.** $1000-2000.

234. **Laughing Clown** lead, KLT; 3 7/8; Germany; **3.** $500-1000.

235. **Indian Bust Profile** lead, KLT; 3 1/2; Germany; **1.** $100-200.

236. **Indian in Teepee** lead; 4 7/8; US; **1.** $30-50.

237. **Indian Chief Arms Crossed** WM, KLT; 4 1/8; Europe; **2.** $150-300.

A	238.	**Amish Man** AL; 5 3/4 x 4 3/4; Reynolds Toys US 1980; **M.** $45-75.
	239.	***Indian Seated on Log** Cl; 3 5/8; A. Ouve, artist US c1970s; **M.** $20-40.
	240.	**Clown, Hands in Pockets** WM; 6 5/16; US; **2.** $60-100.
	241.	***Buster Brown & Tige** Cl; 5 1/2; A.C. Williams US 1910-19 32; **B.** $250-350.
	242.	***Buster Brown & Tige** (paint variation) Cl; 5 1/2; A.C.Wi lliams US 1920s; **C.** $350-450.
	243.	**Halloween "Hag"** AL; 5 7/8; Reynolds Toys US 1981; **M.** $100-150.
	244.	**Leering Clown** pottery; 3 1/2; US; **1.** $100-200.
	245.	**Mother Hubbard** lead, KLT; 4 5/8; Germany; **3.** $300-600.
	246.	**"Mark Twain Bank"** AL; 5 1/4; Reynolds Toys US 1982; **M.** $50-75.
B	247.	**Charles Russell** WM, KLT; 6 1/4 x 4 1/4; Banthrico US 1962; **M.** $40-70.
	248.	**Jack in the Box** pottery; 4 11/16; US c1895; **2.** $100-150.
	249.	**Whizzor Clown** WM; 6 1/2; Banthrico US; **M.** $60-100.

	250.	**Clown Bust** Cl; 4 7/8; George Knerr US 1973; **M.** $300-500.
	251.	**Transvaal Money Box** Cl; 6"; England; **E.** $800-1200.
	252.	**Pinocchio on Drum** WM, KLT; 5 7/8; US; **A.** $30-50.
	253.	**Nodding Clown at Mailbox** lead; 4 x 3 1/2; Austria; **3.** $200-300.
	254.	**Davy Crockett Bust** WM, KLT; 5"; Banthrico US; **M.** $30-50.
C	255.	**Dutch Boy Doorstop** (mfr. conversion) Cl; 8 1/4; US; **D.** $400-800.
	256.	**Mammy Doorstop** (mfr. conversion) Cl; 8 1/4; US c1970s; **M.** $30-50.
	257.	**Sunbonnet Sue (Dolly Dimple)** Cl; 7 1/2; US c1970; **M.** $50-100.
	258.	**Man Sitting on Cigar Box** lead & iron; 8 1/2; US; **3.** $500-800.
	259.	**Jimmy Durante ("Schnozzola")** WM; 6 3/4; Abbot Wares US; **M.** $150-250.
	260.	**"Mr. Peanut Bank"** plastic; 8 1/4; US 1930s to present; **M.** $20-30.
	261.	**Baby in Egg** lead, KLT; 7 1/4; US; **2.** $300-500.

A 262. ***"Transvaal Money Box"** (cigar added) Cl; 6 1/8 x 4 1/2; J. Harper Ltd. England. $800-1200.

263. **Porky Pig at Tree Trunk** WM; 4 7/16 x 5 3/4; Metal Moss Mfg. Co. US late 1930s; **1.** $80-150.

264. **Porky Pig** 5 3/4; Cl; Hubley US 1930; **C.** $300-500.

265. **Porky Pig at Barrel** WM; 4 7/16 x 5 3/4; Metal Moss Mfg. Co US late 1930s; **1.** $80-150.

266. **Porky Pig on Haunches** lead KLT; 5 1/8; US; **1.** $40-60.

267. **Scrooge McDuck** (glasses missing) plastic; 6"; Oymk-tuote -Ab, Mfr.; copyright: Disney; Finland; **M.** $25-40.

268. **Scrooge McDuck** plastic; 6"; Oymk-tuote-Ab, Mfr.; copyright: Disney; Finland; **M.** $25-40.

269. **"Redskins" Pig** AL; 6 1/2; Reynolds Toys US 1983; **M.** $40-70.

B 270. **Bugs Bunny at Barrel** WM; 5 1/2 x 5 3/4; Metal Moss Mfg. Co. US late 1930s; **1.** $80-150.

271. **Policeman (round)** tin litho; 2 3/8 diam.; Germany late 1800s; **3.** $250-400.

272. **Sailor Boy** lead, KLT; 4 1/8; Europe; **3.** $800-1500.

273. **Jockey** (head lifts off) tin; 2 1/4; Germany late 1800s; **3.** $400-600.

274. **Boy with Empty Pockets** lead, TL; 3 7/8; Germany; **3.** $1000-2000.

275. **Grandpa Dukes** (removable hat) tin; 2 1/8; Germany late 1800s; **3.** $400-600.

276. **Soccer Player** lead; 4 1/2; Europe; **2.** $500-1000.

277. **Clown (round)** tin litho; 2 1/4 diam.; Germany; **3.** $250-400.

278. **Bugs Bunny at Tree Trunk** WM; 5 1/2 x 5 3/4; Metal Moss Mfg. Co. US late 1930s; **1.** $80-150.

C 279. **Minstrel Growing Bank** tin; 5 3/4; see #304; England; **2.** $80-150.

280. **Daffy Duck at Tree Trunk** WM; 4 1/4 x 5 3/4; Metal MossMfg. Co. US; **1.** $80-150.

281. **Pinocchio** comp., TT; 5 1/8; Crown US; **1.** $100-200.

282. **Man in Barrel (Barrel with Arms)** Cl; 3 5/8; J.& E. Stevens US late 1800s; **D.** $600-1200.

283. **Man in Barrel** (converted inkwell) Cl; 3 3/4; US; **D.** $300-400.

284. **Jimminy Cricket** comp.; TT; 5 7/8; Crown US c1940; **1.** $150-250.

285. **Daffy Duck at Barrel** WM; 4 1/4 x 5 3/4; Metal Moss Mfg. Co. US late 1930s; **1.** $80-150.

286. **Andy Panda** comp.; 6"; Arkon Plastics Co. US c1940 US; **2.** $40-70.

A 310. **Scottish Boy** lead, TL; 4 1/8; Europe; **3.** $800-1500.

311. ***Professor Pug Frog (Frog Bank)** Cl; 3 1/4; A.C. Williams US 1905-1912; **C.** $300-500.

312. **Colonial Woman** Staffordshire; 2 1/4; England c1890; **3.** $100-200.

313. **Snowflake with Ball** lead, TL; 3"; Europe; **3.** $600-1000.

314. **Keystone Cop** pottery; 3 1/4; Austria; **3.** $100-200.

315. **"Shakespeare"** WM; 4 1/4; US; **3.** $100-150.

316. **Girl at Barrel** lead, TL; 2"; Germany 1908; **3.** $300-500.

317. **Colonial Gentleman** Staffordshire; 2 1/4; England c1890; **3.** $150-250.

318. **Dog at Barrel** glass; 3"; L.E. Smith Co." US; **2.** $200-300.

319. **Mecki** comp.; 4 3/8; Germany; **2.** $25-50.

B 320. ***Foxy Grandpa (Grandpa Bank)** Cl; with screw; 5 1/2; Wing 1900; Hubley US 1920s; **C.** $250-400.

321. **Girl with Basket of Flowers** lead; 5 5/8; Vanio US c1938; **1.** $75-150.

322. **Woman at Beehive** lead; 4 1/2 x 3 1/4; Austria 1861; **3.** $400-600.

323. **Mother with Child** porcelain; 7 3/4 x 7 1/4 x 4; Porcellaine Royale, W. Germany 1979; **M.** $40-60.

324. **Whistler** WM; 5 1/2 x 4 1/8 D; US; **3.** $100-200.

325. **Baby with Raised Arms** WM, KLT; 4 1/2; US; **2.** $150-300.

326. ***Foxy Grandpa (Grandpa Bank)** Cl; with turnpin; 5 1/2; Wing US c1900; **C.** $400-600.

C 327. **Minuteman** WM, KLT; 8 1/8; Banthrico US 1941; **1.** $50-100.

328. **Junior Minuteman** comp.; 5 5/16; US 1941; **1.** $50-100.

329. **The Spirit of '76** WM, KLT; 6"; Banthrico US 1976; **M.** $25-40.

330. **Republic Pig** Cl; 7"; Wilton Products US 1970; **M.** $40-60.

331. ***Republic Pig** Cl; 7"; Unicast Foundry US 1968; **M.** $40-60.

332. **Davy Crockett with Rifle** WM, KLT; 5 3/8; Banthrico US; **M.** $50-75.

333. **Astronaut on Moon** (paper flag) WM, KLT; 6 1/2; Banthrico US; **M.** $50-75.

334. **Toy Soldier, SBCCA** Cl; 7 1/2; Laverne A. Worley US 1982; **M.** $35-45.

A	335.	**Peg Legged Pirate** WM, KLT; 5 1/4; US 1955; **M.** $25-40.
	336.	**Peg Legged Pirate** Cl; 5 1/8; US; **M.** $15-25.
	337.	**Seated Humpty Dumpty** WM, TT; 5 1/2; US; **M.** $20-30.
	338.	**"Humpty Dumpty"** tin, TT; 5 1/4; J. Chein & Co. US 1934; **1.** $200-350.
	339.	**Seated Humpty Dumpty** Cl; 5 3/8; Edward K. Russell US 1974; **M.** $40-60.
	340.	**Jack and Jill** WM, TT; 4 7/8 x 4; US; **M.** $20-30.
	341.	**Pistol Packing Pirate** WM, KLT; 6 1/4; US; **1.** $75-150.
B	342.	**Dog's Head** ceramic; 4 3/8 x 5 3/16; Staffordshire, England c1890; **2.** $200-300.
	343.	**Dog with Clock** lead & steel, KLT; 2 3/8; Europe c1914; **2.** $150-200.
	344.	**Dog in Doghouse** lead, KLT; 1 13/16; Europe; **2.** $200-400.
	345.	**Bird Dog** AL; 4 x 7 1/2; **M.** $30-50.

346.	**Puss in Shoe** pottery; 3 1/16 x 5 3/4; Wm. S. Reed, designer US patented 1884; **3.** $250-350.
347.	**"Feed the Kitty"** nickeled lead, KLT; 4 7/8 x 3 3/4; B.H. Hockswender & Assoc., US 1930s; **1.** $50-100.
348.	**"Baby's Bank"** celluloid; 5 1/4; US; **1.** $25-40.
349.	**Kitty Bank** Cl; 4 3/4; Hubley US 1930s-1946; **A.** $100-200.
350.	**Cat with Bow** Cl, KLT; 4 1/8; Hubley? US 1930s?; **C.** $150-300.
351.	**Cat with Toothache** lead, KLT; 4"; Europe; **2.** $300-400.
352.	**Cat with Ball** Cl; 2 1/2 x 1 13/16 x 5 11/16; A.C. Williams US 1905-1919; **C.** $250-500.
353.	**Cat with Ball** Cl; 2 1/2 x 1 1/2 x 5 5/8; US; **C.** $250-500.
354.	**Seated Cat** lead, TL; 3 3/4 x 3 1/2; Germany; **3.** $500-800.
355.	**Seated Cat on Base** silvered lead, TL; 4 1/2 x 2 x 2 1/2; Germany 1920s; **2.** $250-450.

C

A

356. **Dog with Letter Pouch** pottery; 5 1/4; US; **1.** $150-200.

357. ***Boxer (Bulldog)** Cl; 4 1/2 x 3 7/8 D; A.C. Williams 1912 -1928, Hubley US; **A.** $100-150.

358. **Cat on Tub** Cl; 4 1/8 x 1 7/8 diam.; A.C. Williams US 1920s-34; **B.** $150-250.

359. **Dog on Tub** Cl; 4 1/16 x 2 diam.; A.C. Williams US 1920s- 34; **B.** $150-250.

360. **Wood Carving;** 4 3/16 x 2; A.C. Williams; US. $800-1200.

361. **Spaniel Begging** lead, TL; 4 3/8; Europe; **1.** $300-400.

362. **Whippet on Base** (conversion) Cl; 3 1/2 x 5; US; **1.** $75-125.

363. **Bulldog with Sailor Cap** lead; 4 3/8; Germany 1930s; **2.** $250-400.

B

364. ***Cat with Bow, Seated** Cl; 4 3/8 x 2 7/8; Grey Iron Casting Co. US c1922; **D.** $300-500.

365. **Cat with Bow, Seated** Cl; 4 3/8 x 2 7/8; John Wright US; **M.** $20-30.

366. **Seated Cat with Soft Hair** Cl; 4 1/4 x 2 7/8; Arcade US c1910-1929; **B.** $150-300.

367. **Seated Cat with Fine Lines** Cl; 4 x 2 15/16; US c1912; **B.** $150-300.

368. **Cat with Long Tail** AL; 4 x 6 1/2; US; **M?** . $300-500.

369. **Cat with Long Tail** Cl; 4 3/8 x 6 3/4; Grey Iron Casting Co.? US c1910s; **E.** $1500-2500.

370. **Seated Cat with Blue Bow** lead, TL; 4 1/8; Germany; **2.** $500-800.

371. **"Lindy's Kat Bank"** silvered lead; 4 3/4 x 4 1/2; Hewter Corp. US 1907; **C.** $100-200.

C

372. **Bulldog (large)** Cl; 6"; John Wright 1960s-present; **M.** $40-60.

373. **Spaniel (large)** Cl; 10 1/2 L; John Wright 1960s; **M.** $30-50.

374. **Nipper (large)** pottery; 9"; Sarsaparilla Japan; **M.** $30-50.

375. **Nipper (small)** pottery; 6 3/8; Sarsaparilla Japan; **M.** $20-30.

376. **Nipper, Flocked** WM; 6"; US c1920s; **2.** $150-250.

A 377. **Bonzo with Suitcase** WM; 5"; Arthur Shaw & Co. England 1933; **2.** $150-250.

378. **Dog on Red Ball** tin & lead, KLT; 4 3/8; Germany; **2.** $200-300.

379. **Bulldog on Ball** lead & tin, KLT; 4 1/4; Germany; **2.** $250-350.

380. **Bassett Hound** Cl; 3 1/8; US; **E.** $1200-1800.

381. **"Deco Dog"** AL; 4"; base, 5 1/4; Reynolds Toys US 1981; **M.** $50-75.

382. **Basset Hound**, White KLT; 4"; Vanio US c late 1930s; **1.** $100-150.

383. **Basset Hound**, Red WM, KLT; 3 1/2; US; **1.** $80-120.

384. **Begging Dog, Small** lead, KLT; 3 1/2; Europe; **2.** $250-400.

385. **Spaniel, Seated** WM, iron KLT; 4 1/2; US; **1.** $100-150.

B 386. **Edison Dog at Phonograph** lead brass & tin, KLT; 3 3/4 x 4 1/4; Europe c1907; **3.** $400-700.

387. **Dog with Ball** lead & tin, KLT; 2"; Europe; **2.** $250-400.

388. **Dog with Doghouse** lead & tin, KLT; 2"; Europe 1914; **2.** $150-250.

389. **Dog with Drum** lead & tin, KLT; 1 3/4; Europe 1914; **2.** $150-250.

390. **Begging Dog with Ball** lead & tin, KLT; 2 1/8 diam.; Europe; **2.** $200-300.

391. **Cat Playing Piano** bronze & metal; 2 1/16; Europe; **3.** $1000-1500.

392. **Dog with Trunk** lead & tin, KLT; 1 3/4; Europe 1914; **2.** $150-250.

393. **Three Sided Doghouse** sterling, KLT; 2 3/4; McChesney Co. US c1920; **2.** $400-600.

394. **Dog in Doghouse** tin, KLT; 2"; Stollwerck, Germany; **2.** $150-200.

395. **Ornate Doghouse** sterling; 2 11/16 x 3 3/4; Germany 1859; **3.** $300-500.

C 396. **Bulldog, Seated** Cl; 3 7/8; Hubley US c1928; **B.** $250-400.

397. **Dog Head with Long Snout** pottery; 2 1/2; US; **2.** $150-200.

398. **Cat Head** pottery; 3"; US; **3.** $100-150.

399. **Bulldog with Collar** lead, TL; 3"; Europe; **2.** $600-1200.

400. **Boxer Head** lead, TL; 2 5/8; Europe; **1.** $200-400.

401. **Dog in Clown Suit** lead, TL; 4 3/8; Europe; **3.** $600-1200.

402. **Bonzo** lead, mechanical bank; TL; 3 1/2; Europe; **3.** $2000-3000.

403. **Bulldog, Standing** (converted paperweight) Cl; 2 1/4; Arcade US c1910-1913; **C.** $150-250.

404. **Pug** lead, TL; 2 3/4; Germany; **2.** $400-800.

405. **Pugdog, Seated** Cl; 3 1/2; Kyser & Rex US 1889; **B.** $200-400.

A 406. **Dog on Basket** bisque; 5 3/4; **2.** $150-250.
   407. **"Lost Dog"** CI; 5 3/8; Judd? US 1890s?; **D.** $500-800.
   408. **Forlorn Dog** WM, KLT; 4 3/4; US; **B.** $75-125.
   409. **Spitz** CI; 4 1/4 x 4 1/2; Grey Iron Casting Co. US 1928; **D.** $350-500.
   410. **Dog with Floppy Ears** lead, TL; 5 11/16; Europe; **2.** $500-800.
   411. **Husky** CI; 5"; Grey Iron Casting Co.? US c1910s; **D.** $600-1200.
   412. **Labrador Retriever** CI; 4 1/2 x 6; US; **C.** $300-500.
B 413. **Boston Bull, Seated** CI; 4 3/8 x 5 5/8; Hubley US 1930s-1 940; **B.** $250-350.
   414. **"Cutie"** CI; 3 7/8; Hubley US "1914" US; **B.** $100-200.
   415. **Dog Smoking Cigar** (conversion) CI; 4 1/4; Hubley? US; **E.** $400-600.
   416. **Puppo** CI; 4 7/8; Hubley US 1920s-1930s; **B.** $250-350.

   417. ***Fido** CI; 5 x 3 3/16 x 3 7/8; Hubley US "1914"-1946; **A.** $80-150.
   418. **Spaniel with Trap** CI; 3 3/4 x 6 L; Hubley 1930s US; **B.** $150-300.
   419. **Scottie, Seated** CI; 4 7/8 x 6; Hubley US 1930-1940; **B.** $100-200.
C 420. **Scottie, Seated, (large)** WM; 6"; "Vanio" US "1935"; **1.** $60-100.
   421. **Boston Bull Terrier** CI; 5 1/4 x 5 3/4; "Vindex Toys" US c1931; **B.** $200-300.
   422. **Wirehaired Terrier** CI; 4 5/8 x 5 3/4; Hubley US 1920- 1940; **B.** $200-300.
   423. **Boston Bull Terrier** AL; 4 7/8 x 5 1/4; US; **1.** $40-60.
   424. **Policeman Dog** lead; 4 1/2; Europe; **3.** $1000-1500.
   425. **Boston Bull Terrier** AL; 5 3/8 x 5 5/8; "Vindex Toys" US c1931; **B.** $100-150.

A 426. **Scottie** comp., TT; 5"; US; **1.** $20-30.
427. ***Six Scotties in Basket** WM, KLT 4 1/2; Vanio US late 1930s; **1.** $75-125.
428. **Tiny Scottie** Cl; 3 1/8; US; **D.** $400-600.
429. **Scottie with Ball** WM, KLT; 3 1/4; Vanio US late 1930s; **1.** $75-125.
430. **Fala with Crinkled Paint** Cl, metal trap; 2 3/4; US c1930s; **C.** $200-350.
431. **Scottie, Art Deco** nickeled lead, TL; 4 1/2 x 4 1/2; Germany c1935; **1.** $200-300.
432. **Scottie, White** WM, KLT; 4 3/4; Vanio US late 1930s; **1.** $40-70.
433. **Scottie** WM, KLT; 4 7/8; US; **1.** $40-60.
434. **Scottie, Red** WM, KLT; 5 1/4; US; **1.** $40-60.
B 435. **Scottie, Standing** Cl; 3 5/16; US; **C.** $150-250.
436. ***Retriever with Pack** Cl; 4 11/16 x 5 1/4; US; **C.** $100-200.

437. ***St. Bernard with Pack, (large)** Cl; 5 1/2 x 7 3/4; A.C. Williams US 1901-mid 1930s; **B.** $100-200.
438. **Water Spaniel with Pack ("I Hear a Call")** Cl; 5 3/8 x 7 7/8; US "1900"; **C.** $150-300.
439. ***St. Bernard with Pack, (small)** Cl; 3 3/4 x 5 1/2; A.C. Williams US 1905-1930s; **A.** $60-100.
440. **Newfoundland** Cl; 3 5/8 x 5 3/8; Arcade US 1910-mid 1930s; **B.** $200-300.
C 441. **RSPCS Dog** (collection box) Comp.; 6 5/8 x 8 3/8; Pytram Ltd., Surrey England; **2.** $150-250.
442. ***Puppo on Pillow** Cl; 5 5/8 x 6; Hubley US c1920s; **C.** $250-350.
443. **Fido on Pillow** Cl; base: 7 3/8 L; Hubley US c1920s; **C.** $300-500.
444. **English Setter** (converted doorstop) Cl; 8 1/2 x 15; John Wright US 1970; **M.** $40-70.

A 445. **Seated Elephant with Turned Trunk** Cl; 4 1/4; US; **D.** $600-1000.

446. **Elephant on Wheels** Cl; 4 1/8 x 4 3/8; A.C. Williams US 1920s; **C.** $300-500.

447. **Elephant with Bent Knee** Cl; 3 1/2 x 4 7/8; Kenton US 1904; **D.** $400-600.

448. **Elephant with Pack** comp., KLT; 3 5/8 x 5 3/8; Hausser, Germany c1929; **2.** $150-250.

449. **Art Deco Elephant** Cl; 4 3/8; US; **B.** $200-300.

450. **Art Deco Elephant ("GOP")** Cl; 4 3/8; US; **C.** $300-600.

451. **Worcester Salt Elephant** WM, KLT; 4 3/16; Baudis Metalcraft Co. US; **1.** $75-150.

B 452. **"McKinley/Teddy" Elephant** Cl; 2 1/2 x 3 1/2; US 1900; **E.** $1200-1800.

453. **"McKinley/Roosevelt"** Cl; 2 1/2 x 3 1/2; US 1900; **E.** $500-800.

454. **Elephant, (small);** 2 1/2" x 3 1/2"; Wing US c1900; **C.** $150-200.

455. **Elephant, Swivel Trunk** Cl; 2 1/2 x 3 1/2; US; **D.** $150-250.

456. **Jelly Bean King** AL; 3 7/8; Reynolds Toys US 1981; **M.** $100-150.

457. **Elephant with Howdah, (small)** Cl; 2 1/2 x 3; A.C. Williams US 1934; **B.** $100-150.

458. **Elephant (hinged back)** silvered lead, TL; 2 1/2 x 5 1/8; Germany 1920s; **2.** $250-350.

459. ***Elephant with Howdah, (medium)** Cl; 3 x 4; A.C. Williams US 1912-1934; **A.** $60-100.

C 460. **Elephant with Tin Chariot** (turnpin) Cl; 8"; Wing (Chariot-Gibbs) US 1900-03; **E.** $1200-1500.

461. **Seated Elephant, Trumpeting** WM, KLT; 5"; "Vanio 1936" US; **1.** $40-70.

462. **Circus Elephant** Cl; 3 7/8; Hubley US 1930-1940; **B.** $250-450.

463. **Hoover/Curtis Elephant "GOP"** Cl; 3 3/8 x 4 3/4; Hubley US "1928"; **E.** $1000-2000.

464. **Elephant Playing Drum** WM, KLT; 4 1/2; Arthur Shaw & Co. England 1933; **1.** $100-150.

465. **Small Elephant with Chariot** (turnpin) Cl; 7"; Hubley US1 906; **E.** $1200-2000.

466. **Chariot** (part of #465) Cl; 2 15/16 L; Hubley 1906

A	467.	**Elephant #465 with Chariot**; 2 1/2 L; Hubley US 1906; **E.** (See #465) $1200-2000.		475.	**Elephant with Raised Slot** Cl; 4 1/2 x 6 1/8 L; US; **C.** $250-350.

467. **Elephant #465 with Chariot**; 2 1/2 L; Hubley US 1906; **E.** (See #465) $1200-2000.

468. **Elephant/GOP 1936** (same as #463) Cl; 3 7/16 x 4 5/8; Hubley US 1936; **E.** $1200-1800.

469. **Stiff-Legged Elephant** Cl; 3 1/2 x 4 5/16; Harris Toy Co. US 1904; **D.** $400-600.

470. **Elephant #465 (no chariot holes)** Hubley US 1906?; **B.** $150-250.

471. **Nixon/Agnew Elephant** (recast of #472) Cl; 2 5/8 x 4; US 1968; **M.** $40-60.

472. **Elephant with Tucked Trunk** Cl; 2 3/4 x 4 5/8; Arcade US 1910-32; **A.** $100-200.

473. **Tiniest Elephant** AL; 1 3/4 x 1 11/16; Reynolds US 1982; **M.** $30-50.

B **474.** ***Elephant with Howdah (large)** Cl; 4 7/8 x 6 3/8; A.C. Williams US 1910-30s; **B.** $100-200.

475. **Elephant with Raised Slot** Cl; 4 1/2 x 6 1/8 L; US; **C.** $250-350.

476. ***Elephant with Howdah** Cl; 4 3/4 x 6 3/4; A.C. Williams US 1905-34; **B.** $100-200.

477. ***Elephant with Howdah (small)** Cl; 3 1/2 x 5; A.C. Williams US 1905-20s; **A.** $75-150.

478. **Elephant, Trumpeting** WM, KLT; 6"; Banthrico US; **M.** $40-60.

C **479.** **Elephant with Chariot, Large** Cl; 4 3/4 x 6 7/8; chariot, 4" L; Hubley US 1906; **E.** $2000-3000.

480. **Elephant #479 (no chariot holes)** Hubley US 1906; **C.** $300-400.

481. **Elephant** (converted doorstop) Cl; 5 x 7; US; **C.** $50-100.

482. **Elephant, Trumpeting** Cl; 7 1/4 x 9 3/4; John Wright US 1971; **M.** $40-80.

A 483. **Elephant on Tub** Cl; 5 3/8; A.C. Williams US c1920s; **B.** $150-250.

484. ***Elephant on Tub, decorated** Cl; 5 3/8; A.C. Williams US 1920s-1934; **B.** $150-300.

485. **Elephant with Ball** lead & tin, TL missing; 2 5/8; Europe **2.** $600-900.

486. **Elephant on Bench on Tub** Cl; 3 7/8; A.C. Williams US 1920s-1930; **B.** $100-150.

487. **Elephant with Blanket** Cl; 3 1/8 x 5; Kenton US 1936-40; **D.** $800-1200.

488. **Donkey with Blanket** Cl; 3 7/8 x 5 3/4; Kenton US 1936-40; **D.** $800-1200.

489. **Donkey "I Made St. Louis Famous"** (slot under belly) Cl; 4 11/16 x 5; Harper US c1904; **E.** $2000-3000.

490. **Donkey (see #489)** (slot under belly); Harper US 1903; **E.** $1500-2000.

B 491. **Donkey with Rectangular Saddle** lead, TL; 3 5/8 x 3 1/2; Germany; **1.** $100-200.

492. **Donkey** Comp.; 4 1/2 x 5 3/8; Hausser, Germany 1929; **2.** $150-250.

493. **Donkey (hinged front quarter)** lead, TL; 3 3/4 x 4 3/4; Germany; **2.** $200-300.

494. **Elephant** pottery; 1 3/4 x 2 1/4; US; **2.** $100-200.

495. **Donkey** pottery; 2 1/4 x 2 3/4; US; **2.** $150-250.

496. **Donkey (hinged neck)** lead, TL; 4 3/16 x 4 1/2; Germany; **2.** $200-300.

497. **Donkey (facing left)** lead, TL; 4 x 4; Germany; **1.** $100-150.

498. **Donkey (hinged saddle)** lead, TL; 3 5/8 x 3 3/8; Japan; **1.** $100-150.

C 499. ***Donkey (small)** Cl; 4 1/2 x 4 5/8; Arcade 1913-1932;   A.C. Williams 1910-1934; US; **A.** $80-150.

500. ***Donkey (large)** Cl; 6 13/16 x 6 1/4; A.C. Williams US c1920s; **C.** $200-350.

501. **Westpoint Mule** lead, TL; 4 7/8 x 5 1/8; Japan; **1.** $200-400.

502. **Donkey on Base** Cl; 6 9/16 x 6 1/4; US; **D.** $300-400.

503. **Donkey with Saddle Bags** silvered lead; TL; 5 x 6 1/4; base, 8 3/4 x 4 3/4; Germany, 1920s; **1.** $150-250.

504. **Prospector's Mule** WM; 6 1/4 x 8 1/2; US; **A.** $40-60.

505. **Donkey with Drum** lead & tin, KLT; 3 7/16; "Germany"; **2.** $400-600.

A 506. **Prancing Horse with Belly Band** Cl; 4 1/2 x 5; US; **D.** $300-400.

507. **Saddle Horse** Cl; 4 3/8 x 5 1/2; Grey Iron Casting Co. US 1928; **D.** $400-600.

508. **Good Luck Horseshoe** (Buster Brown & Tige) Cl; 4 1/4 x 4 3/4; Arcade US 1908-32; **B.** $250-450.

509. ***Horse on Tub, Decorated** Cl; 5 5/16; A.C. Williams US 1920s-34; **C.** $150-300.

510. **Horse on Tub** Cl; 5 5/16; A.C. Williams US 1920s; **C.** $150-300.

511. **Good Luck Horseshoe** (paint variation); see #508; US c1908; **C.** $800-1000.

512. **Horse on Wheels** Cl; 5" Base: 4 1/4; A.C. Williams US c1920; **C.** $300-500.

B 513. **Prancing Horse on Oval Base** Cl; 5 1/8 x 4 7/8; Hubley; A.C. Williams 1920s; US; **B.** $100-200.

514. **Prancing Horse on Oval Base ("Beauty")** Cl; 4 3/4 x 4 7/8; US; **D.** $300-500.

515. **Rocking Horse (SBCCA)** Cl; 5 5/8 x 6 x 2; Knerr US 1975; **M.** $350-550.

516. **Rocking Horse Bronze**; 5 7/8; Rockers, 5 7/8 L; Roadview Farms US; **E.** $200-400.

517. **Prancing Horse** Cl; 4 1/4 x 4 7/8; Arcade 1910-1932; A.C. Williams 1910-1920s; Dent US; **A.** $75-125.

518. **Prancing Horse, Made in Canada** Cl; 4 1/8 x 4 3/4; US; **D.** $250-400.

C 519. **Large Horse with Bridle** Cl; 9 1/2 x 10; Knerr US 1973; **M.** $200-300.

520. ***Prancing Horse on Platform Base (large)** Cl; 7 3/16 x 6 9/16; Arcade 1910; A.C. Williams 1910-1934 US; **A.** $150-250.

521. ***Prancing Horse on Pebbled Base** Cl; 7 1/4 x 6 1/2; US; **B.** $150-250.

522. **Work Horse on Base** (converted doorstop) Cl; 9 x 7 5/8; US; **D.** $100-200.

A   523.   **Saddle Horse (small)** Cl; 2 3/4 x 3 3/16; A.C. Williams US 1934; **C.** $150-250.

524.   **Horseshoe with Wire Mesh** Cl; 3 1/4; Arcade US 1910-25; **B.** $100-150.

525.   **Show Horse** Cl; 5 7/8 x 6 5/8; Lane Chair Co. US 1973; **M.** $40-60.

526.   **Thoroughbred** Cl; 5 1/4 x 6 7/8; Hubley US 1946; **M.** $40-60.

527.   **Work Horse with Flynet** Cl; 4 x 4 5/8; Arcade? US 1910s?; **D.** $500-800.

528.   **Same as #523** (rare, painted version) US; **D.** $200-300.

B   529.   **Same as #517 and #518** (base added?) US; **A.** $50-75.

530.   ***Work Horse** (slot in belly) Cl; 4 1/4 x 4 15/16; Arcade U S 1910s; **C.** $150-250.

531.   **"My Pet"** (slot in belly same as #530) Arcade US 1920s; **C.** $200-300.

532.   **"Beauty"** Cl; 4 1/8 x 4 3/4; Arcade US 1910-32; **A.** $100-150.

533.   ***Work Horse** (same as #532) Cl; Arcade US 1910s; **A.** $100-150.

534.   **Horse, Standing** Cl; 4 3/8 x 5; Virginia Metal Crafters, Inc. US; **M.** $30-40.

535.   **"Tally Ho"** Cl; 4 1/2 x 4 3/16; Chamberlain & Hill, England; **C.** $150-250.

C   536.   **Ox** (factory con version) Cl; 4 3/8 x 6 3/4; Kenton; US; **C.** $75-125.

537.   **Bull on Base** Cl; 4 x 5 7/8; US; **D.** $100-200.

538.   **Elsie the Borden Cow WM**; 6 3/4; Master Caster Mfg. Co.; **M.** $100-200.

539.   **Same as #537** (conversion); US; $150-250.

540.   **Milking Cow** Cl; 4 3/16; J.&E. Stevens?; **E.** $250-400.

A   541.   ***Polish Rooster** Cl; 5 1/2; US; **E.** $1200-2000.

542.   **Bull with Long Horns** Cl; 3 11/16 x 5; US; **M.** $30-50.

543.   **Rooster on Basket** comp.; 5 1/2; Hausser, Germany 1929; **2.** $200-300.

544.   **Holstein Cow** Cl; 2 1/2 x 4 5/8; Arcade US 1910-1920; **C.** $350-600.

545.   **Same as #544** (paint variation) Arcade US 1910-1920; **C.** $250-500.

546.   **Hen on Nest** Cl; 3 x 3 3/8; US early 1900s; **E.** $1500-2000.

547.   ***Rooster** Cl; 4 5/8; Arcade US 1910-1925; **B.** $150-250.

548.   ***Rooster** Cl; 4 3/4; Hubley; A.C. Williams US 1910-34; **B.** $150-250.

B   549.   ***Hen** Cl; 6"; US; **E.** $800-1500.

550.   **Rooster Head** lead, TL missing; 3 1/2; Europe; **2.** $350-600.

551.   **Crowing Rooster** lead, KLT; 5 13/16; US; **2.** $150-250.

552.   **Bull's Head** pottery; 3"; **3.** $100-200.

553.   ***Cow** Cl; 3 3/8 x 5 1/4; A.C. Williams US c1920; **B.** $100-200.

554.   **"Weaver" Hen** Cl; 6"; US 1970s; **M.** $30-40.

555.   ***Aberdeen Angus Bull** AL; 4 1/8 x 7 3/8; US; **2.** $75-150.

C   556.   ***Amherst Buffalo** Cl; 5 1/4 x 8; US c1930s; **C.** $300-400.

557.   **Buffalo (large)**; 5 x 8; US 1970; **M.** $40-60.

558.   **Trick Buffalo** Cl; 5 1/2 x 9 3/8; US; **D.** $1000-2000.

A
559. **Bison** pottery; 2 1/2 x 5 1/8; US; **1.** $150-250.
560. ***Buffalo (small)** Cl; 3 1/8 x 4 3/8; Arcade 1920-25; A.C. Williams 1920s-34; US; **B.** $100-200.
561. **Possum** Cl; 2 3/8 x 4 3/8; Arcade US 1910-1913; **D.** $450-650.
562. **Buffalo on Base** WM; 4 x 5 3/4; Banthrico US; **M.** $40-70.
563. **Billy Possum ("Possum & Taters")** Cl; 3 x 4 3/4; J.M. Harper US 1909; **E.** $4000-6000.
564. **Buffalo Lying Down** ("Expo 1901") pottery; 3 1/8 x 6 1/2; US 1901; **2.** $200-300.

B
565. **Rabbit Lying Down** Cl; 2 1/8 x 5 1/8; US; **D.** $250-450.
566. ***Begging Rabbit** Cl; 5 1/8; A.C. Williams US 1908-1920s. $150-250.
567. **Rabbit with Carrot** Cl; 3 3/8; Knerr US 1972; **M.** $100-200.
568. ***Seated Rabbit (small)** Cl; 3 5/8; Arcade US 1910-20s; **B.** $150-300.

569. **Rabbit on Base** Cl; 2 1/4 x 2 13/16; US "1884"; **E.** $800-1500.
570. ***Large Seated Rabbit** Cl; 4 5/8 x 4 3/8; Wing pre 1906; Hubley 1906-20s US; **C.** $200-400.
571. **Rabbit with Hinged Back (small)** lead, TL; 3 3/8 x 4 3/8; Germany; **1.** $150-300.
572. **Rabbit with Hinged Back (large)** lead, TL; 3 3/4 x 4 1/4; Germany; **2.** $150-300.

C
573. ***Oscar the Goat** Cl; 7 3/4 x 9 1/4; US; **M.** $75-125.
574. ***Rabbit Standing** Cl; 6 1/4 x 5 5/8; A.C. Williams US 1908 to mid 1920s; **C.** $250-400.
575. **Basket of Corn** Cl; 2 1/4 x 3 diam.; J.M. Harper US 1907; **E.** $1200-1800.
576. **Rooster (large)** Cl; 6 3/4; US c1913; **F.** $1200-1800.
577. **Mexican Pig** pottery; 6 7/8 x 7 1/4; Mexico 1950; **M.** $20-40.

A	578.	**Standing Pig** Cl; 3 x 5 5/16; Shimer Toy Co. US c1899; **C.** $200-300.		590.	**Repro. of #587** Cl; 3 5/16 x 3; Knerr 1968; **M.** $30-50.

A 578. **Standing Pig** Cl; 3 x 5 5/16; Shimer Toy Co. US c1899; **C.** $200-300.

579. **Grinning Pig** lead, KLT; 2 5/8 x 4 3/16; Europe; **1.** $75-125.

580. **Downcast Pig** lead, KLT; 3 1/4 x 5 1/16; Europe; **3.** $250-350.

581. **Painted Pig (SBCCA)** porcelain; 1 3/4; Porcellaine Royal, W. Germany 1978; **M.** $20-30.

582. ***Seated Pig** Cl; 3 x 4 9/16; A.C. Williams US 1910-34; **A.** $50-100.

583. **Pig with Curly Hair** lead, TL; 2 7/8 x 5 1/2; Germany; **1.** $150-250.

584. **Sleek Pig** nickeled Cl; 3 1/8 x 6 3/4; US; **B.** $100-200.

B 585. **Large Turkey** Cl; 4 1/4 x 4; A.C. Williams US 1905-1912; **D.** $400-600.

586. **Small Turkey (wood carving)**; 3 1/2 x 3 3/8; A.C. Williams. $1000-1500.

587. ***Small Turkey** Cl; 3 3/8 x 3 3/16; A.C. Williams US 1905- 35; **B.** $150-250.

588. **Great Northern Goat** lead, TL; 3 1/2 x 4; Europe c1912; **3.** $1000-2000.

589. **"Red Goose Savings Bank"** tin & paper; 2 3/8 x 1 3/4 diam.; US; **2.** $75-125.

590. **Repro. of #587** Cl; 3 5/16 x 3; Knerr 1968; **M.** $30-50.

591. **Hen House with Rabbit** lead, KLT; 4 3/8 x 3 1/2; Europe 1908; **3.** $600-1000.

592. **"Red Goose Savings Bank"** tin & paper; 2 x 1 3/4 x 1 3/8; F.L. Rand Co. US; **1.** $40-70.

593. **"Chicken Feed Bag"** Cl; 4 5/8 x 3 7/8; Knerr 1973; **M.** $150-250.

C 594. **"Two Kids"** Cl; 4 1/2 x 4 1/2; Harper? US; **D.** $1200-1800.

595. **Lamb (small)** Cl; 3 3/16 x 4 1/8; US 1880; **C.** $250-350.

595a. **"Red Goose Penny Bank"** tin; 1 11/16 diam.; US; **2.** $40-70.

596. **"Feed My Sheep"** lead; 2 3/4 x 4 1/8; US; **1.** $100-150.

597. **Owl** Cl; 4 1/4 x 2 1/2; Vindex US c1930; **C.** $200-400.

598. **"Be Wise Owl"** Cl; 4 7/8 x 2 1/2; A.C. Williams US 1912-20s; **B.** $150-300.

599. **Owl on Stump** Cl; 3 5/8 x 2 5/8 US; **M.** $50-75.

600. **Lamb painted** Cl; 3 1/4 x 5 1/2; John Wright US 1970; **M.** $20-30.

601. ***Lamb, large** Cl; 3 1/4 x 5 1/2; Grey Iron Casting Co US 1928; **C.** $250-350.

A   602.   **"Bismark Bank"** Cl; 3 3/8 x 7 3/8; US c1883; **C.** $250-350.

603.   **"Decker's Iowana"** Cl; 2 5/16 x 4 3/8; US; **B.** $100-200.

604.   **Seated Pig with Hinged Back** lead, TL; 2 3/4 x 4 3/8; Germany; **1.** $150-250.

605.   **Pig on Pedestal** lead, KLT; 4 1/2 x 3 7/8; Austria; **3.** $350-550.

606.   **Pig with Bow** Cl; 2 15/16 x 5; Shimer Toy Co. US 1899; **C.** $200-350.

607.   **Pink Pig** Cl; 2 3/8 x 4 3/8; John Wright US 1970; **M.** $20-30.

608.   **Bismark Pig** Cl; (See #602) US c1880s; **B.** $100-200.

B   609.   ***"The Wise Pig"** Cl; 6 5/8 x 2 7/8; Hubley US c1930-36; **A.** $100-250.

610.   **"Red Goose Shoes"** Cl; 3 3/4; Arcade US c1920s; **B.** $200-300.

611.   **"Red Goose Shoes"** (Hood Ornament) Cl; 5 3/4; Arcade US c1920s; **D.** $400-600.

612.   **Squatty "Red Goose Shoes"** Cl; 3 7/8; Arcade US c1920s; **D.** $350-550.

613.   **"A Christmas Roast"** Cl; 3 1/4 x 7 1/8; US; **C.** $250-400.

614.   **Goose Bank** Cl (See #610) Arcade US c1920s; **C.** $150-250.

615.   **Duck Bank** Cl; 4 7/8; A.C. Williams US 1909-35; **C.** $200-300.

616.   **Duck on Tub ("Save for a Rainy Day")** Cl; 5 3/8; Hubley US 1930-1936; **B.** $150-300.

617.   ***"The Wise Pig"** lead, 6 9/16 x 2 3/4; Jessie McCutcheon Nelson, designer; US patented 1929; **1.** $100-200.

C   618.   **Piggy Bank** WM; 5 1/2 x 9; United Gift Mfg. Co. US; **M.** $10-20.

619.   **Round Duck** Cl; large Kenton Trap; 4 x 4 7/8; Kenton US 1936-40; **C.** $300-600.

620.   **The Biggest Pig of All** Cl; 7 1/4; **M.** $30-40.

621.   **Pig with Pink Ears** pottery; 3 x 7; **2.** $50-75.

622.   **Standing Pig on Base** (conversion?); Cl; 3 5/8 x 6 5/8; US; **B.** $100-150.

A 647. **Nesting Doves Safe** Cl; 5 1/4; J.M. Harper US 1907; **E.** $3000-5000.

648. **Cockatoo with Ball** lead, TL; 3"; Europe; **2.** $300-500.

649. **Brementown Musicians** lead; 5 3/8 barrel; 1 5/8 at top & bottom; Germany; **3.** $1200-1800.

650. **Pelican with Ball** lead, TL; 3"; Germany; **2.** $300-500.

651. **Stork Safe** Cl; 5 1/2; J.M. Harper US 1907; **D.** $1000-2000.

652. **Rabbit with Cabbage** lead, TL; 3"; Germany; **3.** $600-1200.

653. **Bird House (tall)** silvered lead, KLT; 4 3/16; Germany 1907; **3.** $400-700.

654. **Tiny Parrot with Ball** lead, TL; 2 1/8 (globe); Europe; **2.** $200-350.

655. **Bird House (short)** silvered lead, TL; 3 11/16; Germany c1907; **2.** $400-600.

B 656. **Cockatoo** WM, iron KLT; 5"; **2.** $200-300.

657. **Female Parrot** lead, TL; 3 1/2; Germany; **2.** $400-600.

658. **Elf with Tree Stump** lead, TL; 2 5/8; Germany; **3.** $300-500.

659. **Chipmunk with Nut** Cl; 4 1/8; US; **D.** $1500-2000.

660. **Squirrel with Nut** Cl; 4 1/8; US; **D.** $600-1000.

661. **Tree Stump** lead, TL; 2 7/8; Germany; **2.** $200-300.

662. **Parrot Head** lead; 3"; Germany; **2.** $300-500.

663. **Sandpiper** lead, TL; 3 3/4; Germany; **2.** $400-600.

C 664. **Songbird on Stump (Bird Toy Bank)** Cl; 4 3/4 x 4 11/16; A.C. Williams US 1912-1920s; **D.** $400-700.

665. **White-winged Parrot** lead, TL; 3 7/8; Germany; **2.** $400-700.

666. **Tree Stump (short)** lead, TL; 2 1/2; Europe; **2.** $200-300.

667. **Two-piece Egg** (combo. opening) tin; 2 5/16; "Steel Corp. of S.F., California" US 1922; **1.** $60-100.

668. **Parrot on Stump** (conversion) CL; 6 1/4; US; **C.** $250-450.

669. **Poll Parrot** tin; 1 1/2 x 1 5/8 diam.; US; **1.** $60-100.

670. **Baby Bird** lead, TL; 3"; Arthur Shaw Co. England; **2.** $400-600.

671. **Female Parrot** lead, TL; 4"; Germany; **2.** $400-700.

672. **Male Parrot** lead, TL; 5 1/8; Germany; **2.** $600-1000.

A   **673.** **Pelican on Base** WM; 6 1/4; Banthrico US; **M.** $30-40.

674. **Long-beeked Cockatoo** lead, TL; 4"; Germany; **2.** $600-1000.

675. **Frog (SBCCA)** porcelain; 2 5/8; Tresor-Verlag W. Germany 1980; **M.** $20-30.

676. **Old Abe with Shield** Cl; 3 7/8; US c1880; **E.** $800-1500.

677. **Gold Eagle** Cl; 5 3/4 x 3 5/8 x 2 1/2; John Wright US 1970; **M.** $20-30.

678. **Wisconsin War Eagle** Cl; 2 7/8; US c 1880; **E.** $1000-1800.

679. **Pelican** Cl; 4 3/4; Hubley US 1930s; **D.** $800-1500.

680. **Frog on Lattice** (construction) lead frog, iron base; 4 1/2; US; **D.** $350-500.

B   **681.** **Beehive Registering Savings Bank** Cl; 5 3/8 x 6 1/2 x 2; US c1891; **C.** $300-500.

682. **Bee-covered Hive** silvered lead; 3"; American Art Works, Inc. US; **B.** $100-200.

683. *****Beehive Bank** Cl; 2 3/8; Kyser & Rex US 1882; **C.** $300-500.

684. **Beehive with Brass Top** Cl; 5 1/2 x 5 7/8 diam.; W.M. Gobeille US; **E.** $600-1000.

685. **Beehive** WM; 3 3/4; Banthrico US; **M.** $30-50.

686. **Beehive "Industry Shall Be Rewarded"** Cl; 4 1/8 x 5 1/2; John Harper Ltd. England c1897; **E.** $600-900.

C   **687.** **Mountain Goat** WM; 6 1/2; Banthrico US; **M.** $40-60.

688. **Penguin (large)** chalk; 8"; US; **M.** $150-250.

689. **Penguin on Base** comp., TT; 4 3/4; Crown Toys US; **1.** $50-75.

690. **Hanging Stork** Cl; plaque, 10 x 6 7/8; bank, 9 x 6; John Harper Ltd. England 1914; **E.** $600-900.

691. **Penguin (small)** tin, TT; 5 3/4; Animate Toy Corp. US; **3.** $100-200.

692. **Frog (Mfgr's. conversion)** Cl; 4 1/8; "Iron Art" US 1973; **M.** $40-60.

A 693. ***Bear Stealing Pig** (correct paint) Cl; 5 1/2; US; **D.** $800-1500.

694. ***Teddy Bear** Cl; 2 1/2 x 3 7/8; Arcade US 1905-1925; **B.** $150-250.

695. **Bear with Top Hat** lead, TL;' 5 1/4' Europe; **2.** $800-1500.

696. **Honey Bear** Cl; 2 1/2 x 2 5/8 x 1 11/16; US; **E.** $700-1200.

697. **Bear with Arms Folded** lead, TL; 3 13/16; Europe; **3.** $400-700.

698. ***"Teddy" Bear** Cl; (see #694) Arcade US 1910-1925; **B.** $200-300.

699. **Downcast Bear** lead, TL; 2 1/2 x 3 5/8; Germany; **C.** $250-350.

700. **Panda** pottery; 3 3/8; **1.** $40-60.

701. ***Bear Stealing Pig** (repaint) Cl; 5 1/2; US; **D.** $500-700.

B 702. **Pooh Bank** Cl; 5 x 4 7/8; US 1977; **M.** $30-40.

703. **Grisley Bear** lead, tin KLT; 2 3/4; "Made in Japan"; **1.** $150-200.

704. **Angry Bear** lead, TL; 3 x 4 1/4; Germany; **1.** $200-250.

705. **Seated Panda** WM; 4 15/16; "Vanio, 1938" US; **1.** $100-200.

706. **Cinnamon Bear** WM, iron trap; 3 7/8; Germany; **2.** $150-250.

707. **Bear with Pole on Shoulders** pottery; 3 3/4; Czechoslovakia; **1.** $75-125.

708. **Walking Polar Bear** pottery; 2 x 4 1/4; **1.** $40-60.

709. **Panda on Log** comp0.; 4 7/8; Japan; **1.** $40-60.

C 710. ***Bear on Hind Legs** Cl; 6 1/8; John Harper Ltd. England 1911; **C.** $150-250.

711. **Bear on Hind Legs** AL; 6"; John Harper Ltd. England; **2.** $100-150.

712. **Bear on Hind Legs** brass; 5 7/8; England; **C.** $60-100.

713. ***Mean Standing Bear** Cl; 5 1/2; Hubley "US 1906; **B.** $200-300.

714. **Bear Seated on Log** Cl; 7"; US; **E.** $500-800.

715. ***Begging Bear** Cl; 5 3/8; A.C. Williams, 1910s; Arcade 1910 1910-1925 US; **B.** $100-200.

716. ***Polar Bear** Cl; 5 1/4; Arcade c1920; A.C. Williams c1917 US; **C.** $350-550.

717. ***Bear with Honey Pot** Cl; 6 1/2; Hubley US 1936; **B.** $150-250.

A 718. **Hippo** Cl; 2 x 5 3/16; US; **E.** $5000-8000.
719. **Hippo** nickeled Cl; (see #718) 2 x 5 3/16; US; **E.** $5000-8000.
720. **Baby Brumas** AL; 6"; England; **2.** $100-150.
721. **Rhino** Cl; 2 5/8 x 5; Arcade US 1910-1925; **C.** $400-700.
722. **Hipporhino** lead; 2 1/2 x 4 3/4; made in Lima, Ohio c1970s; **M.** $40-60.
723. **Well-dressed Hippo** lead, TL; 4 3/8; Europe; **3.** $1000-2000.
724. **"Whale of a Bank"** Cl; 2 3/4 x 5 3/16; Knerr US 1975; **M.** $100-150.

B 725. **Fish** lead, TT; 4 x 4 3/8; Germany; **3.** $200-300.
726. **Fish (mech.)** lead, KLT; 2 1/4 x 4 7/8; Europe; **1.** $300-400
727. **Bony Fish** lead; 1 5/16 x 3 3/16; **M.** $80-125.
728. **Alligator** lead; 2 7/8; "Germany"; **3.** $400-600.

729. **"Turtle Bank"** Cl; 1 x 2 1/16 x 3 7/16; US; **F.** $3000-4000.
730. **Alligator (mech.)** lead; 3 1/2; "Germany"; **3.** $1500-2000.
731. **"IFC" Fish** lead; 2 7/16 x 6 7/8; US; **3.** $800-1200.
732. **Sea Lion (Seal on Rock)** Cl; 3 1/2 x 4 1/4; Arcade US 1910-1913; **C.** $400-650.

C 733. **Alligator on Rock** WM; 5 3/8; US; **B.** $75-100.
734. **Swan** lead, TL; 4 1/4 x 5 5/8; Germany; **2.** $200-350.
735. **Reindeer on Base** Cl; 10 x 8; John Wright US 1973; **M.** $75-125.
736. **Small Reindeer (Elk)** Cl; 6 1/4 x 4 7/8; A.C. Williams 1910-1935; Arcade 1913-1932; US; **A.** $75-150.
737. **Large Reindeer (Elk)** Cl; 9 1/2 x 5 1/4; A.C. Williams US 1910-1935; **B.** $150-300.

96

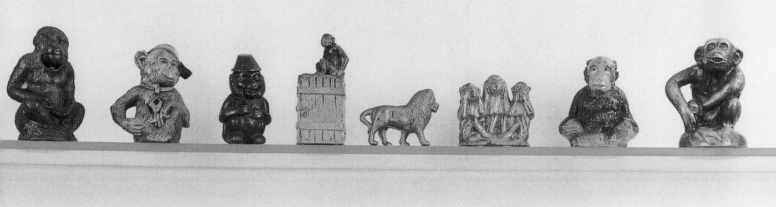

A | 738. | **Monkey with Moveable Jaw** lead; 5/ x 3 3/4; French?; **3.** $400-600.
| 739. | **Monkey Smoking Cigarette** lead, TL; 4 1/2; Europe; **2.** $800-1500.
| 740. | **Monkey with Removable Hat** bronze; with hat, 3 7/8; without, 3 3/8; US; **D.** $1000-2000.
| 741. | **Monkey on Cage** comp.; 5 x 2 3/8; Hausser, Germany c1929; **2.** $150-300.
| 742. | **Lion, small** Cl; 2 1/2 x 3 5/8; A.C. Williams US 1934; **C.** $100-150.
| 743. | **Three Wise Monkeys** Cl; 3 1/4 x 3 1/2; A.C. Williams US 1910-1912; **C.** $300-450.
| 744. | **Gorilla** lead, Cl trap; 4 1/4; US; **2.** $200-400.
| 745. | **Monkey, Scratching** lead; 4 **7/8; 1.** $50-75.
B | 746. | ***Lion on Tub, Decorated** Cl; 5 1/2; tub, 2 1/2 diam.; A.C. Williams US 1920s-1934; **B.** $150-300.
| 747. | **Lion on Tub,** small Cl; 4 1/8; tub diam. 2"; A.C. Williams US; **B.** $100-150.
| 748. | **Wood Carving;** r 3/16 x 2 diam.; A.C. Williams. $800-1200.
| 749. | **Beaver with Ball ("Canada")** lead; 4 3/8; **2.** $500-800.

| 750. | **Canadian Beaver** Cl; 2 1/2 x 8; "W-S S"; US; **F.** $4000-5000.
| 751. | **Seated Royal Lion** Cl; 5 x 4 1/4; John Harper Ltd. England 1911; **D.** $500-800.
| 752. | **Lion on Rock** lead, TL; 3 x 3 15/16; England; **2.** $100-200.
| 753. | **Lion on Tub, plain** Cl; 7 3/8 x 2; A.C. Williams US 1920s; **B.** $100-200.
C | 754. | **Lion, Tail Right** Cl; 5 1/4 x 6 1/4; A.C. Williams US 1905-1931; **B.** $100-150.
| 755. | ***Lion, Tail Right** Cl; 4 x 4 7/8; Arcade 1910- 1913; A.C. Williams 1905-1931; US; **A.** $60-90.
| 756. | **Lion, Fine Haired Mane** Cl; 3 13/16 x 4 7/8; US; **A.** $60-90.
| 757. | **Lion, Ears Up** (Turnpin) Cl; 3 5/8 x 4 1/2; A.C.Williams 1934; Arcade 1932; US; **A.** $60-90.
| 758. | **Quilted Lion** Cl; 3 3/4 x 4 3/4; US; **D.** $350-500.
| 759. | ***Lion, Tail Right** Cl; 3 1/2 x 4 15/16; A.C. Williams US 1920s; **A.** $50-75.
| 760. | **Lion on Wheels** Cl; 4 1/2 x 4 5/8; A.C. Williams US 1920s; **C.** $250-450.

	A	761.	**Harris Lion** WM; 6 x 2 1/2 x 5 1/8; Banthrico US 1950s; **M.** $25-35.

<table>
<tr><td>A</td><td>761.</td><td>Harris Lion WM; 6 x 2 1/2 x 5 1/8; Banthrico US 1950s; M. $25-35.</td></tr>
</table>

A 761. **Harris Lion** WM; 6 x 2 1/2 x 5 1/8; Banthrico US 1950s; **M.** $25-35.

762. **Large Lion, Tail Right,** Cl; 5 1/4 x 5 1/4; US; **B.** $100-150.

763. **Lion, Tail Left** Cl; 3 3/4 x 5 3/8; Hubley US 1910-1929; **B.** $125-175.

764. **Lion, Tail Between Legs** Cl; 3 x 5 1/4; US; **B.** $100-200.

765. **Lion, Tail Left** Cl; 4 x 4 7/8; US; **C.** $100-200.

766. **Harris Lion (Oval Base)** WM; 6 x 4 5/8; Banthrico US 1950s; **M.** $30-40.

B 767. **Camel, Large** Cl; 7 1/4 x 6 1/4; A.C. Williams US c1917-1920s; **C.** $350-550.

768. **Camel, Small** Cl; 4 3/4 x 3 7/8; Hubley; A.C. Williams US c 1920-1930s; **B.** $125-200.

769. **Oriental Camel** Cl; 3 3/4 x 5 3/8; US; **D.** $600-1000.

770. **Kneeling Camel** Cl; 2 1/2 x 4 13/16; Kyser & Rex US 1889; **D.** $600-1000.

771. **Camel with Pack** comp.; 4 x 4 1/2; Hausser, Germany 1929; **2.** $150-250.

772. **Camel with Hinged Back** silvered lead; 5 x 5 3/4; Germany 1920s; **1.** $200-300.

C 773. **Lion** (converted doorstop) AL; 7"; US; **1.** $100-150.

774. **Stegosaurus** cast bronze; 3 3/4 x 7 1/4; Copyright Nelles US 1979; **M.** $50-75.

775. **Three Wise Monkeys** lead; US; **1.** $20-30.

776. **Tyrannosaurus** WM; 5 1/2; Rush Metal Products, Inc. US; **M.** $20-30.

777. **Brontosaurus** WM; 8 1/2; US; **M.** $30-40.

778. **Rhesus Monkey** (converted doorstop) Cl; 8 1/2; US; **C.** $150-250.

A 779.   **World's Fair Globe on Base** wood & paper Cl; 5";
          US c1893; **D.** $600-900.

    780.   **Liberty Bell 1905** Cl; 3 3/4 x 3 5/16; J.M. Harper
          US 1905; **C.** $250-350.

    781.   **Globe Bank** Cl; 5 3/4; Enterprise Mfg. Co. US 1875;
          C. $200-350.

    782.   ***Liberty Bell ("1926")** Cl; 3 3/4 x 3 7/8 diam.;
          Grey Iron Casting Co. US 1928; **C.** $75-125.

    783.   **"Columbia Savings Bank"** Cl, wood & paper;
          5 3/4 x 5 1/2; Hermann Schedler, designer US 1889;
          E. $1500-2000.

    784.   ***Washington Bell** Cl; (see #782) 3 3/4 x 3 7/8
          diam.; Grey Iron Casting Co. US 1900-1905; **C.**
          $100-150.

    785.   **Glove on Wire Arc** Cl; 4 5/8 x 2 3/8 diam.; Arcade
          US 1900-1913; **C.** $250-450.

B 786.   **Washington Bell with Yoke** -- 1932 Cl; 2 3/4 x 2
          5/8; Grey Iron Casting Co. US. 1932. **C.** $100-150.

    787.   **Universal Globe** tin litho; 4"; Cribben & Sexton Co.
          US; **2.** $250-450.

    788.   **German Olympics Bell** porcelain, KLT; 4"; Hein-
          rich & Co. "Bayer Ostmark" Germany 1936; **3.** $100-
          150.

    789.   **Globe on Arc** Cl; 5 1/4; Grey Iron Casting Co. US
          1900-1903; **B.** $150-300.

    790.   **Japanese Olympics Bell** metal, KLT; 3 1/2; 1940;
          3. $100-150.

    791.   **Globe on Wood Base** metal & paper litho; 4 1/4;
          Miller Bank Service Co. US c1930s; **B.** $50-75.

    792.   **"Miniature Liberty Bell"** Cl; 3 1/2 x 1 3/4; Penn-
          craft; **M.** $30-40.

C 793.   **Promotional Bell** metal & wood; 4 x 3 3/4;
          Banker's Savings & Credit System Co. US 1919; **1.**
          $20-30.

    794.   **"World's Fair '93" (small)** pottery; 4 3/8 x 6; US
          1893; **3.** $600-900.

    795.   **"Musical Bank" with Eagle "1776-1876"** Cl;
          6 5/8 x 4 1/2; A. Feigl, designer US 1876; **F.** $5000-
          10,000.

    796.   **"Bank of Liberty and Peace"** Cl; 5 3/4; US 1916;
          F. $2000-2500.

    797.   **"Musical Bank"** Cl; 5 11/16; A. Feigl, designer US
          1876; **E.** $4000-6000.

    798.   **"Globe Bank"** tin, KLT; 4 3/8; Chein US c1934-
          1977; **1.** $30-40.

    799.   **Bicentennial Bell** AL; 4 1/2 x 4 1/4; US; **M.** $20-
          30.

A 819. **Crosley Radio, large** Cl; 5 1/8 x 4 1/2; Kenton US 1931-1936; **D.** $800-1200.

820. **Crosley Radio, small** Cl; 4 5/16 x 4; Kenton US 1931-1936; **C.** $300-500.

821. **"Radio Bank"** Cl; 3 5/16 x 2 5/16; Hubley US 1928; **C.** $150-300.

822. **"GE" Radio** Cl; 3 7/8 x 2 3/8; Arcade US 1932-1934; **C.** $150-250.

823. **"Zenith Radio"** (paper dial) WM; 3 9/16; US; **2.** $80-125.

824. **"Sunny Suds" Record Player** brass; 4 1/2; US; **B.** $75-125.

825. **"Brunswick" Record Player** brass; 5"; US; **B.** $75-125.

826. **"Templeton Radio"** Cl, steel sides; 4 5/16; Kenton US 1930-34; **C.** $400-600.

B 827. **"Majestic" Radio** Cl, steel back; 4 1/2; Arcade US 1932-1934; **A.** $50-75.

828. **Piano, Candy Container** (sliding tin closure) glass; 2 3/4; US; **2.** $200-300.

829. **Radio Bank (3 dials)** Cl, metal sides & back; 3 x 2 7/8 x 4 5/8; Kenton US 1927-1932; **B.** $200-350.

830. **Radio Bank (3 dials, large)** Cl, with metal sides & back; 3 1/2 x 3 1/8 x 6 3/16; Kenton US 1927-1931; **C.** $250-450.

831. **Radio Bank (2 dials)** Cl, metal sides & back; 3 3/8 x 4 1/2 x 3 1/4; Kenton US 1924-5; **C.** $150-300.

832. **"Musette" Piano** lead; 2 1/2 x 4 x 1 3/15; US; **2.** $150-250.

833. **Radio with Combination Door** Cl, metal sides & back; 4 1/2 x 3 5/8 x 2 3/16; Kenton US 1936- 40; **A.** $100-200.

C 834. **U.S. Mail Bank (combination lock)** Cl; 6 7/8 x 4 3/8 x 2 1/2; O.B. Fish US 1903; **D.** $350-550.

835. **U.S. Mail (large combination trap)** Cl; 4 3/4 x 3 1/2/ x 2 ; Kenton US 1904-10; **C.** $100-200.

836. **U.S. Mail (small combination trap)** Cl; (see #835) 4 3/4 x 3 1/2 x 2; Kenton US early 1900s; **B.** $100-200.

837. **U.S. Mail, narrow** (hinged coin slot) Cl; 4 3/8 x 2 3/4 x 1 11/16; Kenton; A.C. Williams US 1912-1931; **A.** $60-100.

838. **U.S. Mail, small** Cl; 3 5/8 x 2 3/4 x 1 11/16; A.C. Williams, 1912-1931; Kenton, c1904-1910 US; **A.** $60-80.

839. **U.S. Mail** Cl; 3 1/2 x 2 1/2 x 1 5/8; Arcade, 1913; A.C. Williams US 1908-34; **A.** $50-80.

840. **"R.L. Berry's Piano Bank"** steel, KLT; 5 1/8 x 5 7/8 x 3; US; **B.** $75-125.

A   841.   ***Standing Mailbox, large** Cl; 5 1/2 x 2 1/2 x 2 1/4; Hubley US 1928-1936; **B.** $150-250.

842.   **Standing Mailbox, small** Cl; 3 3/4 x 1 7/8 x 1 1/2; Hubley US 1928; **A.** $60-90.

843.   **Phone Bank, penny toy** tin; 3 1/2; Germany; **3.** $200-300.

844.   **Pay Phone** tin; 6 3/4 x 3; US 1924; **2.** $75-125.

845.   **"Postal Savings Mailbox"** Cl; 6 3/4 x 3 3/4; Nicol US c1920s; **D.** $250-450.

846.   **Letter Box** tin, KLT; 5 7/8 x 4; England; **2.** $75-100.

847.   **Pillar Box, "VR"** Cl; 5 5/16 x 3; late 1800s England; **F.** $800-1200.

848.   **Air Mail Bank on Base** Cl; 6 3/8 x 2 5/8 x 2 3/4 base diam.; Dent. US 1920; **C.** $600-1000.

B   849.   **"U.S. Mail" with Eagle** Cl; 5 1/8 x 3 1/2 x 1 3/4; Kenton US c1932-34; **C.** $100-200.

850.   **"U.S. Mail" with Eagle** Cl; 4 1/8 x 3 1/2 x 2 3/4; Kenton US 1911-31; **B.** $100-150.

851.   **"U.S. Mail Bank" with Eagle** Cl; 4 1/8 x 3 1/4 x 1 3/8; Kenton US 1932-34; **B.** $75-100.

852.   **"U.S. Mail" with Eagle** Cl; 3 5/8 x 2 1/2 x 1 3/8; Kenton US 191-31; **B.** $50-100.

853.   **"U.S. Mail"** Cl; 3 5/8 x 2 1/2 x 1 1/4; A.C. Williams US 1912-1931; **A.** $50-75.

854.   **"U.S. Mail"** (slot in rear) Cl; 4 1/4 x 3 1/4 x 1 1/4; A.C. Williams US 1920s; **A.** $50-75.

855.   ***"U.S. Mail" with Eagle** Cl; 4 x 4 x 1 7/8; Hubley US 1906; **B.** $100-150.

856.   **"U.S. Mail"** (hanging) Cl; 5 1/8 x 3; A.C. Williams US 1921-34; **A.** $60-100.

C   857.   **"Pay Phone Bank"** Cl; 7 3/16 x 3 11/16 x 3; J. & E. Stevens US patented 1926; **D.** $600-1000.

858.   **"U.S. Mail" on Platform** Cl; 7 1/4; base, 4 11/16 x 4 3/4; US late 1800s; **E.** $1000-2000.

859.   **"U.S. Bank", Eagle Finial** Cl; 9 1/4 x 4 1/8 x 3 5/8 base diam.; US 1890s; **E.** $1000-2000.

860.   **"U.S. Letter Box"** tin; 9 3/4; US 1920s; **3.** $75-125.

861.   **"U.S. Mail" on Victorian Base** Cl; (same box as #855) Hubley US 1906; **D.** $800-1500.

A 862. **"National Iron Safe"** Cl; 4 3/8 x 3 1/2 x 3 3/8; US; **D.** $250-500.

863. **"Fidelity Safe" large** (turnpin) Cl; 3 5/8 x 2 5/8 x 2 5/8; Kyser & Rex US c1880; **C.** $150-300.

864. **"Fidelity Safe" medium** (turnpin) Cl; 3 x 2 1/4 x 2 1/4; Kyser & Rex US c1880; **C.** $100-200.

865. **"The Daisy"** Cl; 2 1/8 x 1 3/4 x 1 1/2; Shimer Toy Co. US 1899; **B.** $100-200.

866. **"Pet Safe"** Cl; 4 1/2 x 2 3/4 x 1 3/4; US; **C.** $200-400.

867. **"The Daisy"** (paint variation) Cl; (see #865) 2 1/8 x 1 3/4 x 1 1/2; Shimer Toy Co. US; **B.** $100-200.

868. **"Johnstown Savings Bank"** lead, KLT; 2 1/4 x 4 1/8 x 2 1/4; A.C. Rehberger US; **2.** $100-200.

869. **"Safe"** Cl; 3 1/4 x 2 1/2 x 2 1/4; J. & E. Stevens US 1891; **A.** $50-100.

870. **"Bank of England"** Cl; 4 1/2 x 4 3/16 x 4 1/8; England 1882; **E.** $500-800.

B 871. **"Puzzle Try Me"** Cl; 2 11/16 x 2 3/8 x 2 5/16; Abe & Geo. Abrams, designers US patented 1868; **E.** $500-800.

872. **"Dime Savings"** Cl; 2 1/2 x 1 15/16 x 1 3/4; Shimer Toy Co. US 1899; **D.** $400-800.

873. **Red Ball Safe** Cl; 3 x 2 7/16; US; **C.** $200-400.

874. **"Savings Bank" Candy Container** glass; 4 x 3 13/16 x 2 3/4; US; **1.** $100-200.

875. **"Kodak Bank"** Cl; 4 1/4 x 5 x 2 3/4; J. & E. Stevens US 1905; **C.** $200-400.

876. **"Star Safe"** Cl; 2 5/8 x 2 x 2; Kyser & Rex US 1882; **B.** $200-400.

877. **"Penny Trust Co." Candy Container** (tin sliding clos.); 2 7/8 x 2 1/8 x 1/8; US; **1.** $100-150.

878. **Columbia Bank** Cl; 2 5/8 x 2 2/14; Columbia Grey Iron Casting Co. US 1897; **B.** $50-100.

879. **Mosler Safe** tin; 1 7/8 x 1 3/8 x 1; Mosler Safe Co. US c1919; **2.** $100-150.

C 880. **"Roller Safe"** Cl; 3 11/16 x 2 7/8 x 2 3/4; Kyser & Rex US 1882; **B.** $100-200.

881. **"Young America"** Cl; 4 3/8 x 3 1/8 x 3 1/8; Kyser & Rex US 1882; **B.** $150-250.

882. **"Arabian Safe"** Cl; 4 9/16 x 4 1/4 x 4 1/8 ; Kyser & Rex US 1882; **B.** $150-250.

883. **"Japanese Safe"** Cl; 5 3/8 x 4 5/8 x 4 5/8; Kyser & Rex US 1882; **C.** $150-250.

884. **Safe with Geometric Designs** Cl; 5 3/8 x 4 3/8 x 4 3/8;Kys er & Rex US 1882?; **C.** $500-800.

885. **Floral Safe (National Safe)** Cl; 4 5/8 x 4 1/8 x 4 3/16; Kyser & Rex 1882?; J. & E. Stevens US 1898; **C.** $200-400.

886. **"Sport Safe"** Cl; 3 x 2 1/4; Kyser & Rex US 1882; **B.** $100-150.

<table>
</table>

A 887. **National "Safe"** Cl; 3 3/8 x 2 1/2 x 2 1/4; J. & E. Stevens US 1896-1928; **A.** $50-75.

888. **"Safe Deposit"** Cl; 3 5/8 x 2 3/4 x 2 1/2; Shimer Toy Co. US 1899; **A.** $50-100.

889. **"Security Safe"** Cl; 4 1/2 x 3 1/4 x 2 1/4; SU 1894; **A.** $200-300.

890. **"Security Safe"** Cl; 6 x 4 1/8 x 2 3/4; US 1894; **B.** $200-400.

891. **"Security Safe Deposit"** Cl; 3 7/8 x 2 13/16 x 2 3/8; Kyser & Rex? US 1881; **B.** $100-150.

892. **Church Window Safe** Cl; 3 1/16 x 2 1/4 x 2 3/16 Shimer Toy Co. US 1890s; **A.** $75-150.

893. **"I X L" Safe** Cl; 3 x 2 1/4 x 2 1/4; Kyser & Rex US 1881; **A.** $150-250.

894. **Scrollwork Safe** Cl; 2 3/4 x 2 5/16 x 2; US early 1900s; **B.** $75-125.

B 895. **"Time Safe"** Cl; 7 1/16 x 3 3/4; E.M. Roche Co. US; **D.** $500-800.

896. **Jewel Safe** Cl; 5 3/8 x 3 3/4 x 3 1/4; J. & E. Stevens US c1907; **C.** $300-500.

897. **"Junior Safe Deposit"** Cl; 4 5/8 x 3 3/8 x 2 1/8; US; **C.** $150-250.

898. **"Junior Safe Deposit"** Cl; 4 1/2 x 3 1/4 x 2 1/8; US 1892; **C.** $150-250.

899. **"My Secret Safe"** tin; 4 3/4 x 3 5/16 x 1 7/8; "AN-FOE" pre WWII "Germany"; **2.** $75-125.

900. **"Child's Safe, Fireproof"** tin; 5 1/2 x 4 x 3 1/4; Chein US 1906; **3.** $100-200.

C 901. **"Fidelity Trust Vault" (with Lord Fauntleroy)** Cl; 4 7/8 x 3 7/8 x 4 1/2; J. Barton Smith Co. US 1890; **C.** $600-1200.

902. **"Watch Dog Safe"** Cl, brass handle; 5 1/8 5 1/8; US; **F.** $3000-4000.

903. **"Fidelity Trust Vault" (with Lord Fauntleroy)** Cl; 6 1/2 x 5 7/8 x 5 3/8; J. Barton Smith Co. US 1890; **D.** $600-1200.

904. **"Metropolitan Bank"** Cl, 5 7/8 x 4 1/8 x 4 1/8; J. & E. Stevens US c1872; **C.** $300-500.

905. **"New York Bank"** Cl; 4 1/4 x 3 x 3; J. & E. Stevens US c1872; **C.** $250-400.

906. **"Bank of Columbia"** Cl 4 7/8 x 3 3/4 x 3 3/8; Arcade US 1891-1913; **C.** $300-500.

A 907. **White City Barrel #1 on Cart** Cl; cart, 5" long; Nicol US patented 1894; **D.** $400-500.

908. **White City Barrel #1** Cl; 4"; Nicol US patented 1894; **B.** $100-200.

909. **Barrel** Cl; 2 3/4 x 2 (diam. at top); Judd US c1873; **C.** $100-150.

910. **White City Puzzle Safe #12** Cl; 4 7/8 x 3 5/8 x 3 3/8; Nicol US 1893; **C.** $250-350.

911. **White City Pail** Cl; 2 5/8 x 2 5/8; Nicol US 1893; **B.** $100-200.

912. **"Penny Register" Pail** Cl; 2 3/4 x 2 3/4; Kyser & Rex US c1889; **C.** $100-200.

913. **White City Puzzle Safe #10** Cl; 4 5/8 x 2 3/4 x 2 3/4; Nicol US 1893; **B.** $150-250.

914. **"Time Lock Puzzle Safe No. 326"** Cl; 4 5/8 x 2 3/4 x 2 3/4; Nicol US 1893; **B.** $150-250.

B 915. **Basket Bank (smooth)** steel; 2 7/8 x 3 3/4; Chas. A. Braun, designer US patented 1902; **A.** $60-100.

916. **White City Barrel (large)** Cl; 5 1/8 x 3 3/8 diam.; Nicol US 1893; **C.** $250-350.

917. **Basket Bank (woven)** Cl; 2 7/8 x 3 3/4; Chas. A. Braun, designer US patented 1902; **A.** $75-125.

918. **Beer Keg on Support** nickeled brass; 3 1/16 x 1 5/8 diam.; US; **D.** $250-450.

919. **Fruit Basket Puzzle Bank** Cl; 2 3/4 x 3 1/2; Nicol US 1894; **C.** $400-600.

920. **"Little Millionaire"** nickeled brass; 2 7/8 x 2; Vertago Mfg. Co., Boston US 1924; **C.** $60-100.

921. **"Dime Registering Coin Barrel"** Cl; 4 x 2 1/2 diam.; Kyser & Rex US 1889; **C.** $150-250.

922. **"White City Puzzle Safe" #357 (small)** Cl; 2 11/16 x 2 3/16 x 1 9/16; Nicol US 1893; **C.** $300-500.

923. **"White City Puzzle Safe" #357** (no ferris wheel) Cl; (see #92) 2 11/16 x 2 3/16 x 1 9/16; Nicol US 1895; **C.** $300-500.

C 924. **"Cash Register Savings Bank"** (factory conversion) Cl; 4 3/4 x 3 3/4 x 4 3/4; Hubley US 1906; **D.** $600-800.

925. **Cash Register with Mesh** Cl; 3 3/4 x 3 5/16 x 2 7/16; Arcade UYS 1910-1925; **B.** $100-150.

926. **"Crystal Bank"** Cl and glass; 3 7/8 x 2 11/16 diam.; Arcade US 1910-1925; **A.** $75-125.

927. **Bird Cage Bank ("Crystal Bank")** Cl and mesh; Arcade US 1910-25; **A.** $75-125.

928. **Treasure Chest (small)** Cl; 1 7/8 x 2 3/4 x 1 7/8; US; **C.** $100-200.

929. **Treasure Chest (large)** Cl; 2 3/4 x 4 x 2 5/8; John Wright US 1970; **M.** $20-30.

930. ***"Junior Cash" Register (small)** Cl; 4 1/4 x 3 1/2 x 3; J. & E. Stevens US c1920s; **B.** $100-200.

931. ***"Junior Cash" Register (large)** Cl; 5 1/4 x 4 5/8 x 4 1/8; J. & E. Stevens US c1920s; **C.** $150-300.

A   932.   **"Thrift Bank"** AL; 5 1/8 x 2 7/8 x 2 7/8; US; **3.** $60-100.

933.   **"National Savings Bank"** WM, KLT; 4 3/8 x 3 1/4 x 2 3/4; US; **1.** $50-80.

934.   **R.C. Allen Cash Register** (conversion) WM; 3 3/4 x 3 x 3 3/4; US 1958; **M.** $10-20.

935.   **Pirate Chest** WM; 3 1/8 x 4 x 3; US; **1.** $10-20.

936.   **Pirate Chest on Base** lead, ST; 2 5/8 x 3 3/8; US; **1.** $30-40.

937.   **One-Armed Bandit ("Slot Bank")** WM; 4 x 2 1/2; Dodge, Inc., L.A. US; **1.** $20-30.

938.   **Barrel with Clothespins** wood; 3 1/8 x 2; 1891; **2.** $20-30.

939.   **Barrel (deposit developer)** wood & metal; 2 15/16; Bankers Thrift Corp. US; **1.** $20-40.

940.   **Barrel on Cart,** metal; 4 1/4 x 3; US; **1.** $40-60.

B   941.   **Strongbox** heavy steel; 3 1/4 x 4 3/8 x 2 1/8; US patented 1891; **1.** $30-50.

942.   **Strongbox** heavy steel; 2 3/8 x 4 3/8; US; $30-50.

943.   **Indian Head Penny** Cl; 3 1/4 diam.; G. Knerr US 1972; **M.** $60-80.

944.   **Dollar Sign** (2 tiny slots in side) tin; KLT; 4 x 2 5/8; US; **2.** $50-75.

945.   **Buffalo Nickel** Cl; 3 7/8 diam.; G. Knerr US early 1970s; **M.** $75-125.

946.   **Trunk on Dolly** Cl; 2 5/8 x 3 9/16 x 2; Piaget US 1890; **D.** $300-400.

947.   **"Phoenix" Dime Register Trunk** Cl; 3 3/4 x 5 x 2 5/8; Piaget US 1890; **C.** $150-250.

C   948.   **Savings Chest** Cl; 4 5/16 x 6 1/4 x 3 11/16; Van Elyen-Henstep, Detroit US 1892; **D.** $400-600.

949.   **Mourner's Purse** lead with brass handle; 5 x 5 x 3 1/4; US c1880s; **3.** $200-300.

950.   **Wall Safe** metal & comp.; 8 x 8; Leister Game Co., Toledo US 1963; **M.** $40-50.

951.   **Bean Pot** (nickel registering) Cl; 3 x 3 7/16 diam.; US; **C.** $250-350.

952.   **Jewel Chest (Coffin Bank)** Cl; combo. lock; 6 1/8 x 4 5/8; US 1889; **C.** $300-500.

A 953. **Dormer Bank** Cl; 4 3/4 x 3 1/4 x 3 3/4; US; **E.** $4000-6000.

954. **Castle Bank,** small Cl; 3 x 2 13/16 x 1 13/16; Kyser & Rex US 1882; **C.** $400-800.

955. **"San Gabriel Mission"** (musical) Cl; 4 5/8 x 3 3/4 x 2 9/16; US; **F.** $6000-10,000.

956. **Church Towers** Cl; 6 3/4 x 6 1/4 x 2 1/4; US; **D.** $800-1200.

957. **San Gabriel Mission** (lead pattern); 4 11/16 x 3 3/4 x 2 9/16; US. $2000-4000.

958. **Takoma Park Bank** Cl; 3 3/4 x 3 5/8 x 3 1/4 US c1916; **E.** $600-1200.

959. ***Villa Bank (1882 Church)** Cl; 5 7/8 x 3 3/8 x 2; Kyser & Rex US 1882; **C.** $450-750.

B 960. **Little Brown Church** AL alloy; 4 x 2 3/8 x 5 3/16; Hout, metal manufacturer; **M.** $20-30.

961. **Little Brown Church** pottery; 3 1/2 x 4 x 2 5/8; **M.** $20-30.

962. **"Estberg Fan Bank"** brass; 4 1/2 x 3 3/4 x 3; Denmark c1904; **B.** $100-200.

963. **"Den Danske Landmands-bank"** brass; 4 1/2 x 3 3/4 x 3; "Hansen & Jensen" Denmark c1904; **B.** $100-200.

964. **Banken Skanderborg Omebn** brass; 4 3/8 x 3 3/4 x 2 7/8; Denmark; **C.** $100-200.

965. **Rochester Clock** Cl; 4 7/8 x 4 1/8 x 3; US; **D.** $400-600.

966. **Stollwerck Church** tin; 3 3/8 x 1 5/8 x 2 1/2; Germany c1908; **2.** $250-450.

967. **Lilliput, Still** Cl; 4 7/16 x 2 7/8 x 3 3/8; J. & E. Stevens US 1875; **E.** $800-1200.

C 968. **Lichfield Cathedral** Cl; 6 1/2 x 2 3/16 x 3 1/2; Chamberlain & Hill, England c1908; **C.** $350-500.

969. ***Lichfield Cathedral** brass; 6 5/8 x 3 3/8 x 2; Chamberlain & Hill, England c1908; **C.** $300-400.

970. **Riverside Bank** lead; 5 3/8 x 3 1/2 x 2 15/16; American Badge Co., Inc. US; **3.** $200-300.

971. **Dordrecht** Cl; 7 1/8 x 5; Holland 1800s; **D.** $800-1200.

972. **Stave Church** metal; 7 x 3 5/8; Scandinavia; **2.** $150-250.

973. **Westminster Abbey** Cl; 6 1/4 x 3 5/16 x 1 3/8; Sydenham & McOustra? England c1908; **B.** $200-300.

974. **Westminster Abbey** Cl; 6 3/8 x 3 1/2 x 1 5/8; Sydenham & McOustra? England c1908; **B.** $250-350.

A 975. **Church with Two Chimneys** sheet brass with KL door; 3 7/8 x 2 3/4 x 3 1/2; US; **B.** $200-300.

976. **Tabernacle Savings** Cl; 2 1/4 x 5 x 2 1/2; Keyless Lock Co. US; **E.** $1000-2000.

977. **St. Paul's Church** lead; 6 1/8 x 3 x 4 1/8; A.C. Rehberger US; **2.** $250-450.

978. **"St. Luke's Tower"** lead; 5 5/8 x 5 x 2 3/8; A.C. Rehberger US; **2.** $200-400.

979. **Cologne Cathedral** silvered lead; 3 3/4 x 1 3/4 x 3 1/4; Germany 1920s; **2.** $150-250.

980. **Cologne Cathedral** ("Dom-Koln") silvered lead; 4 1/8 x 1 1/2 x 3 3/4; Germany 1920s; **2.** $150-250.

981. **"Chapel Mite Bank"** silvered lead; 4 3/8 x 3 1/6 x 3 5/8; US; **1.** $100-200.

B 982. **New Church** Cl; 6 5/8 x 3 1/2 x 5 3/4; Chicago Hardware Foundry 1950s; **M.** $400-800.

983. **Blackpool Tower** lead with hinged, KL base; 5 7/16 x 3 1/2 x 3; Germany 1920s; **1.** $200-400.

984. **Blackpool Tower** Cl; 7 3/8 x 4 3/8 x 2 7/8; Chamberlain & Hill, England c1908; **1.** $250-450.

985. **Blackpool Tower** silvered lead; 4 9/16 x 3 1/2 x 2 1/16; Germany 1920s; **1.** $200-300.

986. **New England Church** Cl; 7 1/2 x 4 x 7 1/2; US; **C.** $450-750.

C 987. **Church on Base** tin; 12 1/2 x 5 1/2 x 5 3/8; George W. Brown US c1870s; **3.** $1000-1500.

988. **Old South Church** Cl; 5 5/8 (to top of tower) x 4 x 6 3/8; 9 3/4 to top of spire; US; **D.** $4000-6000.

989. **Ornate Church** (glass windows) Cl; 8 1/2 x 3 7/8 x 4 3/16; **F.** $600-1000.

990. **Old South Church** Cl; 5 5/8 (to top of tower) x 4 x 6 3/8; 9 1/4 to top of spire; US; **E.** $6000-10,000.

991. **Old South Church** Cl; 13 x 4 1/2 x 7 1/2; US; **E.** $10,000-15,000.

A 992. ***Colonial House (House with Porch)** Cl; 4 x
3 7/8 x 2 3/4; A.C. Williams US 1910-1934; **A.** $100-
200.

993. **Colonial House (House with Porch)** Cl; 3 x 2 5/8
x 2 1/8; A.C. Williams US 1910-1931; **A.** $75-150.

994. **Tudor Home** lead; 3 1/8 x 4 1/8 x 2 1/8; Europe; **2.**
$150-250.

995. **"Little Red School House"** tin; 1 3/4 x 1 15/16;
US; **2.** $60-100.

996. ***House with Basement** Cl; 4 5/8 x 4 5/8 x 3 7/8;
Ohio Foundry Col, Cleveland US 1893; **D.** $2000-
3000.

997. **House with Chimney Slot** Cl; 2 7/8 x 2 13/16 x 2;
US; **D.** $600-1000.

998. **"Town Hall Bank"** Cl; 4 5/8 x 3 1/4 x 2 1/4; Kyser
& Rex US 1882; **C.** $500-800.

999. **Bungalow Bank (Cottage with Porch)** Cl; 3 3/4
x 3 x 3 1/4; Grey Iron Casting Co. US 1918-1928; **C.**
$300-500.

B 1000. **One Story House** Cl; 3 x 2 1/4 x 2; J. & E. Stevens
1883; Grey Iron Casting Co. US 1903; **A.** $75-125.

1001. **One Story House** C; 2 7/8 x 2 3/16 x 1 15/16;
Kenton US 1927; **A.** $100-150.

1002. **Two Story House** Cl; 3 1/16 x 2 1/8 x 1 13/16; A.C.
Williams US 1931-1934; **A.** $100-150.

1003. **Quadrafoil House** Cl; 3 1/8 x 2 1/4 x 2; Stevens;
Wing; Arcade 1902-1913; Kenton c1904-1926; US;
A. $100-150.

1004. **Pavillion** Cl; 3 1/8 x 3 x 2 1/2; Kyser & Rex US
1880; **D.** $450-650.

1005. **Oriental Bank (Oval)** Cl; 3 x 2 3/4 x 1 15/16; Kyser

& Rex US 1880; **D.** $500-800.

1006. **Snappit Still** Cl; 4 x 3 3/8 x 3 1/8; H.L. Judd US
1890; **D.** $600-1000.

1007. **Six-Sided Bldg.** Cl, twist pin; 2 3/8 x 2 7/8 x 1 3/4;
US; **D.** $400-600.

1008. **Two Story (Six Sided)** Cl; 3 3/8 x 2 7/16 x 2 3/8;
US; **C.** $250-400.

1009. **One Car Garage** Cl; 2 1/2 x 2 x 1 7/8; A.C. Williams
US 1927-1931; **B.** $200-300.

1010. **Two Car Garage** Cl; 2 1/2 x 2 1/2 x 1 7/8; A.C. Williams US 1927-31; US; **B.** $200-300.

C 1011. ***1876 Bank** Cl; 3 3/8 x 3 x 2 3/16; Judd US 1895;
B. $200-300.

1012. **1876 Bank** Cl; 2 7/8 x 2 3/8 x 2; Judd US 1895; **B.**
$150-250.

1013. **"Wanamaker" Bank** tin; 2 1/4 x 3 1/4 x 2 5/8; Stollwerck, Germany 1908; **1.** $150-200.

1014. **Red Riding Hood Hut** lead, TL; 2 3/8 x 2 5/8 x 2;
Europe; **2.** $200-400.

1015. **Temple of Jehol** tin; 3 1/8 x 3 1/4 x 3 1/4; Green
Duck, Chicago US 1933; **2.** $150-250.

1016. **Hansel & Gretel** tin; 2 1/4 x 2 1/2; Stollwerck, Germany c1890; **2.** $150-250.

1017. **"Harleysville Bank"** Cl; 2 5/8 x 3 x 5 1/4; unicast
Foundry US 1959; **M.** $100-150.

1018. **"Beverly State Savings Bank"** tin; 2 5/8 x
3 11/16 x 2 1/4; Banker's Thrift Corp. US late 1920s;
1. $30-40.

1019. **Home Bank** Cl; 4 x 3 1/2 x 3 1/2; H.L. Judd US
1895; **C.** $300-500.

A 1020. **Ironmaster's House (combo. trap)** Cl; 4 1/2 x 2 3/4 x 2 7/8; Kyser & Rex US 1884; **D.** $800-1200.

1021. **Lincoln's Cabin** pottery; 2 3/8 x 3 /4 x 2 3/8; Austria; **1.** $40-60.

1022. **Log Cabin, center chimney** Cl; 2 9/16 x 3 7/16 x 2 3/4; US; **C.** $250-450.

1023. **Log Cabin, side chimney** Cl; 2 1/2 x 3 1/4 x 2 3/4; Kyser & Rex US 1882; **C.** $250-400.

1024. **Cabin with Shake roof** Cl; 3 3/8 x 2 13/16 x 2 1/4; England; **D.** $500-700.

1025. **Old Shawneetown** Cl; 2 7/16 x 3 4/8 x 2 5/8; US; **M.** $40-60.

1026. **Old Shawneetown** Cl; 2 7/16 x 3 5/8 x 2 5/8; Bergbower US 1970; **M.** $40-60.

1027. **Ironmaster's House (combo. door)** Cl; 4 1/4 x 3 3/4 x 2 5/8; Kyser & Rex US 1884; **D.** $1200-1800.

B 1028. **CMS Straw Hut** (collection box) comp.; 5"; England; **1.** $50-80.

1029. **Gingerbread House** Cl, KLT; 3 7/8 x 4 1/4 x 3 1/8; France; **E.** $2000-3000.

1030. **Lucky Cabin** Cl; 4 1/8 x 6 x 3 1/8; John Wright US 1970; **M.** $40-60.

1031. **TB Hut,** lead; 4 x 2 3/4; US c1920s; **1.** $150-250.

1032. **"Lincoln Bank"** brass; 2 1/2 x 3 1/2 x 2 1/16; US; **C.** $100-150.

1033. **Gingerbread House** silver plate, KLT; 3 3/4 x 4 3/8 x 3 5/16; Denmark; **1.** $75-125.

1034. **"Indian Hut"** (CMS) comp.; 3 3/14 x 5 x 3 1/8; England; **1.** $75-125.

C 1035. **The Cottage Bank,** tin; 6 1/8 x 5 1/8; George W. Brown US 1870s; **3.** $1000-1500.

1036. **Cottage,** tin; 4 x 4 1/2 x 4 1/8; George W. Brown US 1870s; **3.** $800-1500.

1037. **Chelsea House,** tin & wood; 6 7/8 x 10 1/8 x 7; England; **3.** $300-400.

1038. **Cottage,** tin; 4 1/2 x 4 3/8 x 4 3/8; Bing, Germany 1908; **2.** $350-450.

1039. **Cottage,** tin; 5 7/8 x 5 3/8 x 5 3/8; George W. Brown US 1870s; **3.** $1000-1500.

A

1040. **"Woolworth Building on base."** Cl; 8 1/8 x 2 5/8 x 3 1/8; Kenton US 1915; **E.** $2000-3000.

1041. **"Woolworth Bldg."** Cl; 7 7/8 x 1 3/4 x 2 1/4; Kenton US 1915; **B.** $150-250.

1042. **Woolworth Bldg.** Cl; 5 3/4 x 1 1/4 x 1 9/16; Kenton US 1915; **A.** $100-200.

1043. **Woolworth Bldg.** ceramic; 5 1/4 x 2 x 2 1/4; 1940s; **1.** $75-125.

1044. **"Woolworth Bldg."** (wood base) lead, KLT; 5 3/8 x 2 x 2 5/8; **1.** $50-100.

1045. **"Woolworth Bldg."** lead; **(#1044 without base); 1.** $50-100.

1046. **"Empire State Bldg."** silvered lead; 5 5/8 x 2 3/4 x 1 15/16; US; **1.** $75-125.

1047. **"Empire State" Bldg.** silvered lead; 7 3/4 x 2 3/4 x 1 5/8; US; **1.** $75-125.

1048. **"Washington" Monument** Cl; 6 1/8 x 2 1/8 x 2 1/8; A.C. Williams US 1910-1912; **B.** $300-400.

1049. **"Washington" Monument** Cl; 7 1/2 x 2 1/2 x 2 1/2; A.C. Williams US 1910-1912; **C.** $400-500.

B

1050. **Capitol Bank** Cl; 5 1/8 x 3 5/8 x 1; Don Duer- Riverside Foundry US 1981; **M.** $20-40.

1051. **National Bank of Los Angeles** silvered lead; 4 1/8 x 3 1/4 x 3 1/4; A.C. Rehberger US; **2.** $250-350.

1052. **"The White House"** silvered lead; 1 5/8 x 3 7/8 x 2 11/16; US; **1.** $100-150.

1053. ***U.S. Treasury Bank** Cl, sheet metal base; 3 1/4 x 3 1/4 x 3 3/4; Grey Iron Casting Co. US 1925-1928; **C.** $300-500.

1054. **"The Capitol"** silvered lead; 3 3/8 x 4 1/2 x 3 1/4; W.B. Mfg. Co. US; **1.** $100-150.

1055. **"Washington Mansion"** silvered lead; 2 1/4 x 4 x 2 3/8; US; **1.** $100-150.

1056. **"Savings Bank"** metal; 5 13/16 x 4 1/8 x 2 3/8; Master Lock Co. US; **1.** $150-250.

C

1057. **"Travel & Transportation Bldg."** WM; 3 1/4 x 5 1/4; Pref. Bank Service Co. US 1933; **1.** $200-300.

1058. **Temple,** metal; 4 5/8 x 4 1/8 x 4 3/8; S. Africa; **3.** $250-400.

1059. **People's Bank,** sheet metal & zinc alloy; 3 5/8 x 9 x 6; US; **2.** $500-700.

1060. **Aurora National Bank,** silvered lead; 5 5/8 x 3 1/4 x 3 3/4; Banthrico US; **M.** $100-150.

1061. **Masonic Temple,** brass; 6 x 5 5/8 x 2 3/4; US 1892; **D.** $800-1500.

A   1062.   **Recording Bank** Cl; 6 5/8 x 4 1/4 x 2; US 1891; **C.** $300-500.

1063.   **Administration Building** (combo. trap) Cl; 5 x 5 1/4 x 1 5/8; Magic Introduction Co., US patented 1893; **D.** $400-700.

1064.   **"Century of Progress"** Cl; 4 1/2 7 x 2; Arcade US 1933; **D.** $1500-2000.

1065.   **"Columbia Magic Savings Bank"** Cl; 5 x 5 1/4 x 1 5/8; Magic Introduction Co. US 1892; **B.** $300-400.

1066.   **"The Hub"** (mech.) Cl; 5 x 5 1/4 x 1 5/ 8; Magic Introduction Co. US 1892; **C.** $600-800.

B   1067.   **Chicago Bank** Cl; 6 3/8 x 5 3/4 x 3; John Harper Ltd. England 1893; **E.** $2000-4000.

1068.   **Arc de Triomphe,** electro-bronzed lead; 3 3/4 x 3 1/8 x 2 1/4; Europe; **1.** $75-150.

1069.   **Columbia** Cl; 4 1/2 x 3 1/2 x 3 1/2; Kenton US 1893-1913; **D.** $600-800.

1070.   **Columbia (large trap)** Cl; 5 3/4 x 4 1/2 x 4 1/2; Kenton US 1893-1913; **C.** $600-800.

1071.   **Eiffel Tower on Base** metal, KLT; 5 1/2 x 2 5/8 x 2 5/8; Europe 1920s; **2.** $150-200.

1072.   **"World's Fair Admin. Bldg."** Cl; 6 x 6 x 2 1/2; US 1893; **D.** $1500-2000.

C   1073.   **Columbia Bank** Cl; 8 3/4 x 7 x 7; Kenton US 1893-1913; **D.** $800-1200.

1074.   **Eiffel Tower** Cl; 8 3/4 x 5 1/2 x 5 1/2; Sydenham & McOustra, England 1908; **D.** $600-1000.

1075.   **Eiffel Tower** Cl; 10 3/8 x 5 1/4 x 5 1/4; England; **F.** $1500-2000.

1076.   **Eiffel Tower** Cl; 8 1/2 x 5 1/2 x 5 1/2; Robert Brown, Wales 1981; **M.** $50-100.

1077.   **Columbia** Cl; 7 x 5 3/8 x 5 3/8; Kenton US 1893-1904; **C.** $500-700.

A	1078.	**State Bank** Cl; 8 x 7 x 5 1/2; Kenton US c1900; **D.** $700-1200.
	1079.	**State Bank** Cl; 6 3/4 x 5 1/2 x 4 1/4; Kenton c1900; Grey Iron Casting Co. 1899 US; **C.** $500-800.
	1080.	**State Bank** Cl; 5 7/8 x 4 5/8 x 3 1/2; Kenton US c1900?; **A.** $200-300.
	1081.	**Deposit Bank (large print)** Cl; 4 1/4 x 3 x 2 3/8; Columbia Grey Iron Casting Co. US 1897; **B.** $150-250.
	1082.	**Deposit Bank (small print)** Cl; 4 1/4 x 3 x 2 3/8; US; **B.** $150-250.
	1083.	**State Bank** Cl; 4 1/8 x 3 1/16 x 2 3/8; Arcade 1913-1925; Grey Iron Casting Co. US 1889; **A.** $100-200.
	1084.	**City Bank** Cl; 3 1/4 x 2 1/4 x 1 7/8; Grey Iron Casting Co. US 1903; **C.** $200-300.
	1085.	**State Bank** Cl; 3 x 2 x 1 3/4; Kenton US c1890; **B.** $150-200.
	1086.	**Jarmulowsky Bldg.** Cl; 7 3/4 x 2 1/8 x 5; C.G. Shepard & Co., J. & E. Stevens US; **D.** $1500-2500.
B	1087.	**Space Heater (Bird)** Cl; 6 1/2 x 4 x 4; Chamberlain & Hill, England c1892; **B.** $100-200.
	1088.	**Castle** Cl; 4 x 3 3/8 x 3 1/8; John Harper Ltd. England; **D.** $800-1000.
	1089.	**Nurnberg** Silvered lead; 3 x 1 5/8 x 3 7/8; Germany; **2.** $250-350.

1090.	**Space Heater (Cupid)** Cl;/ 6 1/2 x 3 5/8 x 3 5/8; England c1895; **D.** $400-600.
1091.	**City of Nurnberg** silvered lead; 2 1/2 x 3 1/2 x 1 3/4; Germany; **2.** $200-300.
1092.	**Space Heater (Bee)** Cl; 6 1/4 x 4; England c1890; **D.** $500-700.
1093.	**Stuttgart Bank** lead; 3 1/4 x 3 3/4 x 1 5/8; Germany; **2.** $250-350.
1094.	**Spaceheater (Flowers)** Cl; 6 1/2 x 3 7/8 x 4 1/8; England c1890; **B.** $150-250.
C 1095.	**"City Bank" with Crown** Cl; 5 1/2 x 4 1/4 x 2 7/8; Thos. Swan, designer, US Patented 1873; **D.** $1200-1800.
1096.	**"Pearl Street Bank"** Cl; 4 1/4 x 4 1/4 x 2 1/2; US; **C.** $600-800.
1097.	**"City Bank" with Teller** Cl; 5 1/2 x 3 1/4 x 4 3/8; H.L. Judd US; **D.** $800-1200.
1098.	**City Bank with Teller** (brass pattern); 5 3/8 x 3 1/4 x 2 1/2; H.L. Judd US. $600-1000.
1099.	**City Bank with Teller** Cl; 5 1/4 x 3 x 2; H.L. Judd US; **C.** $250-450.
1100.	**United Bank** Cl; 2 3/4 x 4 1/4 x 2 3/4; A.C. Williams US; **B.** $400-600.
1101.	**City Bank with Chimney** Cl; 6 3/4 x 4 3/4 x 4 3/4; Thos. Swan, designer US patented 1873; **D.** $2000-3000.

A   1102.   **"Shakespeare Savings Bank"** china; 4 3/4x 4 1/8 x 2 1/2; England c1920; **1.** $40-60.

1103.   **"Van Wickle Library"** Al; 2 7/8 x 6 x 2 1/4; US; **1.** $100-150.

1104.   **"Reid Library, Lake Forest College"** Cl & porcelain; 3 1/2 x 5 1/4 x 2 1/8; US 1930; **C.** $500-800.

1105.   **Shakespeare's Home** brass; 2 5/8 x 6 1/8 x 2 1/4; England; **B.** $100-200.

1106.   **"Ferris Wheel Bank"** (conversion) Cl; 4 1/8 x 5 1/2 x 1 3/4; US; **D.** $200-300.

1107.   **Davenport House** pewter; 4 1/4 x 4 x 3 1/2; C. Metzke US 1935; **2.** $100-150.

B   1108.   **The Flags Bank (SBCAA)** Cl; 3 1/4 x 6 square; Littlestown Hardware & Foundry Co. US 1976; **M.** $50-100.

1109.   **Outhouse** bronze; 6 1/2 x 7 1/8 x 5 1/8; E. $800-1200.

1110.   **County Bank** Cl; 4 1/4 x 5 1/4 x 2 3/4; John Harper, Ltd. England c1892; **B.** $300-400.

1111.   ***City Bank, with Director's Room on Top** Cl; 4 1/8 x 3 3/8 x 2 7/16; John Harper, Ltd. 1902; Chamberlain & Hill, England; **B.** $200-300.

1112.   **Double Entry** Cl; 5 3/4 x 5 1/2 x 4 1/2; John Wright US 1960s; **M.** $40-60.

1113.   **Egyptian Tomb** Cl; 6 1/4 x 5 3/4 x 2 1/8; **D.** $400-600.

C   1114.   **Castle with Two Towers** Cl; 7 x 4 5/8 x 3 1/8; John Harper, Ltd. England c1908-1911; **D.** $800-1200.

1115.   **Lighthouse** Cl; 10 1/4 x 5 1/2 x 5 1/2; US 1891; **D.** $2500-4000.

1116.   **Palace** Cl; 7 1/2 x 8 x 5; Ives US 1885; **D.** $1500-2000.

1117.   **Lighthouse** tin; 7 x 3 1/2 diam.; Germany; **2.** $150-250.

1118.   **"Columbia Tower"** Cl; 6 7/8 x 3 1/8 diam.; Columbia Grey Iron Casting Co. US 1897; **D.** $600-1000.

1119.   **Jarmulowski Bldg.** (side view of #1086) US; **D.** $1500-2500.

A   1120.   **Four Tower** (painted) Cl; 5 3/8 x 4 1/4 x 3 1/4; Ohio Foundry Co. US 1949; **M.** $100-200.

1121.   ***Four Tower** Cl; 5 3/4 x 4 1/4 x 3 1/4; J. & E. Stevens US 1895-1906; **C.** $400-500.

1122.   **Roof "Bank"** Cl; 5 1/4 x 3 3/4 x 3 1/4; J. & E. Stevens US 1887; **B.** $200-300.

1123.   **"Cassa"** brass; 6 1/4 x 4 1/4 x 5 5/8; France; **D.** $400-800.

1124.   **Roof Bank** Cl; 5 1/4 x 3 3/4 x 3 1/4; Grey Iron Casting Co. US 1903-1928; **B.** $200-350.

1125.   **Double Door** Cl; 5 7/16 x 3 7/8 x 3; A.C. Williams US 1905-1920s; **B.** $250-350.

1126.   **Home Savings Bank** Cl; 5 7/8 x 4 1/2 x 3 3/8; Shimer Toy Co. 1899; J. & E. Stevens 1896 US; **C.** $400-700.

B   1127.   **Office Building** wood; 5 3/4 x 4 1/4 x 3 3/8; c!(circled) Shackman, Japan; **M.** $50-100.

1128.   **Church** (sliding wood trap in base) wood; 4 3/4 x 2 7/8 x 3 3/8; **1.** $20-30.

1129.   **"National Savings Bank"** wood; 5 1/4 x 5 3/8 x 3 7/8; **2.** $60-100.

1130.   **Building with Pillars** wood; 4 7/8 x 3 5/8 x 2 5/8; Norway?; **2.** $75-125.

1131.   **Oriental Building** inlaid wood; 3 1/4 x 6 1/2 x 2 1/8; **2.** $60-80.

1132.   **Henry's House** wood; 6 1/4 x 6 1/8 x 5; US 1929; **3.** $300-400.

C   1133.   **Eagle with Ball, Building** Cl; 10 3/4 x 5 1/2 x 4 1/2; US; **E.** $5000-8000.

1134.   **Eagle Bank** Cl; 9 3/4 x 5 1/2 x 4 1/4; US; **D.** $1000-2000.

1135.   Lighthouse **("Light of the World")** Cl; 9 1/2 x 4 7/8 diam.; Lane Art US 1950s; **M.** $75-125.

1136.   **Bureaux Caisse** Cl; 8 3/4 x 6 1/2 x 6 1/2; France; **D.** $450-650.

1137.   **Bureaux Caisse** Cl; 10 5/8 x 6 1/4 x 4 5/8; France; **D.** $700-1000.

A   1138.   **Birth Bank (large)** brass & steel; 7/34 x 5 1/16 x 2 7/8; England c1860; **B.** $150-250.

1139.   **Villa** Cl; 3 15/16 x 3 7/16 x 2; Sydenham & McOustra, England c1908; **D.** $700-1000.

1140.   **Birth Bank** brass & steel, ST; 5 3/8 x 3 3/4 x 2 1/8; England c1860; **B.** $100-200.

1141.   **Birth Bank with Clock** brass & steel, ST; 7 1/2 x 4 x 2 1/2; England c1840; **B.** $150-250.

1142.   **Victorian House** Cl; 4 1/2 x 3 1/4 x 2 1/2; J. & E. Stevens US 1892; **B.** $250-400.

1143.   **Victorian House** Cl; 3 1/4 x 2 3/4 x 1 7/8; J. & E. Stevens US patented 1898; **B.** $200-300.

1144.   **Birth Bank (swivel trap)** brass; 6 3/4 x 5 x 1 7/8; England c1860; **B.** $100-150.

B   1145.   **Cupola Bank** Cl; 5 1/2 x 4 1/4 x 3 3/8; Vermong Novelty Works 1869; J. & E. Stevens US 1872; **B.** $500-800.

1146.   **Cupola Bank** Cl; 4 1/8 x 3 3/8 x 2 3/4; J. & E. Stevens US 1872; **A.** $250-450.

1147.   **Cupola Bank** Cl; 3 1/4 x 2 5/8 x 2 3/16; J. & E. Stevens US 1872; **A.** $200-400.

1148.   **"Banque"** (key lock opens roof) brass; 5 1/2 x 4 x 3 3/16; **B.** $200-400.

1149.   **Bird Bank ("Bank New York")**; Cl; 5 7/8 x 3 7/8 x 3 1/8; US; **D.** $800-1200.

1150.   **Crown Bank on Legs, small** Cl; 4 5/8 x 4 1/4 x 3 1/2; US; **D.** $1500-2000.

1151.   **Crown Bank on Legs, large** Cl; 4 7/8 x 4 1/4 x 3 1/4; US; **D.** $1500-2000.

C   1152.   **Napoleon Bank** brass; 6 x 3 5/8 x 2 7/8; France; **E.** $500-700.

1153.   **Pagoda Bank** Cl; 5 x 3 x 3; England 1889; **D.** $500-700.

1154.   **House with Knight** Cl; 7 1/4 x 4 1/2 x 3 1/8; US; **D.** $500-700.

1555.   **Gladiator** brass; 5 3/8 x 4 3/8 x 3 5/8; US; **C.** $600-1000.

1156.   **"Caisse"** AL; 6 x 3 3/4 x 3; France; **1.** $100-200.

1157.   **"Park Bank"** Cl; 4 3/8 x 4 x 3 3/8; US; **E.** $3000-5000.

1158.   **Finial Bank** Cl; 5 3/4 x 4 3/8 x 3 1/4; Kyser & Rex US 1887; **C.** $600-900.

A | 1159. | **"Flat Iron Building Bank"** Cl; 8 1/4 x 4 3/4 x 6 1/8; Kenton US 1904-1913; **D.** $2500-3500.

1160. **"Flat Iron Building Bank" (small trap)** Cl; 5 3/4 x 4 3/4 x 4 1/2; Kenton US 1904-1926; **B.** $400-600.

1161. **Flat Iron Building (no trap)** Cl; 5 1/2 x 3 x 3 1/2; Kenton US; 1912-1926; **B.** $250-400.

1162. **Flat Iron Building** Cl; 3 3/16 x 2 x 2 3/16; Kenton US 1912-1926; **C.** $450-650.

1163. **Temple Bar (Gateway to City of London)** Cl; 4 x 4 1/8 x 2 1/2; England; **D.** $600-1000.

1164. **Statue of Liberty** Cl; 6 1/16 x 2 1/4 x 2 1/4; A.C. Williams US 1910-early 1930s; **A.** $150-250.

1165. **Statue of Liberty** Cl; 6 3/8 x 2 1/4 x 2 3/8; Kenton US 1910-1931; **B.** $200-400.

1166. **Statue of Liberty** Cl; 9 5/8 x 3 3/8 x 3 7/16; Wing c1900; Kenton US 1911-1932; **C.** $900-1600.

B | 1167. | **Presto** Cl; 4 1/16 x 3 9/16; Kenton? US 1911-1913; **B**. $75-150.

1168. **Presto "Bank"** Cl; 3 5/8 x 2 3/4 x 1 3/4; A.C. Williams US 1905-1934; **A.** $60-80.

1169. **Presto "Bank"** Cl; 3 5/8 x 2 3/4 x 1 3/4; A.C. Williams US 1905-1934; **A.** $60-80.

1170. **Rose Window** Cl; 2 3/8 x 2 3/8 x 1 1/2; England; **D.** $300-400.

1171. **Presto Trick Bank** Cl; 4 1/2 x 4 x 2 1/2; Kyser & Rex US c1892; **B.** $400-600.

1172. **Fort** Cl; 4 1/8 x 2 3/8; Kenton? US 1910s?; **C.** $400-600.

1173. **Tower** Cl; 4 1/8 x 2 3/8; Kenton US 1911-1915; **C.** $400-600.

1174. **Mosque** Cl; 2 7/8 x 2 7/16 x 1 5/8; US; **A.** $60-100.

1175. **Mosque (3 story)** Cl; 3 1/2 x 2 1/2 x 1 5/8; A.C. Williams US 1920s; **A.** $75-125.

C | 1176. | **Domed Mosque "Bank" (combin. door)** Vl; 5 1/8 x 5 1/8 x 3 1/8; Grey Iron Casting Co. US 1903-1928; **C.** $400-600.

1177. **Domed Mosque "Bank"** Cl; 4 1/4 x 4 1/8 x 2 3/8; Grey Iron Casting Co. US 1903-1928; **A.** $150-250.

1178. **Domed Mosque "Bank"** Cl; 3 1/8 x 3 1/8 x 2 15/16; Grey Iron Casting Co. Us 1903-1928; **B.** $150-250.

1179. **Villa** Cl 5 9/16 x 4 7/8 x 3; Kyser & Rex US c1894; **C.** $600-1000.

1180. **Domed "Bank"** Cl; 3 x 2 x 1 3/4; A.C. Williams US 1899-1934; **A.** $50-75.

1181. **Domed "Bank"** Cl; 3 5/8 x 2 1/4 x 1 3/4; A.C. Williams US 1899; **B.** $60-100.

1182. **Domed "Bank"** Cl; 4 1/2 x 3 1/4 x 2; A.C. Williams US 1899-1934; **A.** $60-100.

1183. **Domed "Bank"** Cl; 4 3/4 x 4 x 2 3/8; A.C. Williams US 1899-1934; **A.** $75-125.

A   1184.   **Multiplying Bank** Cl; 6 1/2 x 4 1/16 x 5 1/8; J. & E.
Stevens 1883; **D.** $1500-2500.

1185.   **John Brown Fort** Cl; 3 x 2 3/4 x 2 11/16; US; **B.**
$100-150.

1186.   **Alamo** WM; 2 1/4 x 4 x 3 1/8; US; **1.** $75-125.

1187.   **Alamo** Cl; 1 7/8 x 2 3/4 x 3 3/8; Alamo Iron Works
US c1930s; **C.** $400-600.

1188.   **Fort Dearborn** WM; 4 3/8 x 4 1/8 x 2 3/4; Preferred
Bank Service Co. US 1933; **1.** $150-250.

1189.   **Fort Mt. Hope** Cl; 2 7/8 2 3/4 x 2 3/4; US; **D.** $300-
500.

1190.   **Fort Dearborn** Cl; 5 3/4 x 4 3/4 x 4 1/2; US 1933;
D. $1500-2500.

B   1191.   **Windmill** brass; 4 3/4 x 3 x 2 3/4; **C.** $100-150.

1192.   **"La Salette"** silvered lead; 3 3/4 x 3 7/8 x 3; Japan;
1. $60-100.

1193.   **Amish Barn** WM, iron trap; 3 5/8 x 3 1/2 x 3 3/8; **M.**
$50-75.

1194.   **Battle of Gettysburg** Cl; 4 3/4 x 7 1/4 x 3 3/4;
Wilton Products Co. 1960; **M.** $50-100.

1195.   **Covered Bridge** Cl; 2 1/2 x 6 1/8 x 2 3/8; John
Wright c1960s; **M.** $30-40.

1196.   **Administration Building Bethel College** Cl;
2 7/8 x 5 1/4 x 3 7/8; Service Foundry US 1935; **A.**
$100-200.

C   1197.   **Home Savings Bank** (chimney missing) Cl; 9 5/8 x
6 7/16 x 8 1/4; US; **D.** $600-1000 complete.

1198.   **Tower Bank** Cl; 6 7/8 6 7/8 x 2 1/2; Kyser & Rex US
1890; **D.** $900-1600.

1199.   **"Globe Savings Fund" Bank** Cl; 7 1/8 x 5 11/16 x
4; Kyser & Rex US 1889; **D.** $2500-5000.

1200.   **"Coin Registering Bank"** Cl; 6 3/4 x 5 3/8 x 4 1/4;
Kyser & Rex US 1890; **E.** $6000-10,000.

1201.   **Home Savings** Cl; 10 1/2 x 6 1/4 x 8 1/8; US; **D.**
$800-1200.

1225. **Crown Bank** Cl; 5 x 4 3/8 x 3 1/4; J. & E. Stevens 1873-1907; Grey Iron Casting Co. US 1903-1928; **C.** $800-1200.

1226. **Crown Bank** Cl; 3 5/8 x 3 1/8 x 2 3/8; J. & E.Stevens 1873-1907; Grey Iron Casting Co. US 1903-1928; **B.** $300-500.

1227. **Crown Bank** Cl; 3 x 2 1/2 x 2 1/8; J. & E. Stevens 1873-1907; Grey Iron Casting Co. US 1903-1928; **B.** $250-450.

1228. **Moody & Sankey** Cl; 5 x 4 1/4 x 3 1/2; Smith & Egge US patented 1870; **D.** $3000-5000.

1229. **New Bank** Cl; 5 1/4 x 4 3/8 x 4 1/4; J. & E. Stevens US 1872; **E.** $2500-4000.

1230. **Crown with Tower** Cl; 3 3/16 x 2 3/4 x 2 3/8; J. & E. Stevens?; US; **D.** $800-1000.

1231. **"Home Bank" (Crown)** Cl; 3 1/8 x 2 5/8 x 2 1/4; J. & E. Stevens US patented 1872; **C.** $600-1000.

1232. **"Home Bank" (Crown)** Cl; 5 1/4 x 4 5/16 x 3 1/4; J. & E. Stevens US patented 1872; **C.** $1500-2500.

1233. **Building with Belfry** Cl; 8 x 3 5/8 x 4; Kenton? US; **E.** $5000-7000.

1234. **Penthouse** Cl; 5 7/8 x 2 1/2 x 2 1/2; A.C. Williams US; **D.** $1000-1500.

1235. **Triangular Bldg.** Cl; 6 x 3 3/8 x 2; Hubley US 1914; **D.** $500-700.

1236. **"Home Savings Bank" with Finial** Cl; 3 1/2 x 2 1/2 x 2 1/8; J. & E. Stevens US 1891; **C.** $300-400.

1237. **"Home Savings Bank" Dog Finial** Cl; 5 3/4 x 4 3/8 x 3 5/16; J. & E. Stevens US 1891; **C.** $250-450.

1238. **Skyscraper** Cl; 3 9/16 x 1 7/8 x 1 7/8; A.C. Williams US 1900-1931; **A.** $75-100.

1239. **Skyscraper** Cl 4 3/8 x 2 1/8 x 2 1/8; A.C. Williams US 1900-1931; **A.** $100-150.

1240. **Skyscraper** Cl; 5 1/2 x 2 1/2 x 2 1/2; A.C. Williams US 1900-1931; **A.** $100-150.

1241. ***Skyscraper (six posts)** Cl; 6 1/2 x 4 x 3; A.C. Williams US 1900-1909; **B.** $300-500.

1242. ***Independence Hall** Cl; 10 x 9 3/8 x 8; Enterprise US 1875; **D.** $1000-2000.

1243. **Independence Hall** Cl; 8 1/8 x 15 1/2 x 4 1/8; US 1875; **E.** $4000-6000.

1244. **Independence Hall** Cl; 8 7/8 x 6 11/16 x 6 1/4; Enterprise US 1875; **C.** $800-1500.

A   1245.   **Lighthouse** WM, KLT; 5 1/4 x 3 5/16; Vanio US 1937; **2.** $100-200.

1246.   **Marietta Silo** Cl; 5 1/2 x 1 7/8; US; **D.** $600-800.

1247.   **Indiana Silo** Cl; 3 1/2 x 2; US; **E.** $1000-1500.

1248.   **Cottage with Tree** comp., KLT; 3 1/2 x 3 1/2; Hausser, Germany; **2.** $200-300.

1249.   **Snappit (mech.)** Cl; 4 x 3 1/4; H.L. Judd US c1895; **C.** $600-1000.

1250.   **Administration Building** glass; 3 1/4 x 2 1/4 x 2 1/4; US 1893; **1.** $150-250.

1251.   **Millport Bay Tower** boxwood; England c1880; **2.** $75-125.

1252.   **Clay Head Barrel** boxwood; 3 1/4; England c1880; **2.** $60-80.

1253.   **Pump & Bucket** WM, KLT; 4 1/2 x 3 1/8; Vanio US late 1930s; **2.** $100-150.

B   1254.   **Cupid with Mushroom** silverplate; 4 1/4; Germany 1900; **3.** $800-1200.

1255.   **Cupid with Money Bag** lead; 3 x 3 3/4; Germany; **3.** $500-700.

1256.   **"Union Dime Savings Bank 1882"** Cl; 3 13/16 x 2 1/4; US 1882; **E.** $200-1200.

1257.   **Victorian Recording Bank** Cl & etched glass; 6 x 4 1/2; US; **F.** $2000-4000.

1258.   **Silver Dollar Bank** lead; 3 x 2 1/2; US; **3.** $300-500.

1259.   **"Wurzburg" Basket** WM, KLT; 1 3/4 x 3 5/8 x 2 7/8; Germany c1920s; **2.** $150-250.

1260.   **Tankard** lead; 3 5/8; Germany c1920s; **1.** $150-250.

1261.   **"Goody Bank"** tin; 2" diam.; US; **1.** $50-75. Vertising Corp. US; **2.** $50-75.

C   1265.   **Jewel Chest** metal; 2 1/8 x 2 3/8 x 1 1/4 ; France c1700s; **3.** $200-400.

1266.   **"Put Money in Thy Purse"** Cl; 2 3/4 x 3 1/2 x 1 9/16; US c1886; **E.** $600-1000.

1267.   **Jewel Chest, Horse-drawn** metal; 2 5/8 x 6 1/4; France c1700s; **3.** $300-500.

1268.   **Satchel** heavy steel; 3 3/8 x 5 3/4 x 2 1/2; US; **C.** $250-450.

A   1269.   **"Full Dinner Pail"** tin, KLT; 2 1/8 x 3 1/8; US 1896; **3.** $400-600.

1270.   **Tiny Tot** (conversion) wood & iron; 3 1/4 x 2 1/2 x 2 1/2; Arcade; A.C. Williams US 1902-1932; **A.** $50-75.

1271.   **Remington Typewriter** WM; 1 3/8 x 2 7/8; National Products Corp. US 1939; **1.** $75-150.

1272.   **Underwood Typewriter** WM; 1 3/8 x 2 3/4; National Products Corp. US 1939; **1.** $60-100.

1273.   **Wooden Shoe** (screw top); 1 3/4 x 4 1/4; **1.** $20-30.

1274.   **Wooden Puzzle Bank;** 2 3/4 x 3 13/16 x 2 3/4; c1929; **2.** $50-75.

1275.   **Ivory Viewer;** 2 1/2 x 2; Germany 1920s; **3.** $400-600.

1276.   **Melon Bank** pottery; 2 7/8 x 3 1/2; **3.** $100-200.

B   1277.   **Roly Poly Monkey** tin; 6 x 3 1/2 diam.; Chein US 1940s; **2.** $350-450.

1278.   **Jazz Band** tin, KLT; 4 x 3; **3.** $350-450.

1279.   **Umbrella** tin; 6 1/4 x 3 1/4; US; **2.** $50-75.

1280.   **"Puzzle Picture Box"** tin TL; 2 1/4 diam.; England; **3.** $200-300.

1281.   **Jug with Flowers** pottery; 4 1/2 x 3 1/8 US; **2.** $100-150.

1282.   **Acorn** pottery; 3 1/8 x 3 1/4; US; **2.** $75-125.

1283.   **Orange** lead, KLT; 3 x 3; Germany; **2.** $200-300.

1284.   **Pickle** metal, KLT; 3 7/8 x 2 1/8; US; **2.** $400-600.

1285.   **Buckeye (SBCCA)** Cl; 3 1/2 x 3 1/4; Lou Filler US 1973; **M.** $30-50.

C   1286.   **"Freedman's Bureau"** wood; mech.; 5 1/4 x 6 1/2 x 3 3/4; Seco US c1882 or earlier; **3.** $1000-1500.

1287.   **Loaf of Bread** (collection box) comp.; 4 x 5; England; **2.** $40-60.

1288.   **Frying Pan (Pan American Exposition)** tin; 11 3/4 x 6 x 1 1/4; US 1901; **3.** $400-600.

1289.   **Red Cross Bed** (collection box) comp.; 2 1/2 x 5 5/8; England; **2.** $75-100.

1290.   **"Uncle Sam's Register Bank"** cold rolled steel; 6 1/4 x 4 1/2 x 5 1/4; Durable Toy & Novelty Corp. US 1912--present; **1.** $25-50.

A 1291. **Creased Gourd** pottery; 6 1/4; **1.** $50-75.
   1292. **Teardrop Gourd** pottery; 5 3/4; **1.** $50-75.
   1293. **Ear of Corn** chalk; 8 1/2; **3.** $100-200.
   1294. **Dotted Gourd** pottery; 5 1/8; **1.** $40-60.
   1295. **Round Gourd** pottery; 4 5/8 x 4 1/8; Mexico; **1.** $40-60.

B 1296. **Queen's Doll House** tin; 3 5/16 x 4 5/16 x 2 11/16; Chubb Safe Co. England early 1920s; **1.** $75-100.
   1297. **George VI Coronation Bank** tin; 3 x 2 9/16; England 1937; **1.** $30-50.
   1298. **Punch & Judy** tin, KL in roof; 2 7/8 x 2 1/2; Germany; **2.** $250-400.
   1299. **Punch & Judy** tin; 4 1/4 x 3; "Made in England"; **1.** $125-200.
   1300. **Punch & Judy** tin; 2 3/4 x 2 1/8; Germany; **2.** $450-700.
   1301. **Royal Wedding (Chas. & Diana)** tin; 3 x 2 1/8; England 1981; **M.** $20-30.

C 1302. **"Sixpenny Piece Bank"** AL; 3 1/8 x 3 1/4; Reuben Wineberg, England 1954; **M.** $75-100.
   1303. **Collection Box** wood & paper; 3 3/4 x 4 15/16; England; **2.** $60-80.
   1304. **Bedpost** brass; 7 3/8 x 2 1/2; England; **B.** $60-80.
   1305. **Dime Bedpost** brass; 5 1/8 x 1 3/4; England; **B.** $60-80.
   1306. **Teapot** metal and wood, KLT; 3 5/8 x 4 7/8; England c1908; **2.** $100-150.
   1307. **Cup & Saucer** brass; 1 3/4 x 4 1/2; England c1920; **C.** $50-100.
   1308. ***Bear Stealing Honey** CI; 7 x 4 1/4; Sydenham & McOustra? England c1908; **B.** $300-400.
   1309. **Milk Can** brass; 4 11/16 x 2 3/4; England; **A.** $50-70.
   1310. **Milk Can** brass; 3 1/2 x 2 3/4; England c1922; **B.** $50-80.

A 1311. **Coronation Crown (Elizabeth II);** 3 1/4 x 3; "Made in England" PGP 1953; **M.** $50-75.

1312. **Coronation rown (flocked);** 3 1/2 x 3; "Made in England" 1953; **M.** $50-75.

1313. * **"Our Kitchener"** Cl; 6 11/16 x 4; Sydenham & McOustra? England 1914; **C.** $250-350.

1314. **"Dreadnought Bank"** Cl; 7 x 7 1/2; Sydenham & McOustra? England c1915; **D.** $700-1000.

1315. * **"Coronation Bank" (George V)** Cl; 6 5/8 x 4 1/8; Sydenham & McOustra? England 1911; **C.** $250-350.

1316. **Coronation Crown (Edward VII)** Cl; 3 9/16 x 3 1/8; John Harper, Ltd. England 1901; **D.** $250-350.

1317. **Coronation Crown (Elizabeth II)** Cl; 3 3/16 x 3; England 1953; **M.** $75-125.

B 1318. **Jeweled Crown** metal, KLT; 3 11/16; Japan; **C.** $100-150.

1319. **"Coronation Bank" (George V)** Cl; 6 5/16 x 7 3/8; Sydenham & McOustra? England 1911; **E.** $800-1000.

1320. * **"Our Empire Bank" (George V & Mary)** Cl; (See #1315) Sydenham & McOustra? England 1911; **C.** $200-300.

1321. **"Our Empire Bank"** Cl; (See #1319) Sydenham & McOustra? England 1911; **F.** $1000-1500.

1322. **Coronation Crown (Elizabeth II)** Cl; 4 3/8 x 4 1/8; England 1953; **M.** $200-400.

C 1323. **Alice in Wonderland** brass; 4 1/2 x 3 15/16 x 4; England 1909; **E.** $500-800.

1324. **Prince & Princess of Wales** zinc alloy; 6 3/4 x 4 3/16 x 1 3/4; Robert Brown, Wales 1981; **M.** $40-60.

1325. **English Throne (Elizabeth II)** AL; 3 3/8; Reuben Wineberg, England 1953; **M.** $40-60.

1326. **English Throne** Cl; 8 1/8 x 4 5/8 x 2 3/4; John Harper, Ltd. England 1953; **M.** $75-125.

1327. **English Throne** AL; (See #1325) Reuben Wineberg, England c1953; **M.** $40-60.

1328. **"Victorian Coin" Bank** tin; 5 3/8; England c1900; **2.** $75-125.

1329. **"Royal Bank" (George V)** Cl; 5 1/4 x 5 3/4; Chamberlain & Hill, England 1910; **D.** $300-500.

A 1330. **GE Refrigerator, small** Cl; 3 3/4 x 2; Hubley US 1930-1936; **A.** $100-200.

1331. **GE Refrigerator, large** Cl; 4 1/4 x 2 1/8; Hubley US 1930-1936; **C.** $150-250.

1332. **Majestic Ice Box** Cl & sheet metal; 4 1/2 x 2 5/8; Arcade US 1932-1934; **D.** $300-500.

1333. **Norge Refrigerator** WM; 4 x 2 1/8; US; **1.** $60-100.

1334. **"Servel Electrolux"** WM; 4 x 1 7/8; US; **1.** $60-80.

1335. **"Electrolux"** WM; 4 x 2; US; **1.** $60-80.

1336. **"Frigidaire"** WM; 4 x 2 1/16; National Products Corp. US; **1.** $60-80.

1337. **"Save for Ice" (ice box)** Cl; 4 1/4 x 2 13/16; Arcade US; **D.** $400-800.

1338. **"Kelvinator"** (door opens) Cl; 3 7/8 x 2 1/2; Arcade US 1932-1934; **C.** $150-300.

B 1339. **"Magic Chef"** WM, ST; 3 1/2 x 2 7/8; US; **1.** $60-80.

1340. **"Estate Stove"** WM; 3 x 2 15/16; US; **1.** $75-125.

1341. **Roper Stove** (burner covers lift up) Cl & sheet metal; 3 3/4 x 3 3/4 x 2 1/4; Arcade US; **C.** $300-500.

1342. **Roper Stove** Cl & sheet metal; 4 x 3 7/8; Arcade US; **B.** $300-500.

1343. **Dot Stove** Cl; 2 1/2 x 3 1/2, top piece: 2"; John Wright US 1970; **M.** $20-30.

1344. **Oak Stove** Cl; 2 3/8 x 3 1/4; Shimer Toy Co. US 1899; **E.** $200-300.

1345. **Dot Stove** Cl; 2 1/4 x 3 1/4, top: 1 13/16; Grey Iron Casting Co. US 1903; **C.** $150-250.

C 1346. **Hot Point Electric Stove** Cl; 6 x 5 5/8; Arcade US 1925; **D.** $1000-2000.

1347. **"Star Stove"** (conversion) Cl; 2 5/8 x 3 7/8, stove pipe: 2 1/2; US; **C.** $30-40.

1348. **Pot Bellied Stove** Cl; 5 3/4 x 2 1/4; Knerr US 1968; **M.** $30-50.

1349. **Gas Stove** Cl & sheet metal; 5 1/2 x 4; S. Bernstein Co., N.Y. City US 1901; **C.** $200-300.

1350. **"Eureka" Gas Stove** tin; 5 1/4; John Wright & Co. England; **1.** $100-150.

1351. **"York Stove"** Cl; 4 x 4 x 2 3/4; Abendroth Bros., N.Y. US; **D.** $350-450.

1352. **Queen Stove** Cl; 3 3/4 x 5 3/8, stove pipe: 2 7/8; John Wright Us 1975; **M.** $30-40.

<table>
<tr><td>A</td><td>1353.</td><td>Fireplace tin, KLT; 4 5/8 x 5; Burnett Ltd. England; 2. $100-200.</td></tr>
</table>

A   1353.   **Fireplace** tin, KLT; 4 5/8 x 5; Burnett Ltd. England; **2.** $100-200.

1354.   **New Heatrola Bank** Cl; 4 1/2 x 2 5/8 x 2 5/8; Kenton US 1927-1932; **B.** $150-300.

1355.   **"Champion" Heater** (w/combination) Cl; 4 1/8 x 2 3/4 x 2 3/8; US; **C.** $200-350.

1356.   **Reliable Parlor Stove** Cl; 6 1/4 x 4; Schneider & Trenkamp Co. US; **E.** $600-900.

1357.   **Parlor Stove** Cl; 6 7/8 x 2 3/4; US; **C.** $350-500.

1358.   **Coal Scuttle** lead; 3 1/4; US; **2.** $150-250.

1359.   **"Thermo X Gas" Fireplace** tin; (See #1353); Burnett Ltd. England; **2.** $100-200.

B   1360.   **Penn. Dutch Dowry Chest** AL; 2 3/8 x 3 3/4 x 2 3/8; G.B. Fenstermaker US; **M.** $40-60.

1361.   **Fish Keg** AL, KLT; 2 3/8 x 2 7/8; C.L. Poole Co. US; **M.** $40-60.

1362.   **Marshall Stove** Cl; 3 7/8 x 2 7/8; US; **B.** $100-200.

1363.   **Mellow Stove** Cl; 3 9/16 x 3 1/8; Liberty Toy Co. US; **B.** $100-150.

1364.   **Gem Stove** Cl; 4 3/4 x 3; Abendroth Bros. US; **C.** $150-250.

1365.   **Mo-He-Co Furnace** Cl; 4 1/4 x 2 5/8; US; **D.** $250-450.

1366.   **Penn. Dutch Dowry Chest** AL; 2 1/8 x 3 1/2 x 2; G.B. Fenstermaker US; **M.** $40-60.

1367.   **Dry Sink** Cl; 3 x 2 3/4 x 1 1/2; John Wright Us 1970; **M.** $50-75.

C   1368.   **Singer Sewing Machine** tin; 5 1/4 x 4 1/2 x 2 3/4; Germany c1910; **3.** $600-800.

1369.   **Singer Electric Sewing Machine** tin & iron; 5 1/8 x 41/2 x 2 3/4; Germany c1925; **3.** $500-700.

1370.   **Richmond Ice Cream Freezer** Cl; 4 1/4 x 2 5/8; Grey Iron Casting Co. US c1910; **D.** $250-400.

1371.   * **"The North Pole Bank" (Ice Cream Freezer)** nickeled Cl; 4 1/4 x 2 5/8; (See #1373) Grey Iron Casting Co. US 1922-1928; **D.** $300-500.

1372.   **Brass Pattern for Bank #1371;** 4 1/4 x 2 5/8. $600-800.

1373.   * **"The North Pole Bank"** (painted version) nickeled Cl; 4 1/4 x 2 5/8; (See #1371); Grey Iron Casting Co. US1922-1928; **E.** $800-1200.

1374.   **Safe Harbor Chair** WM; 3 1/4 x 2 1/2; Banthrico US; **1.** $75-125.

1375.   **Rocking Chair** Cl; 6 3/4 x 2 9/16 x 4; C.J. Manning, designer US 1898; **E.** $3000-4000.

A 1398. **"Tommy's Tin Hat"** tin; 1 5/8 x 4 1/16; England c1917; **2.** $150-250.

1399. **"Buddy Bank"** metal; 1 7/8 x 3 11/16; Stronghart Co. US cWWI; **1.** $75-125.

1400. **Bullet Head (Empire State)** metal; 4 1/2; US c1940s; **1.** $150-250.

1401. **Helmet with Eagle (small)** tin, KLT; 1 1/2 x 3 5/8; Japan cWWI; **1.** $60-80.

1402. **Helmet with Eagle (large)** tin, KLT; 1 3/4 x 4 3/8; Japan cWWI; **1.** $60-80.

1403. **War Bonds Bullet** tin, TT; 5 3/4 x 2 7/8; cWWII; **1.** $100-200.

1404. **Japanese Helmet with Star** tin, KLT; (See #1401); Japan cWWII; **2.** $60-80.

1405. **German Helmet** tin, KLT; 2 5/8 x 4 1/8; Germany; **3.** $250-350.

B 1406. **"The Tank Bank"** Cl; 3 1/4 x 7 1/4; John Harper, Ltd. England; **C.** $300-500.

1407. **Dime Bullet Bank** (conversion) brass; 7 3/16; US; **A.** $50-100.

1408. **"Preparedness" Bullet** metal; 6 1/16; Harmo Electric Co. US WWII?; **1.** $50-100.

1409. **"Bullet Bank" (Buster Brown Shoes)** metal; 4 1/4; US cWWII; **1.** $40-60.

1410. **NRA Eagle** WM; 6"; Preferred Bank Service Co. US early 1930s; **2.** $100-200.

1411. **Bullet (Woolworth Bldg.)** metal; 3"; & K Co. cWWI US; **2.** $100-200.

1412. **Bullet** (bank promo.) metal; 4"; Stronghart Co. US cWWI; **1.** $100-150.

1413. **Bullet Bank with Cross** brass; 6 5/8 x 2 7/8; England c1918; **2.** $60-100.

1414. **"The Tank Bank" ("119")** Cl; 3 5/8 x 7 3/8; John Harper, Ltd. England; **D.** $300-500.

C 1415. **"USN" Bullet** steel; 2 7/8; & K Co. US; **2.** $60-100.

1416. **"1 Pounder Bank"** Cl; 8"; Grey Iron Casting Co. US 1918; **B.** $100-150.

1417. **"Tank Savings Bank"** Cl; 9 1/2 x 4; Ferrosteel US 1919; **C.** $300-500.

1418. **"Boyco Kick in Canteen"** tin, screw top; 4 1/4 x 4 1/4; US; **3.** $250-400.

1419. **Tank** Cl; 3 5/8 x 8 1/4; England 1918; **D.** $250-400.

1420. **1 1/2 inch Shell Bank;** 8 1/16; Ferrosteel Mfg. Co. US 1919; **B.** $100-150.

1421. **"42 Centimeter" Bullet** Bank brass; 5"; Europe 1915; **D.** $100-200.

A   1439.   **Battleship Maine** Cl; 6 x 10 1/4; J. & E. Stevens US 1902; **D.** $3000-6000.

1440.   **"Maine" (small)** Cl; 4 5/8 x 4 1/2; Grey Iron Casting Co. US 1897-1903; **C.** $300-500.

1441.   **"Maine" (large)** Cl; 5 1/4 x 6 5/8; Grey Iron Casting Co. US 1897-1903; **E.** $2500-5000.

B   1442.   **Indiana Paddle Wheeler** Cl; 3 5/8 x 7 1/8; patented by Robert J. Sellentine US 1896; **F.** $10,000-20,000.

1443.   **Wilhelmshaven Touring Boat** silvered lead; 3 x 7; Germany early 1900s; **2.** $200-300.

1444.   **Ocean Liner** lead, hinged trap art; 2 3/4 x 7 5/8; **2.** $200-300.

1445.   **Ocean Liner** lead, KLT; 2 3/8 x 7 1/8; **2.** $200-300.

C   1446.   **"Koln" (Cologne) Touring Boat** silvered lead, KLT; 3 7/8 x 7 1/2; (piece of smoke missing) Germany early 1900s; **2.** $250-350; complete.

1447.   **"Lindau Bodensee" Touring Boat** silvered lead; Germany early 1900s; **2.** $250-350.

1448.   **"Mainz" Touring Boat** silvered lead, KLT; 3 x 7 1/4; Germany early 1900s; **2.** $200-300.

1449.   **"Homburg" Touring Boat "Rathhus"** silvered lead; 4 3/8 x 7 3/8; Germany early 1900s; **2.** $250-350.

D   1450.   **"Oregon" (small)** Cl; 3 7/8 x 4 7/8; J. & E. Stevens US 1891-1906; **C.** $300-500.

1451.   **Oregon (lead pattern);** 4 1/2 x 5 1/16; J. & E. Stevens. $600-800.

1452.   **Oregon (large)** Cl; 4 7/8 x 6; J. & E. Stevens US 1898-1906; **C.** $500-800.

1453.   **Barge** Cl; 1 1/4 x 5 3/4; Welker-Crosby? US; **F.** $5000-8000.

1454.   **Tug Boat** Cl; 3 9/16 x 5 7/16; Welker-Crosby? US; **F.** $8000-12,000.

A   1455.   **Treasure Ship** WM; 4 1/2 x 3 1/4; Japan; **2.** $250-400.

1456.   **Freighter** wood; 4 x 18 1/4; Redi Houl? US; **3.** $200-300.

1457.   **Fortune Ship** Cl; 4 1/8 x 5 3/8; England?; **E.** $1500-2000.

B   1458.   ***Steamboat with Small Wheels** Cl; 2 3/8 x 7 7/16; Kenton? US; **D.** $300-500.

1459.   ***Steamboat** Cl; 2 7/16 x 7 5/8; A.C. Williams US 1912-1920s; **B.** $300-500.

1460.   **Arcade Steamboat** Cl; 2 3/8 x 7 1/2; Arcade US 1910-25; **C.** $300-500.

1461.   **Steamboat (6 holes)** Cl; 2 11/16 x 8 1/8; US; **D.** $300-600.

C   1462.   **Gunboat** Cl; with mast, 2 3/4 x 8 1/2; w/out mast, 1 5/8 x 8 1/2; Kenton? US; **E.** $1500-2000.

1463.   **"Oregon" Gunboat** Cl; w/mast, 5 1/4; w/out, 2 3/8; length, 11" Kenton? Us; **F.** $2000-4000.

1464.   **Gunboat (pulltoy)** Cl; w/mast, 2 7/8; w/out, 1 3/4; length 8 1/2" Kenton? US; **E.** $1500-2000.

D   1465.   **Noah's Ark** comp.; 2 5/8 x 5 3/8; Hausser Germany 1929; **2.** $150-250.

1466.   **Life Boat** tin; 15"; England c1910s; **3.** $200-400.

1467.   **Floating Dispensary** (collection box) comp.; 2 3/8 x 8 1/8; England; **2.** $75-100.

A   1483.   ***Model T Ford (2nd casting)** Cl; 4 x 6 5/16; Arcade US 1920s; **D.** $600-700.

1484.   ***Model T Ford (1st casting)** Cl; (see #1483); Arcade US 1923-25; **E.** $1200-2000.

1485.   **Gas Pump** Cl; 5 11/16 x 2 1/8; US; **C.** $500-700.

1486.   **Auto (4 passengers)** Cl; 2 3/4 x 5 11/16; A.C. Williams US c1910?; **E.** $500-700.

1487.   **Auto (4 passengers)** Cl; 3 1/2 x 6 3/4; A.C. Williams US 1912-1931; **D.** $600-800.

1488.   **Auto (wood carving);** (see #1486); 2 1/4 x 5 1/8. $800-1000.

B   1489.   **Yellow Cab** (rubber tires) Cl; 4 1/4 x 7 7/8; Arcade US 1921; **D.** $1500-2500.

1490.   **Double Decker Bus** Cl; 2 1/4 x 3 1/2; US; **E.** $1200-1800.

1491.   **Checker Cab** Cl; (see #1489 & 1493); Arcade US 1921; **D.** $2000-3000.

1492.   **Model T ("Garber's Garage")** lead, KLT; 2 5/8 x 4 1/8; American Art Works, Inc. US; **3.** $250-400.

1493.   **Yellow Cab** (steel wheels) Cl; (see #1491 & 1489) Arcade US 1921; **C.** $1500-2000.

C   1494.   **Auto with Hinged Roof** lead; 2 x 5 3/16; Germany c1910; **2.** $200-300.

1495.   **Auto with Hinged Roof** lead; 2 5 3/16; Germany c1910; **2.** $200-300.

1496.   **Horse-drawn Cannon and Limber** Cl & steel; 7 1/2 x 17; US patented 1895; **F.** $600-1000.

1497.   **Auto lead,** KLT; 2 1/4 x 5 3/16; Germany c1910; **2.** $200-300.

133

A   1498. **"Armoured Truck Bank"** metal; 2 3/4 x 5 1/4; Callen Mfg. Corp. US; **M.** $20-40.

1499. **"Armoured Bank"** sheet metal; 2 13/16 x 3 1/4; Marx US patented 1937; **2.** $100-150.

1500. **Brinks Truck** metal; 3 7/8 x 8 1/4; US; **2.** $75-125.

1501. **Truck & Trailer** metal; 2 3/4 x 9 3/4; Marx US patented 1937; **3.** $100-200.

B   1502. **Autobank (Cadillac)** WM, KLT; 2 7/8 x 8 1/4; Banthrico US 1950s; **M.** $200-400.

1503. **Autobank (Pontiac)** WM, KLT; 2 7/8 x 7 3/4; Banthrico US 1950s; **M.** $200-400.

1504. **Autobank (Ford)** WM, KLT; 2 7/8 x 8; Banthrico US 1950s; **M.** $200-400.

1505. **Autobank (Mercury)** WM, KLT; 2 7/8 x 7 3/4; Banthrico US 1950s; **M.** $200-400.

C   1506. **Autobank (Oldsmobile)** WM, KLT; 2 7/8 x 7 7/8; Banthrico US 1950s; **M.** $200-400.

1507. **Autobank (Chevrolet)** WM, KLT: 2 7/8 x 7 3/4; Banthrico US 1950s; **M.** $200-400.

1508. **Autobank (Dodge)** WM, KLT: 2 7/8 x 8 3/16; Banthrico US 1950s; **M.** $200-400.

1509. **Autobank (Chevrolet)** WM, KLT: 2 7/8 x 7 3/4; Banthrico US 1950s; **M.** $200-400.

D   1510. **"Mercury Eight"** WM; 1 7/8 x 4 7/8; US; **A.** $75-125.

1511. **Auto** lead; 5 3/4; US; **B.** $75-125.

1512. **Taxi** (battery operated) metal & plastic; 3 1/2 x 6 1/4; Japan; **M.** $20-30.

1513. **Passenger Bus** metal; 1 7/8 x 6 1/8; Germany; **M.** $40-60.

1514. **Gas Truck** metal; 2 1/4 x 6 1/8; Marx US patented 1937; **1.** $75-125.

A   1515.   **1955 Thunderbird;** 7"; Banthrico US ©1974; **M.** $15-25.

1516.   **1937 Packard** V-12; 6 3/4; Banthrico US ©1974; **M.** $15-25.

1517.   **1936 Cord;** 6 3/4; Banthrico US © 1974; **M.** $15-25.

1518.   **1930 Duesenberg;** 6 3/4; Banthrico US © 1974; **M.** $15-25.

B   1519.   **1955 Jaguar;** 6 7/8; Banthrico US ©1974; **M.** $15-25.

1520.   **1937 Rolls Royce;** 7"; Banthrico US © 1974; **M.** $15-25.

1521.   **1953 Corvette;** 6 7/8; Banthrico US ©1974; **M.** $15-25.

1522.   **1927 Lincoln Brougham;** 7 3/4; Banthrico US © 1974; **M.** $15-25.

C   1523.   **1929 Ford;** 6"; Banthrico US © 1974; **M.** $15-25.

1524.   **1906 Oldsmobile;** 5 1/2; Banthrico US © 1974; **M.** $15-25.

1525.   **1902 Nash Rambler;** 3 3/8 x 5 3/16; Banthrico US © 1974; **M.** $15-25.

1526.   **1900 Baker Electric;** 3 5/8 x 4 3/4; Banthrico US © 1974; **M.** $15-25.

1527.   **1926 Pontiac;** 6"; Banthrico US © 1974; **M.** $15-25.

D   1528.   **TNT Delivery Truck;** 2 1/2 x 4 1/4; c1965; **M.** $20-40.

1529.   **1913 Ford Model T Van "Go Hawks";** 3 11/16 x 4 7/8; Ertl, Hong Kong; **M.** $15-25.

1530.   **1913 Ford Model T Van "Heinz";** 3 11/16 x 5 7/8; Ertl, Hong Kong; **M.** $15-25.

1531.   **1913 Ford Model T Van "Ford";** 3 11/16 x 5 7/8; Ertl, Hong Kong; **M.** $15-25.

1532.   **1913 Ford Model T Van "Home of the Handyman";** 3 11/16 x 5 7/8; Ertl, Hong Kong; **M.** $15-25.

1533.   **UPS Truck;** (See #1528); **M.** $20-30.

A   '1534. **Hall Clock with Paper Face** Cl; 5 1/4 x 2 3/16; Hubley US 1914-1920s; **C-D.** $300-500.

1535. **Ornate Hall Clock, Paper Face** Cl; 5 7/8 x 2 15/16; Hubley US 1914-1920s; **D.** $400-600.

1536. **Hall Clock with Cast Face** Cl; 5 3/16 x 2 3/16; Hubley US c1920s; **E.** $400-600.

1537. **Clock with Movable Hands** Cl; 4 7/16 x 3 7/16; Judd? US c1890?; **E.** $500-800.

1538. **"Cash Register Savings Bank"** Cl; 5 5/8 x 4 5/8; US c1889; **E.** $1000-1500.

1539. **World Time Bank** Cl & Paper; 4 1/8 x 2 5/8; Arcade US 1910-1920; **C-D.** $250-400.

1540. **Hall Clock** Cl; 5 5/8 x 3 1/4; Arcade US 1923; **C-D.** $400-700.

1541. **"Grandfather's Clock"** Cl; 5 3/8 x 3; England? late 1800s; **E.** $800-1200.

B   1542. **Clock with Movable Hands** Cl; 4 3/4 x 4 1/2; Chamberlain & Hill, England c1892; **E.** $600-800.

1543. **"Grandfather's Clock"** Cl; 7 1/8; (See #1557 for reverse); **F.** $2000-4000.

1544. ***"A Money Saver"** Cl & steel; 3 1/2 x 2 15/16; Arcade US 1909-1920s; **B.** $75-125.

1545. **Gold Dollar (Eagle Clock)** Cl & Steel; 3 1/2 x 2 15/16; Arcade US 1910-1913; **C.** $100-200.

1546. ***"Time is Money"** Cl; 3 5/8 x 3 1/16; A.C. Williams US 1909-1931; **B.** $75-125.

1547. **Hall Clock** (operates) lead, KLT; 7 1/2 x 3; "Made in U.S.A."; **1.** $150-250.

1548. **Street Clock** Cl & Steel; 6 x 2 1/2 wide at base; A.C. Williams US 1920s-1931; **D.** $600-1000.

1549. **"Sun Dial"** Cl; 4 5/16 x 2 1/8 sq. at base; Arcade US 1910-1916; **E.** $1500-2000.

C   1550. **Mantle Clock** lead; 3 7/8 x 6 7/8; "Made in U.S.A."; **1.** $50-100.

1551. **Carriage Clock** steel, KLT; 5 3/8 x 3 5/8; US patented 1901; **2.** $50-100.

1552. **Clock with Clown & Cat** tin; 2 x 1 1/4; **1.** $100-150.

1553. **Mantle Clock** lead, KLT; 6 7/8 x 6 7/8; Ingram Co. US; **2.** $100-200.

1554. **Clock with Clown & Dog** tin; 2 x 1 1/2; **1.** $100-150.

1555. **"Time is Money" Clock** iron & tin; 4 7/8; H.C. Hart Co. US patented 1885; **E.** $800-1000.

1556. **Swivel-Head Clock** lead; 5 1/4 x 4 3/8; B.D. Corp. US 1930; **1.** $75-125.

136

A 1557. **Reverse of #1543.** $2000-4000.

1558. **"Coin Registering Bank"** metal; 7 x 5 1/8; Kingsbury Mfg. Co. US c1932; **1.** $30-50.

1559. **"Atlas Mason" Milk Bottle** glass; 3 3/4 x 1 3/4; US; **1.** $15-20.

1560. **1st Federal Savings Bank** metal; 7 x 3 1/2; Banthrico US; **1.** $75-125.

1561. **"Strong Shoulder" Milk Bottle** glass; 3 5/8 x 2; US; **1.** $20-30.

1562. **Mantle Clock** metal; 6 x 6; US; **1.** $75-125.

1563. **"Four Coin Bank"** metal; 7 1/4 x 5 3/4; Kingsbury Mfg. Co. US c1941; **1.** $30-50.

B 1564. **Dime Register (Superman)** metal, slide trap; 2 1/2 square; © D.C. US; **3.** $100-200.

1565. **Dime Register (Jackie Robinson)** metal, press down trap; 2 5/8 square; US; **2.** $350-550.

1566. **N.Y. World's Fair (1964-1965)** metal, press down trap; 2 5/8 square; U.S. Steel US 1961; **1.** $75-125.

1567. **Dime Register (Snow White)** metal, slide trap; 2 1/2 square; W. Disney Productions US 1938; **2.** $100-150.

1568. **Dime Register (Astronaut)** metal, press down trap; 2 5/8 square; Kalon Mfg. Corp. US; **1.** $60-100.

1569. **Dime Register (Liberty Dollar)** metal, press bump to separate; Chein US 1945; **2.** $100-150.

1570. **Dime Register (Thrifty Elf)** metal, press bump to separate; 2 5/8 square; Chein US mid 1950s; **1.** $75-125.

1571. **Dime Register (Daily Dime Bank)** metal, press down trap; 2 5/8 square; US; **1.** $60-100.

1572. **Dime Register (Elf)** metal, slide trap; 2 1/2 square; US; **2.** $75-125.

1573. **Dime Register (Popeye)** metal, slide trap; 2 1/2 square; © King Feat. Synd. US 1929; **1.** $75-125.

1574. **Dime Register (Popeye)** metal, slide trap; 2 5/8 square; © King Feat. Synd. US 1956; **1.** $75-125.

C 1575. **"The Youth's Companion Savings Bank"** tin; 2 x 1 3/4; US; **1.** $100-200.

1576. **Children's Crusade** tin; 4 x 2 7/8 diam.; US 1940; **1.** $50-70.

1577. **Declaration of Independence** tin; 3 1/2; American Can Co. US; **1.** $20-30.

1578. **Puppo** wood; 4 3/8 x 3 5/8; Earl Albright US 1980; **M.** $20-30.

1579. **"Select-O-Matic" Juke Box** tin; 4 1/2 x 3 5/8 x 2 1/2; Haji, Japan; **1.** $75-125.

1580. **"Ideola" Juke Box** plastic; 6 1/4 x 4 x 2 1/4; Ideal US; **1.** $75-125.

1581. **Wurlitzer Juke Box** metal; 3 x 1 3/4; US; **1.** $75-125.

1582. **Cat with Bow** wood; 4 3/8 x 3 1/4; Earl Albright US; **M.** $20-30.

1583. **"Dodge Saves" Barrel** tin; 4 x 3 1/2; Chein US 1920s; **1.** $50-80.

1584. **Ernest Saver Club Bank** tin; 2 1/4 x 3 1/4; US; **1.** $50-70.

A   1585.   **Red Goose Shoe** tin; 2 3/4 x 5 1/4; US; **3.** $100-200.

1586.   **Lady's Shoe** (hinged top) silvered lead; 3 x 6 1/8; Germany 1920s; **1.** $100-200.

1587.   **Lady's Shoe with Mouse** silvered lead; 3 1/4 x 6 1/8; Germany 1920s; **2.** $150-250.

1588.   **Ben Franklin Desk** metal; 4 3/8 x 3 1/4; US; **2.** $50-70.

1589.   **Cradle with Sliding Blanket** silver plate; 3 1/8 x 3 1/4; Scandinavia 1925; **2.** $150-250.

1590.   **Aladdin's Lamp** metal; 4 1/2 x 8 1/4; US; **1.** $40-60.

B   1591.   **Pennsylvania (Bicentennial Bank)** Cl; 2 3/4 x 5; Knerr US 1975; **M.** $75-125.

1592.   **Allcoin Calendar Bank** metal & plastic; 3 3/16 x 4 1/4; M.A. Gerett Corp. US; **1.** $20-30.

1593.   **Rocking Horse (SBCCA)** tin; 3 x 2 1/4; US 1977; **M.** $15-20.

1594.   **Washington D.C. (SBCCA)** tin; 4 7/8 x 4 3/8; Capitol Souvenir Co. Hong Kong; **M.** $15-20.

1595.   **Lion** wood; 3 3/4 x 5 1/4; Earl Albright US 1983; **M.** $15-20.

1596.   **"Lock-up Savings" (SBCCA)** AL; 4 x 3; Reynolds Toys US 1983; **M.** $50-70.

1597.   **Suitcase (SBCCA)** porcelain; 2 7/8 x 3 9/16; Tresor-Verlag, West Germany 1979; **M.** $20-40.

C   1598.   **American League Bats** wood & plastic, 5 1/2 x 4 base diam.; Van Dyne Bros. US 1950s; **M.** $75-125.

1599.   **Covered Wagon** Cl; 6 5/8 x 2 1/8; Wilton Products, Inc.; still available US; **M.** $20-40.

1600.   **Coal & Coke Museum** glass; 4 5/8 x 5 diam.; US 1969; **M.** $40-60.

1601.   **"The Cradle"** AL; 4 1/8 x 6 1/8; US; **2.** $100-200.

1602.   **Shoe House** WM; 5 1/4 x 5 1/4; Banthrico US; **A.** $20-30.

1603.   **National League Bats** plastic; 5 3/4 x 4 base diam.; still available US; **M.** $30-40.

A
1604.	**Alphabet** Cl; 3 7/8; US; **E.** $3000-5000.
1605.	**Coca Cola** Cl; 3 3/4 x 1 7/8; US; **F.** $3000-5000.
1606.	**Waterwheel** Cl & steel; 4 1/2 x 4; US; **E.** $1500-2500.
1607.	**"Camera Bank"** Cl; mech., 4 5/16 x 2 3/8 x 4 1/4; Wrightsville Hardware Co. US late 1800s; **E.** $5000-7000.
1608.	**Baseball on Three Bats** Cl; 5 1/4; Hubley US 1914; **D.** $1200-1800.
1609.	**Map of U.S.** WM, KLT; 2 3/4 x 4 1/2; US; **3.** $400-600.
1610.	**Klondyke Gold Bug** Cl; 3 1/4 x 3 3/8; US; **F.** $1200-2000.

B
1611.	***Merry-Go-Round** nickeled Cl; 4 5/8 x 4 3/8; Grey Iron Casting Co. US 1925-1928; **C.** $400-600.
1612.	**Potato** Cl; 2 1/8 x 5 1/4; Mary A. Martin, designer, US 1897; **E.** $1200-2000.
1613.	**Sen Sen** tin; 2 1/2 x 1 13/16 x 3/16; W & H Co. US 1912; **2.** $100-200.
1614.	***Merry-Go-Round** Cl; 4 5/8 x 4 3/8; Grey Iron Casting Co. US 1925-1928; **C.** $600-1000.

1615.	**Token** brass; 1 3/16 diam.; US; **1.** $40-60.
1616.	**Key** Cl; 5 1/2; Wm. J. Somerville, designer, US 1905; **D.** $450-750.
1617.	***Merry-Go-Round** Cl; 4 5/8 x 4 3/8; Grey Iron Casting Co. US 1925-1928; **C.** $400-600.
1618.	**"Nest Egg" ("Horace")** Cl; 3 3/8 x 4 3/4; Smith & Egge US 1873; **E.** $800-1200.
1619.	**"Lone Ranger Strong Box"** covered metal; 3 7/16 x 3 1/8; Zell Products Co. US; **1.** $100-150.
1620.	**Football** Cl; 2 x 3; (part of bank #10) US; **E.** $200-300.
1621.	**Apple** Cl; 3 x 5 1/4 x 5; Kyser & Rex US 1882; **E.** $1500-2500.
1622.	**"Shell Out"** Cl; 2 1/2 x 4 3/4; J. & E. Stevens US 1882; **D.** $600-900.
1623.	**"Scrappy Bank"** covered metal, KLT; 3 1/4 x 3 1/8; Zell Products Co. US; **1.** $50-100.
1624.	**Football on Stand** Al; 4 1/4; US; **1.** $40-60.

C appears next to 1618.

A	1625.	**Clock Candy Container** glass; 3 5/8 x 2 13/16 x 1 3/4; US; **3.** $200-300.
	1626.	**"Nixe"** Cl; 4 1/2 x 4; US; **F.** $5000-7000.
	1627.	**"Mermaid"** Cl; (See #34); Grey Iron Casting Co.? US; **D.** $450-800.
	1628.	**Cross** Cl; 9 1/4 x 4 5/8; US; **F.** $1200-1500.
	1629.	**Dressmaker's Model;** 6 x 4 5/16 x 2 7/8; Banthrico US; **M.** $60-80.
	1630.	**Elephant with Howdah (short trunk)** Cl; 3 3/4 x 4 3/4; Hubley US 1910; **B.** $200-400.
	1631.	**Damm Yankees** AL; 2 1/4 x 8 3/4; Laverne A. Worley US 1982; **M.** $40-60.
B	1632.	**First National Bank** wood; 5 5/8 x 4 1/2; US c1886; **3.** $150-200.
	1633.	**State Bank** Cl; 5 1/2 x 4; Columbia Grey Iron Casting Co. US 1897; Kyser & Rex US; **B.** $200-350.
	1634.	**"Kress"** Cl; 4 x 3 x 2; US; **F.** $1200-1800.
	1635.	**Presto** Cl; 3 1/4 x 2 1/4 x 1 3/4; US; **A.** $75-125.
	1636.	**Mosque** Cl 2 7/8 x 2 3/8 x 1 5/8; A.C. Williams US 1905-1934; **B.** $100-200.
	1637.	**Fisherman's Cottage** tin; 1 7/8 x 2 1/2 x 1 3/4; "Germany", **3.** $200-300.

	1638.	**"Berliner Bank"** tin; 3 1/8 x 5 x 2 1/2; Germany 1930s?; **2.** $100-200.
	1639.	**"Goteborgs Sparbank"** brass; 6 1/2 x 4 3/8 x 4 3/8; Sweden; **C.** $100-150.
C	1640.	**Brownie** comp.; 6 x 4 1/4; US; **2.** $75-125.
	1641.	**Save & Smile Money Box** (paint variation) Cl; 4 1/4 x 4 1/8; Sydenham & McOustra or Chamberlain & Hill, England; **C.** $300-450.
	1642.	**Donkey** (Bad Accident mechanical) Cl; 3 1/4 x 4 7/8; US; **E.** $300-500.
	1643.	**"Post Office"** (George V) tin; 2 1/4 x 1 1/2 diam.; England 1920s; **2.** $30-40.
	1644.	**Small Ox** (conversion) Cl, riveted; 2 1/2 x 3 1/4; US; **D.** $100-200.
	1645.	**Reclining Cow** Cl; 2 1/8 x 4; US; **F.** $600-1000.
	1646.	**Polish Rooster** Cl; 5 1/2 x 3 3/4; US; **E.** $3000-4000.
	1647.	**Transvaal Money Box** AL; 6 x 4 1/2; England; **3.** $300-400.

A 1648. **Bulldog** lead, TL; 4 1/4 x 2 1/4 x 4; Europe; **3.** $400-600.

1649. **Emperor Franz Joseph & Kaiser Wilhelm** parian ware; 3 5/8 x 2 9/16; England 1912; **3.** $200-300.

1650. **Flower Girl** lead; 4 3/4 x 2 3/8; Germany; **3.** $800-1200.

1651. **Santa** pottery; 6 3/4 x 3 3/16; US; **2.** $150-250.

1652. **Dog with Wash Tub** lead, KLT; 2 x 2 1/2 diam.; Germany; **3.** $250-350.

1653. **Pigs at Stone Wall** pottery; 3 1/4 x 3; Germany; **3.** $200-300.

1654. **"Saratoga" Bulldog** pottery; 2 5/8 x 5; US; **1.** $100-150.

1655. **John Bull** lead; 4 1/2; England; **3.** $400-800.

1656. **Grisley Bear** lead, TL missing; 3 1/4 x 5 1/2; Germany; **3.** $300-400.

B 1657. **Rockingham House** pottery; 5 x 3 3/4; England 1890s; **2.** $150-250.

1658. **Fox Head** Cl; 4 1/2 x 2 3/8; Unicast US 1973; **M.** $40-60.

1659. **Humphrey - Muskie Donkey** Cl; 4 1/2 x 4 1/2; US 1968; **M.** $40-60.

1660. **State Bank (miniature)** AL; 2 1/16 x 1 3/4 x 1 3/8; Reynolds Toys US 1983; **M.** $40-60.

1661. **"New York World's Fair" Bldg.** WM, KLT; 2 1/4 x 2 5/8; US "1939"; **2.** $200-300.

1662. **Washerwoman** tin; 2 3/4 diam.; Germany; **3.** $250-350.

1663. **"Pingree Potato"** Cl; 2 1/4 x 5 1/2; Mary A. Martin, designer, US WWI; **E.** $2000-3000.

1664. **Plymouth Rock "1620"** Cl; 1 15/16 x 3 7/8; US; **E.** $1200-1800.

1665. **Key (St. Louis World's Fair)** Cl; 5 3/4; US 1904; **E.** $500-800.

1666. **Elephant with Raised Trunk** silvered lead, TL; 3 15/16 x 6 1/8; Germany 1920s; **2.** $250-350.

C 1667. **Japanese Safe** (paint variation) Cl; 5 1/2 x 4 5/8 x 4 5/8; Kyser & Rex US c1883; **C.** $300-400.

1668. **Throne ("Geo. III")** Cl; 8 x 4 11/16 x 2; England; **M.** $75-125

1669. **"Guest Hospital"** brass; 10 7/16 x 9 x 5 15/16; England 1931; **E.** $800-1500.

1670. **"Dandy Candy Savings Bank"** tin; 7 5/16 x 3 3/16; Leckie & Gray, England 1920s; **3.** $300-400.

1671. **Kanter's Telephone** tin; 10 x 4 3/8; Kanter Co. US; **2.** $100-150.

1672. **Pig in Tux** (repaint) lead; 5 3/4 x 2 7/8; US 1930s?; **3.** $40-60.

1673.   **Santa with Pack** CI; 6"; Arcade US c1932; **F.** $3500-7000.   Reverse

1674. **Santa with Xmas Bag** pottery; 4 1/4 x 3 4/8; Japan c1930s; **2.** $200-300.

1675. **"Toy Radio Bank"** Cl & sheet metal; dials turn; 2 13/16 x 5 1/2 x 3; J & E Stevens US c1920s-1933; **D.** $500-700.

1677. **Drum** (semi-mech.) tin; 1 3/8 x 2 diam.; Germany; **3.** $200-300.

1676. **Oil Lamp** Cl; lamp, 7 x 5 diam.; cone, 6 1/2; **F.** $600-1000.

1678. **Beehive** lead, trick lock; 2 6/8 x 2 1/4 diam.; Europe; **3.** $300-500.

1679.   **Native Warrior** brass & coconut; 6 1/2; **3.** $500-800.

1680.   **Queen Victoria** pottery; 5 1/2; England, late 1800s; **3.** $700-1000.

1682.   **Peter's Weatherbird (bank & hood ornament);** See #159. **E.** $2000-3000.

1683.   **Mean Standing Bear** Cl; 6 1/4; Hubley US 1910s; **C.** $250-400.

1681.   **Mayflower Refrigerator** Cl; 5 1/8 x 3 x 2 1/8; US 1920s; **D** (embossed on back: "Save 25¢ per day & buy a Mayflower Refrigerator"). $350-600.

1684. **Grinning/Frowning Boy** "This Boy Saves His Money" C1;
4 ¾; Ives? 1800's; F. $15,000-20,000.

1684. **Upside Down** "This Boy Spends His Money".

1685. **The Midget** CI; 2 5/8; Harper
(England); D. $500-800.

1686. **Barrel on Stand** CI; 2 7/8; U.S.; E.
$400-800.

1687. **Walking Bear** CI; 2 3/4; Grey Iron?;
F. $2500-5000.

1688. **Ideal Stove** CI; 3; "Ideal Mfg Co
Det Mich"; E. $500-1000.

1688. **Open** (see #1688)

1689. **Cone-topped Building** CI; 2 5/8;
Kyser & Rex?; E. $500-1000.

144B

1690. **Tall Domed "Bank"** CI; 5 1/2; A.C. Williams; E. $300-600.

1691. **Skyscraper w/Clock** CI; 5 3/8; A.C. Williams; D. $800-1500.

1692. **"Broadcast Bank"** WM; 6 1/4; U.S. 30's-40's; 3. $300-600.

1693. **"1878" Bank** CI; 3 1/4; Judd?; D. $200-400.

1694. **Walking Retriever** AL; 3 5/8; Unknown; 3. $200-400.

1695. **Solid-top Crystal Bank** CI/glass; 3 5/8; Arcade; C. $150-300.

1696. **"Savings" Cash Register CI and mesh;** 3 5/8; Arcade?; C. $200-300.

1697. **"N.P.M.A." Liberty Bell** CI; 3 15/16; Chicago Hardware 1906; E. $1200-2500.

1698. **Egelhoff Safe** CI; 4 3/16; M. $100-200.

1699. **"Old Homestead" Safe** CI; 4 1/4; Shimer Toy Co. 1899; E. $800-1500.

1700. **Four-post Safe** CI; 5; Unknown; D. $300-600.

1701. **Town Hall** CI; 3 5/16; Harper (England); D. $500-800.

1702. **"Broadway" Safe** tin; 3 13/16; U.S. 1920's; 2. $100-200.

1703. **"Wembley Bank"** CI; 3 7/16; Harper (England)?; E. $2500-5000.

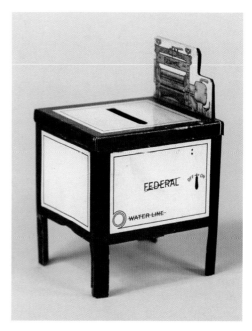

1704. **"Federal" Washer** tin; 4 1/4; U.S. 1920's; 3. $150-300.

1705. **Monument w/Cross** WM; 2; Unknown; 3. $100-200.

1706. **Hairy Buffalo** CI; 2 7/8; Ober MFG. Co.; E. $1500-2500.

1707. **Fluted Urn** WM; 3 1/2; Vanio?; 3. $100-200.

1708. **Walking Santa w/Pack** AL; 5 7/8; Unknown, E. $500-1000.

1709. **"Old Volunteer F.D. Bank"** CI; 5; U.S. 1800's; F. $5000-8000.

1710. **"Home Bank" w/Dormers** CI; 5 1/4; J&E Stevens pat'd 1872; E. $4000-8000.

1711. **Pelican lead,** TL; 4 1/16; Germany; 3. $3000-5000.

1712. **Seated Indian lead,** KLT; 3 1/2; Germany; 3. $800-1200.

1713. **"State Bank" (flat top)** CI; 4 3/16; U.S.; D. $800-1500.

1714. **General U.S. Grant Safe** CI;
144E 5 15/16; JM Harper US 1903; E. $4000-7000.

1715. **William McKinley Safe** CI; 5 7/8; JM Harper US 1903; E. $4000-7000.

1716. **Empire State Savings Bank** CI; 10 1/2; U.S.; D. $1000-1500.

APPENDIX TO THE CATALOG

1. Symbol of the Penny Door. Appears in various forms throughout the catalog. (See index.) Pipe is always replaced. Two originals exist. A cartoonist for the *Westminster Gazette* caricatured General Paul Kruger, who fought the British for that area of South Africa known as the Transvaal. The fighting continued from 1877 until 1881, when Kruger & The Boers obtained brief and limited independence for the Transvaal.

   Front: *Transvaal Money Box*
   Back: *By permission of the proprietors of the Westminster Gazette.*

2. Frederick was King of Prussia from 1740-1786.

3. Front: *American and National League Ball*
   Back: *Design Pat. Appl'd For.*

4. Same pig as Bismark Mechanical, which caricatures Otto von Bismark, (1815-1898), founder of German Empire. Probably an anti-German bank, produced after Bismark halted importation of American pork, in 1883. Bank depicts American businessmen riding sharp-eared pigs against Germany. Pig's ears are indeed razor-sharp.

7. Lloyd George (1863-1945). Was chancellor of the Exchequer in 1911, when he designed Britain's first unemployment insurance. He wanted the employer to contribute 9 pence and the employee, 4 pence.

   Front: *Insurance Bill Bank*
   9 p for 4 p

10. Front: *Official League Ball*
    Back: Design Pat. Pending. See patent papers.

13. Original Hubley tag: *I am the greatest thing on earth, King Midas and behold; he who keeps me always near will never want for Gold.*

14. Billy Bounce was a comic strip character created by W.W. Denslow in 1902. Red and black version is difficult to find. Turnpin closure.

    Front: *Give Billy a Penny.* Probably an earlier bank than #15.

15. Casting of shoes and coin slot is slightly different than #14. This is the typical paint combination and is easier to find than #14.

18. See patent papers.

19. Paint variation. Hard to find.

20. Easier to find this paint variation than numbers 18 and 19.

21. Mahogony carving obtained at A.C. Williams pattern maker's estate auction.

22. Front: *Major League Baseball*

23. Front: *Mother Hubbard*
    Back: *Copyright by J.M. Harper 1907.*

24. See #164 for variation.

25. Back: *Copyright by J.M. Harper 1907.*

26. Tin keylock closure.

    Front: *Souvenir of Windsor, Canada*
    Other banks depict German scenes in center disc.

30. A comic strip character created by Robert Sidney Smith (1877-1935), leading cartoonist of his day. Doc Yak was the lead figure in the strip, which appeared in the Chicago Daily Tribune, circa 1911-1917, when Smith created Andy Gump, who became more popular. The number "348", stenciled on Yak's rump, was the number of Yak's sports car. Yak banks are converted automobile hood ornaments.

31. There is a smaller version of this bank, not known to exist in any collection, which was produced by A.C. Williams in 1904. See patent paper.

32. A comic strip character created by Fred Opper (1857-1938) for the Hearst Syndicate. Strip appeared in San Francisco and New York City in 1900.

34. See variation, #1627.

37. Side: *Pat. Pending*

38. Shovel was cast separately and is often replaced.

39. This was probably never a bank, although there is a rare version that came painted.

40. The feet on this bank are identical to those on the Golliwog Bank, number 85, an English Harper bank. #40 also made in brass. English registry #670140

42. Bank is held together by a screw in the "wall". Bank #43, which we believe to be English, is held together by a screw in each ear.

43. See #42, above.

45. The Boy Scout movement, brought to the United States around 1910, inspired this bank. It was renamed "Soldier Boy" during World War I. This bank, and the Hubley version #47 were both produced before the war, and both were originally Boy Scouts.

49. There is a mechanical version of this bank, also rare, in which the following inscription appears: *Jubilee 1897*

    Back of our bank: *Born May 24, 1819*
    Crowned June 20, 1837
    Married February 10, 1840

50. Philip Henry Sheridan (1831-1888), famed Civil War general for the North.

51. Baby and blanket are nickeled, and the beautiful rosettes seen on #52, are missing. The more difficult bank to cast, #52 was probably dropped in favor of #51. The reproduction is easy to detect; it is painted blue and white, and the coin slot is in the headboard, rather than the blanket.

52. See #51 above.

53. This bank, of which is the only known specimen, turned up in Virginia, several years ago.

54. Caricature of General Benjamin F. Butler, who ran for president of the United States on the Greenback-Labor and Anti-Monopolist Ticket in 1884. In 1878, Arnold Seligsberg of New York City was granted a patent for a bank which fits the description of this one. Bank depicts the general holding a bunch of greenbacks. Inscription: *Bullion and yachts for myself and my friends, dry bread and greenbacks for the people.* Bank is an excellent portrait of Butler.

55. Base: *Big mir mehr viel mehr.* Translates, Bring me more, much more.

56. See variation made in pottery, #1652.

65. Japanese characters at right of drawer translate, *$1000 in gold.* Symbol at left is Daikoku's mallet. See Gods of Fortune, page 177.

66. See *Gods of Fortune*, page 177.

67. See *Gods of Fortune*, page 177.

68. The Japanese God of Fortune carries a mallet, which is called *u chi-deKozuchi.* See page 177.

69. Fukusuki, not a god, is a symbol of good luck for Japanese merchants.

70. English registry #646486
    Front: *I love a Copper*
    Back: *Every Copper Helps*
    This is a double-faced bank. The policeman figure, bank #72, a single faced bank, appears on the reverse side of #70.

71. English registry #551222, Oct. 20, 1909.

72. Base: *Every Copper Helps.* Bank also came in iron or aluminum. English registry #574268.

73. Original design patent issued to Florence Pretz, in 1908. Figure, considered to be good luck, is the symbol of "things as they ought to be."

74. See #73 above.

75. Feet and base: *Do You Know Me?* The figure of Rumplestiltskin, posed the same as the Billiken banks. Someone's wonderful joke? We wish we knew!

77. Base: *#1564.*

78. See Appendix #1.

79. Obviously another take-off on the Billiken banks. Wish we know who made this one, too.

80. Advertising variation.
    Front: *Billiken Shoes Bring Good Luck.*

83. See patent papers.

84. See #83 above.

85. The Golliwog was a character who appeared in the book, *Adventures of Two Dutch Dolls and a Golliwog,* written in 1895 by Florence Upton, an American who lived and wrote in England. This bank was described in 1910 Harper catalog as being done in *attractive colors.* Rd 568461, Aug. 22, 1910.

86. See #85 above.

87. See #85 above.

89. Placard reads: *I'm a comical knave*
    But your money I'll save.
    The more you give me
    The richer you'll be.
    Bank depicts, Tim, a character from English comic strip which appeared in *Chips,* a comic paper. First drawn by Tom Browne in 1896, Percy Cocking took over the task in 1919. The strip continued until 1953.

90. See #89 above. Same bank except for name of character. Made in Germany. English Registry #610047.

92. Date *1981* written on scarf.
    Back: *Save before I melt.*
    This bank is one of a limited edition of 50.

93. Front: *Hang Seng Bank Ltd.*

94. A candy container, it came filled with mints. On top: *Save your pennies and your dollars will take care of themselves.*

95. Back: *Santa's Village, Sky Forest, California.*

97. This bank is a cigarette lighter, as well as a bank.

101. Back: *Reynolds Toys 1982* This bank is one of a limited edition of 501.

103. Base: *Deno Burralli*

107. See Appendix #1.

108. William Howard Taft (1857-1930) was 27th. President of the United States, 1909-1913. Called *Egg Bank* in Arcade catalog.

109. A two-faced bank, depicting Presidential candidate, William Howard Taft *(Peaceful Bill)* and his running mate, James Schoolcraft Sherman *(Smiling Jim).* Smiling

Jim side: *Copyright 1908.*
Peaceful Bill side: *By J.M. Harper*
See #108 above. Election was in 1909.

110. William Marcy Tweed (1823-1878) was a corrupt New York City politician. Boss Tweed gained control of the city's finances and swindled the treasury of millions of dollars. Charges of corruption were brought by *Harper's Weekly,* whose powerful cartoonist, Thomas Nast caricatured Tweed and his political machine, which Nast portrayed as a tiger — the Tammany Hall Tiger.
     Front: *Savings Bank.*
     Back: The face of a tiger is sculpted on Tweed's back.

111. Uncle Sam is the personification of the U.S. Government. Dates from War of 1812, when U.S. Army supply packages were stamped with initials of inspector Samuel Wilson, nicknamed, Uncle Sam.

112. See #111 above.

113. See #111 above.

114. George Washington, (1732-1799) first President of the United States. Bust is separate casting attached with a screw. The number 3 is cast inside Washington's head.
     Back: *Pat Appl'd For.*
     Harper advertised a series of bust banks, including *Lincoln, McKinley,* and *Cleveland* or *Theodore Roosevelt,* but only Washington and Grant, #115, are known to exist.

115. Same as #114, but the number 2 is cast inside Grant's head. Knobs on safe doors are made of brass. Ulysses Simpson Grant (1822-1885) was the 18th President of the United States. Commanded armies of the North late in the Civil War and received General Lee's surrender at Appomattox.

116. See #115 above. This bank produced for Grant Sesquicentennial, Galena, Illinois.

117. Robert Edward Lee (1807-1870) was commander in chief of the confederate armies in the Civil War.

118. Base: *A.C. Rehberger, Chgo.*

119. Front: *George Washington.*

120. Top of base: *Teddy*
     Theodore Roosevelt (1858-1919), 26th President of the United States. Bank was probably made for a short time.

121. Front: *I do not keep money to look at — George Washington*
     Back: *The Prudential Insurance Company of America Home Office, Newark, New Jersey.*

122. Benjamin Franklin (1706-1790) was a famed American statesman, scientist and philosopher.
     Back: *The Franklin Life Insurance Company Founded 1884. Compliments of your Franklin Life Representative.*

124. Charles A. Lindbergh (1902-1974), famous American aeronautical pioneer, made the first non-stop solo flight across the Atlantic Ocean in May, 1927.
     Back: *Lindy Bank C. by G & T 1928 N. Tregor* (artist)

125. Front: *You can bank on Lindy*
     Back: *1929 Copyright Arnold, Oregon, Illinois*

126. There are three known specimens of this bank, none of which has a trap. Bert Whiting thought he had seen one with a closure and slot in the base.

127. Douglas MacArthur (1880-1964), American general who commanded the Pacific theatre in W.W. II. Promoted to General of the Army in 1944.

128. Abraham Lincoln (1809-1865), 16th President of the United States. Civil War President. Originally came painted brown.

129. Front: *February 12, 1809 — April 15, 1865.*
     Back: *Lincoln Trust & Savings Bank, Chicago.*

133. Dwight David Eisenhower (1890-1969), Supreme commander of the Allied Forces during W.W. II and 34th President of the United States.

135. John Fitzgerald Kennedy (1917-1963), 35th President of the United States.

136. Back: *S.E. Bushong Kennott Sq. Pa.*

137. Base of the figure is hollow. This bank was mounted on its base and painted by George Bauer for the 1973

Mechanical Bank Collectors Club of America convention.
Back: *S.E. Bushong Kennott Sq. Pa.*

139. Augustus Saint Gaudens (1848-1907) sculpted the seated Lincoln, located at the Lincoln Memorial, Washington, D.C.

140. Richard M. Nixon (1913----), 37th President of the United States. Resigned the Presidency in 1974, the only American president ever to do so.
Back: *1972 Charlotte Blevins.*

141. Thomas A. Edison (1847-1931), American inventor, who invented, among other things, the phonograph, the incandescent electric lamp and talking motion pictures.

142. Robert Cavelier de LaSalle (1643-1687), French explorer in America.

Back: *LaSalle National Bank, Chicago, Illinois.*

143. Back: *England.*

145. Franklin Delano Roosevelt (1822-1945), 32nd President of the United States. His last term coincided with World War II.

148. The "New Deal" was the name Roosevelt gave to his program to lift the country out of the Great Depression. This bank came copper finished and copper oxydized.

150. Base: *Pat. July 30, 1918.*

151. John Joseph Pershing (1860-1948), Commander in Chief of the American Expeditionary Force, W.W.I, promoted to Chief of Staff, U.S. Army. Recipient Pulitzer Prize in 1932 for *My Experiences in the World War.*

152. Paul von Hindenburg, 1847-1934. German General and Field Marshall, W.W. I and second president of Weimar Republic, 1925-1934.
Front: *Helft Den Ostpreussen* "Help the East Prussians"

153. Commemorates 200th anniversary of Washington's birth.

Back: *T. Fischer, 1915.* Brass key-lock trap.

154. Pattern of perforations and shape of bank's back same as on Tammany Mechanical Bank. Bank also has perfectly fitting Steven's trap. Betty Hale, a dedicated long time member of the SBCCA, and frequent contributor to the club's magazine, *The Penny Bank Post,* makes a good case for the Trust Man being Mark Hanna (1837-1903), a Republican who felt that large corporations and trusts insured general prosperity. The likeness to Hanna is excellent.

157. Mutt & Jeff were the creation of H.C. "Bud" Fisher (1885-1954), cartoonist for the San Francisco Chronicle. Strip began in 1907, with a character named, "A. Mutt," with Jeff making his appearance in 1908. Fisher licensed A.C.W. to make the bank.

158. Base: *Saving Sam.*

159. Character used to advertise children's shoes.

160. Front: *Peters Weatherbird Shoes for Girls.*
Back: *Peters Weatherbird Shoes for Boys.*

161. Lloyd was a famous silent film star. Career began in 1913, and by 1928, he was a very wealthy man. Coins accumulate in rectangular box behind Harold. Slot is in the key-opened trap. There is a similar, rare mechanical.

162. Back: *Copyright by J.M. Harper 1907.*

163. Bank licensed by Campbell Soup Company. Characters created for Campbell by Grace Drayton, circa 1900. See appendix #257.

164. The condition of the specimen pictured is unusually good. The paint used on this bank, and on the Lamb, #595, did not bond well, and most samples of these banks are in poor condition.

165. Back: *Copyright by J.M. Harper 1907.*

167. This bank has a turnpin, rather than a screw as in bank #166. We believe this to be an earlier bank, probably made by Wing.

168. A.C.W. catalog describes this bank as "Aunt Jemima Bank with gold cake turner." See patent papers.

170. Back: *The Young Nigger Bank.*

171. Back: *No. 3000.*

173. See patent papers. This bank is being reproduced under the name, "Hard Luck Charlie."

174. This bank called *Darkey Bank* in A.C.W. catalogs. They probably started to produce it after Hubley's patent ran out.

177. Advertised in catalogs as "Policeman Toy Bank." The name "Mulligan" came from a radio show called *Milligan and Mulligan,* a comedy-adventure starring Don Ameche. Don't know dates that show aired.

178. See #177 above.

179. See #177 above.

183. Iron, key-lock trap in base.

187. Back: *D & S Pat. Pend.* Juliet Low (1860-1927) founded the Girl Scouts of America in 1912.

189. Back: *1930 The Platt & Munk Co., Inc.* Book contains pages with slots for coins. Back of book contained picture stamps. Child put coin in slot and then covered the coin with a stamp. When a page was completed, the stamps revealed a picture. The book held $10.00.

191. Shirley Temple, famous child movie star. Bank pictures her in her role as The Little Corporal.

192. This is a converted doorstop. Woman should be seated on a pillow. Japanese Goddess of Fortune holds a Biwa, a musical instrument. See Gods of Fortune, page 177.

196. Mickey Mouse was the first and most famous of Walt Disney's characters. Featured in movies in the 1930's and in comic strips.

201. See #196 above.

202. Front: *Walt Disney — Crown Toys* Tin twist closure.
See #196 above.

203. See #196 above. *Asco* is trademark of Arthur Shaw & Co., Denver Works, Morfital Lane, Willenhall, Staffordshire, Eng. Made banks in aluminum and soft metal.

204. A souvenir of the 1933-34 Chicago's World's Fair, "A Century of Progress." Printed on trunk: *Minnie & Mickey at the World's Fair. Be Thrifty and Save your coins.* Three buildings at the fair — the Hall of Science, Travel and Transportation and the Federal Building are pictured.

205. Charlie McCarthy was the dummy of Edgar Bergen, the most popular ventriloquist ever in the United States. Bergen had his own radio show and also an early TV show. Charlie and his dummy friend, Mortimer Snerd, also appeared in a comic strip in the 1930's.

206. Wooden jaw moves when string is pulled. Bank has a tin key lock. See #205 above.

207. Wooden jaw moves when string is pulled. Key lock closure. See #205 above.

208. Front: *Charlie McCarthy.* Black wire monacle and string are usually missing on this bank. See #205 above.

209. Front: *Feed me I save you money* See #205 above.

211. This bank came in assorted colors. See patent papers.

214. The chantecler is a character in an old fairy tale, but the inspiration for the bank probably came from a play by Edmond Rostand, first performed in Paris in 1910. Maude Adams, a great lady of the American theatre, appeared in the play in New York City in 1911, dressed in full-feathered costume. We like to think the bank, which probably was American made, depicts her.

215. See patent papers.

216. This was probably an end-of-day bank. It is the same figure that appears on the mechanical bank made by Hubley.

217. Andy Gump was the comic strip creation of Robert Sidney Smith. The Gump series, called "The Gumps," began its run in 1917 and was the first "serial" comic strip. Smith's first comic character was Doc Yak. (See Appendix #30) The Gump strip lasted until 1957. The Arcade toy car with same Gump figure was produced in

1928. A statue of Andy Gump stands in a park in his home town, Lake Geneva, Wisconsin. Bank has been reproduced in lead.

218. Side: *Save $5.00 in this Thrift Bank and open up a savings account with the bank whose name appears on the bottom. They will furnish you with one of the large savings banks.* This bank, licensed by Sidney Smith Corp., fits inside of bank #219, the *large savings bank* referred to. See also Appendix #217.

219. This bank was given to the customer who had successfully filled bank #218. Bank pictures Andy and Bim Gump. See #217 above.

220. Back: *National Shawmut Bank of Boston.*

221. Marked *Germany* on base. Key-lock trap.

222. Shield: *Winnipesaukee.*

223. Bank has hinged top with lock. Tent flap: *White Mts.* Slot is in rear.

224. Back: *Chicago Hdw. Foundry Co North Chicago, Il. Copyright 1905 J.M. Harper.*

225. Headband: *Trade Mark* Sioux Indian Chief Ish Tak Ha Ba, whose name actually translates *drooping eyelid*, lived from circa 1800 to 1880. The Sleepy Eye Milling Company, Sleepy Eye, Minn., produced a number of items under the trade mark.

227. This bank has a horizontal slot at the back of head. Bank looks the same as number 221 from the front, but headdress is cast differently. Key-lock trap.

228. The reproduction of this bank is easy to detect; the arms are cast whole. Arms are split in the original.

229. Back: *Indian Head National Bank* This bank when new in 1978, sold for $5.00. Bank also came in white metal.

231. Back: *Made in Japan.*

235. Shield: *Grand Canyon National Park, Arizona.* Key lock trap.

238. Back of sign: *Reynolds Toys*
This was Reynolds' first still bank, produced in an edition of 35.

241. R.F. Outcault (1863-1928), originated Buster Brown and his famous dog. Outcault's comic strip was introduced in 1902 and was syndicated. Buster was an upper class brat, quite unlike Outcault's first popular comic character, *Yellow Kid*, who was strickly lower class!

243. Back of hat: *Hag.* This bank made in edition of 50.

246. Back of sign: *Reynolds Toys*
Edition limited to 50 produced for the 1982 Still Bank Collectors' Club convention.

247. Side: *C. Dennis, 1962.* Charles Russell, an artist who painted his impressions of the Old West in the 1880's.

248. Base: *2302 J.I.J.*

249. Front: *Whizzor.*
Back: *Home Savings Assn. Kansas City.*

250. Base: *10-19-73.*
Back: *GK.*
A limited edition of 32 banks was cast in 1972. A few were painted as Emmett Kelly, famous American clown.

251. See Appendix #1. A shorter version with no writing.

253. Mailbox slides out of holder. Mailbox and base are tin.
Base: *Trademark Carinet, Registered Austria.*

254. Davy Crockett (1786-1836) American hero, Indian fighter, United States Congressman. With 185 others, held off Santa Anna and his army of 4000 Mexican troops at the Alamo, a mission fortress in San Antonio, Texas. Battle fought for control of the state of Texas. Only one American survived, and "Remember the Alamo!" became the battle cry of Texans who finally defeated Santa Anna.

257. Sunbonnet Sue (Dolly Dimple) was the creation of Grace Gebbie Weiderseim Drayton, who illustrated children's books, produced ads for Campbell Soup Company, among others, and designed paper dolls. She also wrote the Dolly Dimples comic strip. See index for a complete list of banks inspired by her characters. Original Hubley pattern for this bank was for a doorstop.

258. Top: *Cigars Larosa*
Back: *Habana 50*
Sides: *Colorado*

259. The Schnozzola, or nose, of the late American comedian, Jimmy Durante, is featured on this bank.
Back: *Abbot Wares*   *C. Romanelli.*

260. Bank sold since the 1930's by Planters Peanuts.

261. A squeaker inside responds when bank is turned upside down to deposit coin.

262. See Appendix #1.

263. This bank is one of a series of banks copyrighted by Warner Bros. and produced by Metal Moss Mfg. Co. Banks depict popular Warner Brothers characters who appeared in short movies, called Looney Tunes & Merrie Melodies. They also appeared in comic strips. The movies ran from 1929 until 1969. The figures were introduced in this order: Porky Pig, 1936, Petunia Pig and Daffy Duck, 1937, Bugs Bunny, 1938, Elmer Fudd, 1940. Other characters had made their appearance by the mid to late 1940's. In 1941 Looney Tunes and Merrie Melodies were published in comic book form by Western Publishing Co. The symbol © *W.B.C.*, appears either on the tree trunk or barrel, depending on the bank, and on the end of the green base. The names of the characters are either embossed or painted. The special keys are made of heavy metal. See Metal Moss in the Index for complete series of banks.

264. Porky is a Warner Brothers cartoon character. He was born in 1936.

265. See Appendix #263.

266. See #264 above.

267. Scrooge McDuck is a cartoon character created by Walt Disney. Scrooge is Donald Duck's nasty and rich uncle. Duck's glasses are missing on bank pictured.

269. Back: *1983.* Commemorates the Super Bowl victory, of the Washington Redskins' Hogs, members of the teams offensive line. Limited edition of 50.

270. See Appendix #263.

273. Lift hat to remove money.

274. See Bank #401, which is nearly identical.

275. Lift hat to remove money.

278. See Appendix #263.

279. See number 304 for picture of this bank in the extended position.
Back: *To open turn hat   Made in England
Patent No.680237.*

280. See Appendix #263.

281. Walt Disney's version of Pinocchio
© *USA W. Disney Ent.*

283. Converted inkwell. Also came as a lighter.

284. Jimminy Cricket was Pinocchio's sidekick.
Back: *W. Disney Pr.* © *USA Crown Toy Co. Inc.*

285. See Appendix #263.

286. Andy Panda was a Walter Lantz cartoon character. Appeared in short movies.

287. One of Snow White's friends. This Dopey is the Walt Disney version, introduced in 1938.
Back: *Walt Disney Ent. 1938*

288. Base: *7788.*

289. See Appendix number 263.

290. Walt Disney's version of the bull who loved to smell flowers. © *W. Disney Crown Toys.* Tin twist closure.

292. The Kewpie Doll was the creation of Rose O'Neill, who first drew the doll in 1909 and copyrighted her drawing in 1913. Kewpie dolls were made in all sizes and materials, and were still popular in the 1930's. Kewpie is currently undergoing a revival. Ah, nostalgia!

293. See Appendix #263.

295. Front: *S.S. Donald Duck.*
Back: *Walt Disney Ent. Inc.*
Donald Duck ranks second in popularity only to Mickey Mouse among Disney's characters.

298. Sir Charles Spencer Chaplin, (1889-1977) the world-renowned comedian who made his motion picture debut in the United States in 1914.
Base front: *Charlie Chaplin*
Base: *Geo Borgfeldt & Co., N.Y. sole Licensees Pat. applied for Serial No. 2862.*

299. Base: *LE Smith Co. Net Wt. 1 1/2 oz.*
See #298 above.

300. Jackie Coogan was a child-star in the movies. He played a character known as "The Kid," in the 1920's.

301. Base: *Geo Borgfeldt Co. N.Y. Reg. U.S. Pat. Off. Des Pat. # 43680 Serial No 2962 Nt. Wt 3/4 oz.*
See Appendix #292 for Kewpie dates.

302. Happifats was a doll developed by artist Kate Jordan. Happifats' heyday was 1913-21.
Base: *Geo Borgfeldt Sole Licensee. U.S. Pat.*

303. See Appendix #263.

304. See #279 for picture of this bank in its closed position. See also Appendix #279.

305. Caricature of Adolph Hitler. Pig grunts when coin is inserted. Bank was designed to aid savings for War Bonds.
Top: *Save for victory.*   *Make him squeal.*

306. See Appendix #263.

307. Crutch and label, separate castings that are attached with a screw, are often missing from bank.

308. See Appendix #263.

311. Called *Frog Bank* in A.C.W. catalogs.

314. Base: *Austria*

318. Base: *L.E. Smith Co.*

320. Foxy Grandpa was the cartoon creation of Carl Schultz. Character appeared in 1900 in the New York Herald, and continued with the Hearst Syndicate until 1918. Wing produced this bank first, under the name, "Grandpa Bank." Bank appears as "Foxy Grandpa" in Hubley catalogs.

322. Coin held by woman is dated 1861. The following is printed on the bank: *Lamm (1 or c) e wie vie bienen.* Hinged door at rear is key-locked.

323. A limited edition bank, designed by Herr Gawand, a designer of Meissen China. One thousand banks were produced, 100 in a bisque finish, 200 in a plain white glaze, and 700 with gold rings on base, covering white glaze.

324. James Abbott McNeill Whistler (1834-1903), American painter and etcher.
Base: *Art must be developed through industry*
Artist signed on side.

325. Base front: *Please*

326. See Appendix #320.

327. Minutemen were spirited soldiers who served during America's Revolutionary War.

328. See #327 above. *Copyright 1941 Nadine Wendem National Defense Junior Minuteman Bank*

329. Refers to spirit of American Revolution.

330. Back: *Bank on Republic Pig Iron* See Appendix #331

331. Fifteen hundred of these banks were produced for the Foundry Show, Cleveland, Ohio, by the Unicast Foundry, Boyertown, Pa. The bank was not painted. Wilton Products, Inc., which apparently purchased the molds, turned out a painted version in 1970. See bank #330.

332. See Appendix #254.

334. Back: *1982* Bank was painted by Edward K. Russell. Edition limited to 489.

335. *55*

336. This book was probably cast from pattern of bank #335.

338. This bank was first produced in 1934. Ours has a circa 1941 pry-out trap.

342. Glaze on bottom indicates bank was dipped. Bank is being reproduced by Keystone Potteries, Stoke-on-Trent, England.

343. Dog on this bank, and on banks numbered 388, 389 and 392 are identical.

346. Base: *1248* See patent paper.

347. *Spare dimes many times*

349. A Grace Drayton Figure. See Appendix #255.

350. This bank is also found in white metal

353. This bank is a superior casting to #352; maker is not known.

355. Replaced lock on our bank.

360. Mahogany wood carving purchased at A.C.W. pattern maker's estate auction.

362. There is also a paperweight like this bank, but coins would fall through. Ours comes together and retains its coins. Both came riveted but rivet removed in most conversions and a screw added.

365. This bank is made from the same pattern as bank #364, but made many years later by John Wright.

367. This bank has fine lines etched in, rather than the tiny indentations of Arcade's #366.

369. Casting quality and treatment is similar to Husky, #411.

371. Base: *Lindy's Kat Bank Model by APEL sc 1907* There is no coin slot. Had coin container base which is missing.

374. Nipper was the symbol-mascot of RCA Corporation. The original Nipper was a fox terrier, owned by an artist, Francis James Barraud. In about 1895, he painted the dog listening to a phonograph. In 1900, Victor purchased the rights to use Nipper in its advertising.

375. See #374 above.

376. Base: *Radio Corp. America* See Appendix #374.

377. Base: *ASCO Rd: 781602* See Appendix #203

378. Produced in edition of 50 for convention of SBCCA.
SBCCA June 1981
Collar: *Deco Dog*
Base: *Reynolds Toys*

380. Most banks were put together by a screw and boss (threading inside casting to receive screw). Kenton was the exception; most of their banks were closed with a screw and nut. When the nut was visible on a bank, Kenton cast a square receiver on the outside of the bank to hold the nut. The Basset has a cast receiver and nut, as do banks numbered 487, 488 and 445.

388. Same dog as seen in banks numbered 343, 389 and 392.

389. See 388 above.

391. Top of piano is hinged. Key opening in back.

392. Same dog as in banks numbered 343, 388 and 389.

393. Base: *McChesney Co., Newark, N.J.*

395. Bank is pictured on page 95 of *Die Kultur der Sparsamkeit,* (The History of Thrift) published by Deutscher Sparkassenverlag, (The German Bank Assn.) Stuttgart, Germany, 1982.

401. See bank #274, casting is similar.

402. Spring jawed, hinged at neck.

408. Bank advertisement on trap.

411. Casting is quality and treatment is similar to Cat with Long Tail, #369.

413. One of three dogs for which Hubley designed special packaging. This dog, and two others, numbered 419 and 422, were packaged in cardboard doghouses.

414. Back: *Design Pat. 1914* Designed by Grace Drayton. See Appendix #255.

415. There is a screw in base for attaching dog to ashtray. Was probably designed as a desk ornament.

416. Back: *G. Drayton* See Appendix #255.

417. Back of Head: *U.S. Pat. 1914* Designed by Grace Drayton. See Appendix #255.

418. Early version has trap; later version was made in two pieces.

419. A dog house bank. See Appendix #413.

421. Cast inside: *Vindex Toys, Belvidere, Ill.*

422. A dog house bank. See Appendix #413.

425. Cast inside: *Vindex Toys, Belvidere, Ill.*

428. This bank has been seen with an Arcade screw.

430. Franklin D. Roosevelt's famous dog, Fala, was born in 1940 and died in 1952. There is some controversy among collectors as to whether this bank was intended to be Fala. This same casting was also used for an iron ornament, on which the screw seat (boss) has never been drilled. Slot in base plate when a bank.

431. This particular specimen was given to *Axim, 1935.*

437. Advertised in 1934 A.C.W. catalog as coming in "assorted colors" (which no one has ever seen!).

438. Each of the dog's legs has one of the following bits of information: *Copyright   July   20th.   1900.*
Belly band: I hear a call.
Bank came with and without tongue. A clapper moves out of the way when you deposit a coin. Has been considered by some a mechanical bank.

439. Also appears in undated Dent catalog.

440. Arcade catalogs from 1923 and 1925 offered bank in gold bronze. The 1932 catalog advertised red, green and blue.

441. Base: *Pytram Ltd. New Malden, Surrey, Eng. #804.*
A collection box.

442. Back: *G. Drayton* See Appendix #255. Sold in 1946 by Hubley as a doorstop.

443. Same dog as bank #417. Sold in 1946 by Hubley only as a doorstop.

445. See Basset #380. Done in same art deco style. See also Appendix #380. We believe these banks were made by same manufacturer, possibly Kenton.

446. Wheels on this bank also came in solid tin, nickeled, spoked iron, and painted spoked iron.

447. This bank came in another size: 4 1/2 x 3.

451. Front: *Ivory Salt*
Back: *Iodized*
Sides: *Worcester Salt.*
Key-opened trap: *Baudis Metalcraft Co., New York.*

452. William McKinley (1843-1901), 25th President of the United States, ran for the Presidency on the Republican ticket, in 1900, with Theodore Roosevelt (see Appendix number 120) as his running mate. McKinley was assasinated in 1901 and was succeeded by Roosevelt. This bank pictures both of them and the campaign theme, *Prosperity.* The words, *"Pat app. For",* appear on the legs.

453. Different casting than #452.
Side of bank: *McKinley Roosevelt.*

454. This bank also came in a nickeled version. An *X* is cast inside. Elephant is identical to #453.

455. There is an *X* cast inside this bank. The interlock is different than on bank #454.

456. Back: *King   81.*
Bank made in an edition of 1000. Number 1 is owned by Ronald Reagan (1911-   ), 40th President of the United States, whose penchant for jelly beans inspired the bank.

457. A.C.W. 1934 catalog says bank also came in red, blue and green.

458. Under belly: *Germany metal.*

459. A.C.W. 1932 catalog says bank came in red, blue, green or gold.

460. We believe that this is an all-original toy, composed of an elephant made by Wing, pulling a chariot made for Wing by Gibbs. The elephant which was designed to pull the chariot, has *two holes on either side,* one set above the

foreLegs, and another slightly larger set on the flanks. The rear set of holes has a wire bracket running through the elephant's body to hold the metal traces in place. Wing made this elephant first, from about 1900-1903, and then it was produced by Hubley, from about 1906 into the 1930's. Hubley made elephants with and without the sets of holes. Some were designed to pull chariots, and some weren't.

This elephant is basically the same as elephants numbered 463, 465, 467, 468 and 470 except that it has the two sets of holes: There are some casting differences among the elephants, in the belly and legs. Casting of bank: solid foot pads, hollow legs and holes in underbelly. Front legs have part of pads removed and have holes to carry axle and small wheel. 1906 Elephant has closed foot pads.

463. Back: *GOP - 1928.*
Herbert Hoover (1874-1964), 31st President of the United States. His running mate in the 1928 campaign was Charles Curtis. Elephant is the same as #460, but there are no chariot holes, the underbelly and footpads are solid and legs are hollow. See #460 above.

464. Ring Base: *ASCO Rd 781501* See Appendix #203.

465. This bank is probably a conversion of a regular Hubley elephant into a chariot-pulling one. There are no rear holes for pulling a chariot. Elephant has open, hollow legs and large, half-inch holes in underbelly. Footpads are cut out. The Hubley chariot, #466, has room for a driver to stand. (Chariot pictured with bank #467 *does not.)* See Appendix #460.

467. The same elephant as the one pictured in #466, but pulling another chariot. This chariot is 2 1/2 inches long, and there is no room for a driver.

468. Embossed on side: *GOP 1936* The names of the Republican candidates for President that year are not printed on this bank. No one could have beaten FDR that year anyway. For a description of this elephant, see Appendix #463; it's identical. See also Appendix #460.

469. This elephant has solid foot pads, cut-out legs and a solid underbelly.

470. Same as elephant #465, but no holes for chariot.

471. This bank is a recast of #472.
Back: *GOP*
Front: *Nixon '68 Agnew*
Richard M. Nixon was the 37th President of the United States. His running mate, Spiro Agnew, was run out of office even before Nixon. This bank was produced for Nixon's first presidential campaign. See also #1659.

473. Reynolds produced a mechanical bank to honor the 25th anniversary of the Mechanical Bank Collectors' Club of America. The bank is a miniature foundry that produces this elephant still bank.

474. A.C.W. also produced a 3-inch high version of this elephant. See #459.

476. A.C.W.'s 1934 catalog indicates the bank also came in red, green and blue. We have seen the bank with drab paint and red trim. See patent paper.

477. Also came in gold, trimmed with red. See patent papers.

478. Back: *Su Banco De Confianza.* Produced for a Venezuelan bank.

479. This large Hubley elephant was designed to pull a chariot. It has *two* sets of holes to hold the traces. (See Appendix #460 for discussion of chariot elephants.) Elephant has solid foot pads, hollowed legs and a solid underbelly.

480. Same elephant as #479, but no chariot holes.

487. Kenton first produced the Elephant as a toy, the "Cairo Express" in 1911. This bank also came painted black. There is also a version that was printed, *Land on Roosevelt 1936* in raised letters on the blanket. Elephant pairs nicely with #488. See Appendix #380.

488. Pairs nicely with elephant #487. Our favorite pair of banks! See Appendix #380.

489. A souvenir of the Louisiana Purchase Exposition, St. Louis World's Fair, 1904. *Copyright* on underbelly.

490. Same as #489, but no imprinting. *Copyright* on underbelly.

499. This bank also came painted plain gold with colored trim. A.C.W. 1934 Catalog says it came in red, green, blue or gold.

500. Also came painted gold, with brown and red saddle.

502. The legs on this bank are thicker and slightly shorter than on bank #500.

505. Base: *Germany.*

508. *Good luck* is embossed on horseshoe. Horseshoe on this bank is solid. See Appendix #241 for information on Buster Brown and Tige. See bank #511 for an earlier variation of this bank — has holes in horseshoe.

510. By 1934, A.C.W. offered only brightly colored animals. Plain gold ones were no longer available.

511. Rare paint variation of bank #508. Also an earlier version than number 508, as there are holes in the horseshoe.

513. Also came painted plain gold.

514. Name *Beauty* cast in side. Horse similar to bank #513, but pattern of holes in base is different. Also shorter than #513.

515. Symbol of the Still Bank Collectors Club of America. Horse designed by George Knerr and modeled after #516. Eighty four were cast in iron, one in bronze. Each is numbered and dated under rockers.

516. Inside one rocker: *Margaret R.C. Warren SC*
Inside other: *Horses in Bronze, Roadview Farms, solid bronze.*

517. Advertised by Arcade in 1923 and 1925 as "gold bronzed." 1932 catalog offers bank in red, blue and green.

518. *Made in Canada* cast in the side. Possibly recast from original American bank.

519. A limited edition of 15 banks produced by George Knerr. *GK* on bridle stands for Knerr.

520. Body of horse is thicker than on bank #521. Arcade advertised a "gold bronze" version in 1923. Bank also came in black with aluminum hooves. And that colorful 1934 A.C.W. catalog says they had them in "red, blue, green, or black enamel."

521. Manufacturer of this variation of #520 is unknown. It's a heavier bank and the base is thicker.

523. A.C.W. 1934 Catalog says it came in assorted colors.

524. Slot is hidden behind horse's ears.

526. Cast on leg: *Made in USA.*

527. Same horse as numbers 530, 531, 532, 533.

528. Rare, painted version.

529. This bank is the same as banks numbered 517 and 518. Base has been added.

530. Only Arcade seems to have placed slots in animals' bellies. See numbers 489, 490, 530, 531. See also Appendix #527.

531. Same as bank #530, but *My Pet* is cast in the side. See Appendix #527.

532. Arcade 1932 Catalog says bank came in red, blue and green. See Appendix #527.

533. Same as bank #531, but two big holes are cast in belly. See Appendix #527.

535. English registry #624637 cast in bank.

536. This specimen is screwed together; most we've seen are riveted. Ox first appears on Kenton toy, the "Plantation Ox Cart" in 1911. Bank probably made, or converted, later.

537. From Whiting's collection. Bank is riveted and has a cut slot.

538. Elsie was the trademark of the Borden Company. Back: *Master Caster Mfg. Co. Chgo. 12, Ill.*

539. Same as #537, except that this was never a bank. It's a home made conversion.

540. Same cow appears on the Milking Cow Mechanical Bank. The still is *not* one-of-kind.

541. See #1646, paint variation.

544. This bank came in all possible paint combinations of black and white.

545. Same as #544.

546. Bank has been seen with slot in bottom as well as on top. In the Middle Ages, a hen on a nest was a symbol of wealth.

548. Bank also came dull black trimmed with red.

555. Cast inside: *There's Money in Aberdeen Angus.*

556. Bank has a five-inch slot for dollar bills.

558. Some consider a mechanical bank. Tail is twisted and pulled out, allowing head to be turned and removed to get at coins.

562. Back: *J. Contway '69.*

563. One side of base: *Billy Possum*
Other side: *Possum & Taters* This bank is a political dart aimed at President William Howard Taft. The press in Taft's day nicknamed him Billy Possum. See bank #109, another Taft bank made by Harper. Also see Appendix #109.

564. Cast in side: *Expo 1901* This is a souvenir of the Pan American Exposition, a World's Fair held in Buffalo, New York, in 1901.

567. Produced in a limited edition of 225. Intentionally smaller than #568.

569. Side of base: *1884.*

573. Bank was a hardware store promotion piece. Goat came without legs. As a store met a sales quota, store was given a leg-another quota, another leg!

575. Slot is in the base. *Copyright J.M. Harper 1907.*

576. A 12" version seen in Fair Store Catalog dated 1913. #576 and this one have markings identical to A.C. Williams #548.

581. *SBCCA 1978 Convention Lancaster, Pennsylvania.*

582. A.C.W. 1934 Catalog says it came in red, blue, green or gold.

584. Same shape as Bismark pig (#602) but thinner and smaller.

586. Mahogany mold purchased at A.C.W. pattern maker's estate auction.

588. Symbol of Great Northern Railway. This bank is a souvenir of Glacier National Park, and the railway promoted the park in the early 1900's.

589. The Red Goose was the trademark of the Friedman-Shelby Shoe Company, St. Louis. It was first used in 1906. We believe that all of the cast iron Red Goose banks were produced by Arcade. They never appeared in the Arcade catalogs, but were probably given away or sold by the shoe company. Bank #589 shows a boy holding Red Goose Shoes box. Four geese are on the bank; each one has a word printed across its body, either *Red, Goose, School,* or *Shoes.* The company name, *Friedman-Shelby Shoe Co., St. Louis, U.S.A.* is printed on the paper seam.

590. George Knerr did a superb job of reproducing this turkey in a smaller size in 1968. He limited production to 250 birds.

591. Personalized by buyer on the back: *Geoarndek Frohe Fern 1908* (Frohe Fern translates *Happy trip*).

592. Lots of copy on this bank: *Friedman-Shelby All Leather Shoes Red Goose Shoes — They're half the fun of having feet. Savings Bank For Boys For Girls Save The Pennies and Buy Red Goose Shoes* Stamped across bank is the store which gave away the banks to children: *The Leather Store, Escanaba, Mich.* See Appendix #589.

593. Back of bank is marked, *GK,* which stands for George Knerr. Knerr produced 68 of these banks in 1968.

594. We believe there is considerable evidence to support our claim that this is a J.M. Harper Bank. While we cannot prove its identity, here is the evidence as we see it:

    1.   While smaller, the bank presents the two goats in the same position at the tree stump as the

bear and bull on the Harper *Board of Trade* Bank assume on the sack of grain. The names of the banks, *Two Kids* and *Board of Trade* appear in the same place on the bases, which are both painted green.

2. Aluminum colored paint appears on seven known Harper banks, *Board of Trade*, the two *I Made Chicago Famous* pigs, *Little Red Riding Hood*, *The Carpenter*, *Santa Claus*, *Mother Hubbard* The same rather shiny aluminum paint was used on *Two Kids*. The red paint in the goat's mouths is the same deep red found on *Red Riding Hood*, *Santa Claus* and *Mother Hubbard*. The black paint on the *Two Kids* has the same patina as the black paint Harper used so lavishly on its banks. (Only the Liberty Bell, Indian Family, Taft/Sherman and the Basket of Corn are free of this black paint.)

3. The *Board of Trade* is marked *J.M. Harper*. *Two Kids* is not, but Harper did not put their name on either of the pig banks. (Granted, they do have copyrights stamped in them!)

4. Perhaps the most compelling evidence is the subtle kind. When placed alongside the known Harper banks, it seems to belong. (We realize this evidence wouldn't stand up in court.) It would be wonderful to think that some still bank researcher of the future will turn up The truth, but it's unlikely. As Bruce Abell noted, in his pamphlet on Harper co-authored by Norman Bowers, "We are a generation too late to find out about the Harper story."

595. See Bank #164 and Appendix #164.

595A. Back: *Red Goose Shoes - All leather*

596. Front: *Feed My Sheep*

597. Cast Inside: *Vindex Toys, Belvidere, Ill.*

598. Cast in front: *Be Wise Save Money*

600. *Made from original pattern by John Wright. See #601.*

602. See Appendix #4. Mold for this bank probably used to make Bank #4. This bank, with *Bismark Bank* embossed on side, was probably made for the same reason.

608. Same as #602, but unmarked.

609. Base: *J.M.N.* vertical slot in pig's back.
Pig's sign reads:
Save a penny yesterday
Another save today
Tomorrow save another
To keep the wolf away. See #617.

610. This bank was produced later than banks numbered 626 and 628, which are identical, except for inscription. See Appendix #589.

611. Same goose appears on bank #643. See Appendix #589.

612. Also came painted gold gilt. See Appendix #589.

613. Embossed on side: *A Christmas Roast* Same pig as #602.

614. This is the same goose that Arcade produced for Red Goose Shoes, but they sold this one through their catalogs. No imprinting appears on the bank. Same goose as numbers 610, 626 and 628. See Appendix #589.

617. Same as bank #609, but a word has been added to the third line on pig's sign. Reads: *Tomorrow save another one.* The vertical slot appears in pig's head, rather than in its back, as in #609. Twist trap. See patent paper.

618. Trap: *United Gift Mfg. Co. Pat Pending.*

619. Has large Kenton trap. Also came painted blue.

620. An earlier version of this bank advertised the Chicago Stockyards.

622. Slot is under tail.

624. See Appendix #630.

625. One side: *You can bank on the Osborn Molding Machines*
Other side: *A Hog for Production Saves Money.*

626. Same goose as numbers 610 and 628. Inscription is the same as bank #628. Color blue is harder to find. See Appendix #589.

627. This key-wound toy is made of tin and covered with felt. Slot is in drum, and trap is in base of drum. Stamped in left foot: *Made in Germany*
Stamped in right foot: *Schuco.*
Schuco also made three other similar banks, a soldier boy playing the drum, a clown drummer, and a member of the Hitler Youth.

628. See bank #626. See Appendix #589.

629. Belly: *Copyright 1902.*

630. Same as bank #624, but this bank is screwed together and has no trap.

631. Belly: *Copyright 1902*
Variation says on reverse, *Minors exchange.*

632. One side: *Razor Back*
Other side: *Bank.*

633. Base: *77.*

635. Pig holds Austrian coin which says: *Scheidemunze Kkoesterk 1885* (Translates roughly to *vacation savings.*)

636. Base: *czech.slov.*

640. Also came with trap.

642. Base: *41830 MOE-L.*

643. Same goose as #611.

645. *SNK* written in trick key lock.

647. Back: *Copyright by J.M. Harper 1907.*

649. Front: *Bremer Stadtmusikanten* (The Brementown Musicians).

650. Marked *Germany.*

651. Back: *Copyright by J.M. Harper 1907*
Front: *Copyrighted* is etched neatly and deeply.

662. *Monticello, N.Y.* is painted on bottom.

664. Usually found with tail missing or repaired. Bank also came painted plain gold and as a redbird.
Catalog name: *Bird Toy Bank.*

667. Base: *Save dimes the Nest Egg Way. Patented 5-23-22 Mfg. by Steel Prod. Corp. of S.F. Cal.*
End of bank: *Fidelity Building Assn., Dayton, Ohio.*

669. Promotion offered by Poll-Parrot Shoe Company.
One Side: *Poll Parrot Solid Leather Shoes for Real Boys and Girls*
Other side: *You save money every time you buy Poll-Parrot Solid Leather Shoes. They speak for themselves.*

670. *Made in England ASCO.*

673. Cast on back: *Save with Pelican. Mutual Benefit Life Insurance Company, Newark, N.J.*

675. Front: *SBCCA 1980 Convention in Denver, Pa.*

676. Old Abe, a bald Eagle, was mascot of "C" Company, 8th Wisconsin Volunteer Regiment in the Civil War. A soldier made the bird a perch in the shape of a shield. Traveled with Regiment from 1861 'til 1864. Was at Battle of Vicksburg, among others. P.T. Barnum once offered $20,000 for him. Abe attended 1876 Centennial Exhibition in Philadelphia. Died in fire in state capital, Madison, Wis., 1881.

678. See #676 above.

680. Base appears to be same as on the mechanical bank, patented in 1870. Base has also been seen with two turtles on top. Ours would seem to be a construction, but we know of three others.

681. Bank opens when ten dollars in dimes is deposited.

682. Cast in back: *Bank for Savings 260 4th. Ave. N.Y. Chartered 1819.*

683. Kyser & Rex Beehive was patented Aug. 19, 1879. Drawing of Beehive in 1882 K & R catalog shows bees. Our slot is vertical, and catalog's is horizontal. Measurements are the same. (K & R catalog drawing of the Apple Bank shows a lady bug on the apple that is not on the real bank.)

684. Says *Bank* on front, and *Pat Applied For*
Base: W.M. Gobeille Cleveland, Ohio, U.S.A. Bank has iron, key-lock trap.

686. English registry #292270. Harper catalog says it came *maroon bronzed or gold enamelline*

689. Base: *Crown Toy Co.* Has tin twist closure.

690. Front: *SPCA* (Society for the Prevention of Cruelty to Animals) English registry #640673, 8/1/1914.

692. Base: *Iron Art.*

693. Also have seen black bear with white pig.

696. This bank has been seen with an Arcade screw.

697. Trick lock has a sunburst design on it, with letters SNK (Japanese).

698. *Teddy* embossed on side. Same bear as #694.

701. Repainted bank pictured on cover of Hubert Whiting's book was his favorite bank.

702. Bank came filled with Belgian chocolate coins.

710. Marked *Rd. no.* (but no registry number follows.)
1911 Harper Catalog says it came *maroon bronzed*

713. Back: *Pat. Apld. For.* Also came painted white.
This bank was copyrighted by Hubley. They also produced a 6 1/4" one with vertical slot in top of head and a turn-pin.

714. Inside: *B* cast in both sides.

716. White paint is authentic. Also came in gold. Painted white during Peary's race to the North Pole in 1909.

719. Only nickled version known.

721. 1923 and 1925 catalogs advertised this bank painted with gold lacquer.

722. Bank, half hippo and half rhino, made for fun.

724. George Knerr produced 200 of these banks in 1975.

726. Also considered a mechanical. Eyes wiggle when coin deposited. Should be painted green.

729. Could be considered a mechanical. Bank must be turned upside down allowing head to swivel to right revealing coin slot.

730. A mechanical bank. Jaw quivers when coin deposited.

731. *I F C*

733. Medallion on front impressed with: *Silver Springs, Fla.*

736. Antlers are cast separately and are often missing. This bank, without antlers, has been reproduced by John Wright, who calls it *Fawn.* Arcade catalogs say it was made in red, green and blue.

738. A mechanical bank. Weighted jaw moves when coin deposited.

742. Also came in red, blue and green enamel — A.C.W. 1934 Catalog.

743. Front: *Hear no evil, see no evil, speak no evil*
Original wood carving of the Three Wise Monkeys is at the Toshogu Shrine in Nikko National Park, northeast of Tokyo, Japan.

748. Mahogany pattern purchased at A.C.W. pattern maker's estate auction.

749. *Canada* impressed on maple leaf. A souvenir of Canada.

751. 1911 Harper Catalog: *Maroon bronzed.*

752. Has an extra long (1 9/16") coin slot.

755. Another, similar lion has closed footpads, no hole between tail and footpad, and no saw-toothed cutouts in underbelly. Arcade made a lion like #755, but measuring 4 3/4 x 5"

757. Arcade version came in red, green and blue. A.C.W. version came in red, blue, green or plain gold.

759. Dent made a similar lion, measuring 5 1/4" long.

760. Same lion as #759.

761. *Harris Trust & Savings Bank* (a major Chicago bank).

762. Similar to #754, but footpads on this bank are cut out and casting is thinner.

764. Tail is attached to left leg.

766. This lion was purportedly produced for just one year.

767. Also came painted drab, with saddle painted red & gold.

768. Ditto #767.

773. Was also produced in iron. Ours is a repaint.

777. Base: *Sinclair*

778. The base is cast separately.

780. One side: *Liberty Bell Copyright 1905 by J.M. Harper*
Other side: *Proclaim Liberty Throughout the Land, unto all the inhabitants thereof.*
Other side of variation reads: *1906 - WPMA Washington, D.C., Chic. Hdw. Fdy. Co.*

781. Design Patent #8820, Dec. 7, 1875. Produced for 1876 Centennial Exposition, Philadelphia
Top: *Pennies first then dollars*
Base: *Enterprise Mfg. Co., Philada. Globe Bank*
See patent paper.

782. Front: *The Old Liberty Bell Sesqui 1926 Centennial*
Back: *Philadelphia MDCCLIII Proclaim 1776 Liberty.*

783. Design for this bank was patented June 4, 1889. Words *Columbia Savings Bank* appear around the slot. *Shedler's Terrestial Globe won a medal at the Paris Exposition, 1867.* See patent paper.

784. Bank produced for 200th. anniversary of Washington's birth, in 1732. Same as bank #782, but says: *The Old Liberty Bell* and has portrait of Washington.

785. Continents and oceans are named and the Phillippines and Sandwich Islands are highlighted.

786. Washington's portrait, and the dates *1732-1932* cast in bank, which celebrates his 200th. birthday. See bank #784.

788. Eagle, with 5 olympic rings embossed on bank. Souvenir of 1936 Olympic Games held in Nazi Germany. The Swastica also present on bank.

789. J.G. Baker obtained a patent (#8820) for this bank, Dec. 7, 1875.

790. Pictures athletes swimming and running. Olympic rings appear on bank. Trap carries mark, *SNK* on it. Olympic games were scheduled for 1940 in Tokyo, but W.W.II interfered. Held finally in Tokyo in 1964. Japanese characters at top of bell translate, *2600th year since the assension of Emperor Meiji, the first emperor of Japan.* There is a difference of 660 years between Georgian calendar age and the emperor's, so date on bank is 1940. Characters at bell's base translate, *12th Olympic Games.*

791. Map for this bank made by Denoyer-Geppert Co., Chgo., a fine old company.

792. On bell: *Proclaim liberty throughout all the land and to all the inhabitants thereof. Leviticus Chap. 25, Verse 10.*

793. See bank #792 for quote. Also: *Lev. XXV V. 10* This bank was patented Feb. 18, 1919. Bank has the number, 54422, on the base.

794. Front: *World's Fair '93* and *My Expenses to Chicago.*
This bank found in an 1893 Ives Catalog. They apparently distributed it. Bank a souvenir of 1893 World's Columbian Exposition, held in Chicago, to commemorate 400th. anniversary of Columbus' voyage to America. See bank #815.

795. This bank, which has a sliding iron trap, has U.S. Patent #166,978. Bell rings when coin is deposited. See patent paper.

796. Bank anticipates America's entry into W.W.I.
Bell: *Old Liberty Bell. Proclaim 1976 Liberty*
Reverse: *Centennial Money Bank 1876*
Top of base: *Bank of Liberty and Peace*

797. Patented August 24, 1875.
Reverse: *Centennial Bell, 1776-1876.* Bell rings when coin is deposited. See patent paper.

798. This bank was produced continuously from sometime before 1934 until 1977. Ours has a square trap and shield logo.

799. Modern bank promo. bell. Found with many different bank names on yoke.

800. Carries names of 3 Apollo astronauts, Borman, Lovell and Anders. No longer in production, this bank was produced by George Papadakos of The Trojan Horse, cast by John Wright, and sold by Trojan Horse. There was a brass edition of 24, a red, white and blue cast iron edition of 1500, and a gold cast iron edition of 500. See #806.

802. Side of base: *New York World's Fair, 1964-65*
Bottom: *NY. W.F. Unisphere, presented by United States Steel*

803. Side: See bank #792 for wording on liberty bell. In addition, this bank says: *Province of Pennsylvania for the State House in Philad. Pass and Stowe, Philad.*
Top of base: *1776-1976*
Base: *Financial Promotions Co., Harrisburg, Pa.*

804. Top of base: *Globe Savings Bank* Other specimens of this bank have *World's Fair Chicago, 1893* or *World's Fair, St. Louis, 1904* cast in them.

807. Reverse: *The Old Liberty Bell Proclaim Liberty 1776.*

809. On bell: *Proclaim Liberty Throughout All the Land* Arcade 1932 Catalog: *also came with stamped sheet bottom.*

810. Has a two-dial combination. Base *Pat. Appld.*

811. Recast of bank #809.

812. Catalog says it came *electro-oxydized* Ours is also japanned.

813. Same as bell #807. See patent paper.

815. Front: *93 World's Fair   My Expenses to Chicago* See Appendix #794.

816. Top of base: *Souvenir The Sesqui-Centennial International Exposition 1776 Philadelphia 1926 150 years of American Independence.*
Key-lock trap on bell base.

817. Trademark looks like a sailboat with a "y" in it. Key-lock trap is on a hidden internal hinge.

819. Front: *70 Crosley*
Back: *Kenton Toys.*

820. See #819 above.

823. Dial is a paper label.
Back: *Zenith Radio.*

824. We wonder why this company used a record player to advertise washing machines!
Front: *Save for your Sunny Suds.*

825. Front: *Save for your Brunswick.*

826. Came in assorted colors.

828. Back has sliding tin closure.

829. Base: *Kenton Toys, Kenton, Ohio*
Original tag reads: *Kenton Toys To open bank turn center dial to 8. Turn right hand dial to left, stop at 1. Then turn left hand dial to right, stop at 4. Pull open. To lock bank, first turn left hand dial back to 1, then turn right hand dial to 4.*

830. Base: *Kenton Toys, Kenton, Ohio.*

832. Back: *Musette* A lead trap on base is held by two screws. Our bank is minus music stand.

833. Back: *Kenton Toys.*

834. Our combination dial opens at 2 and 7. Bank has a *no-return* coin slot.

835. No-return clapper inside. Large Kenton combination trap. Opens at 4 -outer ring, and 2 -inner ring.

836. Combination trap is similar to one on Magic Safe.

837. Hinged coin slot.

839. Came painted red or green with gold trim.

841. Side: *Air Mail*, with an eagle cast in.

843. Word *notes* appears on writing shelf.

845. Twenty-five envelopes came with bank. Each child in family could put his name and amount of deposit on envelope, and then "mail" his money. The remaining envelope in our bank says, *Postal Savings Envelope.*

847. Queen Victoria's cypher is cast on front. Replacement finial is brass.

849. "Lift-up" variety. Large combination trap.

850. Back: *Kenton Toys.* Large Kenton trap.

851. No Kenton identification on this bank. It can be hung on wall. Slot in rear.

852. No Kenton identification on this bank. Kenton made this bank in two other sizes: Kenton #610 - 5 1/4 x 3 3/4 and Kenton #105 - 5 3/8 x 4 1/2.

853. Also came in red with gold letters.

855. Bank is same as #851. Came with and without square key-lock trap.

856. Back: *Patented Nov. 22, 1921.* Also came red with gold trim. See patent paper.

857. Semi-mechanical; rings when you crank it. Takes 5, 10 and 25 cent coins.
Back: *Made in USA Pat. Appd. For.*
Has Stevens' trap. See patent paper.

858. Front: *US Mail.* Slot is on side. Our key-lock, which belongs on the side, is missing. May have been foreign made for U.S. market.

859. Sides and back: *US Bank.* Key-lock on side.

860. Front: U.S. Letter Box. Lists pickup schedule for 22/27 3rd Ave. Street lamp has frosted glass. Tin slide-trap.

861. Same mailbox as #855.

862. When door is opened, it slides into bank. There is a guard dog on the bank, but this specimen's paint is pale. Designs on bank are stenciled.

863. The 1880 Kyser & Rex catalog doesn't picture the Fidelity Safes, but describes them and their sizes. The sides of bank #864 have the same fleur de lis pattern found on the Star Safe, #876. Casting characteristics are similar.

864. See #863 above.

866. Designed to give illusion of being three-dimensional when viewed from any angle. Clever. Opens on 1 and 7.

868. Top: *Johnstown Savings Bank*

869. Base: *Patented Mar. 31, 1891.* This bank also came in another size: 2 5/8 x 2 1/8 x 2. See patent paper.

870. Front: *Bank of England.*
Back: *L.B. Reg.d. July 7, 1882.*

871. To open, turn safe upside down, turn knob to right until it stops. Turn safe on hinged side. Door falls open. To close, reverse the process.
Top: *Pat. Ap'd. For.* See patent paper

875. Bank has slot hidden under handle. Base: *Pat. Pending 1905.* It is purported that Eastman stopped Stevens' production of this bank, so they removed the name Kodak and put the word *coin* in its place.

877. Face: *Penny Trust Co.* Bank has tin sliding closure.

878. Catalog says it came *japanned and green.*

879. Face: *Fireproof Mosler Safe Co.* This bank was given to Ed Mosler by Hubert Whiting in 1972. We obtained it at the Mosler sale in 1982.

880. Base: *Pat. Jan'y 8.82.* Bank displays four separate roller skating scenes.

882. Base: *Pat. Aug. 8 '82.*

883. See #1664 for painted version of this bank.

886. Base: *Jan. 8, 1882.*

887. Base: *June 2, 1896.*

888. Arcade version of this bank says *Daisy* above keyhole, and is a different size.

889. This bank opens on *4.*

890. Base: *Pat. Feby. 15 1881.* Combination is A5. Kyser & Rex put out a larger safe with the same door seen on this bank, patented Feb. 15, 1883 and March 1, 1888.

893. Patented July 12, 1881.

894. Base: *Kenton Brand.*

895. Back: *E.M. Roche Co., Bloomfield, N.J. Pat. Apl'd For.*

896. Iron gate protecting safe is often missing. See patent paper. Patent papers for safe without *jewel* written on it were granted to Lewis S. Bixler of Hardware and Woodenware Manufacturing Co., in 1911.

899. Back: *Anfoe. Germany.* Bank came with a cypher card which corresponded to letters on the safe's door. Move slowly to letter *L*, then to *M*, *N*, and *O*. Pull lever at left side of bank and it will open.

901. Paper clock: *J. Barton Smith Co., Phila. Pa.* and *Patent Applied For.* Under each of four windows: *Security, Fidelity, Paying Teller,* and *Cashier.* Figures of boy and dog in bank's windows have been called Buster Brown and Tige by most collectors for years. The late Mr. Leslie Lewis believed they were Lord Fauntleroy and his dog. He was right. Buster first appeared in a comic strip in 1902, and the bank dates from 1890. The 1890 Marshall Field Catalog proved Mr. Lewis correct. Lord Fauntleroy and his dog appear in the same catalog as the banks, and the likeness to the figures in the ban's windows is perfect. The book, *Lord Fauntleroy,* by Frances Brunett, was advertised in *Youth's Companion Magazine,* 10/30/90.

902. Bank has round tumbler lock, just like a safe deposit box.

903. See Appendix #901. Two-number combination. Cash drawer inside.

904. Figure of man appears in door of the New Bank Mechanical. Must have been designed by same person. See bank #1229.

906. Base: *Pat. May 5, 1891.* Goddess of Liberty and Uncle Sam are pictured. This bank is nickel plated. There is also a specimen that is finished in copper. Arcade also made a Columbia that is 5".

907. There were so many electric lights on the Midway at the Columbia Exposition that it was named "White City." A few years later an amusement park opened near the site and also adopted "White City" as its name. All White City Puzzle banks operate in the same way: Place wing nut over knob and turn to the left, pressing heavily. Unscrew knob and open bank. To relock turn knob to the right, pressing tightly. This barrel is marked *#1.* The cart is reinforced to hold screw which attaches cart to barrel. See bank #908 for identical barrel, sold without cart. Beware of wrong cart. See patent paper.

908. Has no screw thread for attaching bank to cart. *Pat. Oct. 23, 1894.* Marked *#1.* See Appendix #907 for operation of bank. See patent paper.

909. Same barrel is found on Circus Ticket Taker Mechanical Bank. Patent on the mechanical is 1873. Came with solid base or base with holes. If put together incorrectly, bank appears to have slots at both ends! See patent paper.

910. *Pat. Oct. 23, 1894.* Combination is a fake. See Appendix #907 for operation. Scenes from 1893 Chicago World's Fair, the Columbian Exposition, appear on the bank; the Government Building on the left and right sides, and the Ferris Wheel, first introduced at that fair, on the back. See Appendix #794.

911. See Appendix #907 for operation of bank. See patent paper.

912. Deposit a penny, pull lever to the right, and the deposit is recorded. Bank opens when $1.00 has been deposited. We believe this bank is a Kyser & Rex, as is bank #921. There are many similarities.

913. Rear view of White City Safe #10. This bank has a false combination dial on door (see #910, above). Base has a sliding trap door in which to hide the wing nut opener. See patent paper.

914. Similar to bank #913, except this one has no false combination dial. Base has a sliding trap door in which to hide the wing nut opener. See patent paper.

915. Bank holds $30.00 in dimes. First dime locks bank. Every 15th dime unlocks it. Once locked, it can't be opened with an ax (or so said the advertisement!). Amount of deposit is registered on the dial. This bank is lighter than bank #917. See patent paper.

916. Base has housing for wing nut. Patented Oct. 23, 1894. See patent paper.

917. A heavier bank than #915. See Appendix #915 for description of bank's operation. See patent paper.

918. Barrel is a separate piece. Screw atop barrel separates barrel-halves.

919. Holds nickels, dimes and quarters. Fruit is cast into lid. See Appendix #907 for bank's operation. See patent paper.

920. Bank was designed to be set for numerous combinations. This one works by spelling the word "millionaire." Dial *M,* twist to left, dial *I,* twist to left and dial *L,* and so forth. The number *6* written on the base *may* imply that there were six factory-set combinations.

921. Registers numbers of dimes deposited after lever is pulled. Once locked, bank won't open until $10.00 has been deposited. Kyser & Rex also made a nickel registering bank that opens at $5.00.

922. Back: *Pat. Oct. 24, 1893.* Ferris Wheel appears on back. Slot in rear. See Appendix #907 and #910. See patent paper.

923. Different casting than #922, and the World's Fair scene is missing. Bank came out in 1895, after the Fair was over.

924. We think Hubley added the name "bank" to an existing toy to increase sales. There is no coin slot, and deposits don't drop into cash drawer!

925. Another casting of this bank has been seen. It says *savings* instead of *cash.* Bar at the top of bank is often missing.

927. Has same top as #926.

929. Numbers *1* and *4* are cast inside.

930. Base: *Pat. Apld. For. Manufactured by the J. & E. Stevens Co., Cromwell, Conn. U.S.A.* See patent paper.

931. Same base copy as #930. See patent paper.

933. Front: *National.*
    Back: *National Savings Bank USA.*

934. Front: *R.C. Allen, 1958.* Slot probably cut into paper weight. No coin trap.

935. Pictures Long John Silver, skull and crossbones. Has hinged top. Lock is missing. There is a bank identical to this that says *E.J. Kahn Co., Chicago, Il* on bottom.

939. A common deposit developer. *Save your coins and have barrels of money.*

942. Key-opened bank has slots for dimes, nickels, quarters, halves, pennies and five-dollar gold pieces. Slot in top for bills. This one distributed by Merchants National Bank, Watertown, WI.

943. Knerr produced 560 of these banks in 1972.

945. Replica of 1913 Buffalo Nickel. Knerr gave this bank to friends who visited his home.

946. Bank has combination lock on back, with sliding trap. Base: *Pat. Applied For.* Bank also came with no combination. This bank is resting on a dolly which did not come with bank.

947. Base: *Phoenix, the new improved registering trunk bank. Patd. Apl. 7-91.*

948. Access to main compartment is gained by key. Bank must be unlocked before a deposit can be made. Small compartments within are labeled *Pennies, Nickels, Dimes, Quarters, Half Dollars, Dollars.* Windows at rear of bank show child how much money is in each small compartment. It isn't easy to retrieve money. Lid must be unscrewed to get at compartments.

949. Slot will accept silver dollar.

954. Base: *Patented April 11, 1882.* Was advertised as coming in *assorted colors, relieved with bronze.* See patent paper.

955. In addition to name, *C.S.M.S.* was also printed on front. Bank has a tuning fork inside which rings when coin is deposited. Most do not.

956. A slot on each tower, labeled *1, 2* and *5,* for depositing one-cent, two-cent and five-cent pieces.

957. Lead pattern for bank #955.

155

958. This bank says, *Tacoma Park Bank, Tacoma, Md.* Back door opens with a key.

959. Back: *Pat. Feb. 7 '82.* See patent paper.

960. Bank was sold at the church itself and at a store in Nashua, Iowa.
One side: *Little Brown Church.*
Other: *In the Vale.*

962. *Esbjerg* is a town in Denmark and *Fano* means island. Top of bank says *Oddfellow Ordenens,* Ordenens means "order of". Also says *Sparebosse,* which translates, "piggy bank".

963. *Landmandsbank* is the name of a particular bank.

964. Danish name. *Hjemme Sparebosse* translates: Home Piggy Bank. Front of bank reads, *Banken Skanderborg Omebn. Skanderborg* is the name of a town, and *omebn* means *teller.*

965. Front: *Rochester Trust & Safe Deposit Co.*
Step 1: *Time is Money.* Step 2: *Save Both.* Step 3: *No. 25 Exchange St.*
Back: *#81 Pat. Applied For.*

967. One side: *Halls Lilliput Bank.*
Other side: *Patented 1875-1876.* Similar to Halls Lilliput Mechanical, Griffith #229.

968. English registry #482034.

970. Top: *1st National Bank of Riverside.*
Base: *Made by American Badge Co., Chicago Ill. #467.*

971. Dordrecht is a town about 16 miles from Rotterdam, Holland.
Front: *Wie Spaart Vergaart* which means, Who saves — will be protected.

972. Front: *Sparbanken i Alfvesta* which means, Savings Bank (in the town of) Alfvesta.

973. English registry number: 502035. This or #974 is probably Chamberlain and Hill. Chamberlain's foreman, McOustra, broke away and founded Sydenham and McOustra that year. They were highly competitive.

974. Towers are reinforced in the back, a slightly different casting than #973 — designs in casting are not as deeply cut.

976. Base: *Keyless Lock Co., Indianapolis, Ind.*

977. Front: *1837 Hundredth Anniversary 1937.*
Side: *St. Paul's Evangelical Lutheran Church, Ft. Wayne, Ind.*
Side: *Yea, Lord, Thou knowest that I love Thee.*
Back: *A Century of Grace.*
Base: *A.C. Rehberger, Chgo.*

978. Right side: *Christianity is a towering face.*
Left side: *Let us lift the tower with our sacrificial gifts.*
Top: *State Bank & Trust Co., Evanston, Ill., Depository.*

979. Front: *Dom zu Koln* (Cologne Cathedral)

980. *Dom-Koln.* (Cologne Cathedral)

981. Right Side: *Archdiocese of Chicago.*
Left Side: *Propogation of the Faith. This chapel bank presented by the Foreman Bank, LaSalle and Washington Sts. Depository for the Confraternity.*
Back of Base: *Home and Foreign Missions.*

983. Front: *Blackpool.*
Top of base: *Tower Money Box Save Your Pence*

984. English registry number: 499017. See #973. Possibly same story.

985. Back: *A present from Blackpool.*

986. Has aluminum steeple. Base is sheet metal.

987. Roof: *For Good Little Children.* Has typical Stevens and Brown trap.

989. Slot on roof is just a lateral space. We're not positive this is a bank. Windows are glass. Turn crank to ring bell in steeple.

990. Paper label on bank reads:
OLD SOUTH
Church gathered, 1669
First house built, 1670
This house erected, 1720
Desecrated by Br. Tr'ps, 1775

991. See #990 above for message on paper label.

992. This bank came painted aluminum or gold, with red, blue or green roof.

993. This bank came painted gold with red, blue or green roof.

995. Says *Girls* and *boys* above entrances on either side.

996. Reproduced in 1949 by Ohio Foundry Co. See appendix #1120.

998. Catalog says it came in assorted colors, relieved with bronze. See patent paper.

999. See patent paper.

1000. Catalog says it came with copper bronze finish.

1004. Bank was patented Aug. 10, 1880. Says *Bank* on front. Came with either windows or fancy grillwork on sides.

1005. Patented Nov. 30, 1880. Catalog says it was finished with assorted colors, relieved with bronze or fancy colors. We've only seen this combination.

1006. See bank #1249 for Snappit Mechanical Bank.

1011. Updated variation made by Shrimer, 1899.

1012. Updated variation made by Shrimer, 1899.

1013. Top: *Wanamaker J. Wanamaker, Philadelphia, New York, Paris.* An identical bank says *Stollwerck's Lilliputian Savings Bank.*

1015. Depicts the Golden Pavilion of Jehol, one of the Orient's best loved structures. It was the residence of Chinese rulers. Building was reproduced for Century of Progress, 1933, in Chicago. Bank has an internal metal box within a metal exterior. Combination opens on 3 and 3.

1016. Key-opening on roof.

1018. Front: *Beverly State Savings Bank.*
Base: *B.T. Corp., Chgo.*

1021. *House in which Abraham Lincoln was Born* and *Van Dyke Teas — Our own stores everywhere.*

1022. Turnpin goes through chimney. We have an identical bank with chimney on the left, held together by nut.

1023. Slot in center rear instead of left rear. Windows are different sizes than bank #1022. Catalog advertised assorted and rustic colors.

1025. Newer version than #1026. A brass plate has been substituted for the embossed printing. See Appendix #1026 for copy on plate.

1026. Roof: *This old bank still standing in the land of Lincoln will humbly accept your pennies bearing his image.*
Reverse: *Old Shawneetown First Bank in Illinois 1816.* This bank turned down a loan to the city of Chicago, because they didn't think the city would amount to anything.

1028. *CMS* stands for the Church Missionary Society, London.

1029. Hansel, Gretel and the witch are pictured on bank.
Base: *DRPOSR* and *J-E5.*

1031. Not yet proven to be a bank. Base is missing. Depicts the Woodmen of America Sanitorium in Colorado. Patients had individual cottages.

1032. An interesting bank, as it not only pictures Lincoln's cabin, but the setting around it as well.

1033. Base: *Silver plate Denmark.* There is marvelous detailing on this bank.

1034. See Appendix #1028. Back: *An Indian Hut.*

1035. Has typical Stevens and Brown round lock.

1040. The Woolworth Building, in New York, was constructed in 1913.

1043. This bank also came in green.

1044. Side: *New York — Highest in World.*
Rear: *Population 14,000 people.*
Side: *792 feet high.*

1045. Same as #1044, but no base.

1046. Side: *102 stories.*
Back: *New York City 1250 Feet.* Has screw base.

1047. Face: *Empire State.*
Back: *New York.*

Sides: *1472 Ft. High.*
Has hinged back with separate lock.

1048. The Washington Monument, Washington, D.C., was completed in 1884 and opened to the public in 1888.

1049. See #1048 above.

1050. Don Duer, American Limited Editions, Winter Park, Fla., designed and carved the pattern for this bank. There are two versions, a signed, nickel-plated edition of 25, and our burnished iron edition.

1052. Face: *White House.*
Back: *Washington, D.C.*

1054. Face: *The Capitol, Washington, D.C.*
Sides and back picture: Library of Congress, Union Station, Mt. Vernon.

1055. Back: *Mt. Vernon, Va.* (Home of George Washington)

1056. U.S. Capitol on top of a bank building! There is a series of these odd banks, with historic buildings featured.

1057. *Century of Progress, International Exposition, Chicago, 1933.* Celebrated 100th anniversary of Chicago's incorporation as a city.

1059. Front: *People's United States Bank, St. Louis.*
One side: *The Mail Bank.*
This building was constructed in 1905, and intended to be the first national bank-by-mail house. The toy banks would have been distributed to depositors. Never came to be. Building razed in 1929.

1060. Back: *Lighting your way to security.*

1061. Base: *Chicago, 1892 Masonic Temple Fort Dearborn.*

1062. Back: *The National Recording Bank* and *Pat. Apl. 7 '91.*
Bank registers deposit of dimes when lever is pushed.

1063. Same as bank #1065, but this one is a still bank. Has combination trap. See Appendix #794, and patent paper.

1064. Back: *Chicago, 1934.* Has typical Arcade screw, and sheet metal base. See Appendix #1057.

1065. The Administration Building at the Fair was designed by Richard Morris Hunt.
Front: *1492-1892 Administration Bldg. Columbian Exposition.*
Back: *Columbian Magic Savings Bank — Int. Production Co. N.Y.* A mechanical bank. Tray slides out; deposit coin on tray, slip tray back in. Hinged tray drops depositing coin. See Appendix #794.

1066. The same bank as #1065, except for words, *The Hub*, a department store. Used to advertise various stores in New York.

1067. Bank produced in England to commemorate Columbian Exposition. See Appendix #794.
Front: *Chicago Bank.*
Back: *Chicago 1893.*
English registry #210265.

1068. Souvenir of Paris, showing the Arch of Triumph, with a picture of the Eiffel Tower beneath. Two famous birds with one stone. Hinged key-lock.

1069. Replica of Administration Bldg., Columbian Exposition. (See Appendix #794) Bank came nickel plated or electro oxydized. Base: *Made by the Kenton Hdw. Mfg. Co. Kenton Ohio, USA, #37.*

1070. See #1069 above. This is bank #38.

1072. Back: *World's Fair Administration Bldg. 1893.* Combination is *513.* See Appendix #794.

1073. This bank came nickel plated or electro oxydized. (This one has large Kenton trap.) This is bank #40. See Appendix #1069.

1074. English registry number is 526518. Says *Bank Eiffel Tower* on all sides. The 984' Eiffel Tower was built for the Exposition Universelle, in 1889.

1075. Two sides: *Tour Eiffel Paris.*
Other two sides: *Eiffel Tower Paris.*

1076. Robert Brown, founder of the Museum of Childhood, Menai Bridge, Anglesey, North Wales, produced this bank in 1981. The edition was limited to 250 banks. Brown, a member of the Still Bank Collectors' Club of America, also produced the *Prince and Princess of*

Wales Bank , #1324. Base of #1076: *Eiffel Tower Bank Reg. No. 526518 23 June 1908 Reproduced 1981 by Museum of Childhood Anglesey.*

1077. This bank has large Kenton trap; others have combination traps. See #1069 for copy on base. This bank is numbered *39.*

1081. This came painted bronze with assorted colors, according to catalog.

1082. Has turnpin.

1085. See bank #1633. Another small State Bank was made by Columbia Grey Iron Casting Co., 1897. Slight size variances.

1086. Front: *East Broadway M & L Jarmulowsky.*
Sides: *Deposit your money with Banking House 165 East Broadway M & L. Jarmulowsky where it is safe.* (There is a variation of this bank.)

1087. Above bird: *C & H*, (Chamberlain and Hill). English registry #187029. Catalog calls this the *London Bank.*

1089. Front: *Burg mit Kaiserstallung.* (City with the statue of the emperor.)

1090. English registry number, 247278.

1091. Front: *Burg - Nurnberg.*
Back: *Die Nurnberger Hangenkeinen Siehattin ihn Dennzuyor.* (There's nothing new in Nurnberg.)

1092. English registry number, 202983. Hive should be gilt.

1093. Front: *Stuttgart — Altes Schloss — very old castle.*
Back: *Stuttgart Schloss, or castle.*

1094. English registry #203386.

1095. Back: *Pat. Oct. 7, 1875.* See Bank #1101. Must be the same manufacturer.

1096. Has sheet metal, swivel trap. See patent paper.

1097. Says *Paying Teller* above window.

1098. Brass pattern for banks numbered 1097 and 1099. Front and back pattern for both banks, exact pattern for number 1099.

1100. Both sides: *United Banking and Trust Co.*

1101. See patent paper.

1102. Depressed, glazed base indicates bank has been dipped. Later banks have flat bases and no glaze.

1103. Front: *Van Wickle Library LaFayette College.*

1105. Back: *Shakespeare's House Stratford on Avon.* Has swivel trap.

1106. Made from base for Ferris Wheel Mechanical Bank.

1107. Front: *Pewter Metzke*
Side: © *Metzke.* Replica of the Davenport Home, Savannah, Georgia.

1108. SBCCA bank honoring America's Bicentennial, and the 10th anniversary of the Club. Bank is symbolic of Great Seal of U.S. Richards & Sargent, Inc., Providence, Rhode Island produced the flags and captions, and assembled the bank for Utexiqual Products Div., Executive Designs, inc., Moorestown, N.J. Bank cast and painted by Littlestown Hardware & Foundry Co., Littlestown, Pa. Four enamelware flags are pictured: Stars & Stripes, Grand Union, Betsy Ross, and the Gadsden Flags. Captions under each one describe its history. Base: *Still Bank Collectors Club of America Established 1966 1976 Convention Wyomissing Pennsylvania Edition Limited to 200*
© *SBCCA 1976.*

1109. Slot is hidden under *damen* (women) sign. Door is missing its lock. Hinged potty seat inside, for special deposits.

1110. English registry #180427. Came maroon bronzed, gold enamelline, electro brass or copper relief.

1111. Harper sent out a note with an early catalog, complaining that their bank, the City Bank, was being copied by someone. They may have been complaining about their rival, Chamberlain and Hill, who produced a similar bank.

1113. Bank has factory-made slot, but this piece has also been seen as a bookend. May have been a factory conversion,

157

or perhaps the company produced a set of bookends, with one piece being a secret bank.

1114. English registry #484712. Bank has two coin slots, one in each tower. Catalog says banks came, *maroon bronzed, Indian art black, gold bronzed,* and *venetian bronzed.*

1115. This is both a still and mechanical bank. Tower has mechanized action. Slide nickel in top, push knob to deposit coin. Sides of bank are marked to show accumulation of 100 coins. Bank opens when full.

1116. Marked *IB & CO.* on back. Key-lock trap. Possibly the only Ives' bank.

1118. Came nickeled, bronze or gold.

1119. Side view of #1086.

1120. Beautifully made reproduction of bank #1121. Base: *This is a reproduction of an antique bank made by The Ohio Foundry Co., Cleveland, O. 1893-1949.* Ohio Foundry Co. also made a reproduction of bank #996 in 1949.

1121. Base: *Patented July 25, 1895.* Stevens advertised that the bank came in *fancy colors.* They made it in another size: 3 1/4 x 2 1/4 x 2 1/4. See patent paper.

1122. Says *Bank* over door.

1123. Obviously, bank #1122 was the inspiration for this bank. Has sixteen brass steps.

1125. Our bank may be later than 1920. Casting is quite rough.

1126. Bank holds distinction of being our first building bank.

1127. Veneer, not inlay. Key-lock in roof.

1128. Sliding wood trap in base.

1129. A puzzle bank. Slide piece on front to left, push hidden lever down, and spring-loaded tray on the right pops out.

1130. Design is printed on wood. Handwritten message on back, including the country, *Norway.* Metal-lined coin slot. Key-lock trap.

1131. This bank is a lovely piece, with inlaid wood. Base slides forward, back slips down, roof slides back and off. Slide back up to retrieve money.

1132. We think Henry's grandfather made this bank. Remove chimney to shake out coins. Handwritten on bottom: *Stark, 1929.*

1136. There is another less-detailed version of this bank.

1138. Birth banks are common in England and came in many sizes.

1139. English registry #480274. Back half of bank was used for a number of English banks: 1308; 1313, 14 and 15; 1319, 20 and 21.

1141. Paper face: *R-H Brevete SGDG Paris.*

1143. Patented July 25, 1898.

1152. Two statues of Napoleon Bonaparte (1769-1821), French Emperor, one in the classic pose.

1153. *Applied for 1881 Registered 1889.* If there's a registry number, we can't read it.

1158. Base on this bank is identical to Villa Bank, #959.

1159. Actual Flatiron building was constructed in 1902. Bank has large combination trap.

1160. Has small trap. See #1159 above.

1161. Made without a trap. See #1159 above.

1163. After the great fire of 1666, Sir Christopher Wren (1632-1723), great English architect, planned rebuilding of City of London. Rebuilt St. Paul's Cathedral, and designed the Temple Bar, built between 1670 and 1672.

1164. Symbolizes Liberty enlightening the world. Stands in N.Y. Harbor. Designed by Frederic Auguste Bartholdi of Alsace. Statue a gift from people of France to U.S., in memory of the two countries' alliance in American Revolution. Put in place in 1886.

1165. Back: *1776.* Bank is riveted, with a Kenton coin trap. See Appendix #1160 above.

1166. Riveted bank with Kenton coin trap. This bank originally produced by Wing and Jones and Bixler. See Appendix #1164 above.

1167. Large Kenton trap. A.C.W. made similar one, 4 1/4 x 3 1/2. See also bank #1635, and Appendix #1169.

1169. Arcade made same bank and called it *Jewel* or *castle* in company catalog; bank has *jewel* embossed. A Kenton version of bank said *jewel* and it came in three sizes, produced from 1915-1926. Early A.C. Williams' version says *BA* to left of slot and *NK* to the right. Later version has slot in back, and *Bank* on front.

1173. Also made in aluminum and gold, from 1916-1926.

1176. There is a variation of this bank.

1179. Base: Number 86 or 98 is written on bottom. Not clear.

1180. Banks 1180-1183 were designed by A.C. Williams. See patent papers.

1184. See patent papers.

1186. See Appendix #254.

1187. Top: *Machinery Alamo Iron Works Iron & Steel San Antonio, Tex.*
Front: *The Alamo Founded 1516.* (Date nearly illegible — this is a guess.)
Base: *Made by Alamo Iron Works.*

1188. Says, *Souvenir of Chicago World's Fair 1833-1933 Fort Dearborn.* See Appendix #1057.

1190. Has tin baseplate. Some banks have *1883-1933* written on them. See Appendix #1057.

1191. Pressure-fit trap with release on back of bank. Base: *H.F.* and a symbol.

1192. Sides: *La Salette, Southbridge, Mass. Philippine Missions.* Hinged key-opened trap.

1194. Back:

July 1, 2, 3 1863
Gen. Meade   Gen. Lee
97000 men   75000 men
23000   casualties   28000
Commemorative Bank

Bank designed by Laverne A. Worley, Hanover, Pa., 1960. Edition of 200. Cast inside: *Original 1st run 1960.* Banks cast after 1960 have nothing inside.

1195. Older version of this bank has a bridge painted red.

1196. Base: *Westwood Bronze Memorials Live Forever. Manufactured by Service Foundry, Wichita, Kansas, 1935.* College is in N. Newton, Kansas.

1197. Front: *This is the property of the Home Savings Bank.*

1198. Another specimen has *1891* over door. Brass combination lock on door. Base: *Pat. Apl'd. For 475.*

1199. Combination: Clear to left. Turn right to *N*, back to *C*, and right to *D*. Base: *Patent Apl'd. For 450.*

1200. Front: *1890.* Two coin slots, marked *10 cent* and *5 cent.* Paper label on base: *Twist dome, put coin in and coin falls and registers amount on face of bank.*

1201. Face: *Property of People's Savings Bank Grand Rapids, Mich.* (Many different bank names were used.) This is a budget bank. There are 4 coin slots, two on one side, two on the other. Inside bank are two wood and tin sliding trays. Money was separated inside. Within bank were tin chutes to direct coins to proper compartment.

1202. Front: *1776 Centennial Bank 1876.*
Side: *Proclaim Liberty Throughout the Land.*
Side: *Independence Hall Tower.*
Side: *To all the inhabitants Thereof.*
Lever rings internal bell. Bank's inventor: C.W. Croteau. Patented: September 21, 1875. This bank and #1205 were undoubtedly produced for the Philadelphia Centennial Exposition, 1876. The Declaration of Independence was signed in Independence Hall, and the Liberty Bell hung in its tower until 1976 when it was moved to special exhibition building.

1203. Two coin slots in top. Paper label: *Philadelphia.*

1204. Front: *Independence Hall Birthplace of Independence.*
Rear: *Cradle of Liberty.* Three-pronged, key-opened trap.

1205. Painted variation of #1202. No bell in tower. Lever rings internal bell. See Appendix #1202. See patent paper.

1206. Says, *Birthplace of American Independence. Liberty proclaimed July 4, 1776.*

1207. Side: *Bank of Independence Hall 1775-1876.* See patent paper.

1208. Came maroon bronzed, with or without bell. Ours has bell. Brick walls usually came without bell, smooth walls with.

1211. This bank *may have* been produced for 1876 Philadelphia Exposition.

1212. *Patented Nov. 10, 1874.*

1213. *Patented Nov. 10, 1874.*

1214. *Patented Nov. 10, 1874.*

1216. Number *1076* cast on base.

1217. Number *1074* cast on base.

1219. Number *1072* cast on base.

1221. Front of base: *Independence Hall.* Gilt bells, separately cast and attached on each end of building. Screw-opened trap. See Appendix #1202.

1222. Actual building, built in 1969, was designed by C.F. Murphy and Associates and Perkins and Will.

1223. Side 1: *Boulevard Bank.*
Side 2: *Wrigley Building.*
Chicago's Wrigley Building was built in 1921.

1224. *Sears Tower — Home of Sears Bank & Trust Company.* Built in 1974, this is the tallest building in the world — at the moment! Toy has key-lock trap.

1225. See patent paper. Patented by R. Frisbie, assigned to J. & E. Stevens Co.

1226. This bank was the model for an eighteen-cent U.S. Postage Stamp. First day of issue was May 8, 1981. Commemorates 150 years of Savings and Loan Associations in U.S. Artist was Donald M. Hedin. See patent paper. See *#1225 above.*

1227. See patent paper. See #1225 above.

1228. Dwight L. Moody and Ira D. Sankey: Moody was the leader of a religious revival movement, based in Chicago for a time. Sankey was his musical director.
Back of photographs: *Hannay's Souvenir Cards, 335 Washington St., Brooklyn.* Joel Snyder, noted authority on antique photographic processes, removed a coat of red paint that covered Moody and Sankey's faces. The pictures he found, called albumen prints, date from the 1800's.

1229. Similar to New Bank Mechanical. See bank and Appendix #904.

1231. See patent paper.

1232. See patent paper.

1233. Held by two turnpins — really a puzzle bank.

1235. Clock face says 11:45. Slot is in rear, under small *bank* sign.

1236. See patent paper.

1237. *Patd. Mar. 10 1891.* See patent paper.

1238. In 1905 A.C.W. catalog. Hubley also made several of these with clock faces. See *#1235. See patent paper.*

1239. In 1905 A.C.W. catalog. See patent paper.

1240. Also came with clock face at the top — probably made by Hubley. In 1905 A.C.W. catalog. See patent paper.

1241. In 1905 A.C.W. catalog. See patent paper.

1242. Right side: *Liberty Proclaimed July 4, 1776.*
Left Side: *Birthplace of American Independence.*
Patented Sept. 14, 1875. Made for 1876 Philadephia Exposition.

1243. Base: *Pat. October _____1875.* (stenciled on)

1244. Base: *Made by Enterprise Mfg. Co. Phila. Pat. Sept. 14 1875.* Made for 1876 Philadelphia Exposition.

1245. Has orange plastic light strip. *Copyright 1937 Vanio, Inc.*

1246. *A Marietta silo saves you money.* The Marietta (Ohio) Concrete Company is still in the silo business.

1247. Back: *Indiana Silo Anderson Ind. A good place to put money.*

1249. See bank #1006 for still version of this bank. Also made in size 3 x 3 x 2 1/2.

1250. Tin top pictures Columbia with laurel wreath on her head. The front features a picture of Administration Building, 1893 World's Fair. See Appendix #794.

1251. Front: *View in Millport Bay, Cumbrae.* Sold by A.G. McFarlane, *Jeweller, Millport.* Top of tower lifts off.

1252. Depicts Clay Head, Block Island, R.I. Top third of bank lifts off.

1254. Cupid holds German Pfennig dated 1900.

1257. Has iron, mech. trap. Bank is riveted. *Patent pending.*

1258. 1879 dollar pictured.

1259. Depicts town of Wurzburg in shield atop basket.

1260. Pictures Cologne Cathedral. Front: *Koln a R h dom; Cologne Cathedral on the Rhine.*

1261. Directions for use are on the bank.

1263. Commemorates the pilgrims' landing at Plymouth Rock. Date *1620* embossed on top.

1264. Front: *The Prudential has the strength of Gibraltar.* Rock of Gibraltar is the trademark of the Prudential Life Insurance Company.

1265. Hinged top. Key opening in front. Slot in top.

1266. Front: *Put money in thy purse.*
Back: *Pat. Apld. For.*

1268. A bank promotional piece. Base: *Garfield Savings Bank* in neat, raised letters. Key-opened.

1269. Top: *Full Dinner Pail.* This was the slogan of William McKinley in his successful race against William Jennings Bryan for the Presidency, in 1896. Slot is in the back.

1270. A catalog page indicates this was sold as a bank as well as a toy, but catalog page might have been doctored. Most of the collecting world has declared it a non-bank.

1271. Different casting than bank 1272. Back: *Electrical Products Building Remington Rand Hall, New York World's Fair 1939.* Variation of this bank says on back: *A small deposit 10¢ a day, buys any Remington Portable.*

1272. Different casting than #1273. Back: *New York World's Fair, 1939.* Variation has name *Underwood* on back — nothing else. There are several other typewriter banks.

1273. Part of the top unscrews to release coins.

1274. Japanese scene at top. Child must move three pieces of wood to get key hidden inside. Slide down center piece and key-slot appears.

1275. Revolving viewer at top has four tiny windows with magnifying glass. Through one of them can be seen a picture of the *Ruine Heisterbach.*

1277. Has shield logo and pry-out trap. This specimen made in the 1940's.

1279. Near slot: *Save for a rainy day.*

1280. Six heads (Chinaman, dog, monkey, cat, clown, boy) appear in top section of bank, which must be turned by child to match proper head with proper body. Base: *Rothweirs Chokolate.*

1285. *Ohio The Buckeye State SBCCA 1973 Cin. O.* The late Lou Filler designed and produced this bank for the Still Bank Collectors' Club. Also made one that said only *Ohio The Buckeye State.*

1286. After passage of the 13th Amendment to the Constitution, Congress set up the Freedmen's Bureau for aid and protection of former slaves. Considered a mechanical bank.

1287. Collection box for the Church Missionary Society. Around loaf is written: *We thank Thee O Lord.*

1288. Inside pan: *1901 Pan American Bank.* Ethnology Building from Pan American Exposition, Buffalo, N.Y. is pictured.

1289. Top: *MMA.*

1290. Bank has been in continuous production for more tha 70 years. Opens at $10.00.

1295. Has huge, crude slot. Bottom: *Made in Mexico.*

1296. Back: *Chubb & Safe Co. 128 Victoria St. London by special permission Her Majesty the Queen.* A miniature Chubb safe protects the miniature jewels in this doll house, which was built for Queen Mary by the artists of Great Britain, as a tribute. Her husband, George V, reigned from 1910-1936. The doll house itself is in the State apartments at Windsor Castle.

1297. Coronation souvenir, George VI and Elizabeth, May 12, 1937. Tin came filled with Oxo Cubes.

1300. Wire crank causes Punch to hit devil with baseball bat.

1301. Souvenir, Royal Wedding of Charles & Diana, July 29, 1981.

1302. English registry #872932.

1303. Front: Pictures condition of children before receiving help from the National Society for Prevention of Cruelty to Children.
Back: Happy children after receiving help.

1304. Came in many sizes. Variations have screw tops or bottoms.

1307. English registry #685799.

1308. English registry #502036. Back of bank same casting as back of Villa Bank, #1139.

1310. English registry #694628. Pry-out coin trap.

1311. Base: *Elizabeth June 2 1953 Coronation.* This is St. Edward's Crown, used only for coronations. Was made for Charles II, who acceded to the throne in 1649.

1312. Flocked variation of #1311.

1313. Date *1914* below portrait. Rear of bank same casting as back half of Villa Bank, #1139. This bank identical to Coronation Bank, #1315, except for portrait and date.

1314. Front: *Dreadnought Bank United We Stand.* Back of bank same casting as half of #1139, but peaked roof has been added. Dreadnought was a British battleship, launched 1906, which established the pattern for all big-gun warships.

1315. Same as #1313 except for portrait and date. Back of bank same casting as #1139.

1316. English registry #393170. Base has nine holes in it. Commemorates coronation of Edward VII.

1317. See Appendix #1311 for imprinting on base.

1318. Supposed to be St. Edward's Crown, but not a good replica. See bank #1311. However, cross and orb show up better.

1319. Commemorates crowning of George V and Mary. George V reigned 1910-1936. See Appendix #1315. Back same as Villa Bank #1139. See Appendix numbers 1320, 1321 and 1329.

1320. There was still an Empire when George V and Mary acceded to the throne in 1910. See Appendix numbers 1319, 1321 and 1329.

1321. See Appendix #1320 above.

1322. See Appendix #1311 for imprinting on this bank.

1323. Top: picture of Cheshire cat.
Sides picture: The Duchess, The Mad Hatter, The Queen, and the Knave of Hearts. Where's Alice? Remove slide in base to remove money. When you do, a hinged piece falls out, revealing a picture of Alice. Bank has a spring-loaded false bottom. Bank had provisional patent number, 16808-7.

1324. Souvenir of Royal Wedding of Prince Charles and Lady Diana, produced by Robert Brown, Museum of Childhood, Anglesey, North Wales. Bank was cast by Renaissance Castings, Coventry. At top of bank is crest of the Prince of Wales. Medallion with portrait of the royal pair was struck by Reliable Stampings, Ltd., Birmingham, England.

1325. Same as #1327, but carries portrait of Elizabeth II. Words *Coronation 1953* appear under portrait.

1326. Front: *E II R 1953.*
Back: *Reg. Design App. for HARPER.*

1327. Back: *6 penny piece bank.* See #1325 above.

1328. Lid: *Victorian Coins.*
Front: *Take care of the coins. The pounds will take care of themselves.*

1329. Face: *George V 1910.* This bank produced before he was crowned. John Haley has a bank like this that commemorated the marriage of George V. George and Mary were married in 1867. See Appendix numbers 1319, 1320 and 1321.

1330. Also came painted blue, green and red.

1332. Has sheet metal back and Arcade screw. Came white trimmed in gray, or red, green or blue.

1334. Base: *4019-9 S* Has screw-opened trap. Made by same company as #1335.

1335. Base: *4019-5 Super Cast.* Screw-opened trap.

1336. Back: *Frigidaire.*
Base: *National Products Corp. Made in Chicago USA.* There are several variations of this bank.

1337. Arcade screw. Sheet metal back. *837* on base.

1338. This specimen has a door that opens, revealing a set of cast drawers. Variation has door that doesn't open. Sheet metal back and base and Arcade screw. Catalog says it came with or without legs.

1340. Sides: *Estate.*

1341. Unscrew tin back-plate to remove coins. Two top panels lift up to reveal burners.

1342. Sheet metal base and back. Same as #1341, but no burner covers.

1343. Slot hidden behind door. Inside door: *Cook with cash.* Sides and back are sheet metal.

1346. Back: *Made by Arcade Mfg. Co., Freeport, Ill.*
Arcade first made a toy stove with doors that open, a grease tray, etc. Arcade then sealed the oven door, and voila! a coin chamber. A slot was cast in the rear. Note Arcade decalcomania on warmer door.

1347. A toy converted to a bank.

1348. Limited edition of 150.

1349. Sides and back are stamped sheet metal.
Top: *Save your money and buy a gas stove.*
Base: *Pat. Applied For.* See patent paper.

1350. Sides: *Eureka.*
Front: *Wright's famous Eureka New Century Eureka #410.*
Base: *Eureka Gas Cookers — Thermo X Gas Fires - may be purchased from your gas office, manufacturers - John Wright & Co., Birmingham & London M.B. Cooker booklet will be sent free on application.*

1351. Back: *Abendroth Bros., N.Y.*

1352. This bank was a premium offered by Corning Glass Works. Side piece removable. Right side and rear are sheet metal.

1353. Side: *Burnett Ltd., London.*

1354. Sides and back are sheet metal.

1355. Front: *Champion Thrift Bank.*

1356. Slot hidden beneath hinged top. Red isinglass insets in front panels.
Rear: *The Schneider & Trenkamp Co., Cleveland & Chicago.* Screw-opened base. More commonly found in gilt finish.

1357. Comes apart in eleven pieces. Also came all nickeled and all black painted. Base: *Pat. Applied For.* A puzzle bank!

1358. Side: *Thomas E. Coale Co. Coal Co. Fremont 5040.*
Front: *Thermo X Gas Fire.*

1361. Top: *3176 C.L. Poole Co., N.Y., N.Y.*

1362. *Put your money in a Marshall. Marshall Furnace Co., Marshall, Mich.*

1363. *Save money with a Mellow Furnace Mfg. by Liberty Toy Co., St. Louis, Mo.*

1364. *Gem Abendroth Bros., N.Y. Gem Heaters Save Money*

1365. Front: *Modern Home Heating Co., Allentown, Pa. 229*
Top: *Save Money with Mo-He-Co.*

1368. Top, held on by tabs and key locked, lifts off. Singer emblem on cover, and words, *Nahmaschineh* or sewing machine. An *S* for Singer appears on both sides of brace and on the legs.

1369. Machie is iron, stand is tin. Hinged key lock top lifts up to retrieve coins. *Nahe Elektrish*, or Sew Electric, appears on table. This bank is later than #1368, and since table tops are same size, were probably made by the same company. This logo appears on bank. B OO M

1370. Front: *Richmond Cedar Works, Richmond Va.*
Back: *Save Your money. Buy a Steel Frame Freezer.*
Top: *Bank RCW.* Has small coin trap in base.

1371. Back: *North Pole Bank. Pat. Pending.*
Top: *NP Bank.*

1373. Painted over nickeled finish. The reproduction, commonly found, is painted the same colors but is not nickeled.

1374. Back: *Karpen Guaranteed Furniture Snug Harbor.* Key-opened trap.

1375. Both rockers: *Pat. July 26, 1898.* Back of chair is a pressure fit. It must be removed first to open bank. BUT DON'T DO IT! One of the reasons this bank is rare is because it is so fragile. Old iron is brittle. Watch for repairs on this bank. See patent papers.

1378. *M & M Vol. Fire Dept. 1930-1976.* Bank produced with help of Ralph Dye, to raise money for the McConnellsville Volunteer Fire Department.

1379. Top: *Patented.*

1380. *Pass Around the Hat. Pat. Applied For.* There is a larger version of this hat in a 3-piece casting - different wording.

1381. *Pass 'Round the Hat.*

1383. Ours says, *Uncle Sam Bank* on top. During WWII, bank carried a paper label on top which said, *Save for War Bonds & Stamps.* This bank has a shield logo and a twist-out trap.

1387. *Patented March 20, 1917 U.S. Jan. 28, 1918.* Early Chein?

1390. Front: *Christian Police Association CPA.*

1391. *Wm Livers & Co., Ltd. Newcastle Upon Tyne.* English registry #454734.

1392. Pat. #11485.

1393. Identical to bank #1395 except for lettering.

1394. Huge trap in bottom held closed by latch.

1395. Same as #1393.

1396. Letters stand for: *Ancient Arabis Order of Nobles of the Mystic Shrine.*
There is an identical bank with *Medinah* on it. Has pressure fit metal trap.

1397. Base: *It's usual, you know!* English registry #254734.

1398. English registry #664401.

1399. *Pat. Applied For. Manufactured by Stronghart Co., Chicago, U.S.A.* Slot in base.

1400. Front: *Bank Empire State Building, N.Y.*

1404. Same as #1401, but different insignia.

1405. Base: *DRGM.*

1406. Top: *119.*

1407. This was a real shell. Base: *SMC 1943 20mm. m21A1.*

1408. *Harmo Electric Company, Chicago, Ill. Pats. Pending.*

1409. Front: *When bank is full, shake hard and bottom will fall out.*
Side: *Wear Buster Brown Shoes for Boys for Girls. Brown built shoes for men and women.*

1410. Back: *Prudential Insurance Co. of America.*

1411. Picture of Woolworth Bldg. appears on front.

1412. This was a promotional item distributed by banks.

1413. Dates *1914* and *1918* appear above and below the cross.

1414. Top: *Martin Pat 8925.*

1415. *& K Co.* appears on base.

1416. See patent paper.

1417. Bank is patterned after British Mark III Tank. British invented the tank and first used it in France, 1916. Ferrosteel was so eager to produce the bank that they did so before seeing a picture of a tank. Since they could not imagine a land vehicle without wheels, they gave some to the bank.

1419. Same tank as on English mechanical bank, but made as a still bank. Face: *Patent 1918.* Mechanical was patented (#122123) by Robert E. and Nellie Starkie.

1421. Etched on bank are a series of World War I battles, and the dates they were fought. Dates are in years 1914 and 1915. Top of List: *Das Geheimniss Von.* (The Secret of . . .)

1422. Front: *by UWSS.*
Base: *Bartlett Mayward Co., Baltimore Trigger: P & FC.*

1423. *Spirit of Thrift Afros-Fe Co.*

1424. Also came with iron wheels in a later edition.

1425. There is a variation of this bank.

1428. See #1432. Same bank. A variation has *Los Angeles* on it.

1430. Bank is made of Duralumin, same material used to manufacture the U.S.S. Akron, a giant dirigible of the 1930's.
Side: *Goodyear Zeppelin Airship Dock, Akron, Ohio.*
Other Side: *Made of Duralumin used in Airship Akron, length 1176 feet, width 325 feet, height 211 feet.*
Paper label: *Insert key turn left until loose. Pry out plug with blade of screwdriver or pen knife placed between feet and rim of plug.*

1432. Same bank as #1428.

1433. Turret: *Regd No.* — but no number follows.

1435. This bank has been seen without lettering, dated 1919.

1436. This bank belonged to Heinz, whose name is painted on the bottom.

1438. Pair of steel guns, on either side of bank, are often missing or replaced. Bank produced without forward gun. See patent paper.

1439. Spanish-American War (1898) ended Spanish rule in the Americas. The Spanish sank the U.S.S. Maine in Havana Harbor in 1898, giving U.S. an excuse to enter the war in defense of Cuba. Bank appeared shortly thereafter. This ship has been seen with the following other names on it: *Illinois, Oregon, Massachusetts, Iowa, Kentucky, Texas, Cincinnati, Olympic.* Has combination trap. Turn spotlight and lift out trap.

1440. See patent paper.

1441. *Design patent pending.* Sliding trap in base. See Appendix #1439. See patent paper.

1442. Patent papers for this splendid *mystery* bank were found three weeks before our publishing deadline. The inventor designed a mechanical bank, which probably would have been too fragile to produce. A coin was to be hoisted in a carrier from the "dock," swung over the boat, and a rod with small bell on the end was to be vibrated and the rod would work down a pole, finally depositing coin in life boat. We still don't know who produced this bank, but suspect that it was not made as a mechanical. Spring loaded, key-opened trap. This bank was found in an attic in Indiana. Rumor has it that another one or two exist.

1443. Fancy touring boats used to make trips up and down the Rhine River, between 1888 and 1914. This one stopped at *Wilhelmshaven.*

1446. Same bank as #1447. See Appendix #1443.

1447. Same bank as #1446. See Appendix #1443.

1448. *Mainz National Denkmal Niederwald.* See Appendix #1443.

1449. See Appendix #1443.

1450. Guns are cast separately. They are often missing or replaced. The battleship Oregon helped bottle up Spanish Cervera in Santiago Harbor, Cuba, 1898. See Appendix #1439. See patent paper.

1451. Guns and anchor chains are brass, as is rudder. See Appendix numbers 1439 and 1450. See patent paper. Note extra length in mast.

1452. See Appendix numbers 1439 and 1450. See patent paper.

1453. The barge turned up at a Main auction on 10/16/79, purportedly consigned by Mark Hallet from his important collection of the Newport Clock Museum. Barge comes apart in three pieces. Threaded barrel on deck, when unscrewed, separates deck from hull. Two other restored barges are known to exist.

1454. Tug comes apart in six pieces, the smoke stack alone consists of three. The deck is in two pieces and the hull, one. A turnscrew reaching from the cap to the hull holds the bank together. Both tug and barge are pulltoys, having rings for string.

1455. Oriental treasure ship; carries symbols of the 7 Gods of Fortune.

1456. Hull is wood composition. Rest is wood with brass fittings. Large hatch cover has three slots for different sized coins. Inside: *Pat. Apld. For Redi Houl.* Possibly came as a kit and was converted.

1457. Base: *Brighton 70.*
Deck: *When My Fortune Ship Comes In.*
To remove coins, unscrew mast and lift deck. Bank often repaired.

1458. Wheels and paint are identical to #1474, made by Kenton.

1459. Also came blue enamel with red stacks, and painted all aluminum and all gilt.

1460. Came silver, red, and gold bronzed.

1462. Perforated iron base was cast separately. So-called *Gunboat Diplomacy* took place in the Philippine Islands, 1880-1890.

1463. Masts have been replaced, and the deck has been repainted.

1464. Same wheels and paint as numbers 1458 and 1474. Mast has been replaced. Bank has two slots, one on either side.

1466. Key-locked seating area on hinged top. Shortly after the Titanic sank, these collection boats were placed in pubs and shops. Contributions were used to help families of those who went down at sea. Because of the clamor over deaths at sea, the Royal Maritime Safety Commission was established to set standards for safety on the water.

1467. Back: *Medical Missions. CMS* stands for Church Missionary Society.

1468. Some had believed that Whiting bank #265 was a repaint. We now have seen several painted that way. Also we have seen the one in the 1891 Butler Brothers Catalog which describes it as *painted bright vermillion striped with gold.* The 1897 Grey Iron Casting Co. Catalog advertised the bank as *japanned and assorted colors.*

1470. See patent paper.

1472. A longer and taller bank than #1468. The slot is also longer. Top of bank is more finely cast than #1468. Bank in 1889 Butler Brothers Catalog is bronzed with gilt. Word *bank* is not cast at the top, nor on our bank.

1473. Also a pulltoy; has place for a string.

1475. King's insignia is on the side. Coin trap in base. Edward reigned from 1901-1910. Also was a functional train car.

1476. Back: *Pat. '87.* Bank was patented by Edw. Colby, Nov. 15, 1887. He called it the *Toy Locomotive.* Patent #373223. More common variations of this bank are nickeled.

1477. Front end: *One of the first trains operated in America.*
Back: *Travel to success by Saving.*
Side: *1st train in New York State operated by N.Y. Central.*
Other Side: *Pioneer Train of the Mohawk & Hudson Railroad 1831.*

1478. Tires: *Goodrich heavy duty cord.* Rubber tires do deteriorate, and perfect repros are available. Nickeled driver held in by screw. Lights are often missing, as are the rear tire and license plate. Pressed-steel trap. This is Arcade toy #05. Good repros of the trap are now available. See Appendix #1480 below.

1480. Nickeled driver is screwed to seat. Pressed steel trap. *Arcade #05.* Rubber tires at extra cost were offered in 1924.

1482. Same as #1478, but this one has steel wheels. *Arcade #05.* See Appendix #1480.

1483. A hole in the seat holds the driver.

1484. Same as #1483. Arcade converted this from a toy to a bank by filling in the rear window to make a coin receptacle. It looks rather crude. Later was changed as in #1483. Window filled in entirely.

1485. When wire crank in rear is turned, dial shows price of gas. Hose often missing or replaced with shoestring.

1486. Should have four people in car. One of our people never left the factory. A casting flaw.

1488. Mahogany carving purchased at auction of A.C.W. items.

1489. Has wire screen grill. Driver is screwed in. Bank is the same as banks numbered 1491 and 1493. Patent for the Yellow Cab was filed in 1922. Bank was introduced to the public in 1921.

1491. Bank has replacement wheels that are too small for it. Same as #1489 and #1493, only brown and white.

1492. *American Art Works, Inc. Coshocton, O. #178.*

1493. Same as #1491 and 1489, but has steel wheels. See Appendix #1480.

1494. Engraved on top: *A present from Blackpool to Mrs. Fish Hood: 1923.*

1496. This bank is made of cast iron and steel. Turn gun, line up slots, and deposit coins. *Pat. April 23, 1895.*

1498. Rear door lifts to retrieve coins. Rubber wheels. Rear Door: *Callen Mfg. Corp. Melrose Park, Ill. U.S.A.*

1499. Wooden wheels. See patent paper.

1500. Has combination lock on hinged rear door. Paper label shows people at windows. Doors: *Brinks Armored Truck Bank* with Brinks' insignia.

1501. Has key-wind mechanism. Slot is in trailer. Key-opened drop-door in trailer. Bank has wood wheels. See patent paper.

1510. Slot in hood. Wooden wheels. Tin base with tab-opened trap.

1512. Two 1.5 volt batteries operate. Moves in crazy pattern. Plastic wheels and carriage. Body is metal. A mechanical bank.

1513. Sides and top: *Virserums Sparbank.*
Top: *Nasta Hallplats.*

1514. Slot in rear door, which drops down. Wooden wheels. See patent paper.

1528. Side: *December 1965 Works Managers' Conference Electro Coating.* Screw opened base and wheel plate. Same as #1533.

1533. Side: *UPS United Parcel Service.* Same as #1528.

1534. Back is sheet metal. If paper face is missing, this is a *C* bank; if face is intact, it's a *D.*

1535. Back is sheet metal. Harder to find than #1534. This was probably the original design. Casting it was so tough they simplified it.

1536. Face is cast in.

1537. Movable clock hands. Instead of times of day, has dollars and cents. We think it was made by Judd because of finish, casting style and size.

1538. A registering bank. Push plunger after depositing coin to register deposit. The back leg is cast and attached separately. Has a screw-opened, iron trap.

1539. Top: *12:00 M. Washington.* This bank is an instructional toy, an aid in helping children tell time. Heavy cardboard clock faces do *not* show the time in various

1540. Arcade advertised that the pendulum in this clock, once set in motion, would swing for fifteen minutes. It does. Pendulum is often missing. A double wire hanger at the top gave it stability. If original pendulum is present, it's a *D* bank; if missing, a *C*.

1542. English registry #187212.

1543. Clock set at 9:07. Face: *But it stop'd. Short Never to go again.* See #1557 for rear view of this bank.

1544. Sides are sheet metal. Reproduced in 1979 in bronze for 70th anniversary of the Batavia Bank, Batavia, Illinois. Reproduction (in two pieces) done by Batavia Foundry and Machine Company.

1545. Sides are sheet metal.

1546. Also came dull black trimmed with gold.

1548. Pressed steel back. Back: *Pat. Pending.*

1549. If placed in the sun pointing north, this toy will actually tell time.

1550. There are pirate scenes on front of this operating clock. Was a bank promotional piece. *Made in U.S.A.*

1551. An operating clock. *Pat. Mar. 19, 1901.*

1552. Pictures clown lying down, playing with a cat.

1553. *Ingram Co., Bristol, Conn.*

1554. Clown walking his dog.

1555. Paper face: *H.C. Hart & Co., Detroit, Mich. Patented July 7, 1885.* Ours is missing one hand. Bank's top and base are iron; body is tin. See patent paper.

1556. Base: *B.D. Corp., April 1, 1930.*

1557. See #1543 for front view of bank. To open, swivel top piece to the right, which allows middle section of bank to be pushed up and out. Very elaborate and nicely cast!

1560. Has revolving Westclox pocket watch.

1562. *Made in U.S.A. for Bankers' Development Corporation.*

1564. Comic strip artists were Siegel and Shuster. Strip first appeared in National Comics, 1938.

1565. Jackie Robinson - 1st black ballplayer to play major league baseball.

1568. Patent #2463433.

1569. *First dime locks To open press bump.*

1573. Popeye first appeared in 1929, in a comic strip called *Thimble Theatre.* E.C. Segar created the popular figure.

1574. See #1573 above.

1575. *The Youth's Companion Savings Bank. The Youth's Companion* was a magazine that advertised toys. Has sliding trap.

1576. *Children's Crusade for Children April 22-30, 1940.* Money was collected in school for young war victims. Supurb color litho.

1577. Depicts Thomas Jefferson handing the Declaration of Independence to John Hancock.

1578. Metal trap in base. Back: *SBCCA Conv. 1980 Denver, Pa.*

1579. Actually plays a tune when wound and coin deposited. A mechanical bank.

1581. Back: *Wurlitzer Model 2400.* Plastic cover over record holder.

1583. Adv. piece for Detroit auto dealers. Key trap in base.

1584. *Uncle Don's Ernest Saver Club Greenwich Savings Bank, New York City.*

1589. A promotional piece for banks. This one was for the Beverly State Savings Bank, Chicago, Illinois. Has a Benjamin Franklin homily on it.

1590. This bank was given to *W.S., 1925.*

1591. George Knerr made 160 of these banks, honoring America's Bicentennial year, 1976.

1593. Rocking horse is the symbol of the SBCCA. This piece was a souvenir of the 1977 convention in Wyomissing, Pa.

1594. Shows various monuments in Washington, D.C. Marked *SBCCA Convention 14, Rockville, Md., June, 1981.*

1595. Souvenir for the SBCCA convention, Chicago, Illinois, 1983.

1597. Souvenir SBCCA Convention, Syracuse, N.Y., 1979. Limited edition of 210 banks, 160 in white, and 50 speckled ones (which were a production error).

1598. Ten wooden bats representing the teams in the American League at the time. Rack is plastic. See Appendix #1603.

1600. Front: *Coal and Coke Museum.* Charter member commemorative. Officers' names are on the bottom.

1601. The Cradle is an adoption center in Evanston, Illinois.

1603. Ten plastic bats representing National League teams. Still being made. See Appendix #1598.

1604. Entire alphabet is pictured on bank's 26 facets. An instructional bank.

1606. Bank has a trick slot. Slot in wheel must be aligned with slot in stand in order to deposit coin. To open bank, spread base at sides and lift out wheel.

1607. When lever is turned a picture framed in iron pops up. It is reputed that a famous camera company insisted that this bank be taken off the market, insuring its rarity.

1610. Top: *Klondyke Gold Bug at Home.*

1612. Top: *Bank.* See Pingree Potato, #1670. See patent paper.

1613. *Throat Ease & Breath Perfume.* Registers dimes. Patented July 16, 1912.

1616. See Key Bank #1672. Patented April 7, 1905 (786689) by Wm. J. Somerville, Cleveland, Ohio.

1618. There are three of these banks in different sizes with different inscriptions. Ours says *Nest Egg;* on reverse *Horace.* Bank appeared in 1885 Ives catalog, in the section devoted to their own products. They had a close relationship with Smith & Egge.

1619. *A Cache for Coins.* Back has detailed physical description of the Lone Ranger and Silver, plus Lone Ranger's code of ethics.

1621. This bank was advertised as a bank, a wall ornament, and a paperweight. Leaf is often repaired.

1622. See patent paper.

1625. See patent paper.

1626. Front casting same as *Mermaid* except for name. Back casting is different. Mermaid's blouse was redesigned to handle a larger, wider coin slot. *Nixe* means Mermaid in German.

1627. *Mermaid,* bank #34 reshown for comparison purposes.

1628. Front: *God is Love.*
Back: *Faith, Hope Charity.*
Slot is at top of cross.

1629. Dressmaker's model; pin cushion bank. Slot in rear.

1630. Back: *Be smart. Have fun. Collecting banks is fun. Saving money is smart. 1982.* Bank designer Worley was stationed in the South during W.W. II. Southerners complained to him that Yankees "come down and run all over our alligators".

1632. Paper litho on wood. Front: *First Nat. Bank.* On each window: *Banker Broker.*

1633. See banks #1078-1085.

1634. Says *Kress* on three of the four faces.

1635. See also banks numbered 1167, 1168, 1169.

1636. This mosque is similar to Whiting #341, but has more detailed casting and has five diamond-shaped windows instead of two.

1639. Goteborg is a town in Sweden, and *Sparbank* means *Savings Bank.*

1640. *A Brownie is thrifty.*

1641. See Whiting #46. We had thought that a red bonnet in-dicated a much later rougher casting, or a reproduction. This bank has the same quality of detail and paint as #24.

1642. Same casting as donkey on Bad Accident mechanical, except underside of donkey is closed to retain coins and tail is closed instead of open. Probably an end-of-day conversion, but we have seen another. Riveted.

1643. Front: cypher of George V, who reigned from 1910-1936. Number *96783* appears on bank.

1644. Converted from the Ox Cart, a Kenton toy which appears in their 1911 catalog. Probably not a factory conversion.

1646. Paint variation. This one from the Whiting collection.

1649. *Veribus Unitis.* Austrian Emperor Franz Joseph and Ger-man Emperor Wilhelm are pictured. Made in 1912 to commemorate the visit of Wilhelm to Austria. Wilhelm's support for Austria in 1914 contributed to the outbreak of World War I.

1651. Replica of the Ives Santa. See Santas, numbered 56 and 64.

1654. England's Uncle Sam. Has the Union Jack on his chest. John Bull as a symbol dates circa 1900.

1659. Front: *Humphrey Muskie '68.*
Back: *Democrat.*
Bank is reproduction of #472, and came out at the same time as #471. Hubert H. Humphrey, Senator from Min-nesota, made an unsuccessful run at the presidency that year. His running mate was Senator Edmund Muskie.

1660. In the summer of 1983, the Cooper-Hewitt Museum, the Smithsonian Institution's National Museum of Design in New York City, displayed a collection of architectural banks. Charles V. Reynolds built a model forge which could produce this tiny State Bank. It was also on dis-play.

1662. Don't have proper bottom half of this bank.

1663. During World War I, Mayor Pingree of Detroit suggested that people dig up their lawns and plant potatoes. See Bank #1612, for an earlier potato. See patent paper.

1665. Top: *St. Louis Exposition.*
Bottom:*World's Fair Key.*
Souvenir of the Louisiana Purchase Exposition, The St. Louis World's Fair, 1904. Handle wider and thicker than #1616. Otherwise, they're similar. See #1616.

1667. Paint variation of bank #883.

1668. This is a reproduction of Harper's throne, #1326, with George Third's name instead of Elizabeth's. Wish it were really that old.

1671. Has Bell Telephone symbol on it. Bell rings when receiver is jiggled.

APPENDIX — MISCELLANEOUS

U.S. PATENTS

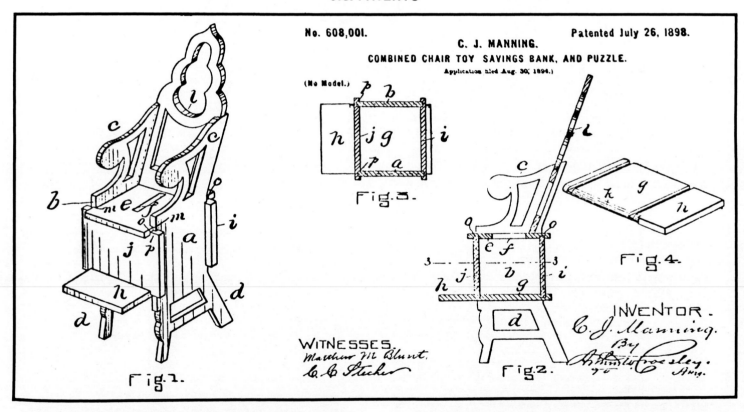

No. 608,001.   Patented July 26, 1898.
C. J. MANNING.
COMBINED CHAIR TOY SAVINGS BANK, AND PUZZLE.
Application filed Aug. 30, 1894.

Patent numbers in this country are issued sequen-tially. Complete papers, including the inventor's draw-ing and written application, can be obtained if the pa-tent number is known. Most still bank patents are de-sign patents and you should so indicate. Send one dollar to:

U.S. Patent and Trademark Office
Office of Public Information
Washington, D.C. 20231

What follows is a series of patent papers we were able to acquire before our publishing deadline. Many of the banks are in this book. Only the inventors' drawings are included, as the written applications for the patents were too lengthy to include. This excerpt, from C.J. Manning's application for a patent on *Rocking Chair*

#1375, will demonstrate how complex and informative the application itself can be:

...the invention consists of a toy savings bank made in the form of a chair, in which the sides and the front and rear and top and bot-tom pieces are grooved to receive the meet-ing edges of the pieces or parts with which they come into contact in such manner that such meeting edges will set into the said grooves and the edge of one piece or part be-ing so formed as that it may be sprung into and out of his holding groove in order to set up or put together the parts to form a toy sav-ings bank or to separate the parts to render it a puzzle to put them together.......

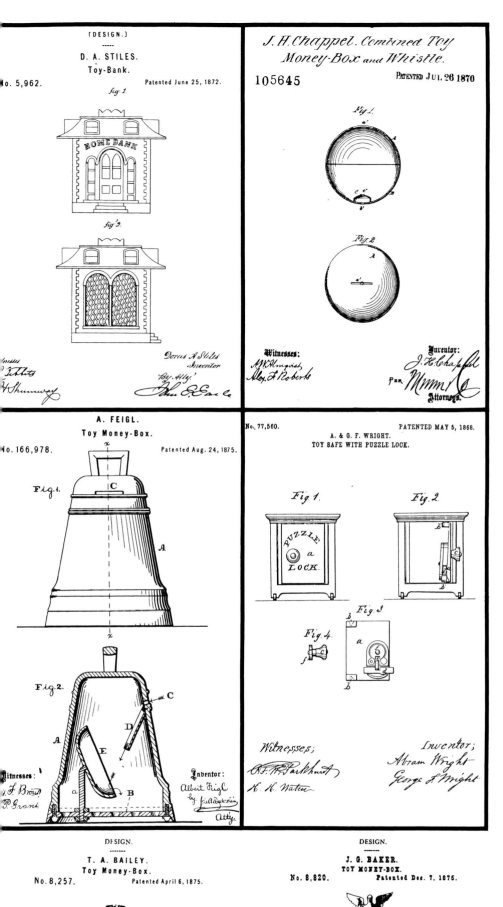

[DESIGN.]

D. A. STILES.
Toy-Bank.
No. 5,962.   Patented June 25, 1872.
fig 1.
fig 2.

Witnesses   Doras A Stiles
                                    Inventor
                             By Atty:

J.H.Chappel. Combined Toy
Money-Box and Whistle.
105645   PATENTED JUL. 26 1870
Fig 1.
Fig 2.

Witnesses: Inventor:
                                    J.H.Chappel
                             Per   Attorneys.

A. FEIGL.
Toy Money-Box.
No. 166,978.   Patented Aug. 24, 1875.
Fig. 1.
Fig. 2.

Witnesses: Inventor:
                                    Albert Feigl
                             by
                                    Atty.

No. 77,560.   PATENTED MAY 5, 1868.
A. & G. F. WRIGHT.
TOY SAFE WITH PUZZLE LOCK.
Fig 1.   Fig 2.
PUZZLE
a
LOCK
Fig 3.
Fig 4.

Witnesses;   Inventor;
                                    Abram Wright
                             George F. Wright

DESIGN.

T. A. BAILEY.
Toy Money-Box.
No. 8,257.   Patented April 6, 1875.

DESIGN.

J. G. BAKER.
TOY MONEY-BOX.
No. 8,820.   Patented Dec. 7, 1875.

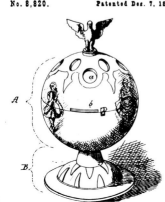

DESIGN.

T. SWANN.
Toy Banks.
No. 6,946.   Patented Oct. 7, 1873.
FIG 1.
CITY BANK
FIG 2.   FIG 3.

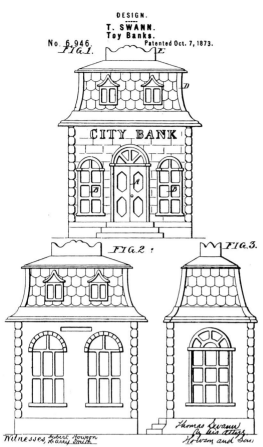

Witnesses   Thomas Swann

R. FRISBIE.
Toy Money-Boxes.
No. 140,358.   Patented July 1, 1873.

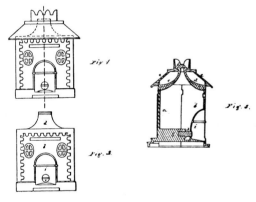

DESIGN.

C. W. CROTEAU.
Toy Money-Bank.
No. 8,655.   Patented Sept. 21, 1875.

165

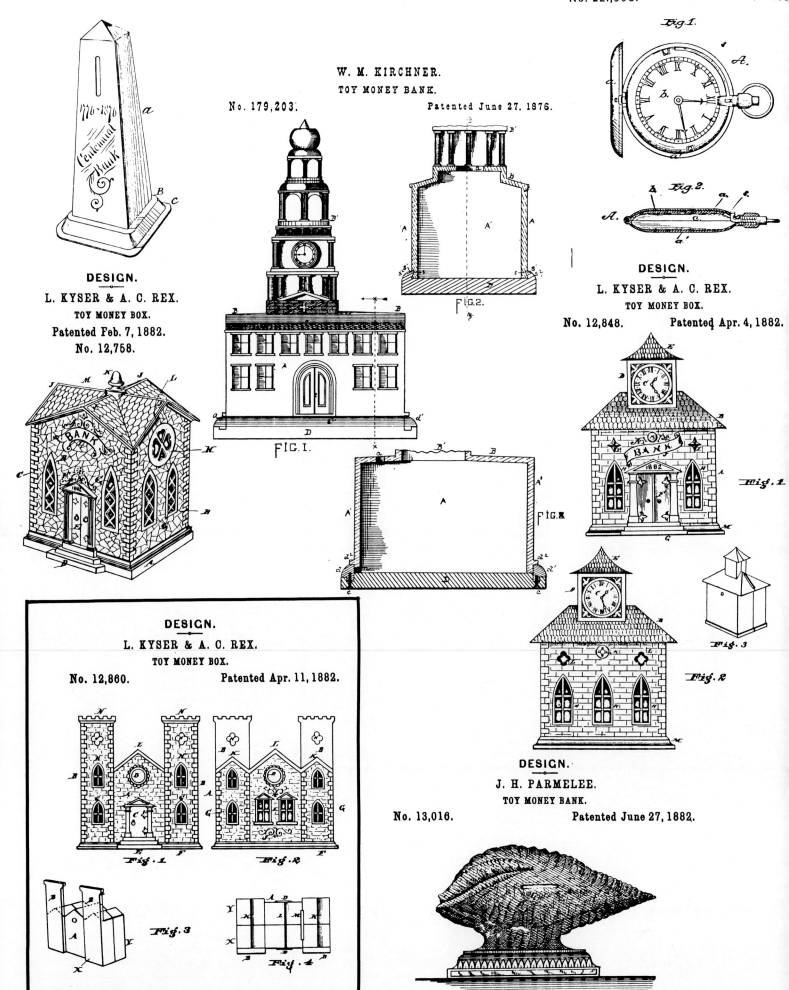

R. F. KANE.
TOY MONEY BOX.
No. 9,231. Patented April 18, 1876.

W. M. KIRCHNER.
TOY MONEY BANK.
No. 179,203. Patented June 27, 1876.

C. A. BAILEY.
Toy Money-Box.
No. 221,998. Patented Nov. 25, 1879.

DESIGN.
L. KYSER & A. C. REX.
TOY MONEY BOX.
Patented Feb. 7, 1882.
No. 12,758.

DESIGN.
L. KYSER & A. C. REX.
TOY MONEY BOX.
No. 12,848. Patented Apr. 4, 1882.

DESIGN.
L. KYSER & A. C. REX.
TOY MONEY BOX.
No. 12,860. Patented Apr. 11, 1882.

DESIGN.
J. H. PARMELEE.
TOY MONEY BANK.
No. 13,016. Patented June 27, 1882.

166

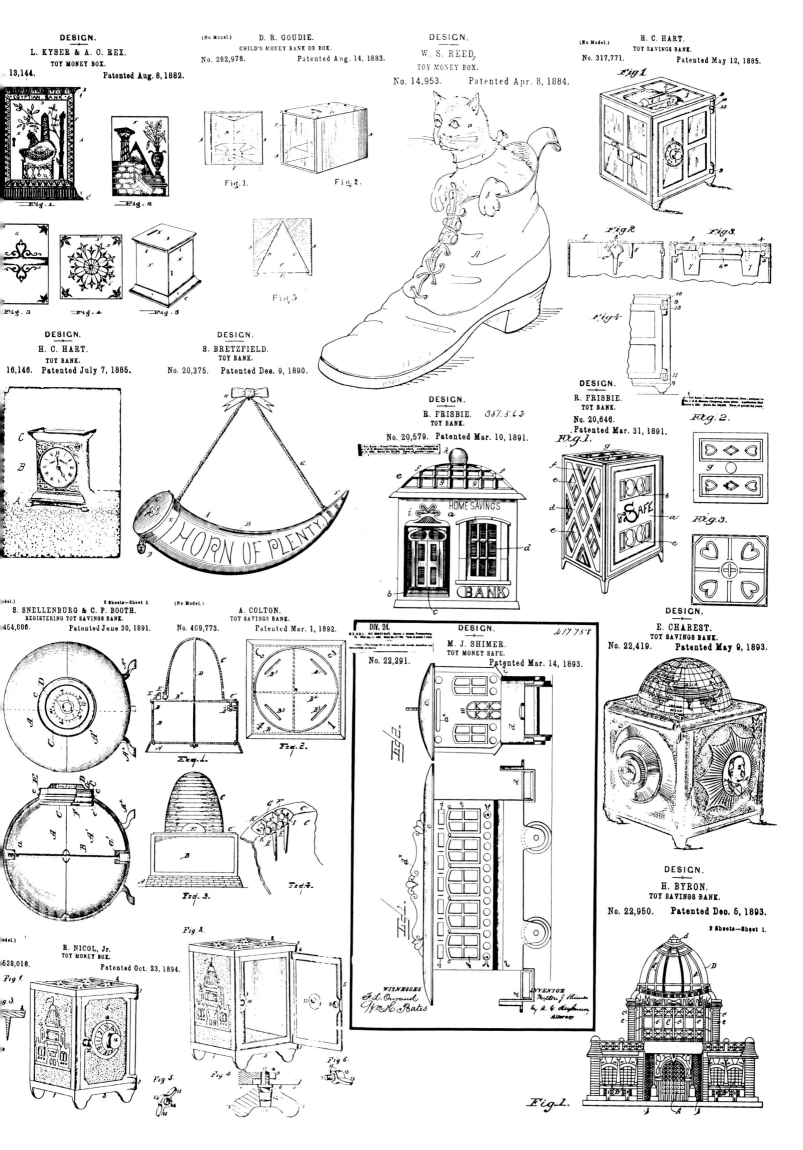

DESIGN.

L. KYSER & A. C. REX.

TOY MONEY BOX.

13,144. Patented Aug. 8, 1882.

(No Model.) D. R. GOUDIE.

CHILD'S MONEY BANK OR BOX.

No. 282,978. Patented Aug. 14, 1883.

DESIGN.

W. S. REED,

TOY MONEY BOX.

No. 14,953. Patented Apr. 8, 1884.

(No Model.) H. C. HART.

TOY SAVINGS BANK.

No. 317,771. Patented May 12, 1885.

DESIGN.

H. C. HART.

TOY BANK.

16,146. Patented July 7, 1885.

DESIGN.

S. BRETZFIELD.

TOY BANK.

No. 20,375. Patented Dec. 9, 1890.

DESIGN.

R. FRISBIE.

TOY BANK.

No. 20,579. Patented Mar. 10, 1891.

DESIGN.

R. FRISBIE.

TOY BANK.

No. 20,646. Patented Mar. 31, 1891.

S. SNELLENBURG & C. P. BOOTH.

REGISTERING TOY SAVINGS BANK.

454,086. Patented June 30, 1891.

(No Model.) A. COLTON.

TOY SAVINGS BANK.

No. 469,773. Patented Mar. 1, 1892.

DESIGN.

M. J. SHIMER.

TOY MONEY SAFE.

No. 22,291. Patented Mar. 14, 1893.

DESIGN.

E. CHAREST.

TOY SAVINGS BANK.

No. 22,419. Patented May 9, 1893.

DESIGN.

H. BYRON.

TOY SAVINGS BANK.

No. 22,950. Patented Dec. 5, 1893.

2 Sheets—Sheet 1.

R. NICOL, Jr.

TOY MONEY BOX.

528,018. Patented Oct. 23, 1894.

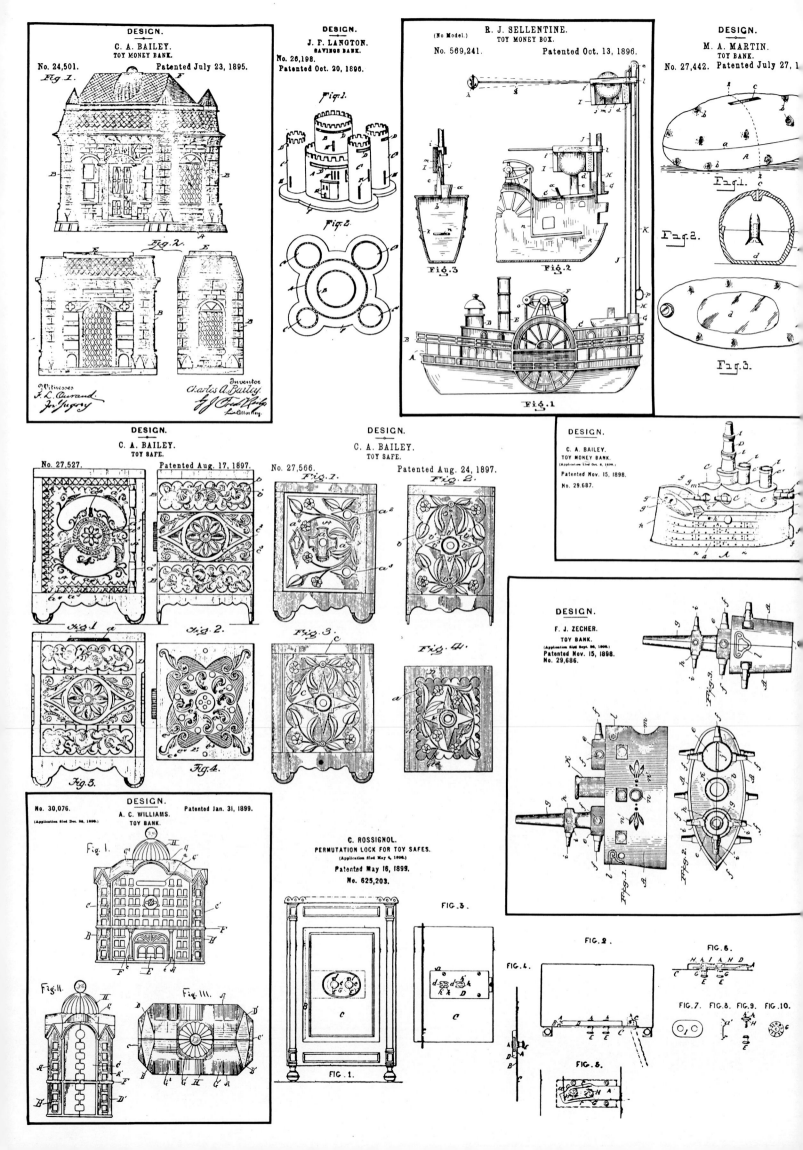

DESIGN.
C. A. BAILEY.
TOY MONEY BANK.
No. 24,501. Patented July 23, 1895.
Fig. 1.
Fig. 2.
Witnesses
F. L. Durand.
Jno. Gregory.
Inventor
Charles A. Bailey.

DESIGN.
J. F. LANGTON.
SAVINGS BANK.
No. 26,198.
Patented Oct. 20, 1896.
Fig. 1.
Fig. 2.

(No Model.)
R. J. SELLENTINE.
TOY MONEY BOX.
No. 569,241. Patented Oct. 13, 1896.
Fig. 3.
Fig. 2.
Fig. 1.

DESIGN.
M. A. MARTIN.
TOY BANK.
No. 27,442. Patented July 27, 1
Fig. 1.
Fig. 2.
Fig. 3.

DESIGN.
C. A. BAILEY.
TOY SAFE.
No. 27,527. Patented Aug. 17, 1897.
Fig. 1.
Fig. 2.
Fig. 3.
Fig. 4.

DESIGN.
C. A. BAILEY.
TOY SAFE.
No. 27,566. Patented Aug. 24, 1897.
Fig. 1.
Fig. 2.
Fig. 3.
Fig. 4.

DESIGN.
C. A. BAILEY.
TOY MONEY BANK.
(Application filed Oct. 8, 1898.)
Patented Nov. 15, 1898.
No. 29,687.

DESIGN.
F. J. ZECHER.
TOY BANK.
(Application filed Sept. 26, 1898.)
Patented Nov. 15, 1898.
No. 29,686.
Fig. 3.
Fig. 2.
Fig. 1.

DESIGN.
No. 30,076. Patented Jan. 31, 1899.
(Application filed Dec. 28, 1898.)
A. C. WILLIAMS.
TOY BANK.
Fig. 1.
Fig. II.
Fig. III.

C. ROSSIGNOL.
PERMUTATION LOCK FOR TOY SAFES.
(Application filed May 4, 1898.)
Patented May 16, 1899.
No. 625,203.
FIG. 1.
FIG. 2.
FIG. 3.
FIG. 4.
FIG. 5.
FIG. 6.
FIG. 7. FIG. 8. FIG. 9. FIG. 10.

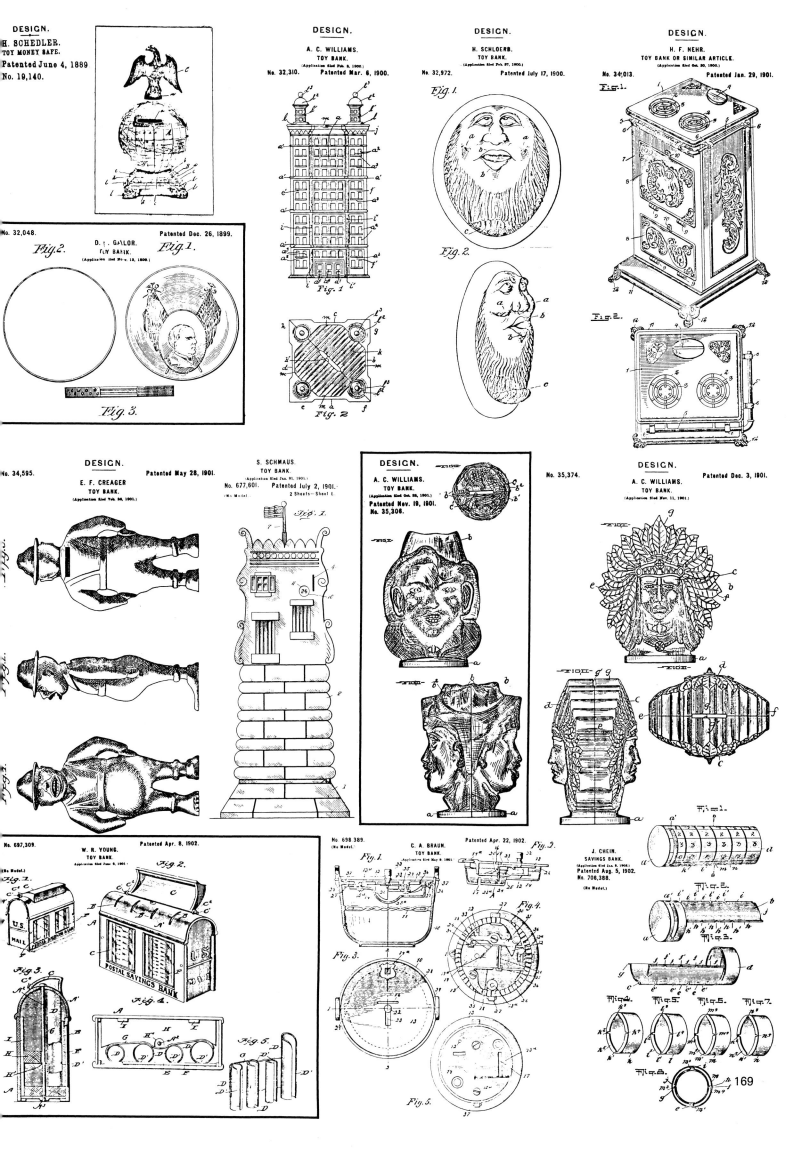

DESIGN.

H. SCHEDLER.
TOY MONEY SAFE.
Patented June 4, 1889.
No. 19,140.

No. 32,048.   Patented Dec. 26, 1899.
Fig.2.   D. I. GAILOR.   Fig.1.
TOY BANK.
(Application filed Nov. 18, 1899.)
Fig.3.

DESIGN.

A. C. WILLIAMS.
TOY BANK.
(Application filed Feb. 3, 1900.)
No. 32,310.   Patented Mar. 6, 1900.
Fig.1.
Fig.2.

DESIGN.

H. SCHLOERB.
TOY BANK.
(Application filed Feb. 27, 1900.)
No. 32,972.   Patented July 17, 1900.
Fig.1.
Fig.2.

DESIGN.

H. F. NEHR.
TOY BANK OR SIMILAR ARTICLE.
(Application filed Oct. 20, 1900.)
No. 34,013.   Patented Jan. 29, 1901.
Fig.1.
Fig.2.

DESIGN.

No. 34,595.   Patented May 28, 1901.
E. F. CREAGER
TOY BANK.
(Application filed Feb. 26, 1901.)

S. SCHMAUS.
TOY BANK.
(Application filed Jan. 21, 1901.)
No. 677,601.   Patented July 2, 1901.
2 Sheets—Sheet 1.
(No Model.)
Fig.1.

DESIGN.

A. C. WILLIAMS.
TOY BANK.
(Application filed Oct. 23, 1901.)
Patented Nov. 19, 1901.
No. 35,306.
Fig.1.

No. 35,374.   Patented Dec. 3, 1901.
A. C. WILLIAMS.
TOY BANK.
(Application filed Nov. 11, 1901.)

No. 697,309.   Patented Apr. 8, 1902.
W. R. YOUNG.
TOY BANK.
(Application filed June 6, 1901.)
(No Model.)
Fig.1.   Fig.2.
US MAIL
POSTAL SAVINGS BANK
Fig.3.   Fig.4.
Fig.5.

No. 698,389.   Patented Apr. 22, 1902.
(No Model.)   C. A. BRAUN.
TOY BANK.
(Application filed May 6, 1901.)
Fig.1.   Fig.2.
Fig.3.   Fig.4.
Fig.5.

J. CHEIN.
SAVINGS BANK.
(Application filed Jan. 8, 1902.)
Patented Aug. 5, 1902.
No. 706,388.
(No Model.)
Fig.1.
Fig.2.
Fig.3.
Fig.4.   Fig.5.   Fig.6.   Fig.7.
Fig.8.

169

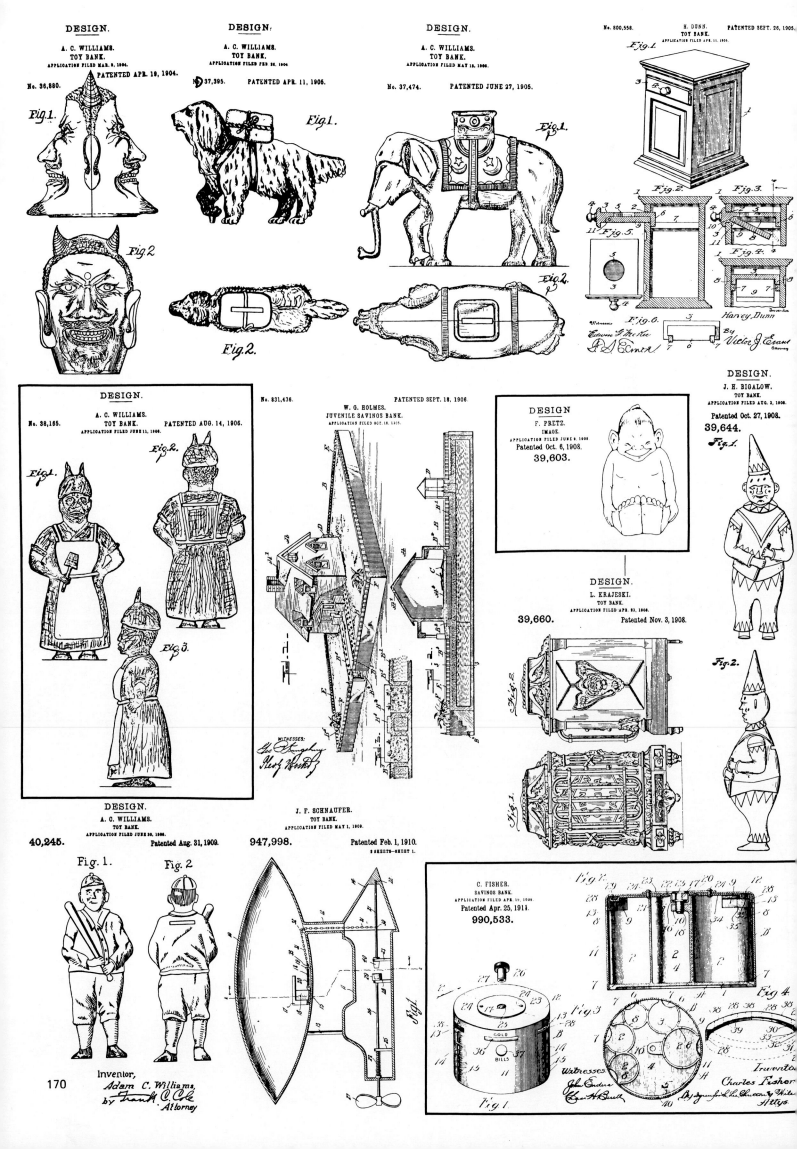

DESIGN.

A. C. WILLIAMS.
TOY BANK.
APPLICATION FILED MAR. 9, 1904.

No. 36,880.   PATENTED APR. 19, 1904.

Fig.1.

Fig.2

DESIGN.

A. C. WILLIAMS.
TOY BANK.
APPLICATION FILED FEB 26, 1904

No. 37,395.   PATENTED APR. 11, 1905.

Fig.1.

Fig.2.

DESIGN.

A. C. WILLIAMS.
TOY BANK.
APPLICATION FILED MAY 16, 1905.

No. 37,474.   PATENTED JUNE 27, 1905.

Fig.1.

Fig.2.

No. 800,558.   H. DUNN.   PATENTED SEPT. 26, 1905.
TOY BANK.
APPLICATION FILED APR. 11, 1905.

Fig.1.

Fig.2.   Fig.3.

Fig.5.   Fig.4.

Fig.6.

Harvey Dunn

By

Victor J. Evans
Attorney

DESIGN.

A. C. WILLIAMS.
TOY BANK.
APPLICATION FILED JUNE 11, 1906.

No. 38,165.   PATENTED AUG. 14, 1906.

Fig.1.   Fig.2.

Fig.3.

No. 831,436.   PATENTED SEPT. 18, 1906.
W. G. HOLMES.
JUVENILE SAVINGS BANK.
APPLICATION FILED OCT. 16, 1905.

WITNESSES:

DESIGN

F. PRETZ.
IMAGE.
APPLICATION FILED JUNE 9, 1908.
Patented Oct. 6, 1908.
39,603.

DESIGN.

L. KRAJESKI.
TOY BANK.
APPLICATION FILED APR. 23, 1908.

39,660.   Patented Nov. 3, 1908.

DESIGN.

J. H. BIGALOW.
TOY BANK.
APPLICATION FILED AUG. 3, 1908.

Patented Oct. 27, 1908.

39,644.

Fig.1.

Fig.2.

DESIGN.

A. C. WILLIAMS.
TOY BANK.
APPLICATION FILED JUNE 30, 1906.

40,245.   Patented Aug. 31, 1909.

Fig. 1.   Fig. 2

Inventor,
Adam C. Williams,
by
Attorney

170

947,998.   J. F. SCHNAUFER.
TOY BANK.
APPLICATION FILED MAY 1, 1909.

Patented Feb. 1, 1910.
2 SHEETS—SHEET 1.

C. FISHER.
SAVINGS BANK.
APPLICATION FILED APR. 19, 1909.
Patented Apr. 25, 1911.
990,533.

GOLD
BILLS

Fig.1.

Witnesses

Inventor
Charles Fisher
Attys.

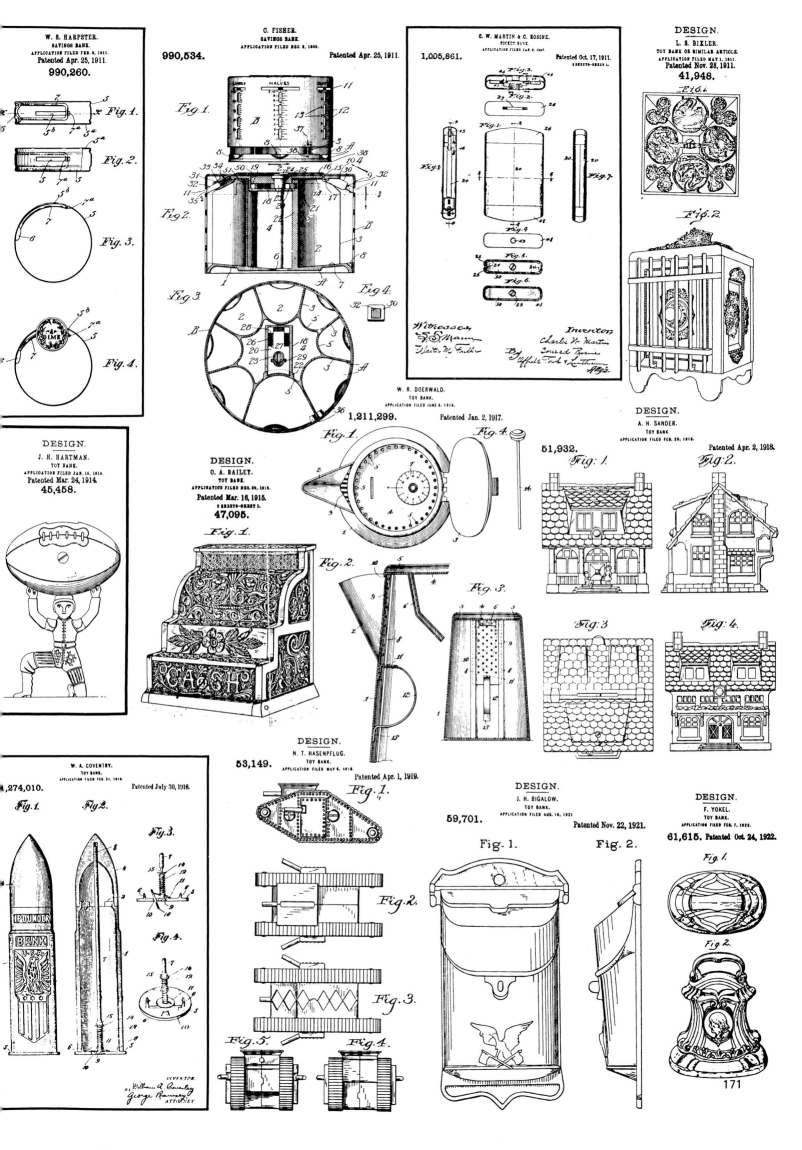

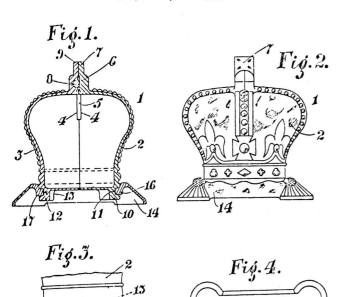

Fig.1. Fig.2. Fig.3. Fig.4. Fig.5.

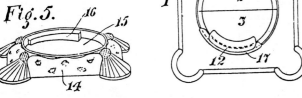

[This Drawing is a reproduction of the Original on a reduced scale]

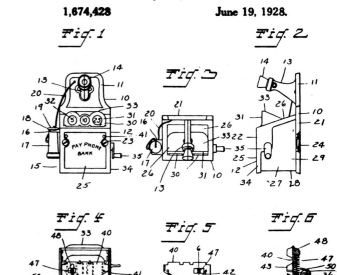

1,674,428   June 19, 1928.

Fig.1 Fig.2 Fig.3 Fig.4 Fig.5 Fig.6 Fig.8 Fig.7

J. McC. NELSON
TOY BANK
Filed Jan. 2, 1929

Dec. 3, 1929.   Des 80,040

M DE CESARE
COIN REGISTERING TOY BANK
Filed Dec. 18, 1935

May 4, 1937.   2,079,202

THE WISE PIG
SAVE A PENNY YESTERDAY
ANOTHER SAVE TO DAY
TO MORROW SAVE ANOTHER ONE
TO KEEP THE WOLF AWAY

THRIFTY

Fig.1.   Fig.2.

INVENTOR
Jessie McCutcheon Nelson,
BY
Hit ATTORNEY

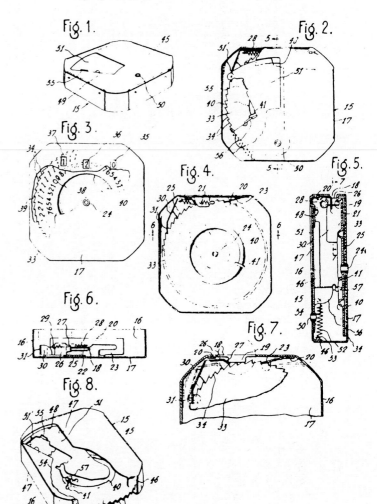

Fig.1. Fig.2. Fig.3. Fig.4. Fig.5. Fig.6. Fig.7. Fig.8.

ENGLISH REGISTRY AND PATENT NUMBERS

Patent Numbers

Most patented English banks are mechanicals, having patentable operating devices. An exception is *Alice in Wonderland*, which is a puzzle bank rather than a mechanical. After filling the bank with coins, the operator pulls a brass plate from a sleeve at the bottom. A hinged plate with Alice's picture (previously hidden) falls down; but alas! No coins fall out. A spring-loaded false bottom holds the coins in place until it is pushed askew, releasing them. This marvelous device was issued Patent #18808/07 in 1909. To trace any English patent, one must know the year in which it was granted, as many of the same numbers were used each year.

Registry Numbers

An English bank which bears an *Rd* or Registry Number can be easily traced, as registry numbers were issued consecutively over many years. Knowing a bank's number can lead to the year it was made. A list of known registry numbers follows; it may help the reader date English banks for which he has a registry number.

ENGLISH PATENTS

Those marked in bold type are exact dates.

33821	Wimbleton, Mechanical	**9/21/1885**
180427	County Bank	c1892
187029	Space Heater/Bird	c1892
187212	Clock with Moveable Hands	c1892
196844	Giant in Tower	**8/13/1892**
202983	Spaceheater/Beehive	c1893
203386	Spaceheater/Floral	c1893
210265	Chicago Bank	c1893
247278	Spaceheater/Cupid	c1895
247326	Football, Mechanical	**1/7/1895**
254734	Top Hat with Gold Band	c1895
292270	Industry Shall be Rewarded/Beehive	c1897
296880	Hoopla	**4/5/1897**
393170	King Edward Crown	c1901
454718	Victorian Coins - tin	c1907
454734	Top Hat - tin	c1907
480274	Villa	c1908
482034	Lichfield Cathedral	c1908
484712	Castle	c1908
499017	Blackpool Tower	c1908
502035	Westminster Abbey	c1908
502036	Bear Stealing Honey	c1908
526518	Eiffel Tower	c1908
542573	John Bull, Mechanical	**5/21/1909**
546486	I Luv a Copper/Two-Faced, brass	c1909
551222	Every Copper Helps; small	**10/20/1909**
568641	Gollywog	**8/22/1910**
574268	Every Copper Helps; large, brass	c1910-1911
581285	Dinah, Mechanical	**3/29/1911**
610047	Poor Weary Willie	c1912
624637	Tally Ho	c1913
640673	Hanging Stork	**8/1/1914**
646486	I Luv a Copper, brass	c1914
664401	Tommy's Tin Hat	c1917
670140	Recruit	c1918
680237	Minstrel Growing Bank	c1920
685799	Brass Teacup	c1920
694628	Milk Can	c1922

766563	Kiltie, Mechanical	**7/29/1931**
768382	Little Moe, Mechanical	**11/4/1931**
775608	Guest Hospital	c1932
781501	Elephant with Drum	c1933
781602	Bonzo with Suitcase	**3/17/1933**
793340	Mickey Mouse/Mandolin	c1934
844290	Jolly Nigger-Starkie's Patent	**8/27/1945**
872932	Six-Penny Piece Bank	c1954

WHITING-PENNY DOOR CONVERSION NUMBERS

1.	164	2.	241	3.	85	5.	34
6.	33	7.	8	8.	177	9.	182
10.	18	11.	10	12.	11	13.	157
14.	45	15.	44	16.	29	17.	168
18.	173	19.	166	20.	176	21.	5
22.	15	23.	320	24.	16	25.	17
26.	36	27.	264	28.	210	29.	211
30.	59	31.	56	32.	61	33.	63
34.	25	35.	181	36.	180	37.	37
38.	38	39.	228	40.	48	41.	31
42.	170	43.	83	44.	84	45.	163
46.	24	47.	13	48.	81	49.	75
50.	74	51.	79	52.	86	53.	358
54.	359	55.	486	56.	509	57.	746
58.	753	59.	483	60.	484	61.	747
62.	480	63.	474	64.	1630	65.	470
66.	445	67.	472	68.	459	69.	457
70.	455	71.	453	72.	450	73.	449
74.	467	75.	446	76.	513	77.	517
78.	520	79.	507	80.	527	81.	533
82.	532	83.	508	84.	508	85.	531
86.	523	87.	512	88.	50	89.	754
90.	755	91.	759	92.	764	93.	763
94.	742	95.	760	96.	568	97.	569
98.	566	99.	574	100.	570	101.	565
102.	396	103.	409	104.	412	105.	357
106.	439	107.	440	108.	435	109.	418
110.	419	111.	405	112.	421	113.	437
114.	413	115.	407	116.	849	117.	837
118.	848	119.	859	120.	858	121.	851
122.	853	123.	852	124.	855	125.	932
126.	842	127.	838	128.	835	129.	1363
130.	1354	131.	1364	132.	1356	133.	1351
134.	1344	136.	821	137.	829	138.	1357
139.	1341	140.	822	141.	820	142.	1440
143.	1439	144.	1452	145.	1462	146.	1452
147.	1454	148.	1459	150.	1461	151.	282
152.	1606	153.	1549	154.	1246	156.	1371
157.	1487	158.	1493	159.	1486	160.	1424
161.	1435	162.	1437	163.	1438	164.	1471
165.	1425	166.	1469	167.	1399	168.	524
169.	1308	170.	974	171.	1428	172.	1539
174.	602	175.	609	176.	608	177.	629
178.	606	179.	582	181.	607	182.	603
183.	578	184.	623	185.	613	186.	541
187.	548	188.	544	189.	542	190.	555
191.	601	192.	595	193.	587	194.	585
195.	736	196.	737	197.	500	198.	499
199.	732	200.	553	201.	767	202.	768
203.	597	204.	598	205.	561	206.	563
207.	556	208.	560	209.	664	210.	549
211.	615	212.	643	213.	612	214.	614
215.	628	216.	1642	217.	1540	218.	1542
219.	1548	220.	1608	221.	1534	222.	1541
223.	1537	224.	1544	225.	1546	226.	1545
227.	1604	228.	976	230.	311	231.	52
232.	946	233.	1481	234.	1479	235.	1253
236.	743	237.	1330	238.	104	239.	524
240.	783	241.	925	242.	927	243.	926
244.	364	245.	369	246.	701	247.	352
248.	366	249.	1457	250.	660	251.	718
252.	721	253.	546	255.	676	256.	770
257.	696	258.	1376	259.	1380	260.	1381
261.	380	262.	594	263.	769	265.	1468
266.	1228	267.	1213	268.	1166	269.	1164
270.	967	271.	1210	272.	955	273.	780
274.	797	275.	786	276.	1172	277.	1375
279.	809	280.	807	281.	782	282.	958
283.	909	284.	923	285.	908	286.	907
287.	913	288.	1153	289.	224	291.	215
292.	1664	293.	1622	294.	54	295.	1262
296.	1266	297.	1023	298.	1020	299.	1621
300.	997	301.	1663	302.	1005	303.	928
304.	1010	305.	1145	306.	1146	307.	1147
308.	1170	309.	120	310.	118	311.	126
312.	150	313.	122	315.	109	315.	875
316.	222	317.	154	318.	110	319.	865
320.	1087	321.	1316	322.	624	323.	616
324.	630	325.	619	327.	717	328.	714
329.	713	330.	715	331.	698	332.	1007
333.	1019	334.	414	335.	349	336.	443
337.	417	338.	416	340.	319	341.	1636
342.	192	343.	6	344.	66	345.	1236
346.	882	347.	885	348.	884	349.	883
350.	881	351.	880	352.	1142	353.	1227
354.	954	355.	1002	356.	1003	357.	1000
358.	1008	359.	1006	360.	1048	361.	1319
362.	1233	363.	1314	364.	1049	366.	1122
367.	1229	368.	1125	369.	1126	370.	1121
371.	1082	372.	956	373.	1226	374.	886
375.	1237	376.	1179	377.	999	378.	1118
379.	1053	380.	1111	381.	959	382.	856
385.	1420	386.	1041	387.	1042	388.	1011

389. 1012	392. 1652	393. 298	395. 828
397. 895	398. 901	399. 1072	400. 1099
401. 998	402. 680	403. 1143	404. 993
405. 949	407. 537	408. 992	409. 1161
410. 1159	411. 1241	412. 1240	413. 1239
414. 1238	415. 1178	416. 1177	417. 1176
418. 1217	419. 1215	420. 1220	421. 1183
422. 1182	423. 1181	424. 1180	425. 1167
426. 1168	427. 1635	428. 1073	429. 1077
430. 1070	431. 1069	432. 1134	433. 1116
434. 1133	435. 904	436. 1101	437. 1198
438. 1200	439. 1199	440. 1538	441. 1078
442. 1085	443. 1081	444. 1633	445. 1080
446. 1079	447. 1242	448. 991	449. 1211
450. 990	451. 1244	452. 1243	

564. 1023	565. 1030	569. 1210	570. 1209
572. 1636	573. 1178	574. 1177	575. 1176
576. 1184	577. 1229	578. 1201	579. 988
580. 991	582. 1116	583. 1004	584. 1201
586. 1169	587. 1168	588. 1298	589. 1296
590. 1104	591. 1059	594. 995	595. 1247
596. 1246	597. 1240	598. 1239	599. 1238
601. 1006	602. 1633	603. 1085	604. 1013
605. 1013	607. 976	609. 1113	610. 1208
611. 1198	612. 1170	614. 1053	616. 1139
617. 1049	618. 1048	619. 958	620. 973
621. 974	622. 1196	623. 1052	625. 1042
626. 1041	627. 1040	628. 1045	629. 1072
630. 217	633. 40	639. 282	640. 20
642. 296	643. 307	644. 55	646. 76
647. 74	648. 80	649. 73	650. 14
651. 79	652. 110	653. 3	654. 39V
655. 45	656. 47	661. 10	665. 278
666. 144	667. 241	668. 508	669. 163
670. 5	671. 38	672. 165	673. 298
674. 299	675. 209	676. 207	678. 6
679. 211	681. 210	683. 271	685. 244
686. 234	687. 233	688. 232	689. 321
690. 285	691. 280	695. 31	696. 30
699. 33	700. 295	701. 259	702. 180
703. 17	704. 255	706. 16	707. 181
708. 141	709. 108	710. 134	711. 133
712. 308	715. 71	719. 195	722. 11
723. 326	725. 123	727. 12	728. 54
729. 115	731. 114	732. 316	733. 167
736. 85	737. 86	738. 275	740. 302
743. 161	747. 43	749. 338	751. 228
752. 224	753. 235	754. 221	755. 231
757. 215	758. 226	759. 237	760. 239
762. 223	763. 7	771. 292	772. 301
773. 314	774. 13	775. 142	776. 185
779. 124	780. 125	782. 25	785. 132
786. 131	787. 176	788. 168	790. 37
791. 273	792. 164	793. 34	794. 201
795. 202	796. 203	797. 36	798. 327
799. 260	800. 1228	801. 23	802. 177
803. 157	806. 170	807. 140	808. 312
809. 216	811. 186	812. 66	813. 192
814. 109	815. 150	816. 159	817. 171
818. 171V	819. 281	820. 182	821. 162
822. 89	823. 90	825. 264	826. 265
827. 311	828. 148	829. 145	831. 120
832. 75	833. 247	836. 28-29	837. 272
840. 103	841. 62	842. 59	843. 61
844. 64	845. 104	846. 105	849. 98
850. 58	851. 97	852. 60	853. 24
854. 158	855. 26	856. 173	857. 191
860. 293	861. 96	862. 8	863. 48
864. 44	865. 1164	866. 1165	867. 1166
869. 300	872. 1	874. 154	875. 149
878. 112	880. 153	881. 136	882. 121
883. 119	885. 84	886. 83	887. 170
888. 1315	889. 1319	890. 1320	891. 1317
892. 1311	893. 1312	895. 1327	896. 1326
897. 1325	899. 1329	900. 1313	901. 1282
904. 1484	907. 1618	910. 667	919. 798
920. 787	922. 779	923. 785	924. 791
925. 783	927. 804	942. 1374	943. 1375
945. 1270V	946. 1270	947. 1601	950. 1353
952. 1364	954. 1362	955. 1363	956. 1365
958. 1337	959. 1371	964. 1590	968. 1310
969. 825	972. 840	975. 1253	977. 821
978. 833	979. 829	980. 831	982. 819
983. 820	985. 822	986. 827	987. 826
989. 823	990. 1330	991. 1331	992. 1338
993. 1332	995. 1334	997. 1333	1000. 1368
1004. 1357	1005. 1356	1010. 1354	1016. 1350
1017. 1349	1020. 1346	1024. 1341	1027. 844
1035. 824	1037. 858	1038. 861	1039. 848
1040. 859	1041. 860	1042. 842	1043. 841
1045. 856	1046. 845	1047. 849	1048. 852
1049. 851	1051. 855	1053. 854	1054. 854
1055. 834	1056. 839	1058. 838	1059. 837
1060. 835-836	1072. 1604	1081. 1608	1082. 1608
1083. 683	1084. 682	1085. 1308	1097. 903
1098. 901	1100. 1425	1101. 1429	1102. 1418
1103. 933	1104. 925	1105. 932	1106. 930
1107. 931	1111. 926	1116. 944	1117. 1545
1119. 1258	1120. 1314	1131. 1485	1132. 1194
1143. 1422	1149. 524	1151. 1278	1152. 1581
1159. 1262	1168. 1263	1170. 1264	1172. 94
1178. 1622	1179. 1420	1180. 1413	1181. 1408
1182. 1400	1183. 1411	1184. 1302	1186. 1481
1187. 1479	1190. 535	1195. 665	1196. 661
1200. 1272	1201. 1256	1202. 1328	1208. 678
1214. 218	1226. 1297	1292. 1583	1346. 1575
1349. 589	1364. 1577	1370. 1576	1372. 1584
1382. 1261	1392. 892	1403. 882	1406. 906
1408. 870	1416. 867	1418. 872	1420. 863
1421. 864	1424. 873	1425. 812	1428. 883
1430. 896	1441. 877	1442. 866	1444. 880
1445. 887	1446. 869	1447. 888	1450. 874
1452. 891	1454. 886	1456. 895	1460. 914
1461. 910	1462. 923	1466. 952	1469. 1360
1470. 204	1471. 935	1472. 936	1473. 928
1474. 929	1478. 1268	1479. 875	1481. 949
1488. 941	1500. 1539	1501. 1552	1508. 1544
1509. 1546	1511. 1537	1513. 1540	1515. 1541
1517. 1535	1521. 1555	1522. 1542	1525. 1548
1527. 1556	1530. 1549	1536. 1423	1537. 1432
1538. 1431	1539. 1428	1540. 1490	1542. 1487
1543. 1478	1545. 1494	1546. 1497	1547. 1525
1548. 1486	1551. 1502	1556. 1507	1559. 1506
1560. 1483	1561. 1523	1565. 1505	1566. 1510

LONG-PENNY DOOR CONVERSION NUMBERS

2. 704	6. 712	7. 710	8. 713
9. 713V	10. 720	11. 714	12. 693
16. 695	17. 696	19. 715-16	20. 698
22. 560	23. 557	24. 556	27. 555
29. 768	30. 767	32. 772	33. 771
34. 770	35. 769	36. 367	37. 371
39. 347	40. 368	43. 398	44. 358
45. 352	46. 350	47. 370	48. 364
52. 349	53. 351	54. 659	55. 553
57. 544	58. 540	59. 736	60. 737
61. 380	62. 444	63. 440	64. 345
66. 377	67. 421	69. 413	72. 357
73. 396	74. 403	75. 401	76. 363
77. 414	82. 318	84. 389	85. 429
90. 379	93. 359	94. 439	95. 437
96. 436	97. 408	98. 399	102. 400
104. 417	105. 443	107. 411	108. 407
110. 405	113. 416	114. 442	115. 376
116. 412	118. 428	119. 433	121. 419
122. 435	124. 430	126. 361	127. 385
128. 418	129. 409	130. 431	132. 422
133. 499	134. 500	135. 492	136. 495
138. 497	139. 497	140. 498	143. 503
144. 496	145. 1642	146. 1059	148. 410
151. 454V	152. 462	153. 472	154. 470
155. 460	156. 44	159. 451	160. 486
161. 483	162. 484	163. 446	166. 450
168. 468	171. 453	172. 452	173. 471
174. 445	177. 447V	178. 447V	179. 447
180. 487	181. 494	183. 464	186. 469
187. 457	188. 457	189. 459	190. 474
193. 455	194. 448	195. 725	197. 731
199. 680	200. 680V	201. 573	202. 594
203. 718	206. 533	207. 532	209. 523
210. 531	211. 513	212. 514	213. 520
214. 521	215. 510	216. 509	217. 512
218. 517	219. 527	220. 507	222. 757
223. 754	224. 755	225. 756	226. 759
227. 758	228. 765	229. 764	230. 742
231. 752	232. 747	233. 753	234. 753
235. 746	236. 760	237. 751	238. 778
241. 741	242. 1277	243. 743	244. 775
248. 740	249. 489	251. 705	253. 639
258. 623	259. 613	260. 331	261. 602
262. 603	263. 631	264. 629	266. 582V
269. 582	270. 641	271. 604	273. 609
276. 606	277. 583	282. 625	286. 561
287. 563	288. 574	289. 652V	291. 565
292. 569	296. 570	297. 568	298. 566
301. 721	302. 732	303. 595	304. 601
305. 596	306. 660	307. 909	308. 939
311. 940	318. 908	319. 907	321. 575
323. 917	324. 919	327. 911	330. 813
331. 782	332. 784	333. 792	334. 786
335. 811	336. 793	341. 816	342. 664
343. 647	345. 663	348. 615	349. 619
354. 616	355. 645	356. 624	358. 676
359. 677	361. 1410	362. 612V	363. 614
364. 628	365. 610	366. 612	368. 549
370. 546	372. 597	375. 598	376. 656
377. 657	378. 668	380. 679	381. 689
383. 548	384. 547	385. 551	386. 543
387. 541	388. 214	389. 651	390. 690
391. 734	392. 586	393. 585	394. 1122
395. 1122	397. 1124	398. 1125	399. 1158
400. 959	403. 1147V	404. 1147	405. 1147
406. 1146	408. 1227	409. 1226	410. 1150
411. 1011	412. 1180	413. 1181	414. 1183
415. 1220	416. 1219	417. 1005	418. 1007
420. 975	421. 1008	424. 997	425. 1163
426. 1087	427. 1090	428. 1094	429. 1092
430. 1233	431. 1134	433. 1133	434. 1179
435. 996	437. 1187	442. 1138V	443. 1141
444. 984	445. 983	446. 985	452. 1152
453. 1123	454. 1088	455. 1114	456. 980V
457. 1064	458. 1067	460. 966	462. 987
466. 986	469. 954	470. 1084	471. 1111
472. 1099	473. 998	474. 1070	475. 1073
476. 1118	477. 1063	478. 1001	479. 1002
480. 1637	482. 1035	484. 1018	491. 1214
492. 1213	493. 1212	494. 1110	496. 963
497. 1075	498. 1074	499. 1071	501. 1047
502. 1046	503. 1632	504. 1162	505. 1159
506. 1172	507. 1190	508. 1188	509. 1061
512. 1010	514. 1016	515. 1029	517. 1430
526. 1019	527. 1232V	528. 1236	541. 999
542. 1143	543. 993	544. 992	545. 1211
546. 1243	547. 1242	548. 1242	549. 1244
550. 1207	552. 1057	553. 1119	555. 1117
556. 967	557. 1020	558. 1032	559. 968
560. 960	561. 1024	562. 1027	563. 1022

1569. 1503	1570. 1493	1571. 1491	1572. 1499
1573. 1500	1575. 1533	1577. 1465	1579. 1439
1580. 1440	1581. 1441	1582. 1450	1583. 1452
1584. 1448	1585. 1446	1586. 1461	1587. 1460
1588. 1458	1589. 1459	1590. 1457	1592. 1464
1593. 1463	1599. 1477	1600. 1475	1602. 1469
1603. 1471	1604. 1474	1605. 1472	1606. 1473
1607. 1424	1610. 1437	1611. 1435	1612. 1414
1614. 1438	1616. 1419	1617. 1417	1621. 1396
1622. 1395	1623. 1394	1625. 1381	1627. 1380
1628. 1379	1629. 1391	1630. 1376	1631. 1387
1632. 1383	1634. 1404	1635. 1390	1636. 1404
1638. 1386	1640. 1266	1642. 1585	1644. 1586
1646. 1587	1649. 1279		

SBCCA/PENNY DOOR CONVERSION NUMBERS

1. 1470	2. 1472	3. 946	4. 946
5. 1312	6. 798	7. 1204	8. 1293
9. 1553	10. 373	13. 1391	14. 846
15. 840	16. 910	17. 464	19. 330
20. 1140	22. 1057	23. 136	26. 1290
27. 984	28. 202	29. 295	30. 1090
31. 376	32. 259	33. 1047	34. 778
35. 1138	36. 1141	37. 1074	38. 890
42. 587	43. 462	44. 683	45. 1382
47. 1013	48. 660	49. 1009	50. 1105
51. 313	52. 699	53. 1613	54. 1554
55. 1261	56. 1615	57. 1018	58. 454
59. 455	60. 393	61. 1431	62. 1474
63. 80	65. 934	66. 245	69. 751
70. 195	71. 1302	72. 1302	73. 417
74. 432	77. 441	80. 1352	81. 960
82. 341	83. 931	84. 930	86. 808
87. 812	88. 1108	89. 1108	90. 970
91. 824	93. 558	94. 65	95. 67
97. 1423	98. 1601	99. 1031	100. 825
101. 646	103. 125	104. 1159	105. 1160
106. 1161	107. 1162	108. 256	109. 176
111. 1061	112. 124	113. 422	114. 833
115. 826	116. 1332	117. 1338	118. 827
119. 951	120. 1610	121. 1378	122. 452
123. 1187	124. 635	125. 945	126. 250
127. 567	128. 1591	129. 593	130. 943
131. 1139	132. 132	133. 132	135. 1285
136. 805	137. 1235	138. 1235	139. 1348
140. 107	141. 510	142. 42	143. 239
144. 659	145. 400	145A. 1379	146. 390
147. 226	148. 90	149. 80	150. 421
153. 1586	154. 388	155. 389	156. 378
157. 343	158. 388	159. 159	161. 1030
162. 777	163. 1329	164. 1272	165. 1272
166. 1441	167. 194	168. 193	169. 1384
170. 342	172. 140	173. 1432	175. 1149
177. 395	178. 410	179. 739	180. 270
181. 278	182. 580	183. 1065	184. 1065
185. 487	186. 488	187. 1342	188. 1341
189. 831	190. 1422	191. 469	192. 1355
193. 1374	194. 1096	195. 1307	196. 854
197. 866	198. 1171	199. 888	200. 1249
201. 1616	202. 1270	203. 908	204. 1088
205. 505	206. 148	207. 1104	208. 208
209. 515	210. 448	211. 771	212. 903
213. 903	214. 257	215. 1144	216. 741
219. 1303	225. 724	226. 645	227. 1110
228. 572	231. 1577	240. 1599	241. 889
242. 1026	243. 597	245. 413	246. 372
248. 918	250. 1485	251. 896	252. 1216
253. 213	254. 1188	256. 573	257. 912
258. 1449	259. 1448	260. 1446	261. 444
262. 306	263. 289	264. 482	265. 1447
266. 1349	267. 912	270. 420	271. 87
272. 355	273. 978	274. 1060	275. 781
276. 789	277. 772	278. 503	279. 279V
280. 391	281. 70	282. 70	283. 986
285. 304V	286. 1420	287. 1408	288. 1413
289. 1312	290. 1205	291. 1135	292. 1155
293. 1201	294. 351	295. 705	297. 419
299. 385	300. 276	301. 384	302. 1619
303. 416	304. 280	305. 285	306. 265
307. 263	311. 800	312. 361	313. 370
314. 303	315. 940	316. 436	317. 451
318. 536	319. 1353	320. 430	323. 1154
325. 834	326. 338	327. 247	328. 60
329. 968	330. 264	331. 1094	332. 218
333. 219	334. 1315	335. 335	336. 336
337. 347	338. 1614	339. 845	340. 996
341. 672	342. 671	343. 861	344. 1195
345. 1017	346. 1445	347. 1414	348. 442
349. 1419	350. 1476	351. 1482	352. 1417
353. 1184	354. 40	355. 857	356. 196
358. 206	359. 206	360. 519	361. 1086
362. 1119	363. 115	364. 1114	365. 1326
366. 1327	367. 953	371. 209	372. 201
375. 767	377. 255	379. 479	381. 522
383. 1350	386. 217	388. 1040	389. 55
391. 668	392. 1346	393. 691	394. 684
395. 417	397. 534	400. 679	403. 656
404. 551	405. 1612	406. 1407	407. 1245
409. 1410	411. 348	413. 71	415. 690
416. 191	417. 193	420. 221	421. 477
424. 272	427. 108	428. 475	429. 476
431. 1281	435. 514	437. 345	438. 1029
439. 651	442. 43	443. 577	444. 199
445. 1151	449. 785	450. 779	453. 596
455. 752	456. 1284	457. 667	458. 677
461. 575	462. 112	463. 1005	464. 1266
467. 1493	468. 1490	469. 1482	474. 1234
475. 1028	478. 408	485. 1550	486. 232

487. 233	488. 221	489. 235	490. 1006
491. 496	492. 493	497. 704	498. 498
503. 403	504. 299	505. 298	506. 731
507. 1429	510. 162	511. 23	512. 1359
518. 612	520. 1460	523. 1064	525. 302
526. 302	527. 641	529. 1102	532. 1296
533. 962	534. 248	536. 1310	539. 32
541. 47	542. 45	543. 46	544. 29
545. 27	546. 371	549. 1158	550. 327
553. 158	563. 363	565. 455	568. 445
572. 1386	573. 1106	574. 1309	577. 214
582. 411	589. 185	592. 260	598. 1201
600. 413	601. 713	604. 175	605. 96
610. 1590	615. 983	617. 900	621. 1323
623. 1190	626. 1392	627. 1586	629. 1404
630. 1402V	631. 287	634. 1277	636. 436
637. 439	639. 994	640. 592	641. 877
642. 948	648. 763	650. 726	651. 1396
656. 1439	659. 981	662. 784	663. 1498
665. 1457	674. 12	675. 461	679. 431
680. 625	682. 1433	683. 892	687. 1579
688. 1580	689. 647	699. 678	700. 518
702. 1409	703. 1421	705. 787	708. 644
713. 1112	714. 237	716. 1473	717. 638
722. 1528	724. 402	729. 579	730. 494
732. 581	733. 1477	735. 1016	737. 1567
739. 1565	740. 1570	748. 160	752. 1084
753. 1100	754. 1022	756. 912	758. 394
766. 1214	770. 404	771. 1658	772. 1276
773. 961	775. 917	776. 951	777. 1247
778. 1163	779. 958	780. 25	787. 1497
788. 1494	791. 758	793. 1262	796. 462
800. 720	801. 1232	802. 897	803. 1555
805. 161	806. 159	808. 734	809. 1377
812. 275	814. 277	815. 1662	816. 1194
818. 1396	820. 76	822. 605	823. 915V
824. 640	827. 428	829. 1588	830. 1588
831. 234	833. 1268	834. 382	835. 207
836. 284	837. 165V	838. 165	839. 26
840. 22	843. 873	844. 1273	848. 429
850. 631	851. 1569	860. 832	863. 1585
864. 300	865. 297	867. 1170	868. 1170V
869. 917	870. 281	872. 56	873. 144
876. 1593	888. 1024	893. 1465	894. 1027
897. 1297	903. 35	904. 1563	905. 3
906. 1390	907. 1475	913. 184	914. 181
915. 184	916. 952	918. 203	919. 350
920. 960	922. 113	923. 244	928. 1196
932. 1113	938. 1075	944. 1422	947. 1292
948. 1294	949. 1291	950. 1258	960. 1360
961. 703	963. 1229	964. 1306	967. 1583
970. 604	971. 583	973. 1562	974. 944
978. 817	982. 670	983. 349	984. 261
985. 653	986. 180	987. 947	988. 71
989. 838	992. 810	993. 1337	994. 749
995. 485	997. 652	998. 656	999. 919
1001. 702	1002. 336	1003. 190	1004. 188
1005. 1367	1006. 1387	1007. 904	1008. 905
1009. 935	1010. 290	1011. 689	1014. 433
1015. 152	1016. 1117	1017. 216	1018. 324
1021. 94	1024. 56	1025. 1035	1026. 769
1027. 105	1028. 106	1029. 95	1030. 587
1031. 585	1032. 98	1033. 1575	1034. 63
1035. 615	1036. 613	1037. 61	1038. 59
1040. 104	1041. 735	1042. 736	1043. 737
1045. 97	1046. 770	1047. 82	1050. 105
1053. 102	1054. 103	1060. 11	1061. 18
1062. 211	1063. 574	1064. 1158	1066. 1158
1067. 1158	1068. 157	1070. 50	1073. 837
1075. 1251V	1076. 126	1077. 1049	1078. 1078
1079. 75	1080. 1164	1081. 150	1082. 54
1085. 892	1087. 310	1089. 1116	1094. 543
1096. 109	1097. 109	1098. 1535	1099. 15
1100. 1019	1101. 366	1103. 999	1105. 744
1107. 992	1108. 884	1109. 885	1110. 1487
1112. 1540	1117. 38	1118. 616	1119. 819
1120. 1539	1121. 241	1122. 164	1123. 1424
1124. 556	1125. 1469	1126. 1471	1129. 1608
1130. 173	1131. 168	1132. 166	1133. 715
1135. 427	1137. 617	1138. 1308	1139. 782
1140. 1538	1142. 597	1147. 798V	1148. 568
1149. 566	1150. 570	1152. 535	1154. 6
1155. 1556V	1157. 1134	1160. 1233	1161. 1368
1163. 1544	1164. 83	1165. 84	1167. 533
1169. 798V	1173. 1364	1174. 643	1177. 598
1178. 1621	1180. 320	1181. 120	1183. 24
1184. 437	1186. 399	1187. 1147	1188. 500
1189. 499	1190. 732	1191. 192	1193. 5
1194. 36	1195. 1097	1196. 1099	1198. 1399
1199. 595	1200. 601	1201. 1254V	1202. 8
1203. 472	1204. 449	1205. 560	1206. 1014V
1207. 391	1210. 182	1211. 743	1212. 415
1213. 925	1214. 927	1215. 926	1216. 524
1217. 1644	1218. 876	1219. 865	1220. 523
1223. 573	1226. 1564	1229. 1571	1230. 1574V
1231. 652V	1233. 31	1234. 1568	1235. 1564
1240. 1567	1242. 1570	1244. 721	1245. 311
1246. 1464	1247. 1622	1248. 454	1249. 606
1250. 1252	1251. 555	1253. 901	1254. 170
1258. 973	1259. 292	1260. 694	1261. 619
1263. 550	1264. 1079	1265. 1080	1267. 1081
1268. 1085	1269. 624	1270. 630	1271. 1479
1273. 282	1274. 1215	1275. 615	1276. 1267
1278. 1319	1279. 1321	1280. 154	1282. 956
1283. 746	1284. 753	1285. 1179	1286. 609
1287. 760	1288. 512	1289. 446	1291. 110
1292. 110	1293. 848	1294. 359	1295. 509
1296. 484	1297. 483	1298. 486	1301. 1450
1302. 1452	1304. 1480	1305. 470	1306. 48

1307. 1199	1308. 1041	1309. 1042	1311. 479
1313. 1198	1314. 124	1316. 965	1318. 526
1319. 525	1320. 517	1321. 508	1322. 531
1323. 459	1324. 457	1325. 759	1326. 742
1327. 763	1328. 764	1329. 754	1330. 755
1331. 757	1332. 474	1333. 1630	1334. 542
1335. 352	1336. 578	1337. 603	1338. 623
1339. 582	1340. 547	1341. 607	1342. 768
1343. 33	1344. 660	1345. 516	1346. 602
1347. 305	1348. 1370	1349. 1246	1350. 1371
1351. 1143	1352. 163	1353. 1545	1354. 676
1355. 1111	1356. 998	1358. 1401	1359. 595-A
1360. 1008	1361. 1226	1362. 1236	1363. 1624
1364. 718V	1365. 682	1366. 1275	1367. 1248
1369. 418	1371. 1227	1372. 993	1373. 1002
1374. 1000	1375. 1004	1376. 786	1377. 1023
1378. 544	1381. 954	1382. 879	1383. 1331
1384. 1528V	1385. 1185	1386. 664	1387. 1172
1388. 1546	1389. 1548	1390. 1481	1391. 828
1392. 1358	1395. 1153	1396. 1007	1397. 1010
1398. 1174	1399. 1175	1400. 1228	1401. 1145
1402. 1146	1403. 1241	1404. 1240	1405. 1239
1406. 1238	1407. 1225	1408. 1237	1409. 1095
1410. 1126	1411. 1124	1412. 1121	1413. 1176
1414. 1177	1415. 1178	1416. 1218	1417. 1220
1418. 1167	1419. 1169	1420. 1183	1421. 1182
1422. 1181	1423. 1180	1424. 1375	1425. 1142
1426. 1122	1427. 1663	1428. 1612	1430. 447
1435. 1549	1436. 1298	1437. 1013	1440. 1430
1442. 66	1443. 1253	1444. 241	1446. 1020
1450. 1318	1451. 230	1453. 1425	1454. 10
1455. 1606	1457. 301	1458. 612V	1459. 696
1463. 114	1464. 1541	1465. 172V	1470. 1435
1471. 1437	1472. 1438	1473. 1492	1476. 549
1477. 693	1480. 13	1482. 552	1484. 1332
1486. 17	1487. 16	1488. 967	1489. 1604
1490. 215	1491. 51	1493. 369	1494. 1642
1495. 380	1499. 538	1500. 1211	1502. 875
1505. 1279	1508. 1508	1509. 228	1510. 177
1511. 44	1512. 1206	1513. 1203	1514. 949
1515. 1053	1518. 561	1519. 809	1520. 835
1521. 224	1523. 1597	1526. 923	1527. 913
1528. 236	1530. 821	1531. 822	1532. 1354
1533. 1043	1534. 559	1535. 356	1536. 881
1537. 880	1541. 520	1542. 1420	1543. 859
1544. 155	1546. 407	1547. 1605	1552. 882
1553. 883	1554. 885	1555. 1552	1557. 856
1559. 851	1560. 853	1561. 842	1564. 1500
1566. 1418	1568. 1265	1569. 1207	1570. 1204
1572. 851	1574. 551	1575. 1357	1576. 339
1577. 594	1578. 358	1579. 414	1581. 319
1584. 1537	1585. 727	1586. 1381	1587. 1380
1588. 1376	1589. 1033	1590. 1486	1595. 37
1596. 7	1597. 93	1600. 1271	1602. 914
1603. 886	1604. 507	1605. 532	1606. 1136
1607. 1087	1608. 717	1610. 895	1611. 1474
1614. 1502	1615. 1505	1616. 1508	1617. 1503
1618. 1507	1619. 1363	1620. 1361	1622. 557
1623. 710	1624. 710	1625. 815	1626. 795
1627. 797	1630. 490	1631. 322	1635. 139
1637. 68	1638. 829	1639. 1073	1640. 1077
1641. 1070	1642. 1069	1643. 1067	1644. 1209
1646. 666	1647. 387	1648. 409	1649. 435
1652. 316	1654. 273	1655. 1659	1656. 471
1658. 271	1659. 891	1660. 1011	1661. 1012
1663. 878	1669. 1173	1670. 1467	1671. 1034
1672. 1289	1677. 314	1678. 398	1679. 397
1680. 636	1682. 1125	1683. 988	1684. 991
1685. 1081	1690. 1166	1691. 1165	1695. 1109
1696. 125	1697. 1152	1698. 210	1700. 379
1702. 253	1703. 976	1704. 1671	1708. 1243
1709. 187	1714. 964	1715. 240	1716. 747
1717. 833	1718. 823	1719. 851	1726. 1534
1728. 1365	1734. 565	1736. 874	1737. 268
1738. 1351	1739. 62	1740. 318	1741. 1230
1742. 997	1754. 740	1756. 1537	1757. 1542
1758. 675	1764. 958	1765. 537V	1766. 1263
1768. 1639	1769. 909	1772. 608	1773. 955
1774. 957	1776. 919	1778. 928	1779. 680V
1784. 783	1789. 663	1791. 385	1794. 546
1795. 1003	1799. 1213	1800. 1212	1801. 541
1803. 1118	1805. 989	1808. 34	1809. 563
1813. 3807	1814. 780	1815. 1440	1820. 1260
1821. 599	1823. 1148	1824. 527	1825. 906
1827. 1389	1829. 156	1830. 325	1831. 357
1832. 405	1833. 714	1834. 402	1835. 702
1836. 1101	1837. 706	1839. 841	1840. 365
1841. 1242	1842. 1244	1843. 465	1844. 840
1845. 396	1846. 467	1847. 460	1848. 513
1849. 85	1851. 57	1852. 649	1853. 307
1855. 123	1856. 987	1857. 1062	1859. 1133
1860. 1625	1863. 1345	1865. 521	1867. 69
1868. 412	1869. 995	1871. 1287	1872. 1555
1873. 1179	1875. 362	1877. 870	1878. 1483
1879. 1393	1880. 1087	1881. 686	1882. 824
1883. 825	1885. 1394	1886. 1395V	1887. 1072
1889. 122	1890. 123	1891. 1356	1892. 1123
1893. 1092	1894. 858		

DUER-PENNY DOOR CONFERSION NUMBERS

2. 1187	3. 1196	4. 984	5. 1210
6. 1209	8. 1050	9. 1064	10. 1067
11. 1069	12. 1070	13. 1077	14. 1073
15. 1063	16. 1118	18. 1074	19. 1075
20. 1162	21. 1161	22. 1160	23. 1159
24. 1190	25. 1189	26. 1017	27. 1244
28. 1242	29. 1211	30. 1243	31. 1202

32. 1247	33. 1086	34. 1185	35. 968
36. 969	37. 1246	40. 1228	42. 1026
43. 990	44. 988	45. 991	46. 1116
47. 1096	48. 1104	49. 955	50. 1164
51. 1165	52. 166	54. 976	55. 1163
56. 1208	59. 1053	60. 1100	61. 1048
62. 1049	63. 973	64. 974	65. 958
66. 958V	67. 1042	68. 1041	69. 1040
70. 1072	73. 1149	74. 1092	75. 1087
76. 1090	77. 1094	78. 1233	79. 1136
80. 1088	82. 1114	83. 1084	84. 1111
85. 1111	86. 1101	88. 1095	90. 1099
91. 1097	93. 1110	94. 1195	95. 1227
96. 1226	97. 1225	98. 1150	99. 1230
100. 1147	101. 1146	102. 1145	104. 1081
105. 1082	106. 1133	107. 1125	108. 1112
109. 1134	110. 1133	111. 1113	112. 1158
113. 1173	114. 1121	115. 1135	116. 967
118. 1184	119. 1229	120. 1005	121. 1153
123. 1157	124. 1004	125. 1004V	127. 1179
128. 1062	129. 1122	130. 1126	131. 1124
133. 1154V	134. 1007V	135. 1006	136. 1006
137. 1085	138. 1085V	139. 1081	140. 1633
141. 1080	142. 1079V	143. 1079	144. 1078
145. 1173	146. 1198	148. 998	149. 1008
151. 1012	152. 1011V	154. 1011V	155. 1011
156. 1180	157. 1181	158. 1182	159. 1183
160. 1220	161. 1219	162. 1217	163. 1216
164. 1218	165. 1215	166. 1169V	167. 1234
168. 1635	169. 1169	170. 1167V	171. 1169V
172. 1240V	173. 1238	174. 1239	176. 1241
177. 1235	178. 956	179. 1178	180. 1177
181. 1176V	182. 1176	183. 1174	184. 1636
185. 1175	186. 982	187. 986	188. 1170
189. 1170V	191. 964	192. 959	193. 1232V
194. 996	195. 996V	196. 1212	197. 1213
198. 1214	199. 1201V	200. 997	201. 999
202. 1029	203. 1019	204. 1232	206. 1231
207. 1231V	208. 1201	209. 1236	210. 1237
211. 1001	212. 1000	213. 993	214. 992
215. 1027	216. 1020V	217. 1020	219. 1023
220. 1022	221. 1023V	222. 1024	223. 1030
224. 1009	225. 1003	227. 1010	228. 1002
229. 1143	230. 1142	231. 1139	

SMALL TIN DIME REGISTERING BANKS*

Astronaut Daily Dime Bank (square, rounded corners)	B
Balfour Budget Bank for Class Ring	E
B and R Pocket Dime Registering Bank (round)	D
Book of Knowledge (square, rounded corners)	A
Boy and Girl (round, flat top) 2 styles	C
Boy and Girl (square, rounded corners)	D
Capitol Building (square, rounded corners) 4 styles	A to D
Captain Marvel (square, rounded corners) 3 styles	D
Chein, Mercury Dime (square)	D
Chein, Thrifty Elf (square)	B
Chein, Uncle Sam (square) 2 styles	D
Clown and Monkey Daily Dime Bank (square, round corners) 2 styles	A and B
Coke (square, round corners)	C
Daily Dime Piggy Bank (square, round corners)	A
Davy Crockett (square, round corners) 2 styles	C and E
Donald Duck Dime Registering Bank (square, round corners)	E
Dopey (square, round corners)	E
Elves Rolling Coins to Bank (square, round corners)	C
Empire State Building - 3 styles	A thru C
Gem Dime Registering (square, round corners)	A
General Electric (square, round corners)	C
Jackie Robinson (square, round corners) 2 styles	E
Keep 'Em Sailing (square, round corners) 2 styles	E
Keep 'Em Flying (square, round corners)	E
Keep 'Em Rolling (square, round corners)	A
Little Cowboy (square, round corners)	E
Little Orphan Annie (round, square top)	E
Lucky Dime Registering (square, round corners) 2 styles	A and C
Magic Dime Registering (round)	B
Marvel Dime Registering (square, round corners)	A
Mickey Mouse (square, round corners) 5 variations, all rated	E
National Bank, Ann Arbor, Michigan (square, round corners	B
New York World's Fair Daily Dime Bank (square round corners)	A
Popeye, 1929 (square, round corners) 2 styles	A
Popeye, 1956 (square, round corners) 2 styles	A
Prince Valiant Dime Bank (square, round corners) 2 styles	B
Sen Sen (small rectangle)	E
Snow White and the Seven Dwarfs (square, round corners) 2 styles	C
Stag Tobacco (small rectangle)	E

Statue of Liberty (square, round corners) 3 styles	A thru C
Superman (square, round corners) 2 styles	D
Treasury Register Bank, 2 styles	A thru C
United Nations Register Bank (square, round corners) 2 styles	B and C
Vacation Daily Dime Bank (square, round corners)	A
World's Scope (square, round corners) 2 styles	C and D

*Courtesy of Gordon P. Jorgensen, from his book, *A Guide to Dime Registering Banks*, available at 29 West Elizabeth Street, Waterloo, New York 13165

SEVEN GODS OF FORTUNE

The authors are indebted to the Japanese Consulate, City of Chicago, for graciously supplying the information on this subject.

The Seven Gods of Fortune are among the most popular deities in Japan. Shrines dedicated to them dot the Japanese landscape, and possessing a picture of a God is regarded as a goodluck charm.

The true origin of the Gods is unknown, but credit for their creation is generally given to Priest Tenkai, a great favorite of Shogun Tokugawa Iyeyasu. Priest Tenkai defined seven attributes of virtue as: 1 Longevity, 2 Fortune, 3 Popularity, 4 Candor, 5 Amiability, 6 Dignity and 7 Magnaminity.

The Shogun was so pleased with Tenkai's explanation of the seven virtues that he told the priest to select seven deities to represent them. What follows is a brief description of each God as Tenkai defined them for the Shogun:

BENTEN: The Goddess of Amiability and the only female god. She represents music and feminine beauty. Benten is usually pictured in a seated position, holding a musical instrument called a biwa.

BISHAMON: The God of Dignity is also the God of Treasure, Fortune and Happiness. Wearing a war helmet and armour, Bishamon holds a threatening halberd in one hand and a tower of treasure in the other. He is the guardian of Budha and is also responsible for bestowing happiness and fortune upon good people.

DAIKOKU: The God of Fortune's smiling face peers out from beneath a flat, black cap. Also a God of Wealth, he is usually seated on two fat straw bags of rice, which represent a rich harvest. He holds a golden mallet in his hand, representing monetary wealth. It is said that when Daikoku shakes the mallet, coins flow in unlimited quantities from the rice bags.

EBISU: Ebisu, the smiling personification of Candor, carries a large fish under his left arm and a long fishing pole in his right hand. His favorite sport is fishing, and the fish represents his success at the sport. Ebisu, also a God of Wealth and Fortune, is worshipped by trades people and shop keepers. He is dressed in the official clothing of the ancient court.

FUKUROKUJU: The God of Popularity has a huge responsibility, for he is in charge of Wealth, Happiness and Longevity. He embodies virtues of the other Gods and is very powerful, though not as popular in Japan as Kaikoku and Ebisu. He is usually pictured as a small, elderly man with a long, bald head. He is often accompanied by a crane, which is the symbol of a long life.

HOTEI: The God of Magnaminity has a huge pot-belly and a fat, smiling face. He dresses in the costume of a Buddhist priest and carries a cloth bag over his shoulder. The bag holds fortunes for those who believe in him. No matter how much demand believers place on the bag, it is never empty.

JUROJIN: The God of Longevity is short of stature, but has too large a head for his body. He holds a long stick, with a small book attached at the top. The book is said to contain the life line of every individual on Earth. Jurojin is often accompanied by a black deer, which is the symbol of long life.

GLOSSARY

"Arcade Screw": A round headed screw without a slot. Had identation on either side of head.

"As found": Refers to the typical condition in which a bank is found.

"As is": 1) Used by an auctioneer to describe the terms of his sale; cautions the buyer that it is *his* responsibility to learn the condition of items being sold. 2) Used by a seller in advertising a single item; a definite warning that something is wrong with the item.

"Average": Usually means approximatelly 60% of original paint remains on a bank, and that the bank is complete and has not been repaired.

Banken: Danish word meaning *bank*.

Bisque: Unglazed porcelain; porcelain without final glaze and firing.

Boss: Threaded spindle or thickening which is cast and drilled inside a bank to receive a screw.

Brass: A copper-based alloy with zinc as the major alloy element.

Bronze: A copper-based alloy with tin as the major alloy element. Further defined by a second alloy element, such as silicon or aluminum.

Bronzed: Having the appearance of copper or bronze, either painted on or applied electrostatically.

Ceramic: Usually fired clay or other materials composed of light metal oxides such as oxides of aluminum, silicon, magnesium and titanium, all fired at high temperatures. The material is fired to set the shape and then the glaze is applied and fired. One of the most common ceramics, glass, is composed of silicon dioxide — heated and formed.

Chasing: A process of decorating by engraving or embossing. Also used to describe the cutting of a screw thread or coin slot.

China: White ceramic, body of which is opaque and fired at a low temperature, then glazed. Glaze and body are then fired at higher temperature to finish the piece.

"Choice": A term used to describe banks which are above average condition — better than usual.

Clapper: A device designed to prevent anyone from spilling or shaking coins from a bank. Clapper is usually on a pivot and makes noise when the bank is shaken.

Closure: The device or part that closes or shuts the bank, holding the coins.

Coin Trap: The device that can be opened to remove coins.

Composition: Any mixture yielding a material from which banks were made, other than ceramic, metal or plastic.

Cross Collectible: Any item collected by more than one collector group.

Deposit Developer: Name given to penny banks distributed by financial institutions whose object was to accumulate enough funds to warrant being put into a bank account. The institution often retained the key.

Draft: A slight taper given a mold to facilitate the removal of a pattern or die.

DRGM: Indicates German registry.

DRPOSR: Indicated French registry.

Elastolin: Trademark of O. & M. Hausser, of Neustadt, Germany. Refers to composition materials from whcih their toys are made.

Electrolysis: The use of an electric current to cause chemical change or cause a bonded deposit.

Electroplate: Creation of a metal flashing over a bank by the use of electrolysis.

Electroplated: A bank that has been covered or coated with a thin layer of metal by electrolysis.

Embossing: Raising or impressing designs or letters on a surface in relief.

Finial: An ornamental, terminating part; in building banks, the separate "peak" of the building.

Flashing: A thin, protective or decorative layer on the surface; also a casting defect of a thin extrusion of metal that escapes at the juncture of the pattern.

Gate: Superfluous piece of metal caused in casting process, as metal filled the hole (gate) through which it was poured. Gate is removed in the finishing process.

Gilded: Covered with, or appearing to be covered with, a thin layer of gold: usually paint containing powdered metal.

Granular: Appearing to be composed of separate grains. Describes the appearance of later cast iron products.

Impressed: Something marked or stamped on a bank, as if with pressure.

Interlocks: A part of the casting designed to keep the two halves of a bank from slipping when assembled. Can be internal or external. Usually takes the form of a protrusion on one half of the casting that fits an indentation on the other half.

"In-the-box": Means that an original box is with the bank; does not necessarily describe the bank's condition. Term is often misused in describing a mint or pristine bank.

Japan: Black enamel or lacquer used to produce a durable, glossy finish.

Jobber: A seller of goods made by others. Selchow and Righter and Butler Brothers were among the largest.

Lead: For purposes of this book, a metal alloy with a high lead content, used to make banks of the white metal family. It is particularly dense and smooth, giving high detail. Takes paint well.

Lithography: An early printing process that yielded particularly bright and complex color schemes.

Malleable Iron: A mixture of iron and carbon with small amounts of manganese, sulphur and phosphorous, cast in white alloy. Capable of being shaped by hammering or pressure. Flexible.

Maroon: A reddish brown or bronze finish. Often used by the English to describe their brown, japanned finish.

Mechanical: Any bank that performs in the process of depositing a coin.

"Mint": A bank that retains 100% of its original paint - no chips - no signs of wear and tear; a much-abused term.

Mold: The space created by the shape or pattern used in casting; the cavity into which the metal is poured.

Money Box: A synonym for penny banks; commonly used in this country in the 1800's and early 1900's. Still used in Great Britain.

Nickeled: A bank that has been given a thin, even layer of nickel applied by electrolysis.

Parian: Unglazed china, fired at a high enough temperature to completely vitrify the clays and other ceramic materials.

Patina: The sheen produced by age on the surface of metal; the thin layer of corrosion caused by oxidation, changing the color of paint or metal.

Pattern: Model of the piece being produced, usually made of bronze or brass, which when pressed in the sand creates the mold.

Penny Door: A Welsh term for *coin trap*; adopted name of the Moore collection.

Playthings: A trade publication for the toy industry; founded in 1903 and still in business.

Porcelain: A fine grind, highly fired white ceramic, the body of which is transluscent; the original, or body firing, is set at a higher temperature than the final, glaze firing.

Pot Metal: *See White Metal*

Pottery: *See Ceramic.*

"Pristine": A bank in unusually fine condition; only a *few* paint chips.

Registering Bank: Any bank that records its accumulation of deposits.

Semi-mechanical: Any performing bank that has moving parts, other than a safe, registering bank or mechanical.

Silvered: A finish of medium grey paint giving the lustrous appearance of silver.

Slush Metal: *See White Metal.*

Sparbanken: Danish word meaning *savings bank.*

Spardose: A German word meaning *money box.*

Sparebosse: A Danish word meaning *piggy bank.*

Sparkassen: A German word meaning *savings bank.*

Spelter: A synonym for zinc; in bank collecting, a metal alloy predominantly made of zinc; in Great Britain, an alloy of tin and lead.

Stroking: A painter's term, indicating the use of different shades or colors to create highlights or depth in finishing.

Transvaal: Formerly part of the Republic of South Africa; the name of the hallmark bank of the Penny Door Collection.

Trick Lock: A small lock used to close hinged European banks; appears to open with a key, but opens when the middle layer of metal is slid outward; usually made of brass.

Turnpin or Twist Pin: A cast iron rod with a head on one end and a wide, flattened surface at the other end; used instead of a screw to hold a bank together.

White Metal: Any one of a number of metal alloys arising from a mixture of metals, having zinc as the primary metal. Synonymous with pot metal, slush metal, spelter, or metal alloy.

BIBLIOGRAPHY

Abell, Bruce and Bowers, Norman, *James M. Harper & The Chicago Hardware Foundry.* Chicago: SBCCA, 1983.

Berenholtz, Bernard and McClintock, Inez, *American Antique Toys.* New York: Harry N. Abrams, Inc., 1980.

Blackbeard, Bill and Williams, Martin, editors. *Smithsonian Collection of Newspaper Comics.* New York: co-published by Smithsonian Institution Press and Harry N. Abrams, Inc., 1977.

Buxton, Frank and Owen, Bill, *The Big Broadcast.* New York: Viking Press, 1966.

Duer, Don and Sommer, Bettie, *The Architecture of Cast Iron Penny Banks.* Winter Park: American Limited Editions, 1983.

Freeman, Ruth and Larry, *Cavalcade of Toys* New York: Century House, 1942.

Harman, Kenny, *Comic Strip Toys.* Des Moines: Wallace-Homestead Book Company, 1975.

Hertz, Louis H., *Handbook of Old American Toys.* Connecticut: Mark Haber and Co., 1947.

_____*Messrs. Ives of Bridgeport.* Connecticut: Mark Haber and Co., 1950.

_____ *The Toy Collector.* New York: Hawthorn Books, 1969.

Jorgenson, Gordon D., *A Guide to Dime Registering Banks.* Waterloo, New York. By the Author, 1982.

Kelley, Dale, ed. *Marshall Field Toy Catalog - 1892-1893.* Des Moines: Wallace Homestead Book Co., 1969.

King, Constance Eileen, *The Encyclopedia of Toys.* New York: Crown Publishers, 1978.

Long, Ida and Ernest, "Kenton Toys". *Collectors' Showcase,* November/December, 1982, pp. 39-43.

Long, Ernest and Ida; Pitman, Jane, *Dictionary of Still Banks.* California: Long's Americana, 1980.

Lowe, David, *Lost Chicago.* Boston: Houghton Mifflin Co., 1975.

McClintock, Inez and Marshall, *Toys in America.* Washington, D.C.: Public Affairs Press, 1961.

Meyer, John, *A Handbook of Old Mechanical Penny Banks,* 1952. Reissued as *Old Penny Banks,* with Larry Freeman. New York: Century House, 1960.

Reed, Jane, ed., *A Celebration of the Queen's Silver Jubilee.* London: IPC Magazines, Ltd., 1977.

Rogers, Carole, *Penny Banks, A History and a Handbook.* New York: E.P. Dutton, 1977.

Schroeder, Joseph J., Jr., ed. *Toys, Games and Dolls - 1860-1930.* Chicago: Follett Publishing Co., 1971.

Stanley, Mary Louise, *A Century of Glass Toys.* Vermont: Forward's Color Productions. (undated)

Thurn, Hans Peter, *Die Kultur Der Sparsamkeit* (The Culture of Thrift). Stuttgart: Deutscher Sparkassen Verlag, 1982.

Trevelyan, G.M., *History of England, Volume III.* New York: Doubleday & Co., Inc., 1953.

Whiting, Hubert B., *Old Iron Still Banks.* Vermont: Forward's Color Productions, Inc., 1968.

Sources
Toy Company Catalogs

ARCADE
1902-3
1904
1908-9
c1911
1923
1925
1929
1932
1934
1940
GEORGE W. BROWN & CO.
The George Brown Toy Sketchbook
COLUMBIA GREY IRON
  CASTING COMPANY
1897
DENT
undated
1920
GREY IRON CASTING
  COMPANY
1903-4
1928
JOHN HARPER, LTD.
1901-2
1911
undated

HUBLEY
1906
1914-15
3 early, undated catalogs
1930
1940
1946
IVES
1893
KENTON
1904
1911
1927
1932
1933
KYSER AND REX
1882
1889?
NICOL
1895
SHIMER
1899

J. & E. STEVENS
1883
1898
1906
1907
1917
1924
1929
STEVENS & BROWN
1870
1872
A. C. WILLIAMS
1894
1905
1906
1908
1910
1912
c1920's
1927
1931

Miscellaneous Source Material

Antique Toy World Magazine
Butler Brothers catalogs, 1889, 1891
Ehrich & Company catalog, 1876
Fair Store, The; wholesale catalog, 1902
Grab, Victor M. Company; early 1900's
Gould & Company catalogs, 1925, 1931
Marshall Field & Company catalogs, 1890-91, 1893-94
Montgomery Ward catalog, 1903
Playthings Magazine; selected issues, 1903-1927
Penny Bank Post, all issues between 1966 and 1983
Selchow & Righter catalogs, 1887-1888, 1894
Strasburger, Oscar & Co.; 1880 catalog
Vergho Ruhling & Company catalog, 1903

INDEX

All italicized numbers are bank numbers; they refer the reader to the color photo section of the book. Note: The material in the Appendix is not indexed. A reader seeking additional information on a particular bank should look up that bank's number in the Appendix.

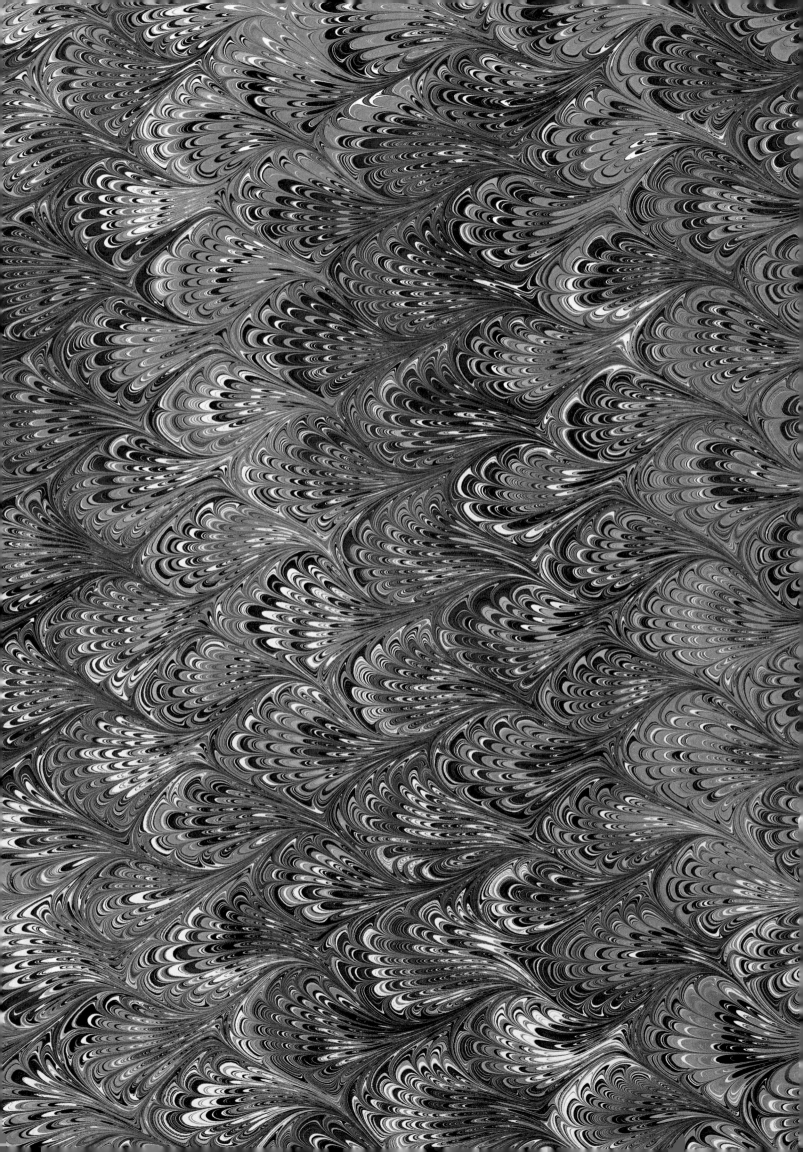